PUBLICATIONS OF THE McMASTER UNIVERSITY
ASSOCIATION FOR 18TH-CENTURY STUDIES

VOLUME ONE
THE VARIED PATTERN:
STUDIES IN THE 18TH CENTURY

VOLUME TWO
THE TRIUMPH OF CULTURE:
18TH CENTURY PERSPECTIVES

The Triumph of Culture: 18th Century Perspectives

EDITORS

PAUL FRITZ • DAVID WILLIAMS

A. M. HAKKERT LTD.

TORONTO

1972

Copyright © 1972 by A. M. Hakkert Ltd.
All rights reserved

Set in Aldine Roman and Caslon Antique
by A. M. Hakkert Ltd.
Toronto, Canada
Printed in Canada

Cover: W. Hogarth, Frontispiece and Tailpiece
to the Catalogue of Pictures
Exhibited in Spring Gardens in 1761

Standard Book Number
88866-520-2
Library of Congress Catalogue Card Number
72-80055

A. M. Hakkert Ltd.
554 Spadina Crescent
Toronto 179, Ontario
Canada

Preface

The second volume in this series contains twenty articles which, we hope, will illuminate in terms of either ideas, personalities or events, certain aspects of the life and culture of the eighteenth century. The articles have been grouped thematically to focus attention on the period's artistic and intellectual activities, science, the nature and dissemination of culture, problems of biography and autobiography, political patronage, and other historical, literary and sociological issues. All the contributors originally presented their work in the form of papers to meetings of the McMaster Association for Eighteenth Century Studies.

The editors wish to dedicate the present volume to R. M. Wiles. Roy Wiles, formerly Professor of English at McMaster University, is the Honorary President of the Association and first Vice-President of the American Society for Eighteenth Century Studies. It is to him that the McMaster Association owes its existence.

We gratefully acknowledge the encouragement and financial support that we have received from McMaster University, and we should like to express our appreciation also to the many members of the Association, and of the McMaster community generally, who have offered valuable help. We should also like to thank our publisher, Alan Samuel and the staff of Hakkert for their expert help and friendly cooperation in the preparation of another volume for the press.

P.F.
D.W.

Toronto, 1972

Editors

P. S. Fritz, Department of History, McMaster University.

D. Williams, Department of Romance Languages, McMaster University.

List of Contributors

J. M. Beattie, Department of History, University of Toronto.

W. J. Callahan, Department of History, University of Toronto.

E. Cappadocia, Department of History, McMaster University.

R. M. Hatton, The London School of Economics and Political Science.

C. Jago, Department of History, McMaster University.

R. Joly, Etudes Françaises, Université Laval.

H. Kalman, Department of Fine Arts, University of British Columbia.

R. Morton, Department of English, McMaster University.

J. B. Owen, Department of History, University of Calgary.

J. H. Plumb, Christ's College, Cambridge University.

L. Rosenfeld, Nordisk Institut for Teoretisk Atomfysik, Copenhagen.

G. Rudé, Department of History, Sir George Williams University.

D. J. Russo, Department of History, McMaster University.

R. G. Saisselin, Department of Foreign and Comparative Literature, University of Rochester.

C. Tracy, Department of English, Acadia University.

R. Van Dusen, Department of German, McMaster University.

R. L. Walters, Department of French, University of Western Ontario.

P. Walton, Department of Fine Arts, McMaster University.

R. M. Wiles, Department of English, McMaster University.

Contents

The
Triumph of Culture:
18th Century Perspectives

Portrait de Madame de Staël en Corinne
by Elisabeth-Louise Vigee-Lebrun

Collection Musée d'art et d'histoire, Genève   *Oil on Canvas*

Tivoli Revisited
or
The Triumph of Culture

In Perrault's *Parallèle des anciens et des modernes* (1688-1697), a provincial President, admirer of the ancient learning, lover of Antiquity, is taken on a tour of Versailles to behold the marvels constructed by modern architects, decorated by modern painters, sculptors, and designers. The President is taken on this tour because he must be made to see, his eyes and his mind must be opened to perceive that the moderns are capable of equalling, and in some cases surpassing, the ancients; that he may realize that to argue in favour of the superiority of the ancients over the moderns is in fact to espouse a mere prejudice — due to pedagogy as well as the work of the imagination, which magnifies that which is distant in space and time. Within the context of the quarrel of the ancients and moderns this is as much as to say that the imagination is the creator of romantic fancies which must be counteracted by the judgment, which must examine, compare, open eyes and mind in order that one may see truly and clearly. For the President, partisan of the ancients, admirer of Tivoli and Frascati, really loves a chimera, an imaginary antiquity, a remembrance of things past. Antiquity is a work of the imagination. Versailles, the work of architects and artists still alive, and its splendid gardens where the President is taken, were by contrast realities, the work of a King as worthy of admiration as Augustus and Maecenas. To paraphrase Henri IV, one may put it that in the view of Perrault, and perhaps Louis XIV, *Versailles vaut bien Tivoli*.

The President's visit to Versailles may be viewed in terms of an issue wider in scope than the historical quarrel between ancients and moderns. One might see it as an aspect of the recurring conflict of art and culture. The President is a cultivated man. He has read the ancients. He knows their work. He has been to Italy, and has visited Tivoli and Frascati, and he has envisaged, or imagined, those noble figures in those settings of serenity and beauty as one may gaze upon a painting by Poussin or Claude. Culture is associated with the past, rather well defined, and even with a specific geographical area which upon a map looks like a boot. Culture is somewhere beyond the mountains. Art, on the other hand, still tied to technique and thought of in terms of function, is an activity, or several such, present, modern, useful, tied to power, wealth, magnificence, grandeur, and in the specific case in question, a certain arrogance *vis-à-vis* the prestige of the birthplace of the arts and the depository of the noblest culture: Italy, happy country endowed not only with all the prestige of Antiquity but also with capable modern artists. Thus Versailles becomes the answer to the Rome of Bernini and Urban VIII.

As for the dialogues one may view these as representing one stage in a continuous dialogue between art and culture; they represent a mental attitude which, viewed within a Vico-like scheme of historical development, belongs to what we shall posit as the world of art, in which instituted religion and monarchy attained their baroque moment and form. In this stage of development one may put it that there existed cultivated circles of scholars, savants, collectors, virtuosi, but that the possession of culture as such is not a national policy, is not judged to be a public good, but rather that art is part of what Sénac de Meilhan in his *Considérations sur la richesse et le luxe* of 1787 referred to as *le faste*, or *magnificence*, which the monarch and the church use as instruments of rule and propaganda. As concerns the art of portraiture, this use of art may be made visible in the baroque royal portrait. As for the Church's use of art as magnificence, one need but enter any baroque church to be aware of its power. Culture, in the world of art thus remains in a sense a private affair of virtuosi and may from a jansenist point of view be subsumed under the general phenomenon of *divertissement*. Religious and feudal values still dominated such a world and counterbalanced the aesthetic appeal of private culture which thus remained but an ornament. All this was to change in the course of the late seventeenth and eighteenth centuries, at least in France, because of the growing power of money which transformed art into luxury. What may be called the transformation of the world of art into that of culture may already be discerned in the period of the Regency at which time the process found an acute observer in the person of the moralist La Bruyère. But the continuing dialogue between art and culture, especially as it bears on the new power of money and luxury, finds further expression in Diderot's *Le Neveu de Rameau*, a short, sparkling literary masterpiece in the form of a dialogue published after his death.

Two characters are involved, or two voices if you will, *Lui*, the great musician Rameau's real nephew — failure, sycophant, eccentric, bohemian about town, earning a living from a few music lessons, living from hand to mouth and from day to day and, at the time *Moi*, the other character or voice meets him, just chased from the table of Bertin, a man involved in finance. *Lui* is amoral, hedonistic, talented but not creative. *Moi*, presumably Diderot himself as *philosophe*, successful editor of the *Encyclopédie*, art critic, friend of Falconet, moral, middle class, hardworking, generous and enthusiastic, is the contrary of *Lui*. These two men are made to meet by chance and there ensues a dialogue touching on genius, talent, the relation of morality to art, society and posterity, issues central to aesthetics. But it also seems to us that the two men, and what they exemplify, also serve admirably to illustrate the different attitudes implied by the world of art and that of culture, with the nephew representing the attitudes of the former and the *philosophe* those of the new world of culture then in the making.

It must not be forgotten that the discussion occurs within the context of a world dominated by luxury and the rich, *fermiers-généraux*, various types of financiers, bankers to the court, and others involved in speculation. Thus it is no wonder that the background of the dialogue is the power of money and luxury, and that the different attitudes expressed by the protagonists come down to a question of spending: ". . . what the devil do you want to spend your money on if not to have a good table, good company, good wines, and beautiful women, pleasures of all colours and amusements of all sorts?" asks the nephew of the *philosophe*, who, on the contrary, thinks not of the pleasures of the day, but of the judgment of posterity. Where the nephew thinks of his pleasure *now* the *philosophe* thinks of his reputation in the future. The mentality of the nephew is still that of pre-capitalist man; it is neither that of the bourgeoisie, nor for that matter of the Christian poor. The *philosophe*, on the other hand, already belongs to the world of the bourgeois in which the risks of damnation have been replaced by those of economic and moral failure; it is a world without sinners and without saints, but looking for new heroes to replace the old.

The genius was such a new hero, for he was a power of the new divinity *nature*; distinct from the feudal hero or the Christian knight or saint, even a bourgeois might be a genius and transcend time, not through feats of heroism or faith and grace, but by work, construction, accumulation, thus contributing to civilization. His look was turned to the future, to posterity, not the instant, and his vision was historical and moral rather than hedonistic. Diderot argued with the nephew, as he did with Falconet, about posterity: ". . . let us forget for a moment the point we occupy in space and duration, and let us extend our vision upon the centuries to come, the most distant régime and the peoples of the future." The passage from art to culture is effected by the genius whose work rises above time, and what might be called the dimension of cultural time: posterity's judgment and history, thus replaces Christian eternity and providence. Needless to say, in the new dimension of culture, the critic as *philosophe* and as man of taste will play an important role, becoming in a sense the interpreter or the reader of the work and works of genius through time. Diderot fits the role to perfection: critic, writer, editor, *philosophe*, he assumes the role of the voice of posterity upon the works of the past and acts as advisor to artists in the present, the moral advisor who would recall to them their duty towards mankind. The man from the middle class becomes the middle man between the artist and the poet on the one hand, the hedonist spectator and reader on the other. The relation of artist to patron is thus changed as the makers of artistic opinion and values gain in importance.

By contrast, the nephew's attitude towards posterity is still dominated by the thought and the reality of death; in this respect it is still close to the old Christian view of destiny; however, the nephew is hardly a Christian, for he does not draw the same conclusion as the man who would above all save his soul by preparing himself for the ultimate judgment. The nephew is rather an enlightened failure, a species of new pagan living in that happy interregnum between the total collapse of the old order and the established form of the new moral-economic order. In any case, posterity is of no concern to him. A genius, a great man, might earn a statue, but "To rot under marble or to rot under earth, is still to rot." His perspective is thus quite different from that of Diderot who believes that the marble above you will preserve the memory of your contribution to humanity. The nephew sticks to the now, the present, and in a sense one may say he espouses life lived as the supreme value, life more than art or beauty or as a means to attain fame; his realism is in a sense very much that of the poor, of the hard life, of the eating while there is something to eat, and his morality, if such it is, is based on hard facts rather than on ideals.

By Christian standards he would be a sinner, one of the poor, having thereby a definite place in the way of providence since the condition of poverty was as pre-ordained as that of the great and powerful. But within the new bourgeois order then in formation, the nephew could only be a wastrel, or at best what he was to Diderot, *un original*, with a very clever way of justifying himself. The nephew sees there is no morality operative in the world at all: "All the species devour each other in nature; all the social conditions devour each other in society." To steal from the rich, to live off them, exploit them, to be their parasite or fool is consequently neither disgraceful nor immoral. It is rather a form of restitution since what the rich possess they do so because it was taken from someone else, somewhere else. The existing unequal distribution of wealth is based on cupidity and power, not on a mechanical-natural system of economic laws presided over by some self-regulating principle. One may thus say, as concerns the world of art, that the system of patronage then obtaining supposed sycophants and parasites of various sorts, men as well as women, genuine artists and poets as well as middling talents and hacks who all lived from the thirst for luxury and pleasure of the

great and the rich. Liberality, spending on luxury and women, was
also a species of restitution. The crumbs of the rich were picked
by those in their entourage, and their vanity and ambition profited
those who could build for them, adorn them, amuse them, flatter
them, and even outwit them, thereby justifying once more the
fable of the bees. It is this which is real, argues the nephew, while
the *philosophe*'s call for an ideal moral life is merely the effect of
a "certain romantic turn of mind." For the *philosophe* moral
action was the supreme good, superior even to art and beauty, for
as Diderot put it: "*Mahomet* is a sublime work, but I should rather
have rehabilitated the memory of the Calas." Such an act too
would pass to posterity. Clearly, art in the service of the luxury of
the rich was insufficient, and it was about to be put in the service
of public morality. Honesty was the best policy; it was best to
make something of yourself and to set aside for a rainy day.

The nephew's policy was to be what he was; he accepted
himself; he did not try to improve himself; and he prided himself
on only one thing, he was not a hypocrite; he lived in accordance
with his character which was to be lazy, foolish, good for nothing.
Virtue, after all, is a constraint and in fact is quite unnatural:
"Virtue makes itself respected, but respect is incommodious;
virtue makes itself admired, but admiration is not amusing." The
nephew was obviously quite free of the categorical imperative. He
was, curiously enough, a free man. He was not governed by any
economic-moral imperatives, but by his own will and temperament; he did not try to imitate a model, stoic, epicurean, or
philosophic. He was not superstitious of culture. One might put it
he was a fool in the Erasmian sense; certainly he did not belong to
the world the Enlightenment was bringing forth. He knew that
everyone was someone else's fool. He did not belong to the family
of Rousseau either; for he blamed no one and no institution for
his failure; he accused no one and nothing and ultimately he
accepted the world for what it was, and in effect wanted what the
world also wants: "Gold, gold. Gold is everything; and the rest,
without gold, is nothing. I want my son to be happy, or what
comes to the same thing, honored, rich and powerful."

The nephew's philosophy is in a sense a justification of
Pascalian *divertissement*; it is neither Christian nor philosophic and

despite his misery, the nephew is closer to Talleyrand's *douceur de vivre*, and to the *fermiers-généraux* he lived off, than to the *philosophe* who was the man who had left Grub Street and forgotten he had to write a semi-pornographic novel to make some money. By contrast, the *philosophe* was already the man of the dimension of culture: he believed in all the right things, Beauty, Truth, Genius, Art, Morality, Posterity, all written with capitals, all worthy of reverance or a special attitude analogous to the cult of the saints allowed within the area of faith. In the world of art, still parallel to institutional Christianity, art was not yet the object of a special cult or veneration nor was a genius regarded as a *bienfaiteur du genre humain*; rather it was the object of private collecting, vanity, cupidity, prestige, love of luxury, at best it might be private scholarship, play, style; but it was not yet the object of that particular veneration which comes from the combination of aesthetic experience, aesthetic theory, historical consciousness, and respect for genius. This would belong to the world of culture.

If Perrault's dialogues marked the moment of the triumph of magnificence in the constant dialogue of art and culture, Diderot's satire was directed rather at the dominant luxury of his times. The effect of the development of aesthetics, the intrusion of the *philosophes* into the world of art, the critique of luxury, combined to create a new attitude towards the arts. In eighteenth century terms one may say that luxury was turned into culture. The gilding disappeared as works of art took on the patina of time.

Madame de Staël's *Corinne*, a rather long novel first published in 1807, may serve to point out some of the salient features of the new mental world of culture. Diderot had not only been a witness of the transition from one world to another, he had also been an active agent which made for the change; but by his death in 1784 the new dimension of culture and the attitudes it implies, the poses, forms, ambiance for its full realization, were still in formation and it was for another generation to assume the new attitudes. David's success came soon after Diderot's death and may be taken as a sign of important changes. Madame de Staël, younger still than David, and brought up in her mother's salon at the feet of men of letters who had been part of the Enlightenment, would be fully conscious of the new dimension of culture, and her novel was a species of vindication of certain points of view presented by Diderot's *Moi* with the *Neveu de Rameau*.

It is also amusing to speculate upon the significance of Madame de Staël's being the daughter of a famous and rich banker who became a minister of state; for the link between money and culture was central to the discussion between Rameau and Diderot. Needless to say, these links are hardly there in *Corinne*; for the case of culture is posed on the level of the most sublime idealism. Culture, as the liberal's view and treatment of art, turns into an "as if" proposition: it is *as if* culture were some essence existing for all time, *as if* emanating from some world spirit or genius irrespective of merely human foibles and material considerations. The reason is simple: it has been dissociated from luxury, which is by definition an aspect of conspicuous consumption, and also it presumably involves and stands for all mankind, poor as well as rich.

Now *Corinne* may be described as a treatise on aesthetics in the form of a novel. Most of the main questions of aesthetic theory are treated in it: the theme of genius versus imitation, the link between national character and culture, the north-south dichotomy so dear to Madame de Staël herself, the differentiations drawn between the arts and their proper limits, the aesthetic experience of nature and art, the differences between the moral and aesthetic character of works of art, all of which turns into a species of grand tour with Corinne as guide. There are echoes of Du Bos, Winckelmann, Lessing, even Charles Nicholas Cochin (*vide* the critique of painting imitating statuary). Also one thinks of Perrault's *Parallèle des anciens et des modernes* and one may think of *Corinne* in terms of a refusal of its premises, for the novel is set in Italy and England; France and Versailles are no longer the setting for the debate of art and culture; the field of enquiry has been widened in time as well as area; it is no longer merely a question of comparing two moments, ancient and modern, but of assessing cultural differentiations. Corinne's guided tour turns into a dissertation upon the nature of culture, art, aesthetic values and experience, and the novel may also be interpreted as a conflict between the moral character and the aesthetic character, in this case the two being represented respectively by Lord Nelvil and Corinne herself. The characters in the novel, Lord Nelvil, Corinne, the Comte d'Erfeuil, Prince Castel-Forte are representations of national character along the lines formulated in the course of the eighteenth century in novels as well as in aesthetic treatises and discussions of the national traits of literature and art.

Lord Nelvil is the deep, brooding, moral, melancholy man of the north; the Comte d'Erfeuil is the amiable, sociable, witty, talkative, brilliant, but of course superficial Frenchman; Prince Castel-Forte is the courtly, charming, warm, and joyful Italian gentleman, joyful in public only, but sad within his own heart; quite clearly his hour upon the stage of history is past. Corinne of course, besides being Madame de Staël, is also Italy, but with certain ties to England since her father had been Lord Edgermond; she is even more than all that, because she is also a genius, a muse, and historical consciousness. Considering Prince Castel-Forte's sadness, one may say that there was good reason for it, indeed for any Italian to be sad; for after all, within the new dimension of culture, Italy, mother of the arts, ancient home of the Romans, had in effect been reduced to a gigantic aesthetic object, a species of transcendant still-life combining nature, antiques, modern works of art and architecture, history and any variety of aesthetic experiences which seemed to be the privilege of non-Italians. Italy, in short, became the privileged terrain of refined cultural experience. The dimension of culture, insofar as it implies a sense of history, insured each nation a specific national past and character, but somehow Italy offered more; it possessed the universal culture, the most beautiful examples of artistic endeavour, and also, the most splendid and smiling and rich landscapes. See Naples and die.

Considering the long fight of the French to declare themselves independent of ancient and Italian artistic prestige, with the rejection of Bernini's plans for the Louvre marking in a sense a turning point in this endeavour, it is clear the French moment was past. It is in this perspective that *Corinne* may be construed as a species of answer to Perrault. And published at the height of Napoleon's power, it could hardly be considered as praise of the age of Napoleon or French artistic achievement. The situation since the age of Louis XIV had been literally reversed. Perrault's President had been to Tivoli and was being shown Versailles to see for himself that the moderns equalled the ancients, and a modern French garden was being opposed to the romance associated with the past in general and with Tivoli in particular. In Madame de Staël's novel, Tivoli regains all its evocative power as in her description of the site, culture and nature unite to create an aesthetic effect upon the spectator:

"At last they discovered Tivoli, which had been the residence of so many famous men, Brutus, Augustus, Meceneas, Catullus, but above all it had been the home of Horace; for it was his verse which had rendered that region illustrious. The house of Corinne was built above the noisy cascade of the Teverone; on top of the mountain, facing her garden was the temple of the Sybil. It was a grand idea of the ancients to place their temples upon the summit of elevated ground. They dominated the countryside as religious ideas dominate all other thoughts. They inspired more enthusiasm for nature, as the sign of the divinity from which it emanates and the eternal recognition of successive generations towards her. The landscape, from whichever point observed, made a tableau with the temple which was the centre or ornament of the whole. Ruins spread a singular charm upon the Italian countryside. They do not bring to mind, like modern edifices, the labour and presence of man; they merge with the trees and nature and seem in harmony with the solitary torrent, image of time which turned them into what they are. The most beautiful sites in the world, holding no traces of a remarkable event, bringing forth no memories, are deprived of interest in comparison with historical countries. What spot was better fitted to be Corinne's home in Italy than a region consecrated to the Sybil, to the memory of a woman animated by divine inspiration? Corinne's home was ravishing; it was decorated with the elegance of the modern manner, yet the charm of an imagination which pleased itself in the beauty of the antique also made itself felt. One could note a rare understanding of happiness, in the most elevated sense of that term, namely that which makes of happiness all which ennobles the soul, excites thought and livens talent."

This passage is an excellent example of the richness and

complexity of the dimension of culture, which might be defined in historical terms as the eighteenth century's contribution to the apprehension of the arts and a further and allied development, namely the aesthetic appreciation of nature. But as the passage indicates, it also implies a sense of history, of the survival of the past, and also a feeling for religion quite different from that associated with orthodox religious thought. Note too that this mental phenomenon, this view of culture, can also be made to fit into a framework of nature and interior decor. The dimension of culture also implied a new vision and form of happiness, quite distinct from that of the *Neveu de Rameau* and the life led by the *fermiers-généraux* and financiers of the eighteenth century of Louis XV. The so-called Rococo had also been the style of a dream of happiness, but by the time of the Revolution and the Empire there were obviously differences of opinion as to whether one ought to reach happiness by the low road or the high road. The generation of Madame de Staël and the readers of the *philosophes* seem to have opted for a happiness associated with the rare atmosphere of sublime heights. Corinne's view of happiness as realized in her interior is not much different from that of Diderot the enthusiast: it is a happiness beyond hedonism, aristocratic, befitting neither the feudal hero, nor the financiers, but rather pertaining to genius, to the great man or woman above the vulgar crowd, which means of course that this new style of happiness is at times, as witness Corinne herself, difficult to distinguish from noble suffering.

Within her house, Corinne had a collection of pictures and these were as tell-tale as the site she had chosen for her country house. The pictures complemented the setting, her sense of history, and along with Corinne herself all these elements were part of an aesthetic-moral unity. The collection was modest: histories, religious and poetical themes, a few landscapes. None of her pictures had many figures in them because she preferred unity of interest to what might be called the aesthetic of the *difficulté vaincue* which the disposition of many figures implied. The first painting described in the novel corresponds to David's "Lictors bringing back the bodies of the sons of Brutus"; its pendant represented Marius being spared by a Cimbrian warrior, and the last of her histories showed Belisarius carrying his dead guide upon his shoulders. All of these illustrated certain moral truths and are indeed excellent examples of what can be defined as literary painting: Brutus exemplified virtues which resembled crime; the Marius illustrated glory as the cause of misfortune, and Belisarius, services being paid for by the blackest persecution.

Besides these pictures, Corinne showed Lord Nelvil a Christ asleep upon the Cross by Albano, a Christ falling under the burden of the cross by Titian, and, as in the case of the histories, these pictures too were chosen with a certain idea in mind, for these were in a sense the answers to pagan history. They relieved the oppressed soul by recalling to mind the religion which was able to console an enslaved universe and bring life into the very depths of the soul and heart while all outside was silence and oppression: Christ was hope.

As for her other pictures, there were four poetries taken respectively from the Aeneid, Tasso, Shakespeare, and Racine, and her landscapes included a rustic scene by Salvator Rosa, a heroic landscape representing Cincinattus being asked to leave his plough in order to command the Roman armies. Finally there was a northern, melancholy, ossianesque landscape which brought tears to Lord Nelvil and prompted Corinne to take up her harp and sing ancient Scottish romances. The visit to the private museum thus ends upon a sublime and tear-filled scene. Corinne's collection was clearly not gathered as an aspect of conspicuous consumption or to satisfy the passion of a *curieux* or an amateur; nor for that matter the taste befitting a *grand seigneur*. There was an idea behind the collection and the arrangement of the pictures, for it outlined in a few monuments or images the stage of European culture reached by the end of the eighteenth century. One might even see in it a certain broadening of the Enlightenment since it even included a historical view of Christianity which was no longer Voltairian, but which was close to that of Chateaubriand's *Génie du Christianisme*, which appeared in 1802; it also included a pronounced taste for nature and for poetry.

Culture as manifest in the work of Madame de Staël, in *De La Littérature* of 1801, and in *Corinne*, may be considered the end result of the Enlightenment. Letters and the arts were thought to be an instrument for the progress and moral improvement of mankind. As such it was considered the expression of thought, and the fine arts too were considered from this point of view. As Sismondi once wrote to Bonstetten about Madame de Staël's relations with objects: "As you know, Madame de Staël is bored if she has to pay attention to *things*, they seem to keep her from pursuing her thoughts."[1] But if she did not much care for things, for the fine arts or for music, both of which she admitted as objects for reverie, she was enamoured of history. Culture was thus a heritage; it was cumulative; it took on value as time passed, as the financiers found in the course of the eighteenth century when they sold their collections. Or on a more intellectual note, as Fontenelle had put it in the previous century, ". . . un bon esprit cultivé est, pour ainsi dire, composé de tous les esprits des siècles précédents."[2]

It was this cumulative character which might tie culture to the idea of progress. But also, already in the time of Madame de Staël, culture came to be considered as the weight of the past upon the present, as a burdensome heritage, and this too came to be expressed in some of the writings of the period. This helps to explain the nostalgia for simpler times and also the *mal du siècle* manifest in such characters as René, a species of anti-hero created by Chateaubriand, Sénancour's Obermann, and Benjamin Constant's Adolphe, all of whom suffer from a byproduct of culture, *ennui*, boredom, one of the psychological problems of the eighteenth century. In the case of *Corinne* culture also implies a certain blurring of the distinctions between nature and history, Christianity and religiosity, art and aesthetic sentiment; but this blurring may be regarded as part of the cumulative aspect of culture, and in the novel it follows from the love of Rome expressed in it, for Rome was not only a city, but the very "history of the world symbolized by various emblems and represented under various forms."[3] Thus culture became in the work and mind of Madame de Staël, "a relationship between history and feeling, between social and political institutions and the human

1. Cf. J. Christopher Herold, *Mistress to an Age*, N.Y. — Indianapolis, 1958, p. 308.
2. Cf. Roland Mortier, *Clartés et ombres au Siècle des Lumières*, Geneva, 1969, p. 66.
3. Herold, *op. cit.*, p. 197.

heart."[4]

Corinne was more than a love novel; for through its protagonists it was also a drama of conflicting cultures and societies.
It was this interest in history which lent the fine arts the prestige
they enjoyed at the end of the eighteenth century; their association with mere luxury, deplored as early as 1719 by the abbé Du
Dos, had been overcome in part through the reforms in history
painting effected by the Academy, in part by the writings of the
philosophes and other critics, but also by the interest of the
antiquarians. Intellectual and aesthetic currents thus joined to
produce what came to be regarded as the universal and true style
of art and beauty, what we call neo-classicism. In fact it was far
less universal than was thought: it was merely the style of the
dimension of culture such as it was understood, or perhaps
misunderstood, at the end of the eighteenth century. It was as tied
to an élite as had been the previous style now disdainfully
described as *rococo* by the partisans of the *retour à l'antique*.

In the seventeenth century, the chevalier de Méré, a writer on
manners, morals, and the qualities befitting a gentleman, had once
disdainfully referred to the Romans as mere bourgeois. The new
régime which came to power after 1789 took the Romans far
more seriously, though the Romans did not have to await the
Revolution to come into their own as models of moral and artistic
emulation. For the French classical tradition, as represented in the
work of Poussin, in the great writers of the seventeenth century,
such as Corneille or Boileau, in Fénelon's admiration for Antiquity, and in the eighteenth century in the works of Montesquieu, Vauvenargues, Rousseau, the *Mémoires* of Madame Roland,
the histories of Rollin and certain of Diderot's writings, had
appealed to men whose turn of mind differed from that of the
more ostentatious and luxurious nobles and financiers for whom
the arts were ornament, luxury, and *divertissement*. In order to
understand the transformation of art into culture it is essential to
take this tradition into account as well as to stress the differences
which existed within the upper classes in regard to luxury and
therefore also the arts. The way of life of the financiers, the

4. *Idem*, p. 198.

luxury of the court, the lavish spending on building, luxury, and women, was far from being approved by all, and there were many who were disturbed by the upward social mobility evident in eighteenth century society. It was judged wrong that money should be able to purchase what in former times had been considered attributes of nobility. To borrow from Sénac de Meilhan, the transformation of magnificence into luxury shocked the more sober of the population to become an object of satire for moralists and playwrights.

In the seventeenth century the bourgeois gentleman Monsieur Jourdain was still the subject of ridicule; but in the course of the eighteenth century, with the growing success of the *fermiers-généraux*, with the very increase in their luxury and riches, their patronage, and also, it must be said, their genuine culture, this was no longer the case. Turcaret, of Lesage's play, was still ridiculous in the early eighteenth century, but by the middle of the same century the reputation of the financiers and *fermiers-généraux* was changing: great wealth, spending on architecture, luxuries, buying noble lands, had succeeded. Indeed, by the end of the Old Régime all but about ten per cent of the *fermiers-généraux* were indeed noble.

In view of this use of art and luxury, and taking the new attitude towards arts and letters propounded by the writers, it might be possible to argue that culture, as it came to be formed in the course of the century, finally reconciled the frugality, morality, and sobriety of the hard working middle class man of affairs or of the robe, with the luxury and all it implied of the very rich and luxurious *fermiers-généraux* and court nobility. Culture in a sense became the bourgeois moral justification of art and aesthetic sentiment, and the history painting of the period of the Revolution provided a fittingly austere basis for this culture. "It is, after all, perhaps, not so surprising to find the 'emancipated' and victorious bourgeoisie erecting a 'Republic of Virtue' in 1793. The 'old' bourgeois way of life died very hard, if it died at all; it was rationally and morally more congruent with the social role of the bourgeoisie in an open class society than were the efforts of so many of the eighteenth century bourgeois to acquire the symbols of noble status."[5] What distinguished the new class in power, a class of lawyers, office holders, bankers, businessmen, rich merchants, doctors, and property owners, was no longer ancient lineage, a glorious past in the service of King and country, nor was its authority based on ancient tradition, lost in time and ultimately claimed to be of divine institution. It was not even a noble way of life, though many had adopted this; rather it was superior ability and knowledge in the realm of practical affairs and political matters of concern to the nation as a whole.

In fact, while the new class in power was no longer the old nobility, it was very much an aristocracy. While the former term could be associated with the ancient feudal order, race, and lineage, the term aristocracy implies something else, for an aristocracy might include nobles as well as non-nobles. One was born a noble; but the aristocrat was such because he possessed wealth and culture, and while an aristocrat might not be noble, a noble might not for all his lineage be an aristocrat.[6] As a character in Balzac's *Ursule Mirouet*, set about 1830, put it, there are no more nobles, only aristocrats. Significantly the man who uttered those words was noble, but broke; he possessed honour, but no fortune. Now as concerns the imaginary world of these new aristocrats, it belonged precisely to the realm of culture, and it was this very culture which served to distinguish them from the old type financier, the more sober bourgeois, or the *grand seigneur*.

The commonly used expression so often heard in recent years, *bourgeois culture*, may strictly speaking be a tautology. As concerns France there may be no other culture, and as concerns the eighteenth century one may consider culture as the bourgeois invention *par excellence*. As such it defined that class's historical attitude towards civilization, morality, private life, luxury, and the arts, and of course, what might be called a gentleman's discipline of leisure and a distinguished way of spending part of one's fortune. By the end of the eighteenth century, the old nobility still had ancestors, pride, the remembrance of past glories, style

5. Elinor G. Barber, *The Bourgeoisie in Eighteenth Century France*, Princeton, 1955, p. 93.
6. On this distinction see R. R. Palmer, *The Age of Democratic Revolution*, Princeton, 1959, vol. I.

and debts. As for the people, it had, as it still does, appetites. The old nobility, as far as its imaginary universe is concerned, had belonged to the world of magnificence and art, while the people had belonged to that of the Christian universe; each had a specific role within the Christian vision of human destiny. In contrast to both, the bourgeois, the learned, the nobility of the robe, had in the course of time come to construct an imaginary universe of their own which came to fruition in the course of the seventeenth and eighteenth centuries, and which, in contrast to the imaginary world espoused by the nobility, was perhaps more literary than that provided by the fine arts.

It must not be forgotten that letters themselves were in the eighteenth century an avenue of social mobility which paralleled that of the financiers: "... men of letters had come to fulfil a function that was felt to be of great importance. This esteem for intellectual achievement opened a channel of mobility to talented men which did not confine them to those activities which were closely associated with the noble style of life."[7] In a sense Diderot's *Moi* pleads for this alternative to *Lui*'s tacit espousal of the financier's style, which by the 1760s was hardly separable from the noble style since the nobility had been infected with luxury.

The history painting which flourished with the school of David was more fitting for this literary mentality than the luxury art of the nobility and the *fermiers-généraux* of the world of art. The Enlightenment heralded the triumph of literary painting because the prestige of men of letters and of culture was high at this time. It manifested itself in art criticism, discourses in the Academy, aesthetic theories and a great many essays on taste as well as antiquarian knowledge. All these manifestations of knowledge, theoretical and antiquarian, historical and even poetical, manifest through language, may all be subsumed under the heading of culture, which thereby turns out to be a possession: the knowledge of the heritage of the past. But though it may be defined as a possession, it is more than the possession of riches, objects of art, luxury, wealth. It may suppose all that, but it is more because it

7. Barber, *op. cit.*, p. 131.

supposes knowledge possessed in such a way as to distinguish its possessor from the old nobility as well as the poor, from the vulgar rich as well as from the pedant whose profession it is to possess knowledge. Thus culture supposes a certain ease, style, worldliness, an amateur status in the best sense of the word. One may wonder how much this differed from the old seventeenth century virtuoso, and on the individual basis it is difficult to deny a similarity; but the range of culture, its possession, was by the end of the eighteenth century more ramified than it had been previously, and it may be that the aesthetic aspect was also quite novel. In the seventeenth century one may say there had been pockets of cultivated men and women in a world of art, whereas by the end of the following century what had been the exception had become what was expected of the well-to-do.

Thus culture was the result of the conjunction of the traits of the nobility with those of the cultivated *fermiers-généraux*, financiers, robe, bourgeois, writers, collectors, and patrons of music, within the milieu of the drawing rooms of certain famous women of the eighteenth century, Madame de Lambert, Madame de Tencin, Madame Geoffrin, Madame Du Deffand, Madame Necker, and also in some of the salons of the cultivated and learned *fermiers-généraux* such as Le Riche de la Poupelinière, Tavernier de Boullongne, Fontaine de Cramayel, Helvétius, Madame d'Epinay, whose salon was frequented by the *encyclopédistes*, Lavoisier who received learned men and many foreign visitors, or Grimod de la Reynière, known above all as a gourmet and therefore probably frequented above all for his table.

It was in these milieux that the old style erudition of the seventeenth century, or letters and poetry as mere amusement as in the time of the *précieux*, became less exclusive, took on the aspect of culture in that knowledge no longer acted as mere ornament, and yet had to possess a certain style to be accepted. The difference between this culture and the imaginary realm of the world of art lies in the strongly historical, moral, civic and intellectual bent of the dimension of culture, as well as with the aesthetic dimension which was often absent from the circles of *érudits* of former times. At its best the new culture was co-extensive with the historical imagination, and it could also attain a certain type of poetry associated with the past; at its worst it was often didactic and moralistic. But it was also capable of assuming the form of an interior dimension or meditative idealism again connected with one's position in time and history. Certainly it was beyond mere décor, even though it did also suppose a décor as witness the art of that period, but it certainly was beyond luxury, for that had in effect been sublimated.

If in its formal aspects it manifested itself as the neo-classicism of the end of the eighteenth century, psychologically it may be regarded as romantic. The imagination ranges in historical time, is enamoured of ideal beauty, and is strongly inclined towards aestheticism. And woman, despised as an object of luxury, makes her re-appearance as an aspect of an ideal and unattainable beauty. This trait of aestheticism is important for it also serves to distinguish the world of culture from that of art. Indeed, aestheticism is a transference, and therefore profanation, of religious sentiment into the realm of art and may thus be termed the mysticism of culture. Archbishop Fénelon played a decisive role in this transferance for he "spread about him the free and poetic religiosity which would take the place of orthodox credos. The abstract spiritualism of some would accommodate itself with a vague deism while others, through a need for a more sensuous imagination, would substitute a divine pantheon for the one God."[8] This influence would be as important as that of Rousseau or Chateaubriand in the make-up of the romantic imagination. Indeed, certain traits of *Corinne* are incomprehensible without the vague religiosity which derives ultimately from *Télémaque*. In her works, as in those of her contemporary Chateaubriand, there is a fusion of diverse traditions into an aesthetic unity which was first effected by the Swan of Cambray. "A nineteenth century critic has said that mythology ends with Fénelon. But one might just as well say that it starts anew with him since through him the Christian and the modern consciousness were able to adopt it."[9] The fusion ended as a rather vague idealism, but it was quite effec-

---

8. Alfred Lombard, *Fénelon et le retour à l'antique au XVIIIe siècle*, Neuchâtel, 1954, p. 119.

9. Lombard, *op. cit.*, p. 138.

tive and helps to explain the eclectic character of much early nineteenth century art, taste, poetry, such as the union of Ossian with antique forms, aestheticism and Christianity, the rather diverse interests which come to make up that rather vague realm of the imagination which becomes culture.

Culture as it constituted itself at the end of the eighteenth century may have been the end product of the Enlightenment, but it needs to be stressed that there was a certain divergence in the minds of the men of the late eighteenth century: a belief in progress, based on material success and science, was coupled with a belief in decadence in the aesthetic-moral realm. How superior the ancients had been in moral, physical, and artistic sensibility, how noble their achievements, how happy they had been to live in the midst of an unspoiled nature! This feeling co-existed with the faith in progress or *perfectionnement* of a Condorcet, and in effect amounted to a rejection of Fontenelle's arguments about the ancients of a century before. Indeed, it amounted to a rejection of a central belief of most of the *philosophes*. The dichotomy is striking but may be explained by the development of two separate realms of endeavour: rational, scientific, practical, empirical thought on the one hand, and the realm of the imagination on the other, the proper field of poetry and sentiment. In the literature of the Enlightenment the two realms had been closely united, at the expense of poetry; but it may be argued that culture, as it constitutes itself in the course of the last decades of the century, separates itself from the Enlightenment's strong interest in the natural sciences to become a matter primarily of the historical and poetical imagination, historical and aesthetical sense. It was in this respect that Madame de Staël was a continuator of the Enlightenment.

But the Enlightenment's concern with history and with art, and at the same time the relegation of religion and Christianity to a historical phenomenon, coupled during the Revolution with the confiscation of Church property, led to another highly important manifestation of culture, namely the foundation of a national museum. This began with the Louvre, the various satellite museums in the provinces, and finally the short-lived Musée Napoléon under the directorship of the remarkable Vivant Denon.

The frame of art of the Old Régime turned into an historical framework for the works of art which were inherited from a recent past or liberated for the greater glory of an Emperor who was well aware of the value of the arts in the process of image making. The establishment of museums at this time testifies not only to the concern for art of the Revolutionaries and the glory of Napoleon, but also to the passing of an historical moment: namely the relegation of the world of art we have posited to the past. Art as the prerogative of the magnificence of the great and the private luxury of the rich, as the instrument of the Church for dominating the imagination of the faithful, turned into an institution associated with a past phase of historical becoming, and its nature would consequently be radically altered.

It is perhaps because of this recognition of the passing of an historical epoch in which art played a central role in society that art was in a sense idealized in the new dimension of culture, beauty assigned a transcendent value, and works of art preserved as precious objects worthy of the attention of the nation rather than merely amateurs, collectors, and connoisseurs. The possession of works of beauty, no matter how acquired, and no matter to what past or society they had belonged, became a national concern. Art as private luxury, as the décor and ornament of the rich was definitely something which belonged to the past. Individuals might still collect, but collecting itself took on a new nature as the works which survived the upheaval of the Revolution and failed to end up in public institutions took on the character of found objects to acquire a poetic dimension if only because they originated from a lost past. Multimillionnaires might still surround themselves with works of art and later turn their homes into museums, like American robber barons of the late nineteenth century; it was felt that the rich ought to have such things because one was morally obligated to be cultivated just as one was morally obligated to pass the private culture on to the public poor. The new status of works of art within the dimension of culture also implied an increased institutionalization by way of the State, since its interest was extended from the production of works of art, already manifest under the Old Régime through the formation of Academies, to their acquisition and preservation, to their existence in time as well as space. The formation of the nation-state must thus also be considered an important formative factor of the new realm of culture.

In the 1750s, in his first published writings, Rousseau had passionately attacked the world of art of his day: the natural man within was stifled by the existence of forms, usages, manners, and the ornate frame of civilization and society. He was a prophet crying in vain, for the progress of civilization was hardly arrested by his writings. Yet his argument went not unheeded; for it was in accord with a sentiment which he shared with others, a sentiment which nostalgically looked back upon a happier and simpler past, and also, it was in accord with the critics of luxury of the eighteenth century. Culture, as it came to take form during and after the Revolution, can well be regarded as a species of conciliation of art and morality, art and sobriety, the union of the past and the present on the level of the imagination in a present, and an idealization of the lost world of art. As concerns luxury, we have already alluded to culture as its sublimation. The loser, despite the continuing success or progress of the arts and sciences deplored by Rousseau, was perhaps less Rousseau himself than the *Neveu de Rameau*, for within the new dimension of culture which would be that of high seriousness, who would dare to refuse a hypothetical statue and immortality as a *bienfaiteur du genre humain* for the pleasures and delights, palpable and not abstract, given by the possession of gold in the present? The *philosophe* triumphed; he had become the man of culture.

If we turn from these rather general considerations to portraiture, the transformations which have occurred become visible as the cultivated man or woman changed appearance and assumed poses and struck attitudes with the changed status of culture within history and society. The traditional portrait in the grand manner, the mythological disguise of court ladies, the unassuming portraits of gentlemen-hunters, men of wit and *aisance*, gave way to meditative men and women as classic inspiration and nature transformed their representation in portraiture into solitary meditations on ruins and the decay of empires, or solitary dreamers in a garden setting. The man of culture whose antecedent might well be traced to the genius of vast and penetrating mind and imagination thus assumed the pose of the superior man, silent, melancholy, profound, responsible, the burdens of thought upon his brow, the smile of sociability of the eighteenth century effaced by the sentiment of responsibility and the weight of experience. The new hero of the dimension of culture may be Obermann, or Corinne, an historical actor like Napoleon, a poetic nature like Goethe, a thinker like Volney, a force like Madame de Staël herself, a historian and minister like Guizot, a beauty beheld like Madame Récamier, a wanderer like Byron. The imagination had broken the frame of art and was free to range and create anew within the dimension of culture. The gardens of Versailles, combining the intelligible beauty of geometric design with the surprises of the *je ne sais quoi,* were quit and abandoned for the more open vistas and memories of Tivoli.

R. G. Saisselin

The Public, Literature
& the Arts
in the 18th Century

Most of us are conscious of the great waves of change which are bearing along the present generation – science and technology, race relations, sexual habits, women's liberation, the revolution of the adolescents. Some are exhilarated as they ride the crest, others fearful that they will be dashed against the rocky shore. Few look back, fewer still realise that the wave they are riding has been lifting and cresting for centuries. None of our present day revolutions has a short ancestry and even that cultural revolution in which we take a certain pride has its origins long ago – its seed bed in the fifteenth century. Its early childhood was certainly long and arduous; lasting longer than one might have expected, but after some three hundred years it burst into vigorous manhood in England in the eighteenth century.

By cultural revolution I mean that process by which literature and the arts have ceased to be the pre-occupation of small, specialised élites and have become available for the mass of society to enjoy. For most of human history there have been two cultures – no, not science and the arts, but the culture of the governing aristocracies and the popular culture of the peasantry. This is as true of China as of Europe. From the late seventeenth century a mass culture, belonging essentially to the middle class, developed, which, if it did not quite obliterate the other two, drove them into smaller and smaller social enclaves. This transformation required three conditions – technological advance, considerable dissemination of wealth and, by no means last, freedom. Without printing there could have been no cultural revolution. It seems to me we always undervalue an invention without which the intellectual achievements of the modern world could never have taken place.[1]

---

1. This view is substantiated in a series of important articles by Elizabeth

Before 1450 there had been several renaissances, propitious times when knots of scholars had been actively encouraged to recover and to study the works of the ancients. But so long as the culture was scribal, such successes as they had could be lost, easily overlooked or forgotten, because they were bound to be enshrined in a small number of manuscripts. For example, John the Deacon exposed the forgery of the Donation of Constantine in the year 1,000 A.D., but his work, which only existed in a few copies, was forgotten, whereas the exposure by Lorenzo Valla four hundred years later was printed in what for a copied MS would have been a very large edition.[2] It became widely available, not to a handful of scholars, but to hundreds. Similarly, within a scribal culture errors tended to multiply, for copyists' mistakes were inevitable, whereas in print texts gradually, but steadily, improved in accuracy. But mainly, of course, print made books available, whereas manuscripts had rarely been so. A monastic library of three hundred books was in the middle ages a very large library:[3] by 1600 three hundred books was not exceptional for a modest country gentleman of bookish tastes. Furthermore, the monastic library would have been composed almost entirely of religious books and a few encyclopaedias, whereas the country gentleman's library, by 1600, would have ranged over history, geography, the classics, as well as divinity. The wide diffusion of secular knowledge could not have taken place without printing: also continuing self-education became possible to a degree that was unthinkable for a purely scribal culture. Printing, therefore, provided the spring to the wide diffusion of literature. And not only literature, but also painting, first through the woodcut and then the etching. And, of course, music too. Think of the boredom and labour involved in

Eisenstein: "Some Conjectures about the Impact of Printing on Western Society and Thought: A Preliminary Report," *Journal of Modern History*, 40, 1968, pp. 1-56; "The Advent of Printing and the Problem of the Renaissance," *Past and Present*, 45, 1969, pp. 18-89; "The Advent of Printing in Current Historical Literature: Notes and Comments on an Elusive Transformation," *American Historical Review*, 75, 1970, pp. 727-743. To some extent Professor Eisenstein's case suffers a little from over-emphasis. See the doubts raised by T. K. Rabb in *Past and Present*, 52, 1971, pp. 135-140. See also Eisenstein's reply, *ibid.*, pp. 140-144.

2. J. H. Plumb, *The Death of the Past*, London, 1969, pp. 79 n. 1, 82.

3. N. R. Ker, *Medieval Libraries of Great Britain. A List of Surviving Books*, London, 2nd. ed., 1964, p. xi.

copying down every song that one enjoyed or every piece of instrumental music that one wished to play. This technological basis has to be stressed, for what it unleashed was in a sense so slow in developing that its revolutionary significance is often overlooked.

The exploitation of printing was curiously slow. Even two hundred years after its invention, the exploitation of its possibilities as far as a mass audience was concerned had not made much progress. Take the London of Pepys.[4] There was only one daily paper — The London Gazette — which contained official matters relating to the Court — proclamations, decrees, promotions and the like, and a little very stale foreign news. Pepys had to go, and almost every day he went, to the Royal Exchange to pick up gossip from foreign merchants to learn what was happening in Europe. Similarly he would spend half an hour or so at Westminster Hall in search of news of the happenings at Court or in Parliament. He haunted taverns, not only because he loved wine, but also because he was avid for the news which was often to be found there. If you happened to live out of London, of course, the situation was worse. A rich man could subscribe to a manuscript letter sent to him by a journalist who, like Pepys, did the rounds and then summarized what he learned for his country correspondents.[5] In consequence it was a world of surprising ignorance, alive with rumours, wonders and marvels. For Pepys, as for most of his dilettante friends, books were precious objects rather than tools — carefully and beautifully bound they were stored in handsome locked bookcases. Still, books were available; large libraries, such as the Earl of Sunderland's, not uncommon, and reading as a pastime, as well as a scholarly pursuit, was well established.

The London of Pepys was not culturally exciting. Certainly

4. For the London of Pepys see the new edition of The Diary of Samuel Pepys, R. C. Latham and W. Matthews, eds., 5 Vols. to date, London, 1970-. Also J. H. Plumb, "The Public and Private Pepys," The Saturday Review, New York, October 24, 1970, pp. 29-31, 71. Reprinted in Plumb, In the Light of History, London, 1972.

5. For a typical newsletter see Historical Manuscripts Commission, 12th. Report, Appendix, Part VII. S. H. Le Fleming MSS, London, 1890, pp. 305-307. For two official newsletter series see Peter Fraser, The Intelligence of the Secretaries of State and Their Monopoly of Licensed News, 1660-1688, Cambridge, 1956, pp. 147-152.

prints of pictures were available, and Pepys bought many, but they were expensive, the editions small and there were not many dealers. Pictures by great masters were rarely to be seen, except by the possessor and his friends. The only easily available pictures for a man or a woman who could afford to dress well were to be seen at the Royal palaces. Charles II was very accessible to his subjects and any well dressed person could get inside the public rooms of Whitehall or Windsor. For the vast majority of men and women, however, paintings were unknown, apart from an amateur portrait by a local artist or a painted inn sign. In music they were a little better served. Even during the Commonwealth church organs had been built and Cromwell himself was fond of music. But public music, apart from church music, was exceptional. The first English opera, *The Siege of Rhodes*, was in effect a play with musical interludes. *The Tempest*, too, was turned by Shadwell into a semi-musical entertainment and occasionally there were musical divertimenti in the theatre. There were no concerts, few public paid performances until the very end of the century. Although popular, the restored theatre of Charles II was poverty-stricken, new plays rare, most were badly acted and vilely produced. Addicted as Pepys was, he was but rarely pleased by what he saw.[6] And theatres were small and sparse. And in the provinces, of course, non-existent. There, one was lucky to enjoy the antics of a few strolling players in a barn. Again, in the country one made one's own music or hired, as Sir Robert Walpole's father did, a pair of fiddlers for an evening for a shilling to play country dances.[7] The

6. See Latham and Matthews, *op.cit.*, Vol. I, pp. 309-10. 5 December 1660: "I dined at home and after dinner went to the New Theatre and there I saw *The Merry Wifes of Windsor* acted. The humours of the country gentleman and the French Doctor very well done: but the rest poorly and Sir J. Falstaffe as bad as any." Vol. II, p. 175. 9 September 1661: ". . . thence to Salisbury Court play-house, where was acted the first time *Tis pitty shee's a whore* — a simple play and ill acted." p. 202. 26 October 1661: ". . . I to the Theatre and there saw *The Country Captaine*, the first time that it hath been acted this 25 years — a play of my Lord Newcastles, but so silly a play as in all my life I never saw, and the first that ever I was weary of in my life." p. 223. 29 November 1661: ". . . I to the Theatre . . . and there saw *Love at first sight*, a play of Mr. Killigrew, and the first time that it hath been acted since before the troubles; and great expectations there was, but I find the play to be a poor thing; and so I perceive everybody else do."

7. See J. H. Plumb, "The Walpoles: Father and Son," in *Men and Places*, London, 1963, pp. 121-146.

cultural poverty of late seventeenth century England was vast — no newspapers, no public libraries, no theatres outside London, no concerts anywhere, no picture galleries of any kind, no museums, almost no botanical gardens and no organised sports. Race meetings happened when gentlemen wagered their horses against each other: football — little better than a riot — occurred on various feast days between villages, prize-fighters were matched, like racehorses, by gentlemen.[8] Nor could the mind be extended by travel, unless one was very rich. Only the aristocratic young could afford to travel to improve their minds. Culturally the seventeenth century was circumscribed to a most remarkable degree. Much more so, one might add, than China of the same date.

Within one hundred years this had almost totally changed: and we can see our own cultural world staring at us in embryo, for it was in the eighteenth century that culture began to develop a mass audience and to take the technology of printing to its furthest commercial limits. Leisure and culture became a profitable speculation in which more and more capital was sunk — an aspect of eighteenth century economic growth almost totally ignored by economic historians. The potentiality for such a development became manifest, however, in that culturally barren world of Pepys. The Civil War had provoked a mass of ephemeral publication in which every shade of religious and political opinion had been earnestly debated. This, of course, had been largely, but not entirely, confined to London and although the flood had abated with the Restoration, neither Charles II nor James II had been able to bring unlicensed printing to a halt. Nevertheless, there was a sharp decline between 1660-1688. Private manuscript newsletter services increased as print declined, but they were expensive and so limited in circulation.[9] Satires on political events and personalities tended also to circulate in manuscript or were sung by ballad singers and often not printed until years later when the danger had passed.[10] But the pamphlet war raged with vigour.

8. Dennis Brailsford, *Sport and Society: Elizabeth to Anne*, London, 1969, pp. 205-6, 213.
9. Fraser, *op. cit.*, p. 39.
10. *Poems on Affairs of State*, Vol. II, 1678-1681, Elias F. Mengel, Jr., ed., New

The growth of coffee houses provided more centres for the dissemination of news, scandal, rumour and argument; and so disturbing did these seem to Charles II that he contemplated suppressing them.[11] But even as early as 1670 it was clear that there was an audience – literate, very politically orientated, even though largely London based.

The first cresting of the wave came after the Revolution of 1688, helped by war, by the rage of party politics, and the lapsing of the licensing laws. With the *Post Boy* and the *Post Man*, the first non-official newspapers began. In 1702 the *Daily Courant* gave London its first daily newspaper. More remarkably, all of these papers flourished. There is a remarkable growth of magazines, but they splutter and die and fail to establish themselves, but they display novel features: much that they print is not in the least concerned with politics or religion, but about the conditions of life or its curiosities and most of them encourage what today would be called "audience participation." *The Athenian Oracle* and its fellows did not last, but the market was there and growing, the right ingredients had not been found. The main road to popular success was to be in the form of the periodic essay concerned with manners, social morality and improvement. Magazines based on this mixture burgeoned in the reign of Queen Anne – Defoe's *Review*, a herculean effort by England's first journalist (he wrote it all himself), the *Medley* and the *Tatler*, which led to the greatest triumph of all, the *Spectator*, of all things a *daily* magazine, but one which so caught the public imagination that it was in demand from New England to Sumatra.[12] Addison and Steele at last found and fully exploited the new and growing middle class audience, an audience which longed to be modish, to be aware of fashion yet wary of its excess, to participate in the world of the great yet be free from its anxieties, to feel smug and superior to provincial rusticity and old world manners, above all to be deeply respectful of the world of

Haven and London, 1965, p. 511.
11. J. H. Plumb, *The Growth of Political Stability in England, 1675-1725*, London, 1967, pp. 43-44.
12. See Donald F. Bond's excellent and definitive edition of *The Spectator*, 5 Vols., Oxford, 1965, Vol. 1, pp. lxxxv-lxxxvi.

commerce and honest trading. These sentiments Addison and Steele skilfully exploited, not with a heavy morality, but by using semi-fictionalized characters such as Sir Roger de Coverley. They provided rich entertainment as well as social education. The key to their outstanding success is contained in the name, *The Spectator*: there was an audience wide enough to participate in life through literature. As T. H. Green so aptly phrased it "that special style of literature . . . which consists in talking to the public about itself. Humanity is taken as reflected in the ordinary life of men."[13] And so, on the success of the *Spectator* one might have prognosticated both the rise of the novel and the growth of a large reading public — spectators living vicariously other people's lives.

Certainly this took place, but more slowly than might have been expected. It was not until the 1740s that Richardson and Fielding began to exploit fully the possibilities of the novel. True, there had been the early successes of Defoe's *Crusoe* and Swift's *Gulliver's Travels*, but these books were nearer to fictionalized tracts than the novel which explored the field of social realism upon which Richardson and Fielding's success was based. But once launched in the forties, the novel spread rapidly. So appealing was this new vogue that, with edges softened a little and language refined, the English novel, again led by Richardson and Fielding, swept France in the 1740s and 50s. As London was full of commercially minded printers, novels, not, however, cheap novels, poured from the presses. Most was imitative trash, meant to fill the idle hours of middle class women and superior servant girls.[14] But the public was there, more numerous than could have been forecast in the late seventeenth century. Just how big this new reading public was is hard to estimate. Editions were not large — the *Spectator* was usually printed in 3,000 copies.[15] Even a very popular paper such as the *Craftsman* at the height of political excitement in the 1730s rarely, if ever, rose beyond 10,000

13. Ian Watt, *The Rise of the Novel: Studies in Defoe, Richardson and Fielding*, University of California Press, Berkeley and Los Angeles, 1967, p. 51. (Quoting from: "Estimate of the Value and Influence of Works of Fiction in Modern Times," *The Works of T. H. Green*, R. L. Nettleship, ed., Vol. III, p. 27.)

14. *Ibid.*, pp. 43-47.

15. Bond, *op.cit.*, Vol. I, pp. xxv-xxvii.

copies.[16] Estimates, such as Dr. Johnson's, give the most popular of all monthly periodicals, *The Gentleman's Magazine*, at no more than 10,000 copies.[17] And the bulk of the public who bought the newspapers, magazines and books lived in London. However, it must be remembered that newspapers and magazines were provided, not only in coffee houses, but also in most taverns; and in the early decades of the eighteenth century coffee houses spread to the major provincial cities. Again, reading aloud was popular, not only to the assembled adults in a family drawing room, but also by the literate to the illiterate. There are plenty of astonished travellers' reports of working men grouped around one who could read to them the latest news of war and politics.[18] And it is to the twenties and thirties that we can trace the beginnings not of the very first circulating libraries — some of them date back to the seventeenth century — but to the rapid exploitation of the circulating library as a profitable line for booksellers. They too spread outwards from London, first to the fashionable spas — Tunbridge Wells and Bath — and then on to major provincial cities — Bristol, Norwich and indeed beyond.[19] By 1760 every town of any size in the West Midlands had at least one circulating library and they could be found flourishing in moderately large villages. Mr. Hanbury of Church Langton, a small village in Leicestershire, was advertising his circulating Library in the Coventry newspapers in 1760 (although his village was some fifteen to twenty miles away).[20] And there was a more exclusive and private development

16. J. H. Plumb, *Sir Robert Walpole*, 2 Vols, London, 1956 and 1961, Vol. II "The King's Minister," pp. 141-143, 179-182.

17. For Dr. Johnson's estimate of *The Gentleman's Magazine* see Watt, *op.cit.*, p. 51. For the circulation of newspapers and periodicals in general see James R. Sutherland, "The Circulation of Newspapers and Literary Periodicals, 1700-30," *The Library*, Series IV, No 15, 1935, pp. 110-124.

18. César de Saussure, *A Foreign View of England in the Reigns of George I and George II*, trans. Van Muyden, London, 1902, p. 162. Also Plumb, *Walpole*, Vol. I, "The Making of A Statesman," p. 31.

19. Paul Kaufman, "The Community Library: A Chapter in English Social History," *Transactions of the American Philosophical Society*, Vol. 57, part 7, Philadelphia, 1967, pp. 50-53. George Barton of Huntingdon was advertising his circulating library in the St. Ives, St. Neots and Peterborough newspapers in 1718. *Ibid.*, pp. 8-9. Also J. H. Plumb, "Reason and Unreason in the Eighteenth Century: The English Experience," *William Andrews Clark Memorial Library*, University of California, Los Angeles, 1971, p. 15.

20. John Money, "Taverns, Coffee Houses and Clubs: Local Politics and Popular

— the Book Club — in which twenty or thirty like-minded men banded together to exchange books and sometimes to meet for a social evening in order to discuss them. This was largely a provincial development, but one which as yet has been scarcely explored.[21] Tamworth (a small town in the Midlands, not far from Dr. Johnson's Lichfield), had several well-established book clubs by the 1770s, most of them associated with local taverns. It is true, however, that these media cater largely for the middle class, professional men and women, or the minor gentry who had to spend so much of their lives isolated in the countryside. However, it would be wrong to think that the growth of publishing and the increase in the reading public, symbolised by the rise of the novel, was confined only to the leisured middle class. Eighteenth century men and women of the lower middle class were eager to participate in the growing affluence of England through self-improvement. They lusted for education: for themselves, for their children. 1744 saw the real foundation of something today everywhere taken for granted — the production of books for children's education and enjoyment. John Newbery published his *A Little Pretty Pocket Book* to teach the alphabet; it was beautifully printed and illustrated, priced 6d, and as an extra selling gimmick — for an extra two pence you could have a ball for your son and a pincushion for your daughter.[22] Of course, there had been children's books before this — horn books for the alphabet teaching and chap books that related fairy stories which, however, I expect were read as much by country folk as by their children, but there had been no systematic and carefully designed children's reading books. Newbery continued to print such books with exceptional success — *and profit*. His *Art of Arithmetic* and *Art of Writing* enjoyed a vast public and he was the first publisher to devise a magazine for young children, *The Lilliputian Magazine*, published in 1751 — a venture which, alas, failed. Newbery — a

Articulacy in the Birmingham Area in the Age of the American Revolution," *Historical Journal*, XIV, No. 1, 1971, pp. 15-47.

    21. For book clubs see Kaufman, *op.cit.*, pp. 26-28. Also Paul Kaufman, "English Book Clubs and Their Role in Social History," *Libri*, Vol. 14, pp. 1-31.

    22. John Newbery, *A Little Pretty Pocket Book*, M. F. Thwaite, ed., Oxford, 1966, p. 2.

typical eighteenth century entrepreneur — had his eye on the middle class market. Even at sixpence his wares were well beyond the means of everyone lower than a tradesman.[23] Nevertheless, other publishers were attempting to push printed matter to the very limits of literacy — not only in cheap chap books and penny ballads or Old Moore's prognostications at a halfpenny a time, but by the "part book" — a device which has had a renewed vogue in Britain this last five or six years. The part-book has two great advantages. The price of a bit of a book can be kept within the means of the poorest section of the market. On the other hand, the profit is enormous, for the total cost of the book soars well beyond what it would be if sold in a single volume.[24] In a desultory way, it had been tried for ballads and poems in Queen Anne's day; (a dreadful poem entitled "A Journey to Hell" had struggled through three parts in 1705), but the boom time came in the twenties and thirties when histories, encyclopaedias, gazeteers and even the Bible were produced in penny and twopenny parts. The avidity for knowledge to which this was the commercial response caught the eye of the provincial newspapers which were being established at this time and more often at their wit's end for material.

These newspapers had begun in the boom time of Queen Anne's wars, but hit the doldrums after the Peace of Utrecht, when many went to the wall. The need for newspapers remained in the provinces largely for a vehicle for advertisement — itself an indication of rising demand — also the eagerness for national and foreign news did not entirely disappear. A few successful newspapers kept going on a diet of news, sex and wonders of all kinds, such as women giving birth to rabbits and the like. Indeed they exploited the untutored appetites of their naive audience with the skill of the tabloid press today, similarly dressing up their pornography in pious condemnation. But they kept alive, and not

23. For John Newbery see Charles Welsh, *A Bookseller of the Last Century. Being some Account of the life of John Newbery and the Books he published, with a notice of the later Newberys*, London, 1875, pp. 106-116. M. F. Thwaite, *From Primer to Pleasure*, London, 1963, pp. 40-51. F. J. H. Darton, *Children's Books in England*, London, 2nd. ed., 1958, pp. 122-140.

24. R. M. Wiles, *Serial Publication in England before 1750*, Cambridge, 1957, pp. 133-194.

only kept alive, but steadily proliferated. By 1760 there were thirty-five provincial newspapers, most of them well established.[25] They give us insight into the increasingly vigorous cultural life of eighteenth century England with their advertisements for schools, for dancing masters, with their news of itinerant salesmen bringing the London fashions, with their notices of assemblies and balls and of their accounts of weekly debates at the local Conversation Clubs. It is from these papers that we learn of the popularity of lectures on science, of the frequency of debate of political and social questions. And we learn, too, of the hunger for the theatre, for music, and for the metropolitan sophistications of life. We glimpse, through them, the birth of that culture-hungry, consumer society which has grown so fast in the last two hundred years.

Only the Netherlands had undergone so thorough a commercial revolution as England did between 1688-1760, but England's population was larger and its revolution more extensive. Long wars stimulated production and by the middle of the century world overseas commerce was beginning to pay handsome dividends. Not only was an exceptionally buoyant home market created, but the burden of labour became much lighter for the men and women who belonged to the minor gentry, the affluent middle class or even to a lesser extent the shopkeepers and tradesmen who lived on the fringe of the middle classes. For the first time there was a leisured middle class to exploit – not rich enough to enjoy their pleasures as the aristocracy had traditionally enjoyed theirs, but longing for the same cultural activities. The first exploitation of this new market came through printers, publishers and writers – of that there can be little doubt. And the stimulus created by this and the new techniques of exploitation which publishers and the bookselling trade devised – newspapers, magazines, libraries, book clubs and the like helped, too, the general exploitation of leisure. Books and papers devoted to manners ran endless essays on the theatre, on music, on dancing, its temptations as well as its delights. Even by satirising the fashionable world they whetted an

25. G. A. Cranfield, *The Development of the Provincial Newspaper, 1700-1760,* Oxford, 1962, pp. 1-28. R. M. Wiles, *Freshest Advices: Early Provincial Newspapers in England,* Ohio, 1965, p. 373.

appetite for it. But the fascination for the social historian is the rapidity with which both the hunger for culture and the increase in leisure were exploited in the eighteenth century – and, of course, exploited at a profit: for the first time the combination of leisure and culture becomes an important industry.

Perhaps one of the most remarkable changes took place in painting and the decorative arts. Unfortunately one can only touch briefly on this huge subject. By the eighteenth century engraving already had a long history, but it had largely been confined to small editions of pictures by great artists which quickly disappeared into the cabinets of the cognoscenti. The only other common engravings were portraits of the great – usually the King, his family and his courtiers. There were also a few allegorical engravings, as well as cheap woodcuts and numerous political satires, but so far the art of engraving had not found its *Spectator*. It did so in William Hogarth,[26] whose *Harlot's Progress* had a similar impact and for similar reasons – a mixture of social realism, dramatically presented, with high-toned morality. Twelve hundred subscribers were delighted with their copies of *Harlot's Progress*; edition after edition flowed from the plates and within twelve months there were eight pirated versions. Hogarth was so enraged that he promoted a Copyright Act which successfully passed the House of Commons in 1735 and gave designers and engravers fifteen years exclusive use of their own productions. A new series by Hogarth, *The Rake's Progress*, soon followed, with a like prodigious success. As Fielding wrote in 1740, "A sober family should be no more without them than without *The Whole Duty of Man* in the house." Indeed, they became the favourite decoration of middle class staircases and dining rooms. Naturally Hogarth followed up his success with a stream of good prints, and imitators abounded. Engraving became immensely profitable. Pictures by English artists from Richardson to Gainsborough were quickly engraved and as quickly sold and so a middle class who could never afford an original modern or old master could festoon their drawing rooms with what was modish in the world of art. By

26. For Hogarth see Ronald Paulson, *Hogarth: His Life, Art and Times*, 2 Vols, New Haven, 1971. Also J. H. Plumb, "Hogarth's Progress," *The New York Review of Books*, Vol. XVII, No. 10, December 16, 1971, pp. 27-28.

the 1780s, England was exporting prints throughout Western Europe — consignments to Spain, even, reaching as much as fifteen thousand pounds at a time. And in London and provincial cities, the print shop became as familiar as a grocer or a draper — and probably more profitable.

Hogarth's act not only stimulated the engraving of fine pictures, but also of satire and caricature — often vicious, often obscene, usually pertinent and sometimes funny — these political cartoons became a symbol of the freedom of English life. In the 1760s when Lord Bute, the favourite of George III, became the object of intense hatred, there were over four hundred derisory prints made about him and one, *The Repeal or the Funeral of Miss Annie Stamp*, dealing with the Stamp Act, sold approximately 16,000 copies.[27] The vitality of this aspect of popular art has rarely been equalled and in Bunbury, Gillray and Rowlandson England produced pictorial satirists of outstanding genius. In no other country could a satirist of the great live both in affluence and public esteem. Elsewhere, except perhaps in Frederick the Great's Prussia or the truly independent America, he would have been clapped in gaol. But participation in art went beyond the cheap engraving — the obvious success and acclaim of British artists made many a young man's pencil twitch and the leisured young ladies of London fancied themselves at drawing and watercolours, dexterity at which became almost as much a mark of gentility as skill in dancing the minuet.

The rich, of course, grew as ever thirsty for costly canvases to adorn their walls. There had been collectors since the days of James I and beyond, but they were few and aristocratic. Now picture collectors became a commonplace in London and the market was as flooded as New York in the twenties with old masters, good, bad and indifferent. Sir Robert Walpole, like any Mellon, set the pace and drove up prices to record heights,[28] but acquired over three hundred splendid pictures which, bought by Catherine the Great from his grandson, became the foundation of the Hermitage collection in Leningrad. But it was this century that

27. *Ex. inf.* John Brewer.
28. For Sir Robert Walpole's collecting activities see Plumb, *Walpole*, Vol. II, pp. 86-87.

began that vast accumulation of paintings which could not be matched by any nation until America entered the art market in the twentieth century. Such a vigorous appetite for painting naturally stimulated other arts — sculpture, architecture and the decorative arts, and here again, England achieved a mass middle class audience that other European nations singularly failed to acquire. But one example must suffice.

The European aristocracy had become increasingly entranced by Chinese porcelain at the turn of the eighteenth century and alchemists and chemists had sought for the materials to make it in Europe, a search that ended with Böttger at Meissen. Other factories and other types of porcelain — soft and hard — quickly followed this initial discovery. The porcelain so made was exceedingly expensive and was designed almost entirely with the noble or luxury market in view. Indeed it proved almost impossible for porcelain factories to survive without lavish royal patronage — attempts in England — Chelsea, Bow, Longton Hall, all went bankrupt, and Louis XV had to rescue the French factories at Vincennes and Sèvres, at times acting as his own salesman.[29] It took the genius of Josiah Wedgwood to exploit properly the huge market that lay beyond the fringes of the aristocratic world. He devised or took over new materials and inventions — basalt, agate, jasper — produced good and expensive vases that could adorn the mantlepieces of the great, pushed his way into royal patronage and at the same time produced vases and flower pots at prices which the middle class could afford — not cheap because that would not have flattered their egos, but *expensive within their means*. And so before the end of the eighteenth century a symbol of middle class culture was as much a Wedgwood vase as a copy of the *Spectator* or Hogarth's *Marriage à la Mode*.[30] And this was true of so many of the decorative arts in

29. For this mania for porcelain see J. H. Plumb, "The Royal Porcelain Craze," *Horizon*, Summer, 1968, pp. 80-89. Reprinted in Plumb, *In the Light of History*, London, 1972.

30. For Josiah Wedgwood see the important series of articles by Neil McKendrick, especially "Josiah Wedgwood: An Eighteenth Century Entrepreneur in Salesmanship and Marketing Techniques," *Economic History Review*, Vol. 12, 1959-60, pp. 408-33; "Josiah Wedgwood and Thomas Bentley: An Inventor — Entrepreneur partnership in the Industrial Revolution," *Transactions of the Royal Historical Society*, 1964, pp. 1-33;

England — furniture such as the French *èbenistes* made for the European aristocracy were beyond the means of lawyers in Norwich or doctors in Bristol or coal traders in Newcastle but, with the elegance retained, indeed improved, but the decoration severely modified, the chairs and commodes and tables of Sheraton and Hepplewhite brought a delight to middle class living which flattered by its reflection of aristocratic taste.[31]

Increasingly in the eighteenth century the aristocracy, the gentry and the financiers became very rich indeed, whilst the middle class living standards steadily became less precarious and more affluent. Some of this wealth in the towns, large and small, seeped down to the shopkeepers, tradesmen, innkeepers and the like. It would be quite wrong to forget the welter of poverty and destitution that still embraced in a deathly vice-like grip the majority of the population, which remained illiterate as well as barbarous, and for whom food, shelter and clothing consumed all of their pitiful earnings, yet the prosperous middle class was sufficiently numerous to begin to change the taste and culture of English society.

So far I have discussed this cultural explosion in terms of media — the spread of printing, of the etching or of the exploitation of the market for more sophisticated goods. But there is always the world of active pleasure, which is just as important as the more passive pursuits. For the first time in the eighteenth century there were sufficient people of sufficient leisure for their exploitation to become professionalized. The prelapsarian myth cultivated by Leavis and his school, and also encouraged by many historians, has pictured the eighteenth and nineteenth century worlds, in contrast to our own, as a world in which cultural participation was the rule: in which people made their own music, made their own games and were not in their idle moments the passive recipients.

In all societies there is a vast amount of self-made culture — one has only to think of the large number of amateur rock groups

"The Enigmatic Urn," *Horizon*, November, 1963, pp. 63-65.

31. The eighteenth century saw the first real growth of leisure shopping; hence the development of the bow-window for shops which enabled more goods to be set out to catch the expectant eye.

or choirs or orchestras or chamber music ensembles, to say nothing of amateur theatricals in our own day, and the same is true of sport. Nevertheless there is a marked change between the seventeenth and eighteenth centuries and once again England led the way, even if it did not always initiate the changes. An excellent example lies in music. Almost everyone who takes delight in music wants to make it. Elizabethan England was full of songsters, full of lute players. Nevertheless, as I mentioned earlier, apart from sacred music, there was practically none that could be publicly heard. The best one could hope for was an interlude at the theatre, or to find a tavern where a girl or boy could sing a country tune or play the fiddle for a country dance. Little or no music was published. The change after 1688 is dramatic. It is true that for the next fifty years orchestras and great musicians, composers as well as executants, were largely supported by aristocratic patronage — one has only to think of the Duke of Chandos's great orchestra at Cannons, for whom first Handel and then Pepusch composed — but public rooms or clubs, open to subscribers, began to develop with rapidity in the reign of Anne and the first Georges — some, like Thomas Britton's — catering for a quite humble public. He converted the loft of his coal house where, for a subscription of 10/- a year and a penny for coffee, one could listen not only to the great English composers, Byrd, Gibbons, Purcell, Locke and Blow, but also to concerti by Correlli and Vivaldi, the court music of Lully and the great German instrumentalist school of Biber and Rosenmuller.[32] Hickford's rooms in St. James's Piccadilly were more fashionable and lasted longer, closing only in 1779,[33] by which time there were a number of flourishing concert halls in London — the Hanover Square Rooms, where Mozart was first popularised, Carlisle House in Soho, the Pantheon in Oxford Street, which was also used as a theatre, and Willis's Rooms, which remained in existence for well over a century. For the size of its potential audience, London was probably as well served with concert halls by 1770 as it is today.

32. For Thomas Britton see *The Oxford Companion to Music*, Percy Scholes, ed., London, 9th. ed., 1955, p. 227.

33. For Thomas Hickford, *ibid.*, p. 227.

And this was only the tip of the musical iceberg. According to Paul Henry Lang, "Toward the middle of the century almost every Town, Castle, University and Church has its orchestra and many musical associations gathered for weekly musical exercises."[34] And the change can be seen in the fare offered by taverns: although many still provided nothing but country songs and dances, an increasing number put on orchestral concerts — Handel's Oratorio *Esther* was performed, for instance, at the Crown and Anchor Tavern — or invested in a Church organ, much to the horror of visiting foreigners, who thought it sacrilegious. As with London, so with the provinces. Starting with the famous Three Choirs Festival (Gloucester, Worcester, Hereford) in 1713,[35] no city of any size was without its musical festivals by the second half of the century.[36] With so wide an audience, middle class taste dominated. For proof one need only turn to the failure of aristocratically supported Italian opera in the 1720s with the incredible popular success of *The Beggar's Opera* which took London so much by storm that in the next decade over a hundred ballad operas were written and produced.[37] Again, the first burst of music publishing came after the Revolution of 1688, when Thomas Cross, John Hare and John Walsh applied the same high pressure methods to music as was common with political pamphlets — that is large cheap editions, as much advertising and puffing as they could find.[38] Walsh, for example, published 600 works in his first twenty-five years.[39] This was but the beginning of a deluge of printed music and there seem to have been about as many musical publishers as ordinary publishers. After 1740, London, the provinces and Ireland doubled their numbers — London reaching the astonishing figure of over 400. Even Scotland

34. Paul Henry Lang, *Music in Western Civilization*, London, 1942, p. 724.

35. For this festival see Watkins Shaw, *The Three Choirs' Festival*, Worcester, 1954.

36. Percy M. Young, *The Concert Tradition*, London, 1965. Birmingham Festival was founded in 1768; Norwich in 1770; Manchester in 1777; Handel Commemorations in London, 1784 and the Yorkshire festival in 1791.

37. John Gay, *The Beggar's Opera*, Edgar V. Roberts, ed.; music edited by Edward Smith, Lincoln, Nebraska, 1969.

38. Charles Humphries and William C. Smith, *Music Publishing in the British Isles*, London, 1954, p. 17.

39. *Ibid.*, p. 18.

became musical. There were six active publishers before 1740, but 59 new ones established themselves before 1800.[40]

As with music, song and dance, so with the theatre. Not only did they increase in London, but the major towns and many minor ones had built theatres by 1750 and expected to see popular London plays acted by some of the leading London professionals.[41] Except for the remoter parts of England, gone forever were the days when a band of strolling comedians took over a farmer's barn for bawdy traditional farces, grotesque melodrama and conjuring tricks, although somewhat more sophisticated mixtures of this kind were to be found in the huge manufacturing towns — Birmingham, Manchester, Leeds — in transition, as it were, to the great music halls of the nineteenth century. Music, dancing, theatre — these were the cultural pastimes for which the prosperous gentry and the new leisured middle class hungered. But their houses were not large enough for private theatres, for private orchestras nor private concerts, nor had they the money to lavish on such conspicuous aristocratic functions. And so it is not surprising that market towns began to build subscription Assembly Rooms, where the social élite of the county could meet for balls, for music, for improving lectures and of course for dramatic performances. Some assembly rooms, such as those at York, were magnificent in conception and design; others were one or two great rooms attached to the leading inn and could double up on occasion for Masonic meetings. Often the subscription was high, which at least kept out the minor shopkeepers and traders, but these Assembly Rooms mark the transitional stage between private and fully public entertainment. As culture seeped through to the masses, and so became more commercially viable, these subscription rooms fell into desuetude. Many, however, remain to remind us of the elegance and sophistication of upper class provincial life in eighteenth century

40. *Ibid.*, pp. 49-346.
41. Allardyce Nicoll, *A History of early Eighteenth Century Drama, 1700-1750*, Cambridge, 2nd. ed., 1929. For the development of the London stage see particularly pp. 271-273; for the provincial theatre see p. 4. See also, *idem, A History of late Eighteenth Century Drama, 1750-1800*, Cambridge, 1927, pp. 3, 232-348. Sybil Rosenfeld, *Strolling Players and Drama in the Provinces, 1660-1765*, Cambridge, 1939.

England.[42] They were, of course, the provincial equivalent of those two wonders of London – Vauxhall and Ranelagh Gardens, where one could dine, listen to music, look at excellent pictures, and of course dance, sometimes masked, sometimes not, and above all partake of that favourite eighteenth century sport of sauntering to ogle the girls.[43]

A similar transitional stage can be seen in the growth of the town dedicated entirely to leisure or retirement – a phenomenon which is now so commonplace in the western world that it is difficult to remind oneself how recent and how significant this development is. Like the readers of the *Spectator* or *Pamela*, eighteenth century men and women, eager for a holiday, liked to have a sound moral excuse for their enjoyment. And so the first holiday centres grew up at spas – Bath and Tunbridge Wells, quickly followed by Scarborough, Bristol Hot Springs, Cheltenham, Harrogate, Matlock and the rest. Brighton, where one took the sea water internally, as well as externally, got off to a slow start, but roared ahead under the patronage of the Prince Regent towards the end of the century, when the spas themselves began slowly to decline, as men and women began to accept frankly the idea of a holiday for holiday's sake.[44] Also men and women may have become healthier as personal and social hygiene improved, for there can be no doubt that the majority of those who went to the spas in the middle of the century usually had some ailment, major or minor, which they hoped the hideous waters might cure. But the main business of spas was amusement – dancing, theatre, music and reading and, of course, flirting and making love. Just as

42. Typical small town assembly rooms, both beautiful eighteenth century buildings, are those at Bury St. Edmunds and Leicester. For Leicester see Jack Simmons, "A Leicester Architect, 1752-1814," *Parish and Empire: Studies and Sketches*, London, 1952, which deals with John Johnson. The Lion Hotel, Cambridge possessed a brilliant eighteenth century assembly room, now demolished, that doubled as a Masonic Lodge. The early assembly room at Brighton is attached to the Old Ship Hotel.

43. For the Vauxhall Gardens see Mollie Sands, "Music not too refined," *Musical Times*, Vol. 91, 1950, pp. 11-15. See also Percy M. Young, *op.cit.*, p. 138. For the Ranelagh Gardens see *ibid.*, p. 140. See also E. D. Mackerness, *A Social History of English Music*, London, 1964, pp. 104-105. It was, of course, Hogarth's idea that Vauxhall Gardens should display contemporary paintings: he never missed a chance of exploiting the market; see Paulson, *op.cit.*, Vol. I, pp. 347-348.

44. For Brighton, see Osbert Sitwell and Margaret Barton, *Brighton*, London, 1935. Also J. H. Plumb, "The Brighton Pavilion," *Men and Places*, pp. 80-97.

it was a little lower down the social scale at Islington or Sadlers Wells, so were the spas nearest to London to which the tradesmen flocked.[45]

All the activities that I have so far described point to the growth of a middle class audience — not a mass audience by our standards — but so large and growing a one that its commercial exploitation was becoming an important industry, and it was a market that had enormous potential for growth. And the seeds of future development were also occurring in one aspect of human living that historians constantly ignore — sport.

Until the eighteenth century, sport had been either for gentlemen or peasants and always something that you made for yourself. If you had a fine horse, you wagered it against your neighbour's, or if you were a racing man you congregated with other racing men at Newmarket or Doncaster and spent a week in challenging those you fancied that you could beat. But it was haphazard; there were conventions rather than rules, and few spectators except those involved in the racing or the business of racing, except maybe for a few neighbouring gentlemen. But steadily throughout the century racing became properly organised — important meetings established elaborate rules drawn up for jockeys and the whole sport became regulated and disciplined — and popular. More and more spectators arrived at the courses for the purpose of watching and gambling. The Derby on Epsom Downs became a semi-national event that drew tens of thousands. What was true of horse-racing became true of cricket: spectators became as important as participants and special grounds — Lords for example — were built to accomodate the crowds who wanted to watch.[46] Indeed, organised sport, which was to become a major

45. G. D. H. Cole, "Town Life in the Provinces," *Johnson's England: An Account of the Life and Manners of His Age*, A. S. Turberville, ed., Oxford, 1933, pp. 215-216.

46. For horse-racing see Robert Black, *Horse Racing in England: A Synoptical View*, London, 1893; *idem, The Jockey Club and its Founders*, London, 1891; T. A. Cook, *A History of the English Turf*, London, 1905, 3 Vols. For the grandstand at Richmond see J. Fairfax-Blakeborough, *Northern Turf History*, 3 Vols., London 1949. What was true of horse-racing was also true of boxing. The first set of rules were introduced in August 1743 by Jack Broughton, the same year he opened his amphitheatre. *Boxiana*, by one of the Fancy, 3 Vols., London, 1812, Vol. I, pp. 49-51; Vol. II, pp. 9-10. Broughton usually took one-third of the takings, *Athletic Exercise or the Science of Boxing Displayed*, London, 1788, p. 17; prices were often high and in

industry in the nineteenth and twentieth centuries throughout the world, began in eighteenth century England, a part of that self-same exploitation of leisure which had stimulated all the arts that adorn the life of man.

Not that many contemporaries thought so: as in our days the spread of culture amongst the masses was regarded as a decline in standards. There was very sharp criticism, an uneasy feeling expressed by Hume, Johnson, Burke, Goldsmith, Reynolds and others that the great age of artistic achievement was past and could not be recovered, that more meant worse. Like Kingsley Amis, they believed that the very act of writing for a mass audience led to coarseness and triviality and to a loss of subtlety and refinement. And then, as now, the quantities of ephemeral trash could be pointed to as a sign of the age's decadence.

What was happening, of course, was the decline of two cultures and the birth of a third. In spite of the Elizabethan theatre, which could and did leap across class boundaries, the culture of England had been either aristocratic or bucolic until the age of Addison and Pope. Although the whole of culture had been under the control of aristocratic patronage, the only vital part to escape that control was popular religion and its two great books, Foxe's *Martyrs* and Bunyan's *Pilgrim's Progress*. Literature, painting and the arts, however, belonged in essentials to the aristocracy. And the peasants, of course, had their crudities — their barn dances, their traditional songs, their farces, distinct from aristocratic sophistication. The new middle class culture grew up between both, absorbing most of what the aristocratic culture had acquired and taking a not inconsiderable amount from the peasantry. But the difference was great — and it lay in the fact of an audience that was large enough to be commercially exploited. Culture became an industry, as it still is. And there was a further dimension, alien both to aristocratic or bucolic cultures. And that was a moral earnestness, a belief that a taste for the arts led to improvement and refinement. This infuses almost every cultural activity of the eighteenth century and, indeed, was even to be a

1786 it cost one guinea to watch the championship of England. *Fistiana: or the Oracle of the Ring*, by the editor of Bell's Life in London, London, 1841, p. 33.

justification of organised sport — that it led to health, to manliness, to the capacity to submerge the self in the team.

And unlike the culture of the nobleman or peasant, this culture was national and poised for growth — it could absorb the lower middle class as well as the upper; in time it would reach down even to the skilled working class. Books, music, painting were no longer private, and leisure itself had become for the first time in our history an industry, and one which became for the next two centuries and probably beyond a major growth point for the world's economies.

We often think of the middle years of eighteenth century life creating the dark satanic mills and the desperate conditions of slum life, but those self-same decades also brought the possibility of cultural enjoyment to the mass of mankind.

J. H. Plumb

Provincial Culture
in Early Georgian England

In this essay the word "culture" has nothing to do with tillage of
the soil or the production of pearls or the development of bacteria
in specifically prepared media; nor is the word used in its wide
sociological sense to embrace every element in the pattern of
human living. It is used to refer to those elements of English
civilization which have to do with the mind — the so-called
"polite" arts: music, reading, the theatre. It is life in the English
provinces rather than in London that will be explored, partly
because most studies in English social history have concentrated
on the capital, despite the fact that most English people did not
live there. Furthermore the focus will be arbitrarily sharpened by
limiting the scope of my survey to what was going on in the
English counties precisely two centuries ago — in the year 1771 —
and the evidence adduced comes exclusively from a source
hitherto little used by others who have written about eighteenth
century life. That source is the local newspaper, and I venture to
bring forward selected examples of the material to be found
therein because, although early newspapers are hard to find, they
give the contemporary picture in remarkably ample detail. I make
no claim that the newspapers published in Bath, Bristol, Canterbury, Norwich, Manchester, Birmingham, and a multitude of other
English towns present the only evidence for what I am calling
provincial culture; obviously much can be learned from letters,
diaries, personal memoirs, accounts of travel, legal records, and the
various documents recording the deliberations at the several levels
of government. The novels, essays, and descriptive verse likewise
throw light on what the times were like.[1] The author of the essay

1. A recent anthology compiled by A. F. Scott, *Every One a Witness: The Georgian
Age*, London, 1970, exhibits the wide range of contemporary documents that may serve
to illuminate the century. On a smaller scale *Eighteenth-Century Prose 1700-1780*,

in the *Connoisseur* number 45 (5 December 1754) might declare, "Even our papers . . . are, I fear, of too fugitive a nature to fall under the inspection of posterity." Yet it turns out — as I hope to show — that those ephemeral half-sheets, in most towns issued only once a week,[2] reveal in one way or another so much of what England was doing and reading and thinking and talking about that no account of English life can be complete if they are ignored. I go so far as to assert that, because the local newspapers have been almost completely ignored, the authentic social history of England has not yet been written.[3]

Before supporting that assertion with specific matter, it should be noted that the English local newspapers comprise an enormous bulk, for there were no fewer than 244 separate provincial newspapers published at one period or another during the eighteenth century, and although 127 of these came to an end before 1771, the year which I have selected for special attention here, and 73 others did not begin until after that year, there were 44 newspapers being issued regularly in thirty-three cities and towns — excluding London — in all corners of England in 1771.[4] Together those forty-four newspapers left no region of the land without a local paper, to say nothing of London papers which were also widely distributed.[5] The total network of coverage was enormous, distribution of those forty-four newspapers went far beyond the towns where they were published. It is impossible to

compiled by D. W. Jefferson, Harmondsworth, 1956, likewise quotes a wide variety of pieces to illustrate not only the conventions of prose style but the *ethos* of Samuel Johnson's century.

2. A few early newspapers published in Exeter and Taunton came out two or three times a week, but in 1771 the only local paper published twice a week was the *Kentish Gazette*.

3. Good use of local newspapers is made by Sybil Rosenfeld in her *Strolling Players & Drama in the Provinces 1660-1765*, Cambridge, 1939; by Cecil Price in *The English Theatre in Wales*, Cardiff, 1948; and by Arnold Hare in *The Georgian Theatre in Wessex*, London, 1958.

4. In 1771 Bristol had three newspapers, and Bath, Birmingham, Exeter, Leeds, Liverpool, Manchester, Norwich, Newcastle, and Sherborne each had two rival papers.

5. In May 1771 the printer of *Bingley's Journal, or, Universal Gazette* which had been running less than a year, sought even more than the two thousand subscribers he said he had in different parts of Great Britain and Ireland. To that end he paid for long advertisements in various provincial newspapers announcing that his *Journal* would be delivered anywhere for thirteen shillings a year. Several printers of local papers actually offered to take in subscriptions for London newspapers. See my *Freshest Advices: Early Provincial Newspapers in England*, Columbus, 1965, p. 35, n. 8.

say how much exaggeration is to be seen in a printer's claim for wide circulation of his paper, for he doubtless wished to impress both his readers and possible advertisers. But extravagant claims would not go long unchallenged, and one should not dismiss as mere window dressing the statement by Cluer Dicey and Son in issues of their *Northampton Mercury* in 1771 that for "above fifty Years" their paper had continued to be circulated in "all the Market-Towns and populous Villages in the following Counties, viz. *Northampton, Leicester, Nottingham, Rutland, Huntingdon, Cambridge* and the Isle of *Ely, Bedford, Essex, Hertford, Buckingham, Berkshire, Oxford, Warwick* to *Birmingham*, and *Stafford*, etc. and by the Post to greater Distances." Simmons and Kirkby, the printers of the *Kentish Gazette*, made a point of listing by name in number 315 (28 May - 1 June 1771) and later issues the thirty-four towns "with many other intermediate Towns and Villages" which they said were "served on the *Day of Publication*," and they added that "on the next Day the Circuit is farther extended into the County of Essex." Corroboration of such claims of wide distribution may be seen in *The Stranger's Assistant and Guide to Bath*, printed in Bath in 1773 by R. Cruttwell for W. Taylor and A. Tennent. That little book has on page 96 the statement that "Persons who live in Bath may ... send parcels every Wednesday evening into the country by the men who carry Cruttwell's *Bath Chronicle*, which is circulated in Bristol, Wells ..." and then come the names of thirty-four other places, followed by these words: "and several intermediate villages, noblemen and gentlemen's seats, etc. to which there is no other direct conveyance. Likewise, to most of the above places, every Monday, by the men who carry *Keene's Bath Journal.*."[6]

If such claims cannot now be either proved or disproved, the same is true of the few extant statements concerning the number of copies printed and sold of any one issue. Surviving figures suggest that well established papers may normally have sold between one thousand and two thousand copies.[7] It is probably

6. For observations on the distribution of local newspapers in the first half of the century see my *Freshest Advices*, pp. 96 f. and 113 f.

7. Even more than two thousand copies of Christopher Etherington's *York Chronicle* were sold less than four years after it was established in 1772, for in several successive issues he printed the names of 2260 regular subscribers to his paper.

not unreasonable to suppose that in any one week the printers of the forty-four provincial newspapers which were being issued in 1771 put between fifty thousand and eighty thousand copies of their papers into the hands of regular buyers, and that the total number of readers far exceeded those figures.

That is my first point. I have provided those dull statistics in order to indicate that, whereas there was not a single local newspaper in England when the century began, by the year of Thomas Gray's death there were many thousands of people all over England who regularly saw a newspaper produced in their own part of the kingdom. That fact alone supports the notion that the eighteenth century saw a cultural explosion.

The evidence for such an outburst becomes more convincing as one examines the newspapers themselves. They all carried domestic and foreign news taken directly from the printed papers that came three times a week from London, sometimes supplemented by late news brought by special courier. Readers in all parts of England could, like William Cowper, peruse every week the "map of busy life, / Its fluctuations, and its vast concerns."[8] Besides reports of facts and rumours from London, from other areas of the British Isles, from the Continent, from America, Asia, and Africa, there was much local news, not only about marriages, elopements, deaths, accidents, robberies, horse races, the assizes, the weather, earthquakes, ecclesiastical appointments, political meetings, exercises of the local militia, and celebrations of many kinds, but also about public lectures, meetings of debating societies, and other activities which can properly be called cultural. To these last I shall return later. There were likewise numerous advertisements – sometimes filling as many as ten of the sixteen columns – and if most of these were concerned with properties for sale or to let, lotteries, innoculation, apologies for insults, animals on show, performers on tightropes, "assemblies," positions vacant, large private libraries for sale, money to borrow or lend, annuity schemes, medicines for every ailment, coaches and "flying machines," as well as other services and commodities of all sorts, there were many announcements about schools for

8. *The Task*, IV, 23-35, 50-119.

young gentlemen or young ladies, detailed notices of plays to be seen in the local theatres, references to circulating libraries, to musical performances, and to recently published books. And there is one other category of material in the provincial newspapers which ought not to be ignored in any attempt to appraise their cultural significance – the contributed prose and verse, considerable in bulk, sometimes original, though seldom distinguished.[9]

The total inventory of prose pieces offered in the local papers in 1771 is extensive enough to justify the assertion made by many of the printers that they intended to provide literary entertainment as well as news for their readers, though there is little to show that the appeal for contributions of "essays and articles of a literary nature" brought response from "men of genius."[10] There were, of course, many direct communications in the form of letters to the printer, such as the complaint in the *Bath Chronicle* number 535 (17 January 1771) that formal balls were being held on the same evenings as performances in the theatre, and a correspondent's censure (in the same paper, number 561, on 18 July 1771) of elaborate and expensive plaster work being installed in a Wiltshire church. A disturbing demonstration of the generation gap in 1771 appears in a long letter printed in William Pine's *Bristol Gazette* number 213 (12 September 1771), in which George Season sought reconciliation with his son William, who had publicly charged him with misusing a bank note in the amount of £350. In the same paper two weeks later William published a bitter reply, ending with these words:

> The last paragraph of your laborious epistle is scurrilous, therefore I despise it. – And was it not for exposing the Parents from whence I sprung, I could fill up a volume, in giving a detail of your cruel usage to me, and my dear deceased Mother; it is past, and I only hint at it, because you endeavour to make the world believe that you are clever, and

9. Details of such matter in the provincial newspapers up to the beginning of the reign of George III will be found in G. A. Cranfield's *The Development of the Provincial Newspaper 1700-1760*, Oxford, 1962, pp. 99-116, and Chapter VII, "Literary Features and Fillers," in my *Freshest Advices*, pp. 303-338.

10. These are terms from the *Marlborough Journal* number 2 (6 April 1771); similar invitations were issued by other printers.

> I an ignoramus. You are my Father, otherwise I would lash
> you; don't provoke further, least I shall particularise your
> brutal behaviour.

Most contributed prose is somewhat more comfortable than those
harsh words. The *Kentish Gazette* had in some issues a special
section entitled "The Kentish Repository for Miscellaneous
Essays" conducted by "Argus: or the Man with a Hundred Eyes."
And there were similar departments in a few other papers. Many
issues of the *Berkshire Chronicle*, published in Wokingham, had
pieces of quite readable prose written by a frequent contributor
who was obviously trying to create a *persona* in the manner of
Isaac Bickerstaff as a means of arousing the interest of readers.
One of his most engaging efforts was written in response to a
teen-age girl's request for "a dissertation on kissing." Scores of
other pieces of prose printed in the local newspapers in 1771
could be cited to show that original contributions were not
negligible.

Often, however, the prose had already appeared in print
elsewhere. Doubtless copied from a London newspaper is the
delightful "Glossary for 1771" in the *Bath Chronicle* number 575
(24 October 1771) in which politics is defined as "Reading the
newspapers" and ball as "A place for grown people to romp in."
In 1771 many issues of William Cruttwell's *Sherborne Weekly
Journal* contained short pieces of prose, and sometimes there were
two or more columns of current fiction. It is worth noting that
readers living away from London were not left wondering what
sort of prose was giving to John Wilkes, John Horne, and "Junius"
such prominence in the reports from the big city. Most of the
provincial newspapers reprinted letters by these controversial
personages which had shortly before appeared in the *Public
Advertiser* or some other London newspaper. One of the most
frequently reprinted letters of "Junius" is the one dated 22 April
1771 beginning "To write for profit without taxing the Press . . ."
Samuel Johnson included scathing remarks about "Junius" in his
pamphlet *Thoughts on the late Transactions respecting Falkland's
Islands* (1771). Several of his strong paragraphs were quoted in the
Kentish Gazette number 304 (19 − 23 April 1771), and two

weeks later the *Gazette* quoted an attack on Johnson for his strictures. The quoted prose in other papers was also more often political than not, but one finds such things as a long letter describing some of the experiences of those who had gone with Banks and Solander on Cook's ship the *Endeavour* to the South Seas in 1768, 1769, and 1770.

The verse offered to readers of the local papers in 1771 is not very impressive, though there was a good deal of it. Remembering George Crabbe's unkind words about amateurish verses printed in newspapers,[11] one should not look for works of genuine poetic merit in the Poets Corner at the top of the fourth page in many papers, except when something by an established author is used. The scholarly world is aware that young Tom Chatterton broke into print a few years earlier than 1771 in the columns of a Bristol newspaper, but no other incipient genius causes a twentieth century reader of the papers printed in 1771 to catch his breath in ecstasy as he reads the verses sent in by hopeful poetasters. Shortly after the opening of the New Assembly Rooms in Bath at the end of September 1771 the *Bath Chronicle* number 573 (10 October 1771) printed a long set of more or less heroic couplets entitled "The Ridotto of Bath, A Panegyrick. Being an Original Epistle from Timothy Screw . . . to his Brother *Henry*, Waiter at *Almack's*." Those jolly and vivid lines were so well received that a few days later they were published separately and sold for twopence. In the *Berkshire Chronicle* of 24 June 1771 are quoted fifteen stanzas of James Beattie's recently published poem, *The Minstrel; or the Progress of Genius*. By comparison – indeed, by any reasonable standard – the original verses sent to that paper by some Oxford undergraduates are pathetically weak. One example will suffice. It is a piece signed "Academicus" in number 2 (14 January 1771) and consists of two stanzas addressed "To a young Lady, with an Impediment in her Speech." The author had a fair sense of rhythm and stanza pattern, but his bizarre assortment of images reminds one of Ned Softly's absurd lines "To Mira" in the *Tatler* number 163 (25 April 1710). Here are the two tender stanzas:

11. *The Newspaper: A Poem*, London, 1785, lines 431-465.

When fair Irene's gentle Voice
   Divides the yielding Air;
Fix'd on her Lips the faultering sounds
   Excess of Joy declare:
There ling'ring round their rosey gate,
   They view their fragrant cell,
Unwilling to depart that mouth,
   Where all the Graces dwell.
Some tuneful accents strike our sense,
   With soft, imperfect sound,
While thousand others die within,
   In their own Honey drown'd.
Yet thro' this cloud, distinct and clear,
   Sweet Sense directs its Dart;
And while it seems to shun the Ear,
   Strikes full upon the *Heart*.

There is not much evidence of a cultural explosion in those lines, but at least there were verses of a sort in most of the local newspapers of 1771, and I believe it fair to assume that readers in general did not disapprove of their presence, whatever they thought of their quality.

It was clearly in response to public demand that a few printers issued a supplement to their newspapers in order to provide more of the entertaining prose and verse than could be fitted into the columns not occupied by news and paid advertisements. I would mention just two such enterprises as evidence that the printers believed there was public interest in *belles lettres*. On 9 April 1771 Joseph Harrop announced in his *Manchester Mercury* number 1031 that beginning two weeks later he would present free of charge to "the steady and uniform Supporters" of his paper successive numbers — eight pages in each — of what he described as "Extracts of so many of the most sensible, ingenious, and witty Pieces, both in Prose and Verse, of Dr. SWIFT's Works, as will make One handsome Volume in Octavo." The other supplementary publication brought out by the printer of a provincial newspaper in 1771 bore a familiar name, though the fortnightly miscellany which Myles Swinney of Birmingham offered at three pence is probably known to very few now. It was called the *British Museum*, and it had a long explanatory subtitle: *Or, Universal Register of Literature, Politics, and Poetry. Containing Instruction and Entertainment for the Fair Sex, the Gentleman, and the Mechanic*. The first number appeared on March 1771, and subsequent numbers came out at regular intervals until mid-September. In its half-year of life it provided its readers with prose fiction, "Lives of Eminent Persons" (Addison, Dr. Boerhaave, Shakespeare, and others), essays from the *Adventurer* and the *Idler*, several poems (Dryden's *Alexander's Feast*, Philips's *The Splendid Shilling*, Addison's *The Campaign*), extracts and reviews of new books (including *Humphry Clinker* and some sharp remarks about *Thoughts on the Late Transactions respecting Falkland's Islands*). If these attempts by Harrop in Manchester and Swinney in Birmingham kept going for something less than a year, it is none the less significant that both men obviously felt that in the areas covered by their respective newspapers there were readers who would welcome more reading matter than the newspapers could provide.[12]

That view must have been shared by the many London booksellers — that is to say, publishers — who paid substantial sums to advertise their new books and pamphlets in the columns of the local newspapers. There is only one reason why T. Davies in Russell Street, Covent Garden, should advertise in several provincial papers the four volumes of Goldsmith's *History of England* at two guineas: he expected that at least a few copies — more than enough to clear the cost of the advertisements — would be purchased by the readers of those local newspapers. And the same argument holds for Dodsley, Bell, Lowndes, Payne, Cadell, Baldwin, and other London publishers who altogether in the course of a year announced the publication of hundreds of books. To give even a few representative titles here would be tiresome. Likewise brought to the attention of readers in the country were

12. Similar enterprises are discussed in my "Early Georgian Provincial Magazines," *The Library*, ser. 5, XIX (1964, published 1968), pp. 187-195. See also my "Middle-Class Literacy in Eighteenth-Century England," in R. F. Brissenden, ed., *Studies in the Eighteenth Century: Papers presented at the David Nichol Smith Memorial Seminar Canberra 1966*, Canberra, 1968, pp. 63 f.

the current London periodicals — the *Gentleman's Magazine*, the *Critical Review*, the *London Magazine*, the *Universal Magazine of Knowledge and Pleasure*, the *Town and Country Magazine*, *Every Man's Magazine*, and the two competing publications both called the *Lady's Magazine* — usually with a detailed listing of the contents of each number.

Not all of the publications advertised in the local papers in 1771 were for adult readers. Following the lead of John Newbery there were in that year two competing publishers of tiny books intended for young readers. The *Northampton Mercury*, for example, listed fifty-five books "for the Instruction and Amusement of Children," printed for T. Carman and F. Newbery, junior, in St. Paul's Churchyard, London, the titles ranging from *The Renowned History of Giles Gingerbread* (price one penny) to *The Holy Bible Abridged* (sixpence) and *A Collection of Letters from eminent Authors* (one shilling). The rival publisher of these Lilliputian tomes was F. Newbery, whose place of business was not in St. Paul's Churchyard but at the corner of St. Paul's Churchyard and Ludgate Street. Each of these rival publishers printed long advertisements warning prospective customers against the other's "paltry Compilations." F. Newbery's list in the *Bath Chronicle* number 555 (6 June 1771) was headed "For the Benefit of all good little Masters and Misses" and included such precious stuff as *The Brother's Gift; or, The Naughty Girl Reformed* (one penny), *Mr. Telltruth's Natural History of Birds* (sixpence), and *The History of Tom Jones Abridged*, with Cuts (one shilling).

The question to be asked at this point is this: how difficult was it for a reader of the *Bath Chronicle* or the *Newcastle Journal* or *Jopson's Coventry Mercury* to obtain a copy of a book or magazine advertised in his local paper? The obvious answer is that he could ask one of the local retail booksellers to order it from the London publisher. But there was another and in many cases probably easier way of getting a book. Whether a reader lived in the town where a paper was published or somewhere else in the region served by that paper's news-carriers, he could order any book which he saw advertised in the paper simply by handing a note to the newsman when he came on his weekly round. The book would be brought right to his door a week or two later along with the newspaper; and in many cases it would cost no more than if purchased over the counter in a London bookshop. The fact is that the printer of a provincial newspaper could afford to deliver it along several country routes, as well as in town, only by selling — and having his newsmen sell — the books and medicines advertised in his paper.[13] Thus the *Northampton Mercury* in 1771 frequently had on the fourth page two or three columns headed with the words, *"The following* BOOKS *and* MEDICINES *may be had of the* PRINTERS *hereof, and of the Men who carry this News."* Some such formula appears in the other local papers. When Simmons and Kirkby, printers of the *Kentish Gazette*, advertised that they sold *The Genuine Letters of Junius*, edited by W. Norton and published in London at four shillings, they added that the volume might be had, "(Carriage free) of all their Newsmen." And when an enterprising London dealer in books, Alexander Donaldson, placed in several provincial newspapers a list of twenty-six works available from him at prices much lower than those charged by the publishers, the local printers of newspapers — among them the printers of the *Berkshire Chronicle* — said they would carefully execute orders for Donaldson's books and would deliver them "free of Carriage" within the circuit of the paper. The same list appeared in the *Northampton Mercury* and in other local papers.

There is one other kind of publication which advertisements in the local papers show to have been readily available to provincial readers who wanted substantial reading matter, whether for instruction or enjoyment. That is the book published in inexpensive weekly or monthly "numbers" — a few sheets folded and stitched in blue paper covers and in that form easily delivered by the newsmen on their regular rounds. It was a form of bookselling which had developed enormously in the second quarter of the century, as I have shown elsewhere.[14] At least twenty-five different works published in "numbers" were advertised in the

13. Printers of local newspapers earlier in the century made money by selling not only books and medicines but many other commodities and by having their newsmen deliver parcels to customers on their regular routes. See the passage quoted from *The Stranger's Assistant*, above, p. 00, and Chapter III, "Distribution and Profits" in my *Freshest Advices*, pp. 93-146.

14. An account of this development is in my *Serial Publication in England before 1750*, Cambridge, 1957.

provincial newspapers in 1771, and they included books of travel, history, Whitefield's *Works*, Hanbury's *Complete Body of Planting and Gardening*, and of course the Bible. All of these were available to country readers through the newsmen or from the nearest bookseller. Two of these "number" books deserve particular attention here, because they were not printed in London but in Birmingham. In that city in 1771 Nicholas Boden not only completed the printing and sale of a *Family Bible* in fascicles, with cuts, but arranged for a large number of distributors of his edition of the plays and sonnets of Shakespeare, with notes and a life of the dramatist, in thirty-eight parts, published fortnightly at fourpence halfpenny, to make "ten neat Pocket Volumes."

There was — as there still is — an alternative to buying a book which one wishes to read. It could be borrowed. Most English towns in 1771 had at least one circulating library, operated either by the local printer of a newspaper or by an independent bookseller. Circulating libraries had begun many years before. As early as 1718 George Barton, a bookseller of Huntingdon with shops in Peterborough, St. Ives, and St. Neots, advertised in Robert Raikes's *St. Ives Post Boy* number 20 (27 October 1718) and following issues that he not only offered for sale "All sorts of bound Books New and Old" and various stationery goods but had "Plays, or any other Books to let out to Read by the Week." In subsequent years there were lending libraries in Bath, Salisbury, Bristol, Liverpool, Leeds, Nottingham, Shrewsbury, Chester, Bury St. Edmunds, Warrington, and other towns. As one would expect, so fashionable a resort as Bath had several circulating libraries, among those functioning in 1771 being William Bally's, Lewis Bull's, and Andrew Tennent's.[15] The standard rates to the subscribers of such libraries are indicated in the notice which appeared in the *Berkshire Chronicle* of 6 April 1772. Elizabeth Cruttwell, bookseller and stationer in the Market Place, Woking-ham, reminded her friends that they could borrow books at her Circulating Library "at 10s. 6d. a Year, 3s. a Quarter, 1s. 6d. a Month, or 3d. a single Volume." And they could get printed

15. The typewritten thesis of V. J. Kite, *Libraries in Bath 1618-1964*, (1966) has in its third section a detailed account of the eighteenth century circulating libraries in Bath.

catalogues for threepence.

Because the libraries in London and the provincial towns have already been discussed by Professor Kaufman,[16] and because Professor Varma is soon to publish a book, *The Evergreen Tree*, dealing explicitly with the circulating libraries, I shall not give further details about this very significant manifestation of a strong interest in reading, except to say that neither Sir Anthony Absolute's condemnation of a circulating library (in the second scene of *The Rivals*) as "an evergreen tree of diabolical knowledge," nor the romantic novels borrowed by Lydia Languish and Isabella Thorpe should be taken as evidence that only frivolous fiction could be found on the shelves of local libraries. One piece of information proves the contrary. When William Frederick, a bookseller and stationer in the Grove, Bath, announced in *Boddely's Bath Journal* number 1407 (3 September 1770) and several later issues that "for the future he must decline the Business of a Circulating Library," he said he was selling off his Library books comprising "Upwards of One Thousand Volumes of Modern Novels and Romances" and "above Nine Thousand Volumes of Books on Various Subjects." There is no reason to suppose that the ratio of non-fiction to fiction in Frederick's circulating Library was abnormal. Certainly the figures are impressive, especially when one remembers that his was only one of several libraries in Bath at the time.

And that is my second point. The vast quantities of literature printed in or mentioned in local newspapers serve as evidence that, so far as the availability of reading matter is concerned, the provinces in 1771 did not lag behind the capital city itself. Books, periodicals, and the newspapers themselves were so abundant that, if reading is a symptom of cultural maturity, there is no justification for perpetuating the notion that the English provinces in the eighteenth century were a hinterland of illiterate peasants and ill-educated shopkeepers.

My third point is that in 1771 the people who lived in provincial cities and towns had opportunity to enjoy the intellec-

16. Paul Kaufman, *Libraries and their Users: Collected Papers in Library History*, London, 1969.

tual stimulus of public lectures and debating societies. "Last Night
the Rev. Mr. Herries, A. M. delivered at the Exchange here, A
Lecture on the Voice, to a genteel and polite audience." So one
reads in the *Manchester Mercury* number 1032 (16 April 1771).
On 3 July 1771 in *Aris's Birmingham Gazette* number 1566 Mr.
Ferguson returned thanks to the ladies and gentlemen who had
subscribed to his three courses of lectures on experimental
philosophy — that is, natural science — and gave notice of a fourth
course, which would be given at Mrs. Sawyer's Assembly Rooms at
six p.m. daily. In *Felix Farley's Bristol Journal* on 5 October 1771
Mr. Donn announced that on the following Monday he would
begin his course of lectures on experimental philosophy and
astronomy at the Mathematical Academy in the Library House on
King Street. In the *Manchester Mercury* number 1052 (3 September 1771) Mr. A. Walker began to advertise his forthcoming series
of twelve lectures on natural and experimental philosophy, stating
that he would discuss "every new and useful Discovery, that has
been made in Astronomy, Use of the Globes, Pneumatics,
Hydrostatics, Hydraulics, Mechanics, Engineering, Fortification,
Magnetism, Electricity, Optics, etc." The subscription for the
series was one guinea for gentlemen, just half a guinea for ladies
and boys. But it was not until ten weeks later that he set a date for
the first lecture in Manchester, explaining that he had only then
finished a series in Liverpool. Walker himself was probably the
author of the report printed as local news in the *Manchester
Mercury* number 1064 (26 November 1771):

> The numerous and polite Appearance at Mr. WALKER's
> LECTURE last Night, is one amongst the many Instances of
> the Town's Attention to ARTS and Sciences. This course is
> confessedly more adapted to every Branch of Business, than
> any ever read in this Town; and has the Sanction of the first
> Colleges in Europe. — We hear the LECTURES are continued
> at six every Monday, Wednesday, Thursday, and Friday
> Evenings, for three Weeks to come.

Two weeks later the *Manchester Mercury* printed the full text of
"The Exordium to Mr. Walker's First Lecture in Manchester." It is
a lucid and dignified statement. Despite his earlier announcement

that he would give only one course of lectures in Manchester, Walker announced in number 1068 of the *Mercury* (24 December 1771) that he would give a second series beginning on 30 December. After that series ended, he said, he would move on to Bolton, where his lectures would begin on 20 January. I have no idea how good or how feeble those "philosophical" lectures were, but they were certainly popular. They did not, of course, begin in 1771; there had been many such series in Newcastle, York, Manchester, Liverpool, Birmingham, Shrewsbury, Bristol, Canterbury, and other centres in preceding years, the subjects ranging from anatomy to architecture, language, botany, chemistry, air, electricity, and the doctrine of colours. Even Samuel Johnson attended at least one philosophical lecture in his own home town. Boswell recorded in his *Journal of a Tour to the Hebrides* that among the dinner guests at Mr. Fraser's house at Strichen on 25 August 1773 was a Dr. Fraser who "remembered to have seen Mr. Johnson at a lecture on experimental philosophy at Lichfield." Boswell added that Johnson remembered being at the lecture.[17]

Another manifestation of interest in things of the mind is to be seen in the various "Conversation Societies" which in some of the larger towns met regularly to debate a wide variety of topics. There is now no way of discovering at what intellectual level those debates were conducted, but it is clear that they attracted enough attention to be reported in the local newspapers. A few examples will serve to show what sort of theme came under discussion at the weekly meetings of the Conversation Society in one city. In number 1018 (8 January 1771) of the *Manchester Mercury* it was announced as an item of local news that the question to be debated at that week's meeting on Thursday evening at seven o'clock in the large room of "the late Angel Inn in the Market Place" would be "Whether is the study of Natural Philosophy, or that of Profane History, more useful to mankind?" In the following issue of the *Manchester Mercury* it was reported that the decision had been in favour of natural philosophy, and the subject

17. *Boswell's Journal of A Tour to the Hebrides with Samuel Johnson, LL.D. Now First Published from the Original Manuscript*, Frederick A. Pottle and Charles H. Bennett, eds, Toronto, 1936, p. 78.

for the next debate was announced: "Whether is a vigorous or an indulgent Mode of Education the best for Youth?" These debates continued in the ensuing weeks, and they sometimes dealt with questions that provoked further discussion. The question discussed on Thursday, 7 February 1771, was "Is it a Duty incumbent upon Parents to Inoculate their Children, as a Means to preserve Life?" When the members of the Conversation Society decided that it was not a duty, a local surgeon wrote a long letter dealing with the arguments that had been presented, and his letter was published in the first three columns of the *Manchester Mercury* on 19 February 1771. It makes interesting reading even now. Later in the year the subjects were such as could still exercise the minds and oratorical powers of mature persons: "Whether is Beauty Real or Imaginary?" "Whether has Gunpowder or Literature been more advantageous to Mankind?" "Whether has Music or Oratory greater Power over the Passions?"

That last question was determined in favour of music, and it is entirely probable that those who participated in the debate knew what they were talking about, for music of all kinds was composed, rehearsed, played, and sung in all corners of England, as any file of any local newspaper can prove. That is my fourth point. There were oratorios, operas, organ recitals, gentlemen's subscription concerts, breakfasts with music, regional festivals, meetings of the St. Cecilia Societies, and of course the great Three Choirs Festival, held every September since 1719 in Gloucester, Worcester, and Hereford by turns. The year 1771 saw not only the usual concerts in Birmingham, Newcastle, Norwich, Salisbury, Manchester, York, and other towns, but in particular the opening of the splendid New Assembly Rooms in Bath on 26 September of that year — an event that was commemorated in Bath in 1971. The *Bath Chronicle* number 567 (29 August 1771) printed a full description of the spacious rooms and magnificent facilities of the place. In the *Manchester Mercury* number 1059 (28 October 1771) is an announcement that "By Desire of the Gentlemen of the Musical Society in Manchester" there would be a performance on the following Friday of Dryden's *Alexander's Feast* as set to music by Handel. The soloists were named and the choruses — the best singers from Oldham, Hey Chapel, and Manchester — were to be "as full as possible." The performance was to be for the benefit of Mr. Wainwright, an energetic local musician who had agreed to play "an Harpsichord Concerto" between the first and second parts.

Special performances of that kind were numerous in the larger English towns; but musical events were not confined to the big communities. I could give details of the annual musical competition in Wokingham, of a performance of Handel's oratorio *Esther* for the benefit of the Musical Club at Oldham, of a performance of *Judas Maccabeus* conducted by Mr. Wainwright at the formal "opening" of the new organ in the parish church of Wigan, of a performance of the same oratorio some months later in the parish church of Ashton-under-line "by a select Band of Vocal and Instrumental Performers, from the Neighbouring Choirs, who have perform'd at *York, Beverley, Liverpool,* etc. . . . with great Applause." All of these performances, and others which I have not mentioned, were announced in the Manchester newspapers of 1771. Similar announcements in other papers of that year make it very clear that good music was to be heard all over England.

It is the same when one looks at the evidence of activity in the provincial theatres, and that brings me to my fifth point. All over the kingdom companies of actors and actresses performed hundreds of plays in scores of playhouses or halls. If anyone ever compiles a list of plays and players seen in the provincial towns and cities during all the years of the eighteenth century — and no such inventory will be possible unless the newspapers are consulted — it will be a more massive report than the eleven fat volumes of *The London Stage*. Even to enumerate the plays, to say nothing of the players, seen in the English provincial towns in the year 1771 would expand this paper to an intolerable length. Here I can only suggest that a detailed study covering the last thirty-five years of the century, carrying forward the account given by Sybil Rosenfeld from 1660 to 1765,[18] would show that theatrical activity kept on expanding: the veteran companies and individual players continued to present both old and new plays, and many new actors and actresses were mentioned in the playbills

18. See above, note 3.

and newspaper advertisements. One new company, Durravan's, performed on Mondays, Wednesdays, and Fridays in Wolverhampton during the early weeks of 1771, and from April to the end of July they were in Northampton. Another company remained in Manchester from midwinter till early March and returned early in December. At Bristol, Bath, Birmingham, Canterbury, and elsewhere there were long series of plays, offered, as usual, on alternate nights. Early in 1771 the *Kentish Gazette* carried announcements of performances of various plays at the New Theatre in Dover, "by The Essex Company of Comedians," and at the New Theatre in Maidstone by Mr. Burton's Company. In number 283 (9 - 12 February 1771) the regional news in the *Kentish Gazette* included a report that "the Portsmouth Company of Comedians open'd at the Theatre at Rochester on Thursday, the 7th instant, and performed *The School for Lovers*, at which there was a brilliant appearance, who all expressed the highest satisfaction at the performance. The Company intend performing Tuesday, Thursday, and Saturday, for this week; and for the remaining part of their stay, they will exhibit Mondays, Wednesdays, and Fridays."

Of particular interest is the performance of an old play, Nicholas Rowe's *The Fair Penitent*, followed by David Garrick's farce, *Lethe; or Aesop in the Shades*, in the town hall at Wokingham on 4 February 1771. What makes this performance noteworthy is that it was presented by some of the local young people. A correspondent wrote to the *Berkshire Chronicle* expressing his approval of their generous action, partly because of their intention of bestowing the profits of the evening on the poor, partly because the young performers would "thereby acquire an easy graceful carriage, and be able to express their sentiments with elegance and propriety."

That reference to the "double bill" offered by the young amateur actors and actresses in Wokingham will remind those who are students of eighteenth century drama in England that long before 1771 it had become customary for a company of players to offer not just a single tragedy or comedy but a whole evening's entertainment, with songs, dances, skits, and a farce to follow the main play. As one example out of hundreds of newspaper advertisements in 1771 I select the announcement in the *Manchester Mercury* number 1018 (8 January 1771). The performance was to be a benefit for Mrs. Wheeler. The main piece was Otway's old tragedy, *The Orphan*. At the end of the tragedy a musical interlude called *Linco's Travels* was to be performed, and after the interlude Miss Polly Wheeler was to offer "a wooden shoe dance." But that was not all. To round out the evening the new comic opera, *The Padlock*, was to follow the wooden shoe dance. The same heterogeneous entertainment was provided in all the public playhouses of the time, obviously because theatre-goers in that "age of exuberance" (as Professor Donald Greene calls it)[19] had come to expect a much longer evening's amusement for their two or three shillings than had been offered to Elizabethan audiences.

That expectation, I must point out, was only satisfied at a considerable risk to the players — not just the risk that their performance might prove unacceptable to the audience but the danger that an informer might report the company for violating the Licensing Act of 1737, which prohibited the performing of plays for hire or gain in any provincial playhouse. That is why some companies in some towns attempted to protect themselves by cautiously announcing that on such and such a date a concert of music would be performed in the local theatre, and that between the parts of the concert would be presented "gratis" a full-length play, followed by the usual farce, also "gratis." That curious subterfuge was still used in 1771, not only in Rochdale and Wokingham and Wolverhampton and other small places but even in Birmingham. No threat of prosecution could stifle the player's eagerness to act or the playgoer's eagerness to see him acting.

What I have presented in illustration of my five points is not so much broad generalizations as specific factual details from widely distributed accounts written in one particular and (I believe) representative year, 1771. During the course of a famous visit to the Western Islands of Scotland not many months after the close of that year Samuel Johnson said in the hearing of James Boswell, "All history, so far as it is not supported by contemporary

19. That is the title of a book of his, published in 1970 by Random House.

evidence, is romance."[20] I have here attempted to demonstrate that, even if one looks only at the local newspapers, there is ample and convincing contemporary evidence that English people throughout the land had an abundance of reading matter, could attend lectures and the meetings of conversation societies, heard much fine music, and saw many plays. These manifestations of cultural activity, I submit, are symptoms that provincial culture was not an embryo unready to be born but a flourishing, healthy adult, alive and well and living in the counties of England.

R. M. Wiles

20. *Op. cit.* (see above, note 17), p. 392, under date 20 November 1773.

The Architecture of Mercantilism: Commercial Buildings by George Dance the Younger

Eighteenth-century mercantilism brought about numerous changes to all aspects of British society, its architecture included. The rapid expansion of trade and commerce was accompanied by a new sensibility which attached positive values to the aggressive transaction of business. What may once have been somewhat difficult to reconcile with religious conscience now became viewed as a virtuous endeavour to be undertaken with pride. Numerous writers stressed the mercantile point of view. John Locke helped to foster the new attitude at the beginning of the century with his acceptance of personal material gain as being natural to man; Mandeville's cynical vindication of greed and avarice gave business a decided boost; Defoe further condoned ruthless commercialism in *The Complete English Tradesman*; and by the century's end the arguments of Adam Smith and the new economists had fully convinced Britons of the need for initiative capitalist enterprise.[1]

The new attitude spawned new institutions, and these in turn required new buildings. Severe strains were placed upon existing architectural programmes by the rapid development of domestic retail commerce, the expansion of international trade and the formation of the overseas trading companies, and the growth of the banking system. Numerous new commercial building types

1. "Mercantilism" is here used in its broadest sense, not as any specific economic doctrine. General references are made to John Locke, *Two Treatises of Government*, London, 1690; John Mandeville, *The Fable of the Bees*, London, 1704 ff.; Daniel Defoe, *The Complete English Tradesman*, London, 1725-27; Adam Smith, *An Enquiry into . . . the Wealth of Nations*, London, 1776. It is a pleasure to thank William L. MacDonald, David R. Coffin, and Philip Pinkus for their helpful suggestions. It should be pointed out that the interpretations expressed in this paper are solely my own responsibility.

emerged in the eighteenth century. Unfortunately, the history of their evolution has never been written.[2]

Important to the development of the new commercial buildings was the architect George Dance the Younger (1741-1825).[3] In his long tenure as Clerk of the Works to the Corporation of London (1768-1816), Dance was faced with numerous opportunities to build for commercial interests. He and his employees — considered here as a single artistic personality — designed many shops, some as part of large urban redevelopment schemes and others for individual merchants; he erected several city markets (not discussed in this paper), one bank, and contributed a mammoth project for redeveloping the Port of London.

Dance's architecture is in many respects "modernistic" while being tied to late-eighteenth-century historicism. It is instructive to see how his mercantile designs attempt to reconcile the apparent contradictions between the progressive spirit of business and the humanistic values of history.

Retail Shops

The English, declared Napoleon (and before him Adam Smith), are a nation of shopkeepers. Retail shopping began its phenomenal growth in the seventeenth century, and by the following century shops had become a familiar part of the urban scene.[4] Shopkeepers were lower in social standing than the great merchant traders or the wholesale dealers, yet were capable of social mobility.[5] Their newly-gained literacy led to a decided thirst for the arts. As beneficiaries of the cultural explosion, they came to epitomize *nouveau-riche* values in their extravagant spending

2. The minimal state of advanced research in this area was revealed by the Society of Architectural Historians' presentation, in their 22nd Annual Meeting (Boston, 31 January 1969), of a paper so general as Michael H. Port, "Commercial Architecture in Northern Europe in the 17th and 18th Centuries: A Survey." See, however, a good summary of English trends in John Summerson, *Georgian London*, first published 1945, rev. ed., London, 1970, pp. 258-268.

3. For Dance's architecture, see Summerson, *Architecture in Britain: 1530 to 1830*, 1953, 4th ed., Harmondsworth, 1963, pp. 273-275; Dorothy Stroud, *George Dance, Architect, 1741-1825*, London, 1971; Harold Kalman, "The Architecture of George Dance the Younger," unpublished Ph.D. dissertation, Princeton University, 1971.

4. Dorothy Davis, *A History of Shopping*, London, 1966, p. 181.

5. E. Lipson, *The Growth of English Society: A Short Economic History*, 1949, 4th ed., London, 1959, p. 80.

and pompous affectation. Addison denounced shopkeepers as "positively the greatest fops in the kingdom."[6] Their taste in architecture, as in the other arts, was often based on somewhat uncertain principles.

Before modern times, retail shops were generally located on the ground floor of residential buildings, either beneath the private dwellings of wealthier shopkeepers, or as part of large blocks of flats. The seventeenth-century London shop was no more than a front room with an enlarged window opening.[7] An instructive comparison may be made between two similar houses built around 1640 and associated with the name of Inigo Jones: the ground-floor shops of the block on Great Queen Street differ from the lower rooms of the Lindsey House on nearby Lincoln's Inn Fields only in their slightly larger windows and the prominent signs.[8]

A more distinctive architectural form began to emerge early in the eighteenth century, probably as part of the new aggressive attitude towards business. Daniel Defoe remarked how, in order to better exhibit their wares, shops now had sash windows with panes of glass as large as twelve inches by sixteen. Defoe disliked the modern tendency to make shops more ornate, particularly the extravagances of "painting and gilding, fine shelves, shutters, boxes, glass doors, sashes and the like, in which they tell us now, 'tis a small matter to lay out two or three hundred pounds, nay, five hundred pounds, to fit up a pastry cook's, or a toy shop."[9]

Sash windows began to extend beyond the plane of the facade, their base probably evolving from the projecting shelf (often a hinged window-board) of the simpler unglazed shop.[10] By the middle of the eighteenth century, the typical shop boasted two projecting bowed windows flanking the entrance. Domestic

6. Quoted in Miriam Beard, *A History of Business*, 1938, I, Ann Arbor, 1962, p. 443. For the relationship between the new middle class and the arts, see Arnold Hauser, *The Social History of Art*, II, London, 1951, part vi, *passim*.

7. Summerson, *Georgian London*, p. 258. Other retail businesses operated from merchants' warehouses, temporary stalls, or hawkers' trays.

8. Both illustrated in Summerson, *Architecture in Britain*, pl. 59.

9. Defoe, *Review*, 1713, and *The Complete English Tradesman*, I, 1725; quoted in M. Dorothy George, *England in Transition*, 1931, 2nd ed., Harmondsworth, 1953, pp. 33-34.

10. T. S. Ashton, *An Economic History of England: The 18th Century*, 1955, London, 1964, pp. 68-69.

quarters occupied the upper floors, generally reached through a separate door to one side.

The shop that survives at 34 Haymarket (1741?) shows this characteristic form.[11] More elaborate is the shop of the silk-mercer Samuel Rybot, 56 Artillery Lane (plate 1), possibly built by Abraham Swan in the 1750s.[12] Surrounding the twin bow windows are finely crafted wooden Doric columns and an entablature. The rules of antiquity are (literally) bent so that the triglyph frieze may reach around the bow. Patterned fretwork decorates the two doors. The ornament, now so much more elaborate than the ground floor of any residence, was certainly felt to attract customers.

This general pattern is found in a number of projects for shops in an album from the City office of George Dance, all probably designed in the 1770s. A shop and house for a Mr. Palmer at the corner of Fenchurch Street and Rood Lane (1777; plate 2) has the familiar bowed windows on its façade.[13] The door lies in the centre of the shop front, inserted between two slender supports which may be of iron. Behind the retail shop lie the merchant's counting house and warehouse. A separate door, located around the corner for privacy, leads to the residence above. Its first and second storeys are joined by a central staircase, bestowing the dignity of a normal residential plan upon the house. Servants and perhaps apprentices sleep in the garrets.

The residential entrance lies beside the shop in a plan for an unidentified merchant (plate 3);[14] whereas in a third shop, designed for a Mr. Warrand in 1774 (plate 4), the extreme narrowness of the Minories site (twenty feet) required omitting this feature entirely and making the house accessible only through the shop.[15]

11. London County Council, *Survey of London*, XX, London, 1940, pp. 97-98 and pl. 90-93.

12. *Survey of London*, XXVII, 1957, pp. 227-236 and pl. 84-86, 90-91.

13. Corporation of London Record Office, Surveyor's Miscellaneous Plans (hereafter CLRO, SMiP), 258. This drawing is one of the few in the album (CLRO, SMiP 90-292) by Dance himself. Many were drawn by Dance's friend and assistant James Peacock.

14. CLRO, SMiP 193-196. Signed by Peacock and by William Browne, the latter probably the builder.

15. CLRO, SMiP 116-123, 138-141, and *passim*. Site identified on CLRO, Surveyor's City Lands Plans, 10.

Shop of Samuel Rybot, 56 Artillery Lane, by Abraham Swan(?)
c. 1756-57, view 1

2

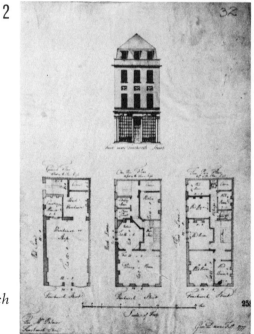

*House and shop for
Mr. Palmer, Fenchurch
Street, 1777, plans
and elevation*

House and shop for an unidentified client, plan of ground floor

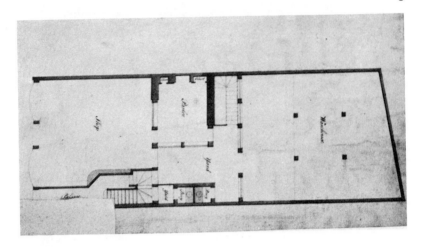

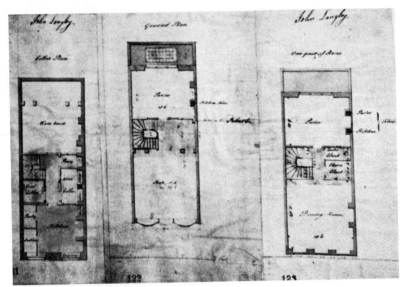

House and shop for Mr. Warrand, the Minories, 1774, plans

The latter two buildings — drawn and probably designed by Dance's friend and assistant James Peacock (c. 1738-1814) — have two storeys and a garret floor above shop level. Each has a parlour behind the shop. The later eighteenth century saw the shop-keeper's living quarters spread to this conspicuous downstairs location in keeping with his new prosperity and affectation.[16]

The three designs by Dance's office offer variations upon the same basic theme, standard for the typical twenty- to thirty-foot-wide shop unit. More generous spaces allowed greater elaboration. The ground floor of a large showroom and residence for the mercer Thomas Moore at the north-west corner of Chiswell Street and Finsbury Square (1775-79; plate 5) contains a spacious shop ("front warehouse") with a domed ante-room, a counting house, two parlours, and two additional warehouses.[17]

The elevation of Mr. Palmer's shop (plate 2) boasts pilasters on either side of the bow windows and a garland frieze above. Other extant sketches for shops from this period in Dance's career consistently show classical ornament on the ground floor. A shop for a Mr. Cholmleys (plate 7) likewise has pilasters and a frieze around its (flat) windows.[18] Another for an unidentified merchant (plate 8) has an anthemion frieze supported by what are certainly circular fluted cast-iron columns; a complex fanlight lies over the door and an elaborate superstructure crowns the merchant's name plate.[19]

Richest in external detail is the shop of the mercer Thomas Moore (plate 6).[20] The bell-flower pilasters, the frieze with rams' heads and swags, and the "cloth" festoons below the windows (fitting for a cloth merchant) contrast markedly with what certainly was an austerely plain brick elevation on the storeys above.[21] Significantly, this pattern reverses that of the few London terrace houses with exterior ornament: the Adelphi, for

16. Davis, *History of Shopping*, p. 195.
17. CLRO, SMiP 151. See Stroud, *Dance*, pp. 132-133 for the identification and discussion of this project.
18. CLRO, SMiP 184.
19. CLRO, SMiP 190.
20. CLRO, SMiP 167A.
21. The adjacent Chiswell Street façades seem to have been plain; see Stroud, *Dance*, pl. 45.

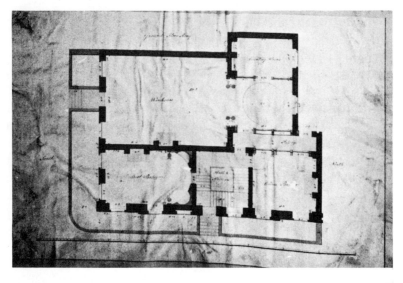

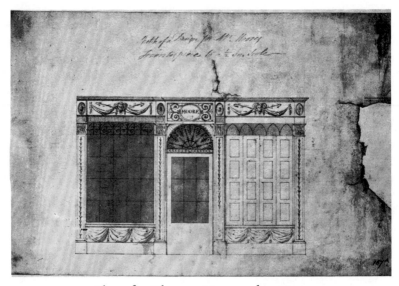

Shop for Thomas Moore, elevation

7

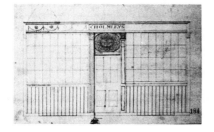

Shop for Mr. Cholmleys,
elevation

8

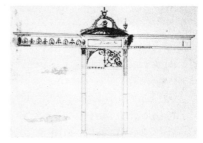

Shop for an unidentified client,
sketch elevation

9

Warehouse and offices for Mines Royal Copper Company, Dowgate
Hill, plans and elevations

example, features pilasters on the upper storeys and plain wall at ground level. Dance's ornament is much more lavish than at the Adelphi, and can be compared only to interior decoration, particularly that of the brothers Adam.

This exterior ornamentation contradicts the expressed taste of Dance's own circle. James Peacock explicitly opposed Adamesque ornament on the exterior of a house:

> Let [the architect] suffer his exterior to be . . . in some measure guiltless of the excess of modern refinement and modern finery; on the contrary, in the interior let him not be afraid to copy the architects of the present day. . . . Here let the nicknackery of the Cabinetmaker, Toy-man, and Pastry-cook preside with impunity.[22]

In retail shops, it seems, the principles of good taste might be ignored in deference to the pressures of commerce. Either the new middle class patrons demanded, or the architects offered, this lavish treatment. Peacock and Dance had on rare occasion resorted to an ornamented upper street façade, as on the west side of Finsbury Square (Peacock, 1777), yet even here the architects aimed at the commercial *nouveaux-riches*. Finsbury Square was expressly intended as a development for "merchants and artisans of the better sort."[23]

The only commercial structures from this period without exterior ornament were apparently those not intended to attract retail trade. The building erected by James Peacock for the Mines Royal Copper Company on Dowgate Hill (plate 9) contains warehouse space, boardrooms, and a counting house, but no shop or residential facilities.[24] Consequently its walls are faced with plain brick from top to bottom. Simple string courses and a

---

22. Jose Mac Packe [James Peacock], *Oikidia, or Nutshells*, London, 1785, pp. 73-74. It was noted above that Defoe had referred to toymen and pastry cooks with similar sarcasm.

23. Michael Hugo-Brunt, "George Dance, the Younger, as Town Planner (1768-1814)," *Journal of the Society of Architectural Historians*, XIV, 4, Dec. 1955, p. 15.

24. CLRO, SMiP 275. Other drawings (by Peacock) for this building are in the British Museum, King's Maps, XXV, 16; and Royal Institute of British Architects (hereafter RIBA), "Dance Leoni," 124.

doorframe serve as the only decoration. The end wall has a large door at each floor through which a derrick passes goods.

The designs discussed thus far were probably all produced in the 1770s. With the passing of this decade and the ebbing of the first wave of British neoclassicism, Dance's treatment of shops changed radically. Sufficient evidence survives from his later work to show that he completely abandoned the use of bay windows with rich ornament around them.

A project for the apothecary shop of William Prowting at Tower Street and Mincing Lane, almost certainly made in 1792, lacks an elevation, but its carefully drawn ground-floor plan (plate 10) shows no evidence of pilasters between the windows.[25]

Unfortunately we possess no other designs for individual shop-houses from these years, but we do have several drawings for full terrace blocks with shops along the ground floor. A design of 1793 for a new six-unit building on the south side of Leadenhall Street (plate 11) shows arched ground-floor openings around the retail shops and rectangular fenestration above.[26] The scheme resembles Dance's contemporaneous elevations for the east side of Finsbury Square; but whereas the residential Finsbury block has ground-floor rustication and recessed lunette panels above, the commercial Leadenhall design entirely lacks cosmetic treatment. The arcading recalls the Italianate "piazzas" of Inigo Jones' Covent Garden houses, as well as the tenement blocks of Italian cities; the connection with the latter will be discussed shortly.

Two decades later, in 1815, Dance designed additional shops and houses for the same area as part of the redevelopment of Leadenhall Market (plate 12).[27] The ground floor of his new block is almost entirely glass, the three upper floors plain brick. The mansard roof and party walls are frankly exposed. Ornament, out of place in Dance's new image of the retail shop, is totally eliminated. In its rectilinear simplicity, the design is surprisingly prophetic of the typical shop front in today's cities.

25. Soane Museum, Dance Cabinet (hereafter SMDC) 3:6:11. The first-floor plan (SMDC 3:6:8) shows iron I-sections used as window mullions. The date is inferred in an entry in CLRO, Clerk of the Works' Journal, 8 Aug. 1792.

26. CLRO, Comptroller's City Lands Plans 227.

27. CLRO, Surveyor's Markets Plans 1207.

House and shop for William Prowting,
Tower Hill, 1792, ground floor plan 10

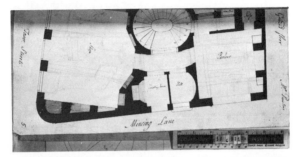

Houses and shops, Leadenhall Street, 1793, elevation 11

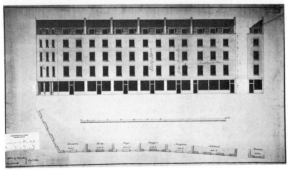

Houses and shops, Leadenhall Market, 12
1815, elevation

Bank for Martin, Stone, and Foote, Lombard Street, 1792, view

Dance's vision of the shop apparently was reversed in forty years. Rather than the ornate thing that the retail shop had been in the 1770s, it was now a wholly unornamented, quasi-mechanistic object. As an expression of an attitude towards commerce, the Leadenhall design may be considered *architecture parlante*, defined by one scholar as "'narrative' architecture, which was expected to tell both the purpose and the character of a building."[28]

The unornamented shop may be seen as a regression to the simpler type of the seventeenth century, perhaps occurring after the shopkeepers' infatuation with elegant living had waned and their social position became more secure. The earlier shops in turn recall the austere type of medieval and Renaissance Italy, and these have been shown by Axel Boëthius to be a continuation, or indeed a conscious revival, of the characteristic tenements with shops — the *insulae* with rows of *tabernae* — of ancient Rome.[29] Many of these "stern utilitarian houses" of antiquity survived into eighteenth-century Italy. Some featured arcaded porticoes or arches, as in Dance's Leadenhall block of 1793, while others were treated with flat window heads.[30] The question arises whether Dance may have been consciously imitating such remains from antiquity, and whether the simplicity of his shops might — paradoxically — be a kind of deliberate neoclassicism. Evidence supplied by Dance's designs for the Port of London, to be discussed below, suggests that this indeed was the case.

Although the common shops designed in Dance's office after 1790 avoided classical ornament, buildings intended for commercial activity of a higher social order did not. The bank that Dance built in 1792 for Martin, Stone, and Foote (later Martin's Bank) at the sign of the Grasshopper on Lombard Street (plate 13) boasts a

---

28. Emil Kaufmann, *Architecture in the Age of Reason*, Cambridge, Mass., 1955, p. 130. Insufficient information on shops by other architects prevents reaching a firmer conclusion concerning this new kind of shop.

29. Axel Boëthius, *The Golden House of Nero: Some Aspects of Roman Architecture*, Ann Arbor, 1960, chap. iv.

30. Axel Boëthius, *The Golden House*, p. 157. See his fig. 76 for an eighteenth-century view of *tabernae* in Florence. Boëthius cites other examples in Rome, Naples, Bologna, and Genoa. The famous tenements at Ostia were excavated only in the twentieth century.

ground-floor façade of finely cut stone. The arched windows are framed by grooved pilasters, bossed capitals, and a tri-fascia frieze.

Even more elaborate are the new additions to the hallowed Bank of England, begun by Dance's protégé John Soane in the early 1790s with the sanction and assistance of Dance himself.[31] The banks might be termed "high" commercial and the shops "low" commercial architecture. Decorum reserved for each its distinctive architectural mode. Buildings for the elite merchant class and for the bankers consistently boasted impressive Roman (and later Greek) ornament. The East India House on Leadenhall Street, designed by Richard Jupp and Henry Holland in the late 1790s, proudly displayed a grand Ionic portico just a few paces away from Dance's undecorated blocks of shops. Dance and his contemporaries came to respect this distinction; only in the more youthful egalitarianism of Dance's earlier career had this discrimination been blurred.

The Port of London

The contrast between "high" and "low" commercial architecture is made clearer in a project by Dance which, if executed, would have ranked among the most ambitious architectural undertakings of all time: his scheme for the redevelopment of the Port of London. British trade soared to unanticipated heights in the last decades of the eighteenth century, and the brunt of the increase fell upon the Port of London. The City exercised a coveted monopoly upon dockage by controlling the legal quays, the only place at which international boats might unload.[32] By 1790 these docks were hopelessly inadequate — not a foot of wharfage had been added since 1666 — and in 1793, the year of the outbreak of war, the first of several parliamentary committees was set up in an attempt to resolve the problem.[33] In 1796 a

31. Dance's role in Soane's design is mentioned in Summerson, "Soane: The Case-History of a Personal Style," *Journal of the RIBA*, S. 3, LVIII, 1951, pp. 84-86; and is discussed more fully in Kalman, "Architecture of George Dance," pp. 121-123.

32. Summerson, *Georgian London*, p. 259. See J. G. Broodbank, *History of the Port of London*, I, London, 1921, *passim*.

33. Proceedings are published in Great Britain, Parliament, *Reports from Committees of the House of Commons*, XIV, 1793-1802 (Misc. Reports, Port of London), London, 1803. The statistic concerning wharfage was reported in 1796, p. 348.

House committee viewed port improvement plans submitted by eight different parties.[34]

The largest and most expensive scheme, submitted by the City of London, had been drawn up by George Dance with the assistance of James Peacock and the civil engineer William Jessop.[35] The City was determined to retain its hold upon the legal quays, a major source of revenue. Its plan therefore strove to increase the capacity of the docks within the City limits while trying not to upset too badly the settled area behind them. Dance, Peacock, and Jessop developed several schemes on the principle of a series of wet docks enclosed by multi-storeyed warehouses.

The definitive City plan (plates 14, 15) was designed in 1796 and submitted to Parliament a few years later.[36] The wet docks are divided into two large basins sufficient each for forty-nine lighters (small boats that unload the larger vessels) and four smaller docks each capable of harbouring nineteen. Towering warehouses set upon the arcaded quays enclose the large basins on all four sides; the boats enter through arches piercing the lower level. Locks neutralize the changing tides. The scheme tries to solve the manifold problems that had plagued the existing facilities. By enclosing the docks the planners hoped to eliminate pilferage. Ramps ("terraces") between the warehouses allow easy access to the goods for commercial carts.

The complex offers a frontage one-third of a mile long facing the Thames, stretching from London Bridge to the Tower. In the centre of the composition the wall of warehouses divides to reveal the grandiose Custom House, as rich in classical detail as the

34. "Committee for mode of providing sufficient accommodation for increased trade and shipping of the Port of London," *Reports from Committees*, XIV, pp. 267-443. In addition to the City scheme here discussed, plans were submitted by Edward Ogle, in collaboration with James Peacock; the Merchants' Plan, by John Rennie and Daniel Asher Alexander; by Samuel Wyatt; the Southwark Plan, by Charles Thomas Cracklow; by Graeme Spence; by Ralph Walker; and four plans by William Reveley.

35. Jessop, a pupil of Smeaton, helped with the technical aspects of the wet docks, canals, and waterworks (testimony of Peacock, Jessop, and Dance, *Reports from Committees*, XIV, pp. 302-315).

36. SMDC 3:11:5, 3:7:4; CLRO, Surveyor's Institutions Plans 1512. An earlier scheme is illustrated in *Reports from Committees*, XIV, opp. p. 384, and described on pp. 277, 385-386. In addition to these docks, the City plan proposed a 102 acre dock in the isthmus of the Isle of Dogs and an identical one at Rotherhithe, as well as a canal from the latter to Vauxhall Canal.

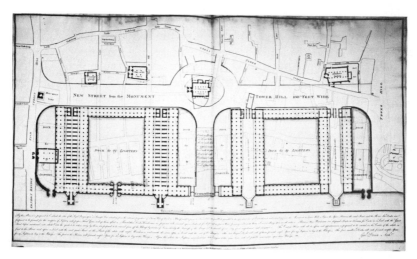

Project for the Legal Quays, 1796, plan

Project for the Legal Quays, elevation

warehouses are devoid of ornament.

The warehouses epitomize a simplicity at once sublime and utilitarian. Stone arcades at water level support the five-storey structures (whose internal beams and floors were to have been of iron) and cover the quays on which customs officers inspect the cargo. The warehouse fenestration consists simply of narrow openings through which cranes may pass the freight. Their regular rhythm slows down only over the arches leading to the docks. The rest is plain masonry. No ornament is provided save four solitary statues at the ends of the loading ramps. The quiet tempo of the surfaces is complemented by the powerful movement of large masses in space. The extreme simplicity of the warehouses expresses the same utilitarian conception of commercial activity as the austerity of Dance's later shops.

A scant twenty yards from Dance's warehouses, yet worlds apart in architectural treatment, stands the Custom House (plate 16), proudly aloof in its pompous classical garb. The Custom House is "high" architecture, the warehouses "low." Different as the two buildings may be in detail, they complement each other in design. The Custom House retains the visual rhythm of the warehouses, sits comfortably upon the same arcuated basement, and keeps its cornice at the same level. The façade features four unfluted Doric columns *in antis* inserted between pilastered fenestrated bays which serve as a transition to the bleakness of the warehouses. Dance experimented elsewhere with this composition, which was thought to have had an ancient Roman source; he employed it in earlier designs in which he sought to recreate a sense of Imperial Roman grandeur.[37] A similar arrangement of parts already existed near the London waterfront on the façade of Samuel Wyatt's recently erected Trinity House (1793-96; plate 17), home of the corporation that looked after lighthouses and other maritime properties.

Although it is left unclear in Dance's drawing, his Doric columns appear to have bases. These, the proportions of the

---

37. RIBA, "Dance Leoni," 33, 34, 60; its probable source is Palladio's reconstructed portico of the "Temples of the Sun and the Moon" (Temple of Venus and Rome), illustrated in *The Architecture of A. Palladio*, Giacomo Leoni, ed., 3rd ed., London, 1742, IV, pl. 25 (this is the book into which the drawings cited above are pasted).

Project for the Custom House, elevation

Trinity House, Tower Hill, by Samuel Wyatt, 1793-96, view

columns, the ground-storey arches, and the enigmatic initials on the parapet[38] show clearly that Dance is trying to convey a Roman rather than a Greek spirit. Just as the power of Rome had held sway over the western world, so too the British navy and merchant fleet could now boast supremacy around the globe. The lion and the unicorn strut in the centre, and above them Britannia rules and waves.

The Custom House is the symbolic entrance to the Port of London and Great Britain; through it passes the produce of the world. It was essential that the building provide a monumental image of the pride and pretentions of the British people, and Roman iconography was best suited as a vehicle. As an architectural programme, moreover, the custom house had a worthy pedigree to be followed with suitable respect.[39] David Laing, architect of the tragically short-lived Custom House which was at last begun in 1813, realized this, as did the designer of its successor, Sir Robert Smirke.[40]

Had the waterfront scheme been erected, boasted Dance, it would have been "a work of such magnitude as to be like undertaking to erect a Palmyra or Balbeck."[41] The comparison with great Roman provincial cities was not gratuitous. For Dance, it seems, had modelled not only the Custom House, but also the warehouses upon ancient Roman sources.

While a student in Italy, in May 1762, Dance had made a sojourn to Anzio, the ancient Roman port of Antium, a short distance south of Rome. The ruins of this great Imperial port were, however, in such poor condition that they revealed disappointingly little to him. As he wrote to his father:

> There are ruins all along the coast for about half a mile but so much destroyed by time and the sea I can make nothing of them. There are also great ruins out in the sea of the antique

38. We may decipher *S.P.L.* as a Londonized version of *S.P.Q.R.*, and *D.O.M.* is the standard dedicatory formula "Deo optimo maximo." The date MMDXX may boast of the futuristic aspects of the design. The rest, however, remains a puzzle.

39. Summerson, *Georgian London*, p. 258.

40. See J. Mordaunt Crook, "The Custom House Scandal," *Architectural History*, VI, 1963, pp. 91-102.

41. Farington Diary (British Museum typescript), 30 July 1796.

port which was semi-circular and of a great extension.[42]

His imagination thus aroused, Dance may have sought the remains of other ancient ports. The ruins of another, more important, port city lay closer to Rome and survived in better condition: Porto (the ancient Portus), the Imperial port of Ostia at the mouth of the Tiber.[43] The remains had apparently been investigated by numerous architects and archaeologists since the Renaissance, including Pirro Ligorio, Antonio Labacco, and Andrea Palladio,[44] and we may suppose that Dance too risked exposure to malaria and made the short journey from Rome to Ostia and Porto. The general form of the buildings was further available on coins.

The hexagonal basin of Porto was surrounded by warehouses, the most impressive being the large Severan magazines. Their ruins are dominated by long rows of arches from which spring groin vaults (plate 18). The brick warehouses behind these porticoes have survived well enough into the present century for a responsible architect to reconstruct them as having been plain cubic masses several storeys high with tall blind arcades along the façades (plate 19).[45] A restored plan by Palladio of these or other

42. Dance to his father, 6 May 1762 (RIBA). Archaeologists have studied the semicircular moles at Anzio but ignored the ruins of its warehouses. L. Linotte, "Sul porto d'Anzio antico," *Giornale arcadio di scienze, lettere, ed arte*, XXIII, 1824, pp. 225-246, XXIV, 1825, pp. 1 ff.; Karl Lehmann-Hartleben, *Die antiken Hafenanlangen des Mittelmeeres* (*Klio*, Beiheft XIV), Leipzig, 1923, pp. 190-191. Canina, *Il Porto neroniano di Anzio*, Rome, 1837, referred to by Lehmann-Hartleben, has been unavailable to me. The ruins at Anzio were further destroyed during the Allied landing on 22 Jan. 1944.

43. G. Lugli and G. Filibeck, *Il Porto di Roma imperiale e l'agro portuense*, Rome, 1935; W. L. MacDonald, "The Design of Roman Imperial Ports," paper presented at the 22nd meeting of the Society of Architectural Historians, Boston, 31 Jan. 1969. O. Testaguzza, *Portus*, Rome, 1970, has been unavailable to me.

44. G. Lugli, "Una Pianta Inedita del Porto ostiense disegnata da Pirro Ligorio," *Rediconti della pontificia accademia romana de archeologia*, XXIII-XXIV, 1946-49, pp. 187-207; A. Labacco, *Libro di A. Labacco appartenente all'architettura*, Rome, 1567; G. Zorzi, *I Disegni delle antichità di Andrea Palladio*, Venice, 1959, p. 102. Ligorio's reconstruction was engraved (1554) and published (1558), the engraving frequently being found in Antonio Lafreri, *Speculum Romanae Magnificentiae*, 1573. See David R. Coffin, "Pirro Ligorio and the Villa d'Este," unpublished Ph.D. dissertation, Princeton University, 1954, I, pp. 17-18.

45. The restorer was the architect Italo Gismondi; his drawings are published in Lugli and Filibeck, *Porto di Roma*, figs. 49-51, and the remains of the Severan magazines are described on pp. 83-85. W. L. MacDonald, who kindly provided me with the reference to this book, believes that this restoration is good.

Porto (Ostia), Severan magazines, reconstructed view by Italo Gismondi 19

warehouses at Porto (plate 20) indicates two rows of cellular magazines set back to back with a narrow corridor between them and a portico in front.[46] Dance's warehouses assimilated several features from these ancient magazines: porticoes (also demanded by Vitruvius[47]), tall and thin fenestration, cubic massing, and double cellular plan.

Dance thus relied upon the architecture of antiquity for both principal parts of his Port of London scheme. Even a "low" commercial building as simple and "functional" as a warehouse may be elevated in significance by following the commercial structures of antiquity — just as Dance's later shops seem to have been inspired by Roman *tabernae*. The "high" commercial Custom House, in contrast, is based upon ideas gleaned from more ornate public architectural sources. Each part expresses its role in the activity of the port: one is the bustling, sweaty, no-frills hub of commercial activity; the other the symbol of the power, the might, and the glory of the awesome British fleets.

Imperial Roman iconography was extended into Dance's monumental scheme of about 1800 for replacing London Bridge.[48] Dance suggested building two new bridges one hundred yards apart, each with a central draw span. One would always be available to vehicular and pedestrian traffic while the other might open to allow a boat to pass.[49] The two bridges lead to a large piazza on either shore; that on the London side has as its central feature Wren's Monument, while an obelisk was intended directly opposite on the South Bank. Each piazza terminates in a crescent, or, more accurately, an exedra. The source of this plan is certainly the Roman hippodrome, in particular the Circus Maximus, which

46. This drawing was in the Burlington-Devonshire collection in England, and Dance could have had access to it. Gismondi restores the plan of the Severan magazines as being a single cell deep with porticoes in front.

47. Vitruvius writes concerning harbours and shipyards: "For round these colonnades [porticus] either docks are to be made, or approaches from the colonnades to the warehouses" (*On Architecture*, trans. F. Granger, V:13, I, London, 1931, pp. 310-313).

48. Select Committee upon the improvement of the Port of London, report of 1800, in *Reports from Committees*, XIV, pp. 543-603, with illustrations and descriptions of seven schemes for a new London Bridge.

49. Dance alone proposed this novel solution: the other competitors put forth "highflying gridirons" which Dance felt to be absurd (Dance to Soane, 28 March 1801, in A. T. Bolton, *The Portrait of Sir John Soane, R. A.*, London, 1927, p. 93).

is long and narrow with two parallel tracks linked by a curve at each end and having a row of monuments down the centre.[50]

The bridge and piazza scheme provides an impressive adjunct to the project for the legal quays, and all are shown together in a perspective rendering by William Daniell (plate 21). What the Parliamentary Committee and all subsequent admirers of the scheme failed to note is that the bridge and the quays are incompatible; the grand piazza on the London side of the river, if executed, would have extended almost as far east as Botolph Lane, eliminating about three hundred feet of the projected docks.[51]

Several features of Dance's project had been proposed a third of a century earlier by the brilliant planner John Gwynn. In *London and Westminster Improved*, Gwynn suggested that the area between London Bridge and the Tower be developed with warehouses over arcades and that a new custom house occupy the central position directly in front of St. Dunstan-in-the-East. The south end of London Bridge, wrote Gwynn, should be "made to open in a spacious circular form," thus anticipating Dance's South Bank piazza.[52] Gwynn's farsighted proposals for the redevelopment of London provided a framework for future planners which was not to be ignored. Dance could not help but be influenced by Gwynn's many exciting ideas, just as John Nash was later to benefit from them in his transformation of London's West End.

Dance's expectations were shattered when the City's scheme for rebuilding the Port of London was passed over in favour of private development by the merchants, his plans being ignored for those by other, younger architects.[53] Many of the features of

50. This conclusion supports the connection between English eighteenth-century planning and the ceremonial structures of ancient Rome proposed by Summerson in "John Wood and the English Town-Planning Tradition," *Heavenly Mansions*, London, 1949. Dance's early biographer speaks of the piazza by the Monument as "an extensive amphitheatrical area" (Samuel Angell, "Sketch of the Professional Life of George Dance, Architect, R. A.," *Builder*, V, 1847, p. 334). In 1760 Dance and G. B. Piranesi had together observed the excavation of the Amphitheatrum Castrense in Rome (Piranesi to Robert Mylne, 22 Nov. 1760, RIBA).

51. Compare the plan of the docks (plate 14) with a plan of London on which is superimposed the bridge scheme (CLRO, Surveyor's Institutions Plans 1511). The docks could not be moved eastward because of the Tower of London, and also because of the alignment of the Custom House with St. Dunstan-in-the-East.

52. Gwynn, *London and Westminster Improved*, London, 1766, pp. 105-109 and pl. IV.

53. See Broodbank, *Port of London*, I, pp. 87 ff.; Summerson, *Georgian London*,

Porto (Ostia), Severan magazines,
reconstructed plan by Andrea Palladio 20

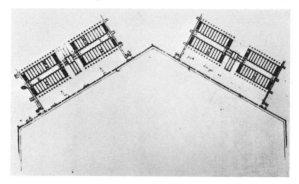

Project for the Port of London, view, painted by 21
William Daniell

London Dock, Wapping, by Daniel Asher 22
Alexander, 1812, view

Warehouse, Bridge Yard, Southwark, 1800, elevation

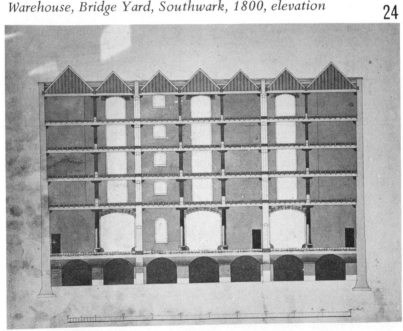

Warehouse, Bridge Yard, section

Dance's design are echoed in the first major warehouse complex erected in the London area, the West India Docks on the Isle of Dogs, begun in 1810 by Ralph Walker and John Rennie. Particularly close to the style of Dance is the London Dock at Wapping (plate 22), begun two years later by Daniel Asher Alexander.[54] Its sheer brick walls, flat parapets, and blocky geometric shape recall Dance's design. But Alexander lacked Dance's supreme restraint; he found it necessary to separate the ground floor from those above with a meaningless broad moulding, and the upper storey is conventionally treated as an attic with its smaller windows.

The only warehouses actually built by the Office of Works were small ones designed in 1800 for the Bridge Yard on the south bank of the Thames (plates 23, 24).[55] The elevations feature rusticated arches at the lower level with tall vertical strips cut into the upper walls as in the warehouses for the legal quays, but all is here on a much smaller scale. The design is less ambitious structurally as well: instead of experimenting with iron, Dance settles for a timber frame. These later warehouses were a timid venture by a defeated man, only a shadow of the great project for the Port of London.

In his Port scheme, as in his later city shops, Dance distinguished between various classes of buildings by adopting different modes. "High" commercial buildings for the merchants and bankers feature compositions and an ornamental vocabulary adopted from the grandiose public architecture of ancient Rome. "Low" commercial buildings, such as shops and warehouses, are simpler in composition and devoid of classical detail; nevertheless they still depend upon sources in similar buildings from antiquity. The "high" and the "low" mode display distinctive characteristics, yet each remains within the mainstream of the architecture of neoclassicism.

H. Kalman

pp. 258-261; Farington Diary, 29 Sept., 29 Dec. 1798; 16 Oct. 1799.

54. For photographs of the West India and London Docks, see J. M. Richards, *The Functional Tradition in Early Industrial Buildings*, London, 1958, pp. 43-46.

55. CLRO, Comptroller's Bridge House Plans 205-49A-G.

Sources of Illustrations

Note: All buildings and projects are located in London and were designed by George Dance or his office unless otherwise noted.

1. London County Council, *Survey of London*, XXVII, London, 1957.

2-9, 11-12, 14, 23, 24. Corporation of London Record Office. Photos by author.

10, 15-16. Sir John Soane's Museum, London. Photos by author: courtesy of Courtauld Institute, London.

13. Martin's Bank, London. Photo by author.

17. National Monuments Record, London.

18, 19. G. Lugli and G. Filibeck, *Il Porto di Roma imperiale e l'agro portuense*, Rome, 1935.

20. G. Zorzi, *I Disegni delle antichita di Andrea Palladio*, Venice, 1959.

21. Guildhall London. Photo by author.

22. John Summerson, *Georgian London*, London, 1945.

The Educated Eye:
Neo-Classical Drawing Masters
& Their Methods

The Neo-Classical movement was based on enthusiastic discovery of the purity and harmony of Greek art, but it has always been understood that this apparently conservative return to the idealism and morality of academic forefathers was connected with radical ideas peculiar to the eighteenth century involving a new and specifically modern conception of the nature of art. Even at the relatively low level of visual culture represented by amateur practice this was the case, and it is the purpose of this paper to examine the way some English drawing masters in the period from about 1790 to 1840 undertook a reform of popular art education based on Neo-Classical attitudes where one can observe the effect of these ideas on traditional practice. This was done primarily through the medium of illustrated books published to satisfy a growing demand among the middle classes for instruction in the fashionable accomplishments of drawing and sketching in water colour. The drawing masters put all their best thoughts about art education, and all their practical experience as teachers into these works, because they hoped that their books would give them some measure of status and influence in an English art world dominated, in theory, by the lofty principles of the Royal Academy. At the same time, what they published had to be both practical and popular, but if we can overcome the usual measure of academic reserve about this, it is possible to recognize that the so-called "drawing books" and related writings can be very useful as a means of focussing our attention on certain developments that are central to an understanding of the origins of modern art.

An early example of a new and more demanding attitude toward amateur art in England can be seen in a short publication which appeared in 1793 with the title, *An Essay on the Study of*

Nature in Drawing. Its author was a drawing master named William Marshall Craig (d. 1828), and his purpose was to attack the popular aims and methods of the best known amateur artist of the eighteenth century, William Gilpin (1724-1804). Craig had just read Gilpin's *Essay on the Art of Sketching Landscape*, published in 1792 in response to widespread interest in the sketches he had made to illustrate his volumes describing British scenery, beginning with *Observations on the River Wye . . .* in 1782. (Plate 2). The purpose of these sketches was to give an imaginative and poetic effect rather than a detailed rendition of a particular place encountered in his travels. Consequently, he used pen, ink and wash in a very free style, usually treating his subjects in monochrome, with only occasional washes of colour. He said that amateurs like himself should avoid colour, and also the human figure, because they required years of training to be dealt with adequately. It was enough to suggest in a general way the kinds of visual pleasure provided in endless variety by the scenery of nature with materials and methods intended only to give "a quick way of conveying picturesque ideas" for the use of those "who draw only for amusement, and are satisfied without colouring and high finishing with an endeavour by a rough sketch to produce a little composition and effect."[1]

This was a very attractive approach for the amateur who might have struggled through page after page of a typical eighteenth century drawing book, copying in careful pen outline engravings of faces, figures, animals, fruit and flowers, as well as landscapes complete with every detail of bush and bridge and castle (Plate 1). Instead of this, Gilpin's essay offered clear motivation, immediate contact with nature, limited subject matter, and a promise of almost instant results. Consequently, his method soon became a fad among well-to-do amateurs who loved to emulate his kind of "picturesque travel" at home and abroad, collecting souvenirs of Nature's beauty in prose, poetry and India ink.[2]

William Marshall Craig's essay was written to disparage this

1. William Gilpin, *Three Essays: On Picturesque Beauty; on Picturesque Travel; and on Sketching Landscape . . .*, London, Third Edition, 1808, p. 153.
2. Christopher Hussey, *The Picturesque . . .*, London and New York, 1927, pp. 83-127.

fad, which he described as a "disease of the pencil," spreading a noxious influence everywhere, causing many amateurs to give up accurate drawing in favour of twirls, flourishes and zig-zags characteristic of the "short-hand kind of representation" favoured by Gilpin and his school.[3] The purpose of this sort of "general imitation," as Craig recognized, was to capture the essence of beauty, identified by Gilpin with unity, a balanced wholeness of "effect" which he had learned to value through his studies of the old masters of landscape painting, Claude Lorraine, Gaspard Poussin and others. Their works demonstrated, for him, that the secret of landscape art lay in the achievement of the kind of composition which enables the eye "to find satisfaction in comprehending the picture as one object,"[4] and Gilpin concentrated his own efforts on suggesting this basic quality of beauty by sketching very generalized forms and broad masses of light and shade. In other words, his concern was with an abstract visual effect, and while Craig acknowledged that "this ingenious and fashionable writer has . . . fairly deduced his practice from his principles,"[5] he regarded the recommendation to represent what he called "abstract ideas" as very dangerous advice for the amateur. Instead of this, the beginner should avoid trying to sketch a whole composition until he has made many drawings of nearby natural objects like a tree, a rock, or a piece of broken ground in clear and distinct outline, and in careful detail. Craig explains further:

> The advantage of beginning by a part rather than sketching the whole is this: The eye can more easily measure a small space or distance than a large one, and a part being accurately drawn becomes a scale, or means of comparison, by which the remaining parts may be successively drawn with a great degree of certainty. Furthermore, as each particular must be impressed upon his mind by attentive observation, the student will insensibly form an intimacy with . . . nature

3. William Marshall Craig, *An Essay on the Study of Nature in Drawing Landscape*, London, 1793, pp. 9, 20.
4. William Gilpin, *An Essay Upon Prints*, London, 1768, pp. 9-10.
5. Craig, *Essay*, p. 11.

... and gradually master those little details in which so much of picturesque beauty consists.[6]

Craig followed up this initial criticism of the Gilpin style with a series of drawing books and lectures expressing his ideas much more fully. The first drawing book appeared in 1806,[7] and it is devoted entirely to landscape since, critical as he was of picturesque sketching, Craig was anxious to capitalize on the popular interest in drawing scenery which Gilpin had excited. It contains thirty-six plates, all careful line drawings in pencil, reproduced by means of soft ground etching, for the student to copy or emulate. They are arranged with the first plates showing single objects like plants, stones, fences, trees, cottages, etc. (Plate 3) followed by groupings of similar forms in landscape "passages," and only at the end are there full-page, finished compositions (Plate 4). The final pages have the clear, linear design and thoughtful balance of large forms which is entirely typical of the Neo-Classical style in general, and one can consider that stylistically they are roughly equivalent, in the realm of landscape, to the figure compositions published by Flaxman in illustration of the Iliad and Odyssey.[8]

The lectures were probably delivered in London in 1806, but they were not published until 1821.[9] In them Craig was more precise in his argument against attempts to represent generalized nature and "abstract ideas." He cited the authority of philosophers John Locke and Thomas Reid in arguing that an abstract idea of a tree, for instance, is a purely intellectual thing, formed when the mind selects common characteristics from all our ideas and sensations of particular trees. As such, an abstract tree has "neither form nor altitude nor dimensions" and cannot be represented in art except by arbitrary symbols like the zig-zags and

6. Craig, *Essay*, p. 18.

7. William Marshall Craig, *The Complete Instructor in Drawing*, London, 1806.

8. Craig's linear style in this book closely resembles that in a series of soft-ground etchings published in 1801-2 by the German artist, J. Philip Hackert (1737-1807) with the title, *Principes pour apprendre à dessiner le paysage d'après nature*. Hackert was a leading figure among Neo-Classical landscape artists on the continent, and his younger brother, J. G. Hackert (1744-1801), lived in England from 1772 until his death.

9. William Marshall Craig, *A Course of Lectures on Drawing, Painting, and Engraving Considered as Branches of Elegant Education*, London, 1821.

scribbles employed by Gilpin, a vicious practice in art, which "leaves the student to his own wild fancies without a criterion to judge of his exertions."[10]

In saying this, Craig demonstrated very clearly his concern to defend and adhere to the empirical tendency in British thought which derived ideas from experience and mistrusted the free use of concepts and generalities which cannot be checked against the evidence of the senses. This was his basic reason for contending that in art education the student should be led from the detail to the whole, from particular sensations to general relationships and conclusions in an inductive way, following the natural order of human experience as described by Locke and his school.

An important advantage of this procedure, in Craig's view, was that it gave the amateur a more practical competence in drawing than Gilpin's sort of random sketching. Craig saw drawing as a means of training the eye to measure forms and spaces accurately, the kind of drawing that could perhaps be used as a tool of science and industry. He commented at length on the practical importance of drawing as a means of transmitting information about mechanical inventions throughout the world. He also recommended the establishment of new schools where students would study art in connection with the mechanic arts and with manufacturing, and all this was appropriate enough, since his lectures were given on the premises of the British Institution for Promoting the Fine Arts, founded in 1805 with the primary aim, as its bylaws state, "to encourage and reward the talents of the artists of the United Kingdom so as to improve and extend our manufactures . . ."[11] Craig's drawing book was also dedicated to the British Institution with the statement that his purpose was to provide a cheap course of drawing for the inferior classes, an undertaking made necessary by "the many and various ways in which *imitative art* connects itself with trades and manufacturing."[12]

These comments emphasize Craig's intention to correct the total preoccupation with esthetic values found among the fol-

10. Craig, *Lectures*, p. 66.
11. John Pye, *Patronage of British Art*, London, 1845, p. 302.
12. Craig, *Complete Instructor*, p. 1.

lowers of Gilpin by including in his instruction elements of the new kind of practical and scientific education that had become a necessity for the middle classes as a result of the Industrial Revolution. Nevertheless, it is also evident that Craig did not mean to recommend a method of drawing that was completely imitative and practical, for after all, the goal which he presents for his students in the last pages of his drawing book of 1806 is the idealization of nature, and he is just as concerned with the classical varieties of response to landscape as Gilpin. This is made especially clear in the revised version of his landscape drawing book which appeared in 1811 with a new essay reviewing the procedure to be followed, and then continues:

> Having gone through the manner of treating ... the various materials of which landscape scenery must necessarily be composed, we come next to consider the principles on which they are to be combined for the purposes of a picture. Combinations of landscape may be divided into three classes, the *rural*, the *beautiful*, and the *grand*. ... [13]

Here he introduces the familiar categories of the Sublime, the Beautiful and the Picturesque with slightly different names. Then he describes their characteristics in some detail, noting the regions of England where each may be found, and the old masters who treated each one best. He urges his students to specialize in one of these classes of composition to be more sure of creating an esthetic unity in their studies from nature. This sort of unity is to be approached by means of careful imitation, but he states in conclusion that he wishes "to impress on the mind of every practitioner that copying should be considered as the means only, not as the end of art."[14]

These words underline Craig's commitment to Neo-Classical idealism. In fact, one might consider the opposition between Craig and Gilpin as a miniature version of the battle fought out in France at an earlier time, and at a much higher level, between Jacques Louis David and artists like Boucher or Fragonard. In a

13. William Marshall Craig, *Instruction in Drawing Landscape*, London, 1811, p. 9.
14. Craig, *Instruction in Drawing Landscape*, p. 10.

different social and historical context, Craig was on the side of rational reform with his concern for clear linear definition, moral seriousness, and social responsibility, while Gilpin's tendency toward impressionistic effects, estheticism, and aristocratic self-indulgence was related to the spirit of the Rococo style and period.

Of course, it was Craig's empiricism that gave his teaching its radical twist and made his idealism so different from Gilpin's, and it reflected a trend which ultimately destroyed the authority of classicism. A symptom of this can be seen in another later work of Craig's where he turns his attention to drawing the human figure.[15] In this, his insistence on working from the part to the whole leads him to attack "the frequent usage of teaching the knowledge of human figures by a scale of proportion," especially as this method is illustrated in drawing books showing "the German practice . . . of producing the forms of human figures by . . . circles, squares, and triangles."[16] He asserts that in his own day this practice had been completely rejected in favour of direct observation. This underscores in a new way his opposition to what E. H. Gombrich has described, with reference in part to the German method described by Craig, as the traditional, natural, and inevitable tendency of the creative process to work from schema to detail, a rule which Gombrich gives in his own well-known formula as, "making comes before matching."[17] Of course, Gilpin was on the side of the "makers," those who believed that beauty could be conceived and expressed initially in very general terms by following certain ideas and principles held in the mind of the artist, with details and secondary effects like colour added later. This approach might also be called "synthetic" compared with the "analytic" approach of Craig, who contended that the ideal whole must be a construction built up with faithfully recorded details of immediate visual experience. Thus Craig's teaching forms a small part of what is called "the history of the struggle against the

15. William Marshall Craig, *Craig's Instructions for Drawing and Understanding the Human Figure*, London, 1817.
16. Craig, *Human Figure*, p. 4.
17. E. H. Gombrich, *Art and Illusion*, London and New York, 1960, pp. 116, 146-178.

Landscape, engraving, 1763

William Gilpin, *View on the River Wye*, aquatint, 1789

W. M. Craig, *Elements of Landscape*, etching, 1806

W. M. Craig, *Landscape*, etching, 1806

George Harley, *Cottage*, colour aquatint, 1829

9

W. H. Pyne, *Castle*, colour aquatint, 1812

David Cox, *Evening: View of Windsor Castle*, colour aquatint, 1813

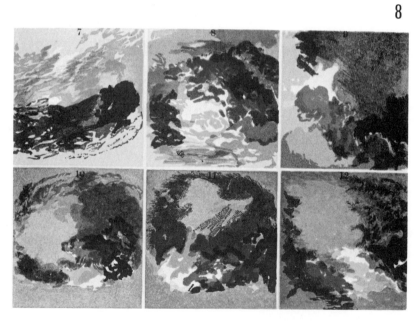

George Barnard, *Contrasts of Colour*, chromolithograph, 1861

J. D. Harding, *Improvement of Claude Lorraine*, wood engraving, 1845

schema" by Gombrich, who sees this as a questionable development in modern art, based on ignorance.[18] Nevertheless, even
among amateurs and their teachers there is something heroic about
an attempt to come to grips with "pure experience."

Other artists joined with Craig in his effort to reform popular
art education along practical and rational lines by publishing
books that reinforced with further comment the criticisms and
procedures he had put forward. "Anti-picturesque" statements
became very common and more sweeping in their scope. W. H.
Pyne (1769–1843), drawing-master, water-colourist and journalist, linked the Gilpin manner with the foreign influence of French
drawing masters who came to England in the eighteenth century
and inspired Gainsborough's sketching style, which was imitated in
turn by his fashionable clients at Bath.[19]

> The Gainsborough mania was long the rage, and there are
> yet some antique beaux and belles of *haut ton* who recollect
> their many friends who, with themselves, were stricken with
> this sketching frenzy, and smile at Bath and its vanities, as
> they talk of the days that are gone.[20]

In this way Pyne made it clear that the sketching craze should
be regarded as an aristocratic fad and folly, only to be laughed at
in his own day, but he noted that its influence lingered on, and
others, like Edward Dayes (1783-1804), a distinguished water-
colour artist, joined him in warning against "French flutter" in
drawing and chiaroscuro.[21] Following another remark published
by Pyne, some came to associate picturesque sketching almost
entirely with the teaching of Alexander Cozens (c. 1710-1786),
who had encouraged his students to make landscapes from more
or less random ink-blots. Typically, Francis Nicholson
(1753-1844) complained about the method of manufacturing
pictures with blotted paper, "which habituates the performer to

18. Gombrich, p. 174.
19. Paul H. Walton, *The Drawings of John Ruskin*, Oxford, 1972, pp. 2-3.
20. W. H. Pyne, "The Rise and Progress of Water-Colour Painting in England,"
Somerset House Gazette I, London, 1823, p. 162.
21. Edward Dayes, *The Works of the Late Edward Dayes*, London, 1805, p. 288;
James Roberts, *Introductory Lessons in ... Painting in Water Colours ...*, London,
1809, p. 13.

every kind of licentiousness," so that "even in the works of the Chinese it is difficult to find anything more unnatural."[22] (An interesting comment because, of course, the best picturesque sketches are quite oriental in spirit.)

They all agreed with Craig, that the best antidote for this disease was a course in careful line drawing with the lead pencil, an instrument which was just beginning to be machine-made and widely available in its modern form, and which was said to give a line superior to that made by pen and ink because it preserved "softness, breadth, and atmosphere."[23] Consequently, most of the drawing books published after Craig by W. H. Pyne (1769-1843), Samuel Prout (1783-1853), David Cox (1783-1859) and others followed his example in illustrating numerous pencil drawings reproduced by soft-ground etching or lithography because "he who devotes his time to the completion of a perfect outline . . . has more than half finished his piece."[24]

Many drawing masters followed Craig in commenting on the utility of accurate drawing in modern times. Francis Nicholson gave first place in his preface to the connection between drawing, mechanics and manufacturing;[25] Prout wrote that children should be taught drawing as carefully as mathematics and languages, and not "as a means of amusing ones self for a vacant hour,"[26] while T. H. Fielding (1781-1851) argued that art should be taught in the universities because a knowledge of drawing and painting can assist some of the most important sciences.[27]

The "analytical" method of instruction was adopted very widely, so that most nineteenth century drawing books gave the student a course that moved from detail to whole, a process which Edward Dayes compared with language instruction, where the master begins with letters and syllables, and these are joined into

22. Francis Nicholson, *The Practice of Drawing and Painting Landscape from Nature in Water Colours . . .*, London, 1820, p. 68.

23. Roberts, *Introductory Lessons*, p. 13.

24. David Cox, *A Treatise on Landscape Painting and Effect in Water Colours . . . with Examples in Outline, Effect, and Colouring*, London, 1813, Edited by G. Holme for *The Studio*, 1922, p. 13.

25. Nicholson, p. i.

26. Samuel Prout, *Rudiments of Landscape . . .*, London, 1813, p. 13.

27. T. H. Fielding, *On the Theory of Painting*, London, 1836, p. 26.

sentences, "but the ultimate end is composing themes to call forth the power of invention, and convey a more exquisite idea of the language. Exactly so should be the process in teaching drawing."[28] This method was applied by W. H. Pyne and others to the handling of colour, a subject not touched on by Craig. In a book published by Pyne in 1812 plates are included which show the student how to proceed, step by step, from outline to full colour (Plate 5).[29] This is based on traditional studio practice in oil and water colour, and it could carry the amateur much farther than Gilpin's casual washes of a single tint. Like Craig's stages in drawing landscape, one impression is added to another until the whole effect is achieved. First, line defines form and colour areas, followed by India ink washes for tonal gradations, and finally local colour is superimposed with washes and touches of transparent water colour.

Of all the manuals of instruction for amateur artists published in this period, the most comprehensive and influential was the *Treatise on Landscape Painting in Water Colour* (1813) by David Cox, a book which was to be reissued in various versions and forms for over a hundred years. It contains a relatively brief text, but it is richly illustrated with seventy-two plates, many of them hand coloured (Plate 7), arranged in three sections devoted to drawing, light and shade, and colour. Like Craig, he offers a course in drawing which proceeds from small forms through larger groupings to finished compositions. The student is then given examples showing how to add light and shade to his outlines with sepia and India ink, and the final section illustrates finished compositions with colour applied over this kind of foundation.

As one leafs through the large number of full-plate landscapes given by Cox, it becomes evident that the analytic procedure, which has been discussed here chiefly with reference to preliminary drawing exercises, can be linked with a class of compositions concerned with light and colour overlapping the traditional categories of Sublime, Beautiful and Picturesque. The last named types are much in evidence, easily recognizable by style and

28. Dayes, p. 260.
29. W. H. Pyne, *Rudiments of Landscape Drawing*, London, 1812.

subject, and Cox presents them as ideals which the student is to hold in his mind as he approaches nature. However, there is also a newer kind of concern to illustrate different times of day, atmospheric effects, and the seasons. There are plates showing Morning, Mid-day, Afternoon, Evening, Twilight, and Moonlight; there is a Hazy Morning, Cloudy Effect, Storm, Rain, a Rainbow, and finally, there are illustrations of Summer, Harvest Time, and Winter. This attention to many varieties of light and colour in nature can be compared with Craig's dissection of landscape form into its constituent elements, and both things proceed from the same idea, that the student must analyze his experience of Nature, considering *form* as a collection of details organized in space, and *colour* as a sequence of effects in time, before he can understand and construct an esthetic whole.

Of course, the ultimate result of this kind of treatment of form and colour, space and time was a breakdown of confidence in an underlying, enduring framework for art and nature, but Cox includes both things in his teaching, and his book shows the amateur how to combine large and simple forms in balanced compositions expressing traditional reactions to the spectacle of Nature, but at the same time include a wealth of detail, and a large measure of fresh observation of light and colour. His book can be seen as the climax of the reform of popular art education initiated by Craig and others where, in accordance with Neo-Classical principles, the goal is idealism, but the method is realistic.

Meanwhile, at a higher level of creative endeavour, J. M. W. Turner was pressing the analysis of light and colour toward new conclusions with unmatched energy and talent. His oils and water colours revealed the dynamism of form, light and space in a way that dazzled his contemporaries and made his art an overwhelming influence in the 1820s. The drawing masters attempted to keep up with these innovations, at a respectful distance, and translate some of them into teachable formulae. For example, the book published by Francis Nicholson in 1823 illustrates the same dramatic view of a castle under four different conditions of light and atmosphere.[30] In the same book there is a description of a method of applying

30. Nicholson, facing p. 42.

colour by means of bold, direct touches of the brush "without preparation," that is, without the kind of preliminary drawing and India ink underpainting of light and shade required by Pyne and Cox. The advantage of this direct method, which must reflect the influence of Turner, was said to be that it would give "great clearness and brilliancy" of colour, but Nicholson shows his awareness that it can also lead the amateur away from classical values when he warns that "without considerable practice, the work will frequently be deficient in harmony, breadth, and above all, repose."[31] A page from a somewhat later book by George Harley (1791-1871) illustrates the new method of adding one patch of colour to another (Plate 6),[32] and in 1839 T. H. Fielding wrote that this way of "merely mixing the colours to the hue required, and laying them in their proper places" was far superior to the old line, plus tone, plus colour process with its "leaden coloured shadows," so "ineffective for producing a natural appearance in painting."[33]

The consequence of this development for amateurs was that their drawing masters nearly gave up trying to provide a systematic, step by step procedure for handling colour. In 1855 George Barnard (fl. 1837-1873) urged his students to try to paint like Turner by "interlacing" the colours, placing them side by side in touches of pure pigment "so that the eye passes rapidly from one to the other and unites them,"[34] but the best that he could give for guidance was a series of plates showing landscape details, analyzed into separate touches, and in one illustration the colours are set down without any apparent reference to nature, in a series of abstract patches, like late Turner water colours in miniature (Plate 8).

At this point, it can be seen that the analytic procedure recommended by Neo-Classical reformers has resulted in the definition of a new goal for amateur art very different from the

31. Nicholson, p. 62.
32. George Harley, *First Principles of Landscape Drawing*, London, 1829.
33. T. H. Fielding, *On Painting in Oil and Water Colours ...*, London, 1839, pp. 88-89.
34. George Barnard, *The Theory and Practice of Landscape Painting in Water Colours*, London, 1855, pp. 118-119.

harmony, breadth and repose which Cox and Nicholson still tried to preserve. It might be described as a "dynamic realism" which, in the realm of colour, results from breaking the total "colour experience" into smaller and smaller component parts, first line with broad washes, then patches, and finally, separate small touches. This pushed the artist and amateur into territory beyond the reach of co-ordinating systems or precepts, leaving him to depend on individual sensitivity alone, the territory to be thoroughly and professionally explored by the Impressionists later in the century.[35]

A comparable development can be traced in the teaching of drawing, with the result that J. D. Harding (1798-1863) was to recommend in 1834 that simple outlines be avoided in favour of broken, separate touches of the pencil, so that the eye would seem to rest on textures and surfaces as it does in nature.[36] Even more significant is the change that came about in discussions of composition. It will be recalled that Craig had forbidden his students any attempt to grasp the whole without reference to details, and they were told to construct their pictures piece by piece, using each detail as "a scale, or means of comparison, by which the remaining parts may be drawn." The problem was how to achieve over-all balance and harmony, and this was dealt with in an ingenious and influential way by John Varley (1778-1842) in his *Treatise on the Principles of Landscape* (1817). He stressed the use of visual contrast as a means of linking and harmonizing the parts of a composition. The picture was to be built up by sequences of contrasting forms, square and round, rough and smooth, light and heavy, etc., to form finally a framework of leading lines giving a series of ascending and descending diagonals which should "balance each other from the different sides of the picture so that a ball running down one of them should be

35. An important and continuing source of inspiration for all English artists pursuing the analysis of colour was the fundamental *Opticks* of Isaac Newton, published in 1704. See Henry Guerlac, "An Augustan Monument: The Opticks of Isaac Newton," *The Varied Pattern: Studies in the 18th Century*, P. Hughes, D. Williams, eds., Toronto, 1971, pp. 131-163.
36. J. D. Harding, *Elementary Art, or, the Use of the Lead Pencil* . . ., London, 1834, p. 25.

impelled up on the other side, and so on in succession until it settles near the centre of the picture."[37] Varley's empirical method of analyzing composition proceeded with many similar metaphors, analogies and figures of speech, all designed to point to a dynamic balance of visual tensions in the work of art, which could be understood rationally as a kind of pictorial machine, without reference to inspiration or intuition, and without mystery. This was regarded as highly "scientific," and others came to use a similar approach. For example, T. H. Fielding, in 1836, defined a picture as "a collection of *foci*, or points of vision, holding their places in a series of gradations, and subject to one great controlling focus, the centre of effect, itself composed of innumerable *foci* of various colours and degrees of light."[38] Of course, all this talk of foci, diagonals, rolling balls and so forth, carried the student far from classical methods of achieving a static compositional balance by means of an ideal framework of verticals and horizontals, with carefully enclosed, plane by plane recession. A new goal had been suggested by the analytical method, defined by Harding as a dynamism of the whole which would create an impression of "infinite, permeable space," achieved by the contrast of forms in every part of the picture, "where all are viewed in connection with those around, and with the whole subject, each part being fitted, adopted, and related to the others, and all together."[39]

Harding was so confident of the validity of the new ideal of dynamic spatial penetration through a structure of calculated contrasts that he undertook to "correct" a landscape by Claude Lorraine according to his principles (Plate 9). The differences are subtle at first sight, but we can see how the new, analytic vision has here resulted in a looser and more informal organization,[40] a

37. John Varley, *A Treatise on the Principles of Landscape* . . ., London, 1817, p. 3.

38. T. H. Fielding, *Theory of Painting*, pp. 60-61.

39. J. D. Harding, *The Principles and Practice of Art*, London, 1845, pp. 71-72.

40. Harding's own explanation may be of assistance. Concerning the lower composition, with its corrections, he writes: "The trees here have different forms and quantities; the building does not repeat either, but possesses a distinct form of its own, and is, therefore, instantly recognized by the mind as a separate object; and all the varieties of form which these lines express, instead of being repeated by others below them and on the foreground, are contrasted and emphasized by straight and other opposing lines; the level of the figures is changed, and the distance beyond them does

development which, in spite of its quest for a scientific method, again tends to leave the student without rule or precept, depending on his own intuitive sense of order.

This marks the end of Neo-Classical idealism in the instruction given to amateur artists in England. Harding's illustration shows the deliberate breakup of classical unity of form in the interest of a new ideal of dynamism and empirical imitation. Of course, the same kind of breakdown can be seen everywhere in the arts early in the nineteenth century, and it had much to do with the freeing of the creative process during the Romantic movement. But it had even more to do with the development of the kind of radical and personal realism which one finds in the art of Courbet, Manet and Cézanne, leading finally to the explosive fragmentation and reconstruction of the visual world which we find in the art of the Cubists and their followers in this century.

P. Walton

---

not in this, as in the example above it, follow any line they suggest. I am aware that in doing this, I am treading on delicate ground, but those who see with unprejudiced eyes must admit that I have made improvements." Harding, *Principles*, p. 67.

"Blot and Insert Where You Please": The Fortunes of 18th Century Play Texts

Eighteenth century plays fell into the hands of actors, and now fall into the hands of editors. The duties of both seem clear: the actor must speak the lines and be heard, the editor must decide on the original intention of his text and a convenient way to present it to his modern readers. It is not easy to put these ideals into practice; the actor is not a parrot, and intentions are hard things to catch. Ancient authors did not leave their manuscripts. Renaissance writers were vigorously edited – one might say abnormalised – by their earliest compositors, and their proofreading seems to have been as blithe as their orthography. Modern writers, aware of the second and third editions as second and third chances, have contracted the disease of revision: which *Oliver Twist*, which *Leaves of Grass* and which stage of a Yeats poem is the writer's intention? On the stage, not only the clowns speak more, or less, than is set down for them.

Even with a non-dramatic text it is hard to find an appropriate form of editorial presentation, if we are to avoid multi-parallel texts, like the great Bible of Erasmus. Do we use modern or old spelling, new or original punctuation, stanza form, pagination, caesura, and so on.

But presentation of a dramatic text is a more particular problem, the possible variations of a reprinted text running from the austere limitation of material to the speeches, the speech tags and the unavoidable *exits* and *entrances*, with the few *asides*, *draws* or *dies* to which most seventeenth century editions confine themselves; through the generally unhelpful additions and interpolations of nineteenth century editors ("Scene, the street outside

Vincentio's house," or "Flinging her from him with disdain"); to the detailed and imaginative stage directions found in a text such as the *New Cambridge Shakespeare* ("The Mart of Ephesus: Antipholus of Syracuse approaches, musing, the chain about his neck"). If we feel sympathetic to this very specific method of play editing, it is no doubt because we recognise that the intention of a play is essentially bound up with its theatrical mode: that the best modern edition might be the best modern performance — because this is financially and scholastically impossible, the editor must do his best to *realise* the theatrical action in book form. Only by doing this as fully as possible — by keeping the staging carefully and constantly in his mind — can the editor keep control over both the most routine stage direction and the rhetorical structure of his piece. Plays, of course, are not written documents: the author's text is his signal to the actors, and the editor's version must be produced in awareness of this, and similarly signal his readers.

This is a comment on the editor's second task — the method of presenting dramatic texts — but it reminds us of the inherent problems in the first task of the play editor, which the present essay will discuss. When Shakespeare writes *Venus and Adonis*, the affair, at least in textual intention, ends with the last stroke of his pen. All the compositor of the first edition and the modern editor must do is to attempt to recapture the intention of the assumed ideal manuscript. But when he writes *Hamlet*, his intention becomes inextricably mingled with the intentions of Burbage, the format of the Elizabethan theatre and the expectation and concentration span of his audience. Who is, indeed, the *author* of what we wish to edit, and how can we hit on the appropriate level of intention? If we had a copy of *Hamlet* in Shakespeare's own hand — the final draft or fair copy which he submitted to the actors — and also a prompt copy representing exactly what happened on the stage in the original performances, we know that these would not be the same. Which would we prefer to read, study, perform, or place in the hands of school-children? History has encouraged us to dodge this issue, partly by taking care to destroy or hide all the manuscripts and all the prompt copies of the Shakespeare plays, but partly by deliberately stressing the role of the *author*, and undervaluing the actors' part in the creation of the work of art. The Greek dramatists produced texts which were, after their first success, legally protected from variation by the actors, so that the works of Aeschylus and Sophocles were as canonical as those of any non-dramatic writers, and indeed were almost in the nature of sacred ritual. While the plays of Shakespeare were never accorded significant respect by the generations of English actors, his written words have from the beginning had an almost magical integrity in the eyes of readers and editors. Heminge and Condell claim that their First Folio presents the plays "offered to your view cured and perfect of their limbs . . . absolute in their numbers, as he conceived them." While it seems almost a necessary condition of a modern production of Shakespeare that the text should be tormented or ignored, modern editors have had little doubt that their task is theoretically simple and of a piece throughout — to get back to the assumed authorial fair copy, the production of the sole playwright's desk. And they traditionally scorn the actions of stage managers to edit and order the plays for presentation, calling such labours, "playhouse corruption."

The obsession of editors of Elizabethan drama with problems of collaboration (an obsession happily diminished in the last two decades) has as its basis again the editor's belief that he can get back to the writer at work, back to the authorial manuscript, catching Middleton and Rowley, Beaumont and Fletcher, at their twin desks. The editor who wants to locate in his mind's eye the ideal manuscript finds it hard to cope with the genially disordered kinds of collaboration that seemed to go on sometimes in the Elizabethan age — the communal development of a play being rather like the development of an oral tradition.

The expressed intention of modern editors of plays performed before 1642 remains simply to discover an author's — or several authors' — intentions. But after 1660, it becomes less easy to think of the author's fair copy as the authoritative embodiment of the only intention that matters, for we are more and more aware of the role of the actors, and aware that their contributions to dramatic literature are vast indeed. "Blot and insert where you please — *I submit myself to your judgment*," says Plotwell, a supposed dramatist in Gay's *Three Hours after Marriage* (1717), to the actors whom he wants to accept and perform the play he hands them. He certainly shows no signs of holding the manuscript sacred in its intentions. Even Phoebe Clinket, the real author of the tragedy, devoted to her text as a mother to her child, is prepared to make sacrifices to get it onto the stage: "I will prevail upon him to strike out some few things." Had the play really existed, our traditional valuation of the author's intentions, conditioned by the study of Sophocles and Shakespeare, would lead us to esteem and print Mrs. Clinket's fair copy. Yet in practice, editors of Restoration and eighteenth century plays have not always followed this custom. Congreve, who hoped to be absolved as a gentleman rather than as a playwright, tidied up his plays for the collected editions, adding touches of extra elegance. Herbert Davis and Kathleen M. Lynch — among the most distinguished and learned of editors of the period — choose to print the texts that are closer to the theatrical performances. Home's *Douglas* we usually meet with in the London edition, which is an abridged acting version, rather than in the slightly fuller Edinburgh edition of a few days later, which seems to be based on an authorial manuscript. Fielding's *The Author's Farce* has been recently edited in the original version, rather than in the more elaborate later text. With a great many plays of the period, it is possible to detect or partially recreate both an acting text and an author's copy — perhaps reworked for publication after the performances. Some basic textual and editorial decisions hinge on the determination of which kind of text is preferred for a modern edition, though sometimes the decision is made on subjective terms. One editor rejects a corrected version because the "improvements" are, in the editor's terms, simply "to be deplored."

Of course, if there is a coherent acting text and a coherent author's text, they may well be both coherent artistic wholes, of differing purpose. Perhaps only on the basis of an aesthetic judgment can we decide which is preferable. For a text of Fielding's *Tom Thumb*, one would certainly feel that the revised text, with all the comic additional footnotes and mock-scholarly paraphernalia (which clearly cannot be acted) is a more meaningful art work than the lively but rather thin parody first performed and printed in 1730. On the other hand, Southerne's *The Spartan Dame* — a great hit of 1710, for which the booksellers paid an unprecedented £120 — was performed with certain omissions, which are only supplied in the fifth edition of 1721. These passages, amounting to some four hundred lines, provide philosophical and moral analysis of Cleombrotus's revolt against his father-in-law, and show the people supporting the uprising and the usurpation. The lines were omitted for political reasons. J. W. Dodds feels that "not a little of the play's force is lost with these excisions," but the piece was a theatrical success without the lines. In the abridged version, the play is a fast-moving, exciting drama of power politics: with the scenes, the action regularly and tediously pauses for a deal of philosophical posturing. One may suspect that the players were happy enough to have the neat, brief, if empty-headed tale of adventure, and that a modern reader would be better served by it too.

What happened to the text of a Restoration or eighteenth century play after the author had produced in his study the "foul papers" which embodied his intentions? Some of the evidence we have from the period suggests a chain of events rather different from that befalling a typical Elizabethan or Jacobean play. The first thing to do was to catch the attention of the players: for an established dramatist or a man under contract to the theatre this was no problem, but a less-well-known figure would need a patron, or an introduction, or a blank cheque. Sir Samuel Tuke and John Crowne aimed high. Tuke noted carefully and explicitly that his *Adventures of Five Hours* was written "by the sacred command of our late most excellent Majesty," and Crowne did not deny the local gossip that said he worked with the King on *Sir Courtly Nice*, showing His Majesty each scene as he wrote it. Dryden's preface to *Mariage à la Mode* is quite specific in its comment on the role played by the Earl of Rochester: "I humbly dedicate to your Lordship that poem, of which you were pleased to appear an early patron before it was acted on the stage. I may go further with your permission and say that it received amendment from your noble hands ere it was fit to be presented. You may please likewise to remember, with how much favour to the author and indulgence to the play, you commended it to the view of His Majesty, then at

Windsor, and by his approbation of it in writing made way for its
kind reception in the theatre."

This is of course to by-pass the problem of getting the
actors to look at your masterpiece. A better known comment on
the sort of introduction an author might expect is to be found in
Pope's lines:

> Bless me, a packet. 'Tis a stranger sues;
> A virgin tragedy; an orphan muse.
> If I dislike it, "Furies, death and rage."
> If I approve, "Commend it to the stage."
> There, thank my stars, the whole commission ends:
> The players and I are, luckily, no friends.

Phoebe Clinket, in *Three Hours after Marriage* is a more explicit
angel. "I'll deposit a sum myself upon the success of it. Well, since
it is to be acted. . . ." We know that the play was presented to the
actors by the author, or his agent, who read it aloud from his
manuscript. Reading aloud would, of course, solve the problem of
the illegibility of foul papers, but the author who was keen to
press his advantage would probably, like Mrs. Clinket, make sure
that he had a readable copy to put straight into the actors' hands.
Colley Cibber tells us what happens, with lively charity towards
the embarrassed participants: "A manager ought to be at the
reading of every new play, when it is first offered to the stage,
though there are seldom one of these plays in twenty which upon
hearing proves to be fit for it, and upon such occasions the
attendance must be allowed to be as painfully tedious as the
getting rid of the author of such plays must be disagreeable and
difficult." The pamphlet *A Comparison between the Two Stages*
(1702) tells a story of how the greedy players dine and drink off
the bill of a wretched author who reads to them one evening at a
tavern. Other stories tell of direct bribery — the actor George
Frederick Cooke was offered £20 by a twice-rejected author who
insisted on reading out his lamentable tragedy of Nero and
Pompaeia in the hope that "through my influence it might be
brought forward." The search for a celebrated writer to affix a
prologue or epilogue, or even, as Southerne's *The Wives' Excuse*
suggests, a whole scene, provided another road to notice.

Once the players accepted the play for production, the careful, letter-perfect prompt copy had to be produced – based on the author's copy (in whatever form) and the source for the *parts* held by the individual actors. Here the question of playhouse alterations comes to the fore. In Fielding's *The Author's Farce*, the manager, aptly called Marplay, swoops into action against the luckless text of the doleful author, Luckless: "I will give you my opinion of it, and if I can make any alterations in it that will be for its advantage, I will do it freely. I will maintain it, let a play be never so good, without alteration it will do nothing." So now the fair copy of the author is used as a basis to produce the – altered – prompt copy. Mrs. Clinket's play, *The Universal Deluge, or the Tragedy of Deucalion and Pyrrha*, is extensively amended on the spot by the players and their tame critic, Sir Tremendous. They make their alterations directly into her own copy: "Absurd to the last degree (*strikes out*), palpable nonsense (*strikes out*), such stuff (*strikes out*), abominable (*strikes out*), most execrable. This thought must out. Madam, with submission, this metaphor, this whole speech." Here, in little, is the modification of the book: the very text which serves as a basis for the transcription of the parts and the prompt copy seems to be vanishing out of the control of the author. The amended prompt copy seems to remain in the hands of the author only if, like Bayes in *The Rehearsal*, he directs the play. At the end of this piece, Bayes has left behind on stage some papers which the actors identify as "foul papers of his," and which contain the "argument of the fifth act" – a draft summary which is no doubt intended to explain to the rather dim-witted actors what their parts mean. Bayes has been carrying this around with him, together with the prompt copy which in a fury he threatens to take away: "I'gad, I'll be revenged on 'em, I'll sell this play to the other house." The stage-keeper pleads, "Nay good sir, don't take away the book – you'll disappoint the company that comes to see it acted here this afternoon." Of course the play cannot be given without the prompt copy – the *book* – close to hand. If the author is the director, the author's copy and the prompt copy may be the same thing – or rather, the prompt copy may have been set up directly from the foul papers (which Bayes seems to keep also close at hand), and no other printable manuscript may exist. But when the manager of the theatre takes over, the theatre prompt book, set up from the fair copy of a less assured author, may well drift further and further from the original during the rehearsals.

There is frequent comment, in dedications and the like, suggesting that the two versions have their own separate identities. In the brief note to *The Beaux Stratagem*, Farquhar states, "The reader may find some faults in the play, which my illness prevented the amending of. But there is great amends made in the representation, which cannot be matched, no more than the friendly and indefatigable care of Mr. Wilks." Does Farquhar mean "amending" literally? It will be suggested later that he probably does. The procedure no doubt varied from play to play, but it seems probable that in the case of an author not closely involved with the playhouse, a fair copy was drawn up by the playwright himself for submission, used to produce the prompt book and then returned to him. (An author's copy would not normally be suitable for marking up as a prompt copy.) If the author is more closely involved, the prompt copy may be set up directly from foul papers, possibly with the author taking part in some sort of communal discussions of the details of the play. Whether the actors normally made changes during the first reading or later during rehearsals is irrelevant, as the changes would in either case be incorporated into the prompt book, but missing from the author's copy. It seems clear, at least from a comment in Boaden's life of John Philip Kemble, that by the end of the century the sophisticated actor assumed that textual authority lay with the author, and that his intentions were to be found in the printed text, while the prompt copies, inaccurate and ignored, mouldered in the theatre office. Kemble's method of preparing the play for presentation, we are told, was "not to order the prompter to write out the parts from some old mutilated prompt copy lingering on his shelves, but himself to consider it attentively in the author's genuine book — not as disputing the judgment of the author, but as suiting the time of the representation to the habits of his audience."

The printing of the play after 1660 seems to have been generally a private deal between the author and the bookseller, and the price paid for a successful play was at first in the neighborhood of £20 – 25. Tonson paid Dryden £20 for *Troilus and Cressida* in 1678, and this was considered a good price. Usually the author relied on the success of the stage version to put him in a good position for bargaining, but sometimes unacted plays were published, out of pique, spite or a sense of injured merit. Pope's comment continues:

> Fired that the house rejects him, "'Sdeath, I'll print it
> And shame the Fools. Your interest, sir, with Lintott."
> "Lintott, dull rogue, will think your price too much."
> "Not, sir, if you revise it, and retouch."

In John Durant Brevel's satiric closet drama *The Confederates*, Bernard Lintott, the bookseller, is personated. He is represented as paling at the news that a play he has bought for £50 will not be staged because of a dispute with the actors:

> I've bought their copy, how my heart does ache.
> Pity, ye gods; if he says true I break.

"Their copy" refers specifically to the authors. They have their own manuscript, which they sell to the bookseller, quite independent of the theatrical event. This is the point at which an author can, if he chooses, fix up his original, sneer at the actors or be graceful to them in a preface, and set down what he thinks will be taking in the closet. Steele, in the introduction to *The Conscious Lovers*, makes a shrewd point. "It must be remembered that a play is to be seen, and is made to be represented with the advantage of action. For the greatest effect of a play in reading is to excite the reader to go see it." Like Farquhar, he praises his manager: "Mr. Cibber's zeal for the work, his care and application in instructing the actors and altering the disposition of the scenes, when I was through sickness unable to cultivate such things myself, has been a very obliging favour and friendship to me." Though the printed text must have been set from a copy that was either the author's or the playhouse's, the implication here is that the manager performed work that was, strictly speaking, the duty of the author: that what we read is an accurate reflection of what we saw on the stage, and that this is substantially altered from the author's original — although altered with his permission and approval. Another writer guarantees the relationship of the printed and the staged text even more explicitly. Vanburgh's The Relapse had been accused of blasphemous and bawdy expressions, and self-righteously (and probably falsely) the author assures us that his text is free of offence and the scandal ill-founded: "if there was any obscene expressions upon the stage, here they are in the print; for I have dealt fairly, I have not sunk a syllable that could be ranged under that head."

But at least one Restoration play is confessedly filthier on the page than on the stage. Thomas Southerne's Sir Anthony Love stars the eponymous heroine, in breeches, Sir Anthony, and has a vivacious caricature of an Abbé whose intended homosexual assault on the young man is thwarted by a timely unveiling of her true sex. This chilling revelation causes the Abbé to retire in some confusion: "I don't use to take the freedom of being so familiar with the ladies." The whole passage was omitted in the representation, rather than "run the venture of offending the ladies."

Obviously, the first task of the editor is to decide on the nature of the text he has before him. Elizabethan and Jacobean plays normally have, in modern editions, some statements about the copy for the text, which early text the author reproduces, and what the nature of its authority is. Unhappily, Restoration and eighteenth century play editions lag behind their ancestors in this respect. With very few exceptions, English dramas of this period are presented to students without any attempt to discuss the basis for their texts. Eighteenth century reprints of pre-1642 plays are generally careful and scrupulous in handling the text, and there is no reason to suppose that they were less diligent with pieces from their own age. But modern editors pay almost no attention to interesting-sounding claims such as those common to reprinted collections of the period: "As performed at the Theatres-Royal, Drury Lane and Covent Garden. Regulated from the Prompt-Books, by permission of the managers. The lines distinguished by inverted commas are omitted in the representation, and those printed in italics are the additions of the theatres."

Variations in the text of The Beaux Stratagem provide a good example of the fortunes of a play text. The collected editions, from 1728, print the scene with Count Bellair in Act III in italics, with the note that the role of the Count was cut out after the first night, and that his part in Act V was given thereafter to Foigard. The 1707 and 1714 editions (usually reprinted in modern anthologies) make no mention of this change, while the reprints at the end of the century (for example, Bell's in 1791) silently incorporate the alterations. The passage in Act III was simply omitted, but the changes in Act V involved transmuting the comedy of Count Bellair's egregious style to the typical fatuities of Foigard, an Irish-Spanish-French-Dutch priest. Some literary skills are involved in this change. Here we have two differing texts, and the editor must decide which best represents the intention he wishes to preserve. The cutting out of the role of Count Bellair may well be an accidental result of a theatrical problem, but the 1728 text is not simply set up from a corrected copy of one of the earlier printings. It appears to come from an independent manuscript source, and from the clarification of various stage directions throughout, and the improvement (one hesitates to say correction) of various passages, seems to be derived from a theatre copy. In its turn, 1728 seems to be the source for the collected editions to the end of the century. Few plays of the period are more frequently anthologised than *The Beaux Stratagem*, and it is distressing to find that its interesting textual history is generally ignored. Collation, through the various early editions, of many Restoration and eighteenth century plays shows frequent similar variation.

The editor of a play of this period should surely take his task as seriously as the editor of an Elizabethan play. He must not take on trust that any edition subsequent to the earliest is set up mindlessly from the earlier edition and has therefore no possible authority. Nor must he assume that the first edition (even when it can be precisely identified) is the most authoritative, and that the particular copy he happens to hold in his hand tells him all he needs to know about it.

John Gay's *Three Hours after Marriage* was first printed, with some press variants, in 1717. This printing is the source for Cooper's edition in the collected works of 1757, and this in turn supplies the test for Whitestone's careless Dublin edition of 1757, re-issued in 1758 and 1761. Bell's edition of 1773, however, is set from a copy of 1717, with a thorough series of alterations, sorting out grammatical disagreements and inconsistencies, and attempting to normalise the fake Polish accent of one of the characters. Somebody has worked carefully through a 1717 text, making regular corrections. A study of Bell's whole series of *Miscellaneous Works* might suggest who, but the various collaborators in the play, all fussy about their texts, lived long after 1717, and may have had some hand in the changes. The 1797 edition of Gay's works uses left-over sheets from 1773. Unlikely though it may seem, then, one copy of the 1797 edition, in a corrected state, might well provide valid readings for an eighty-year-old play, while the intervening editions are no more than careless reprints.

Of course, it is impossible for an editor to work in a void, and there is no long established tradition of bibliographical analysis in this period. Students of pre-Restoration drama have Sir Walter Greg's splendid bibliography, the Malone Society publications, the numerous studies of printers, type-ornaments, woodcuts and so on, together with a variety of noble editions – particularly Jonson, Dekker, and Beaumont and Fletcher (in progress), to say nothing of Shakespeare. But after 1660, until Fredson Bowers' bibliography appears, we have no central reference work, and the background to textual problems is random and sketchy. The fine new editions of Dryden (in progress) and of Steele's plays, and Professor Bowers' 1966 lectures at the W. A. Clark library on Restoration bibliography may persuade us to be patient, and the rewards of patience are illustrated by the frequency of new and interesting discoveries. The story of Dryden's *Sir Martin Mar-All* is a case in point. Bertram Dobell began unravelling the nature of the text for this play in 1922, and since then Hugh Macdonald, R. H. Griffith and James Osborn have worked on it, the issue being brought up to date in the edition from the University of California, incorporating the recent labours of James McManaway and Vinton Dearing. A cancelling during the course of printing this play must drastically have abbreviated the early scenes: a chance survival of part of the cancelled materials shows the existence of a hitherto unsuspected passage, which seems to have been set up directly from foul papers. We are told that Dryden worked on this play with the Duke of Newcastle. Does the cancelled section include some of the Duke's work? Should the editor of a modern text try to incorporate the missing material? In spite of much study of this play, the answers to these questions are by no means clear.

We still need to know a great deal more about the whole process of printing and publishing during the period. Only when our knowledge of the bibliographical world of eighteenth century drama is as full as our knowledge of theatrical history, will editors be able to present students with valid texts, or will the editor be able to share Blakemore Evans's modest hope that he can "at least sometimes explain why there seems to be some dislocation in the text, even though he can rarely do anything to remedy the fault."

R. Morton

Voltaire, Newton
& the Reading Public

Voltaire seems to have a modest but assured place in the history of science. First of all, he is the source for the famous anecdote about Newton and the falling apple.[1] But what is more important, he made Newton's name, and the view of the universe proposed in the *Principia* and the *Opticks* known to the French reading public in two works, the *Lettres philosophiques* of 1734 and the *Eléments de la philosophie de Newton* of 1738. Also Voltaire helped incorporate the new science into the outlook of eighteenth century intellectual life, into the Enlightenment. In France he was among the first, if not the first, to present sympathetically to the general reader the new scientific synthesis, which had been carried out largely outside France and which had made the orthodox French view of the world obsolete. The scientific view proposed, modified and supported by Descartes, Malebranche, Cassini, Fontenelle and many others, no longer described the observable behaviour of nature; Newton's science did.

Voltaire's most extensive scientific work, the one on which his fame as a popularizer of science primarily rests, is the *Eléments de la philosophie de Newton*. In all he wrote some dozen works dealing with science, most of them short, including an *Essai sur la nature du feu et sur sa propagation* and *Doutes sur la mesure des forces motrices*. Here discussion will be limited to the *Eléments de Newton*, which represents Voltaire's attempt to come to terms with the new science, to bring it within his own understanding, incorporate it into his general intellectual outlook, and convert others to his view. Through some ten or twelve different editions, revised and corrected by Voltaire himself, we can follow his

---

1. *Oeuvres complètes*, L. Moland, ed., Paris, 1877-1885, XXII, 520. Voltaire relates the anecdote in the *Lettres philosophiques* and the *Eléments de la philosophie de Newton*.

growth and development as a thinker and artist.

The *Eléments de la philosophie de Newton* was intended for publication from the moment of its conception in 1736.[2] Voltaire's name as author appeared on the title page of the first edition,[3] not the usual case for a work by Voltaire. The original Amsterdam edition of 1738 was followed by a second, somewhat enlarged text printed in Paris the same year. A supplement called *La Métaphysique de Newton ou parallèle des sentiments de Newton et de Leibniz* appeared in 1740. And finally, a complete edition incorporating this supplement appeared in 1741. This edition eliminated about eighty pages of the first edition which were not by Voltaire, and replaced them with new material. This 1741 edition, with a few cancels and a new title page, was reissued in 1744 and 1745.[4] In 1748 Voltaire published the *Eléments de la philosophie de Newton* in the edition of his *Oeuvres* brought out by Conrad Walther in Dresden; from then on the *Eléments de Newton* appears in the many editions of *Oeuvres complètes* published by Walther, Lambert, the Cramers, on to the great posthumous Kehl edition supervised by Beaumarchais and Condorcet.[5] An examination of the text in the editions in which Voltaire himself had a hand reveals that the *Eléments de Newton* was a work he revised throughout his life, and there even remain corrections to some thirty pages, which Wagnière, Voltaire's secretary, sent to Catherine II and which were published in 1970.[6] They have yet to be incorporated into the text of any edition of the work. For forty years Voltaire was sporadically involved with the *Eléments de Newton*. This was the very period in which the Newtonian view was finally assimilated into French science.

2. Best. D 1113. All references to Voltaire's correspondence are taken from the definitive edition edited by Theodore Besterman, now appearing as part of the *Complete Works*, Geneva, 1968-, the number of the letter being given.

3. ELEMENS/ DE LA/ PHILOSOPHIE/ DE NEUTON,/ Mis à la portée de tout le monde./ Par M^r DE VOLTAIRE./ A AMSTERDAM,/ Chez Etienne Ledet & Compagnie. [also Jacques Desbordes]/ M. DCC. XXXVIII./ Referred to as 38A throughout his article.

4. Bibliographical descriptions of these editions will appear in Vol. XV of the *Complete Works*.

5. See William H. Trapnell's "Survey and analysis of Voltaire's collective editions, 1728-1789" in *Studies on Voltaire and the Eighteenth Century*, LXXVII, 1970, pp. 105-155 for bibliographical descriptions of these editions.

6. Published by Andrew Brown in *Studies on Voltaire and the Eighteenth Century*, LXXII, 1970, pp. 62-67.

The earlier editions of the *Eléments de la philosophie de Newton* were expected to convert the reader to Newtonism. They appeared at a favourable moment and reached a large public. The Jesuit *Journal de Trévoux*, already rather hostile to Voltaire, reported some five months after the publication of the first edition that before Voltaire Newton had remained a secret passed on only to scientists.

Newton était un secret, qu'on disait comme à l'oreille, encore y fallait-il de bons entendeurs. . . M. de Voltaire parut enfin, et aussitôt Newton est entendu ou en voye de l'être; tout Paris retentit de Newton, tout Paris bégaye Newton, tout Paris étudie et apprend Newton.[7]

The first reference we have to the work that became the *Eléments de la philosophie de Newton* is in a letter Voltaire wrote to Berger in 1736:

Il est vrai que mes occupations me détournent un peu de la poésie. J'étudie la philosophie de Newton sous les yeux d'Emilie qui est à mon gré encore plus admirable que Newton. Je compte même faire imprimer bientôt un petit ouvrage qui mettra tout le monde en état d'entendre cette philosophie, dont le monde parle et qu'on connaît encore si peu. (Best. D 1113)

Voltaire's aim, as stated in this letter, is to study science so he can write about it so clearly that an ordinary reader will understand it as well. Several years earlier Voltaire had studied science for a few months with Maupertuis as his guide and had composed the four letters on Newton in the *Lettres philosophiques*. There Newton may have appeared to many readers just as one among a host of such curiosities as the Quakers, the Presbyterians, Shakespeare, the Whigs and Tories. At any rate Voltaire does not seem to have helped Newton's cause appreciably in Cartesian France. In 1735 ·and 1736 Voltaire's concern increased for his country, still faithful to erroneous science and

7. *Mémoires pour l'histoire des sciences et des beaux-arts* [commonly known as the *Journal de Trévoux*], août 1738, pp. 1673-74.

relatively unenlightened regarding the Newtonian truth.

Voltaire's contemporaries, as well as some later critics, were incredulous that a leading poet and historian, the author of the *Henriade*, of *Zaïre* and the *Histoire de Charles XII*, should take it upon himself to convert his countrymen to Newtonism, unless the eyes of his celebrated mistress, madame Du Châtelet, the Emilie of the letter to Berger just quoted, exerted sufficient magic to account for his daring step. Voltaire did drop his more usual pursuits and began to study science seriously. Love may work wonders, but I doubt it inspired him to compose the *Eléments de la philosophie de Newton*. Nor was he inspired by his already acquired knowledge of English science. Rather than growing from a solid mastery of Newtonism, the *Eléments* led Voltaire to study carefully for the first time[8] the *Philosophiae naturalis principia mathematica*, the *Opticks*, the *Transactions* of the Royal Society, the *Mémoires* of the Académie royale des sciences, and many other works. An immense intellectual effort was required of Voltaire, extending from the summer of 1736, through his exile in the winter of 1736-1737, when he consulted both 'S-Gravesande and Boerhaave in Leyden (Best. D 1262), and supervised in Amsterdam the printing and engraving of the first chapters of his book, and beyond this to his return to madame Du Châtelet's chateau at Cirey-sur-Blaise and to the submission of a manuscript of the *Eléments* to the academician Henri Pitot in June 1737, when Voltaire hoped to be granted the *privilège* necessary to have his book published legally in France (Best. D 1341).

It is my belief that Voltaire encountered a new vision of the universe, when Francesco Algarotti read aloud to him and to madame Du Châtelet at Cirey late in 1737 the manuscript of his *Newtonianismo per le dame, ovvero dialoghi sopra la luce*. Voltaire wanted this vision made available to the French, and within six months was engaged himself in writing the book which was to

8. At the end of 1735 (Best. D 963, December 1735) Voltaire seems not to have had a copy of the *Principia* at Cirey. In August 1736 (Best. D 1136) he wrote to Paris for a copy of the Coste translation of the *Opticks*. Although it cannot be proved when Voltaire acquired most of the works quoted in the *Eléments de Newton*, his correspondence reveals that in the autumn of 1736 he was reading and digesting some of the leading scientific works of the period.

convert them to what he considered the true science. At that point he discovered how unqualified he was for so bold an undertaking. In reality he had two tasks before him: to educate himself in Newtonism and then to make Newtonism understandable to everyone (*à tout le monde*).

In eighteenth century Holland a publisher claimed his rights to a book by announcing it in the public press, thus notifying other publishers that a text was his property. Two booksellers and publishers, Ledet and Company and Jacques Desbordes, who had undertaken an edition of Voltaire's works and to whom Voltaire had entrusted the publishing of the *Eléments de la philosophie de Newton*, announced both works in the *Gazette d'Amsterdam* for 15 January, 1737:

> Etienne Ledet et Ce et Jacques Desbordes, libraires à Amsterdam, avertissent qu'ils ont sous presse une magnifique nouvelle édition de toutes les Oeuvres de M. de Voltaire, revue et augmentée par lui-même. Lesdits libraires avertissent qu'ils ont aussi sous presse: *Eléments* de la Nouvelle philosophie de M. Newton, mise à la portée de tout le monde, par M. de Voltaire.[9]

Voltaire was in Holland when this announcement appeared and remained there for another six weeks, working closely with Ledet in whose firm the printing was done. After his return to France he stopped sending his manuscript to Holland, having decided to apply for the *privilège* needed for French publication. Voltaire did not want the censor to think he was also intending to publish the work abroad (Best. D 1341). Seven months passed before chancellor Daguesseau's refusal of the *privilège* became known (Best. D 1436), a full year after the announcement in the *Gazette d'Amsterdam*. Finally in March 1738, without Voltaire's permission, the *Eléments* appeared in Holland. The title was not quite as in the *Gazette* announcement. It read simply *Eléments de la philosophie de Neuton, mis à la portée de tout le monde*.

Although rarely satisfied with any edition of his many works, Voltaire was particularly justified in complaining about the first

---

9. Quoted by E. Asse in *Lettres de la M^{se} Du Châtelet*, Paris, 1882, p. 136.

edition of the *Eléments*. Four chapters had never been sent to Amsterdam (Best. D 1502). The publishers had remedied the lacuna by having a mathematician supply about eighty pages of text (Best. D 1505), which presented subjects Voltaire had not intended to discuss. He gave, according to Voltaire, a preposterous explanation of Saturn's ring, and failed to discuss tides, comets, and the precession of the equinoxes, all of which were the true glories of the Newtonian view. These just complaints, however, do not provoke Voltaire's anger as much as the little phrase in the title, *mis à la portée de tout le monde*, which the publishers had added, he claimed, without his knowledge. Newtonism for everyone was a preposterous absurdity (Best. D 1492). Both Voltaire and madame Du Châtelet protest rather too violently against the title to several correspondents. It may be because the quip that there was a typographical error in the title, which should have read *mis à la porte de tout le monde*, had reached Cirey.[10] Nevertheless the phrase does seem to reflect Voltaire's true intentions, as revealed in the letter to Berger already quoted. In a letter to D'Argens written in November 1736 Voltaire had reported he was bringing Newton's philosophy *à la portée du public* (Best. D 1204). In the *Défense du newtonianisme* of 1739 Voltaire expressed the same idea when he wrote: "L'auteur des *Eléments* tâcha de mettre ces vérités nouvelles à la portée des esprits les moins exercés dans ces matières."[11]

Of course Voltaire may be quite correct that his title had been simply *Eléments de la philosophie de Newton*, which is, in fact, the half-title that appears in the first edition just before the dedicatory *Epître* to madame la marquise Du Ch**. And he may be granted his point that only a charlatan or an imbecile could think that Newton's philosophy was within the understanding of everyone, to be read, he writes, between the opera and supper like a verse tale by La Fontaine (Best. D 1502). It was a work that required study. Nevertheless Voltaire felt that anyone who trained his mind to think, who had studied a certain amount could understand his book with a little effort.

10. G. Desnoiresterres, *Voltaire et la société au XVIIIᵉ siècle*, Paris, 1871-76, II, p. 152.

11. M. XXIII, p. 71.

Both Voltaire and madame Du Châtelet acknowledge Voltaire's debt to Algarotti, whose *Newtonianismo per le dame* was the stimulus that set Voltaire to writing his popularization of Newton in 1736 (Best. D 1591).[12] *A la portée de tout le monde* echoes *per le dame* in Algarotti's title. Voltaire, however, was not writing "for ladies" or for any limited audience, not for the young, for example, as other popularizers of science had done. An examination of Voltaire's text bears out that he is aiming at the widest possible reading public: "ceux qui ne connaissent de Neuton & de la Philosophie que le nom seul" (38A, p. 12). Even Newton's geometrical demonstrations will be understood, according to Voltaire, by "tout Lecteur attentif, car les hommes ont une Géométrie naturelle dans l'esprit, qui leur fait saisir les rapports, quand ils ne sont pas trop compliqués" (38A, p. 244). In discussing the refraction of light in his explanation of the rainbow, Voltaire tries to make it understandable to everyone (*tout le monde*). It is his constant concern to define, to illustrate, to simplify, to encourage the reader, to make the complicated understandable and easy (38A, p. 251). The seriousness of purpose is in keeping with the truth he is communicating and the conversion to this truth he hopes to bring about.

This seriousness leads Voltaire to stress the need to instruct at the expense of the traditional literary goal of pleasing. Voltaire condemns consistently the popularizers of science, who have had the greatest popular success in France, because they have been more intent on pleasing or amusing their readers than in helping them to understand, although most of them were also guilty of spreading the errors of Cartesian physics. Fontenelle's *Entretiens sur la pluralité des mondes* was condemned on two counts in the opening sentence of the *avant-propos* to the first edition of the *Eléments de la philosophie de Newton* (38A, p. 9): "Ce n'est point ici une marquise, ni une philosophie imaginaire." Voltaire had in mind Fontenelle's scientist with his marquise dialoguing in her rose garden about Cartesian astronomy. Algarotti's *Newtonianismo per le dame*, dedicated to Fontenelle, presented another marquise whose teacher explained Cartesian science to her, turning

12. For Voltaire's statement see M. XXII, p. 278.

her into a convinced Cartesian. He goes on to explain Male-branche's science, and she becomes Malebranchian. Finally he converts her to attraction at a distance in the final dialogues of his work.

Voltaire is very critical of all popularizations of science that seek popularity through brilliance of style and embellishments. Such ornaments simply did not make the truth any more understandable. "Toutes les mains ne savent pas couvrir de fleurs les épines des sciences." (38A, p. 10) Talk of love that diminished in proportion to the square of the distance between the lovers would not help Newton's cause, even if it amused Algarotti's female readers. Two other very popular works Voltaire attacked for similar reasons were *abbé* Pluche's *Spectacle de la nature* and *abbé* Régnault's *Entretiens physiques d'Ariste et d'Eudoxe, ou physique nouvelle en dialogues*, both of which presented characters whose scientific discussions were interspersed with moral comments on life, on religion, etc. It is worth quoting Voltaire's reaction to the latter as expressed in a letter to D'Argens (Best. D 1342):

> [Régnault] examine la question du vide, et il dit ingénieuse-ment, Voyons s'il y a *du vide ailleurs que dans la bouteille ou dans la bourse*. C'est là le style de nos beaux esprits savants, qui ne peuvent imiter que les défauts de Voiture et de Fontenelle. . . .

Voltaire echoes these sentiments many times; for example, in a passage in *Micromégas*, where the traveller from the world of Sirius converses with the secretary of the Académie des sciences on Saturn, Fontenelle with only the slightest of disguises.

> Il faut avouer, dit Micromégas, que la Nature est bien variée. Oui, dit le Saturnien, la Nature est comme un Parterre dont les fleurs. . . . Ah! dit l'autre, laissez-là votre parterre. Elle est, reprit le Sécrétiare, comme une assemblée de Blondes et de Brunes dont les parures. . . . Et qu'ai-je affaire de vos Brunes? dit l'autre. Elle est comme une Galerie de Peintures dont les traits. . . . Et non, dit le Voyageur, encore une fois la Nature est comme la Nature, pourquoi lui chercher des comparai-

sons? Pour vous plaire, répondit le Sécrétaire. Je ne veux pas qu'on me plaise, dit le Voyageur, je veux qu'on m'instruise. Commencez d'abord par me dire combien les hommes de votre Globe ont de sens.[13]

"Je dois me borner à tâcher de bien concevoir quelques Vérités & à les faire voir avec ordre & clarté," said Voltaire in outlining his purposes in the foreword to the first edition of the *Eléments* (38A, p. 10). Since he was not writing a poem or a play, not a work of the imagination, there was no place for imagining. Voltaire warned a correspondent to beware of allowing himself to be led astray by his imagination, which had its place in poetry, but had to be banished from physics (Best. D 2463).

Voltaire seems then to be advocating and adopting a kind of textbook style. There were, of course, textbooks available in 1736, that explained Newton's view. However, they were either too difficult for the ordinary reader or else not in French. Voltaire urges the reader of the first edition of the *Eléments de Newton* (38A, p. 13) to learn more about Newtonism by reading the works of 'S-Gravesande, Keill, Van Musschenbroek, and Pemberton and thus approach Newton by degrees. The works of these authors were largely in Latin and English. Some were translated into French during the two decades following the publication of the *Eléments.* Newton's *Principia* appeared in French only in 1756, when madame Du Châtelet's translation was published. Presumably the important French scientists of Voltaire's time could read Latin; many had no doubt read the *Principia* in the original but remained Cartesians. Voltaire was not appealing to them. The only important work by any of these Newtonian authors which had appeared in French before Voltaire composed his *Eléments de Newton* was Newton's *Opticks* in the Coste translation (Paris, 1722), a rather forbidding quarto volume, not likely to be read by the readers to whom Voltaire appealed. Voltaire had in all probability consulted the major works by all these authors by the time he wrote the introduction just quoted. He is urging his readers to make a scientific pilgrimage to the

13. Voltaire's *Micromégas*, critical edition by I. O. Wade, Princeton, 1950, p. 123.

source of truth, with Voltaire a Virgil to take the reader on the first stage of his journey.

It is difficult not to use religious imagery in speaking of Voltaire and science, because he sees Newton's law of universal attraction as a divine law dependent directly on God, a basic and eternal truth, which brought Newton as close to the divine as man is likely to come. In the *Eléments* Voltaire quoted (38A, p. 263) the final line of Edmund Halley's prefatory ode to the *Principia: Nec propius fas est mortali attingere Divos.*

Voltaire saw himself as a disciple of the great apostle, who had descended into the abyss, where he read the truths of nature. But he left them there, Voltaire tells us, so it is up to others to follow Newton into the abyss and bring the hidden truths into the light. That is Voltaire's rôle: to study these great Newtonian truths, understand them, then to bring them into the light for others (38A, p. 13).

Enlightenment is one of the keys to the *Eléments de la philosophie de Newton.* In the first edition there is an allegorical frontispiece in which we see light from heaven piercing dark clouds and falling on a mirror held by a goddess. Newton, compass in hand, sits on a cloud in such a position that he can see directly into the mirror. Light is also reflected from the mirror down to an earthbound Voltaire, seated at a table, crowned with laurel leaves and writing. He is surrounded with books and scientific instruments. This is Voltaire, the poet, recording the heavenly truth, revealed to Newton and reflected to him. He passes it on to the public in the volume he is writing.

Two of Voltaire's intentions in writing and publishing the *Eléments de la philosophie de Newton* have become clear: he wrote for all who would read him, the widest possible public, and he regarded the popularization of Newtonism as a serious task. Voltaire had a good idea of the different sorts of readers that were to be found in the reading public. An examination of the text of the *Eléments* reveals these readers. Although Voltaire condemned Fontenelle's *Entretiens* and excluded imaginary marquises, the *Eléments* is not without conversations and characters. In fact Voltaire characterizes his reader by maintaining the dialogue. By writing conversations Voltaire presents two points of view, the view of the enlightened Newtonian author and the view of the readers, who, depending on the situation, share the ignorance or the scientific "prejudices" against Newton then found in France. It is my purpose now to examine these different readers as they emerge from the text of the *Eléments de la philosophie de Newton*.

One reader for whom Voltaire wrote was the beginner, the member of the reading public, who knew little or nothing about science, those who knew nothing of Newton and natural philosophy but the name, as Voltaire wrote in his *avant-propos* (38A, p. 12). He does not want this reader to have to go look up information in other books. When Voltaire discusses the anatomy of the eye, when he discusses mirrors and lenses, which, he says, have been explained correctly in so many books by various authors, he does so because he does not expect the beginner to have to look elsewhere for what he desires to know (38A, p. 48 and p. 59). Voltaire wants his volume to lead the reader all the way to the new and the true (38A, p. 74): "c'est la seule excuse d'un Livre." The question of how we see, the action of mirrors and lenses involve the reliability of the senses, the only source of truth for the disciple of Locke and Newton. If the point is important for the beginner, it is even more important for the disciples of Descartes and Malebranche, who argued that the senses deceive us.

The most important reader, the reader Voltaire had most often in mind and to whom he addresses his arguments, the one with whom he dialogues, is the Cartesian. On page after page Voltaire tries to discredit the Cartesian universe. In the early chapters devoted to light he attacks the view that light was an element everywhere present in the universe. He even rather begrudges Descartes his important contributions to optics, so interested is he in presenting him as a source of error. Descartes invented ingenuous novels instead of performing experiments. He imagined, when he should have been weighing, measuring, calculating and testing.

Descartes a trouvé, à son ordinaire, des raisons ingénieuses & plausibles de cette propriété de la lumière; mais là, comme en tout le reste, mettant son esprit à la place des choses, il a donné des conjectures pour des vérités. (38A, p. 94)

Voltaire expects to instill the greatest scepticism in the Cartesian reader towards the science he may have studied in the schools of his youth or have learned in reading Fontenelle, Pluche, Régnault, Castel, Rohault, or from the public courses that had known immense popularity, especially those given by Polinière earlier in the century and by *abbé* Nollet, who was attracting crowds of men and women of all classes to his Paris laboratory at the very time Voltaire was composing the *Eléments de la philosophie de Newton*.[14]

Voltaire was a master at propaganda. Whenever he espoused a cause, be it science, penal reform, history, toleration, he knew how to put it in the right perspective for the reader into whose hands he hoped his writings would come. He gaged his reader accurately. In the case of the *Eléments de la philosophie de Newton* he imagines his reader to be a rational man, living in a rational world, with great loyalty to the Descartes who had dethroned Aristotle, who had rejected occult qualities, and who had constructed a logical system that seemed to account admirably for the main phenomena of the universe.

Voltaire wants his rational Cartesian to discover that what appears logical is false. Common sense or reason is no test of truth. Voltaire hopes to evoke surprise and wonder in his reader in the face of truth that goes against logic and common sense. Newton's philosophy, he points out again and again, consists of startling paradoxes proved beyond all doubt. Light is not reflected by the solid surfaces of objects. "Examinons ce Problême de la Nature, notre étonnement redoublera. On ne peut s'instruire ici qu'avec surprise" (38A, p. 35). Opaque and transparent bodies defy the most basic common sense:

> Ce sera encore un nouveau sujet de surprise pour ceux qui n'ont pas étudié cette Philosophie, d'entendre dire que le

14. Nollet was not necessarily anti-Newton. In his six volume *Leçons de physique* (Troisième édition, Paris, 1749) he pretends to objectivity, refusing to take sides in the Descartes-Newton controversy.

secret de rendre un corps opaque, est souvent d'élargir ses pores, & que le moyen de le rendre transparent est de les étrecir. L'ordre de la Nature paraitra tout changé: ce qui sembloit devoir faire l'opacité, est précisement ce qui opérera la transparence; & ce qui paraissoit rendre les corps transparens sera ce qui les rendra opaques. Cependant rien n'est si vrai, & l'expérience la plus grossiére le démontre. (38A, p. 41)

More marvels are to follow, even though we ignore their causes (38A, p. 42). Gravitation, the very name of which seems such a strange paradox, is proved to be a necessary law in the construction of the world: "tant ce qui est peu vraisemblable est vrai quelquefois" (38A, p. 269).

For Voltaire, Descartes had at best given ingenuous and plausible reasons, conjectures rather than truths (38A, p. 94). He could not resist the temptation to construct systems. In the few cases where Descartes based his conclusions on experience, they were sound; but in general it takes only a few experiments and some mathematics to ruin Descartes' ideas.

In the *Eléments de la philosophie de Newton* Voltaire puts the Cartesian at a disadvantage by writing passages of dialogue, where the adversary speaks in the third person and Voltaire answers in the first person, finally bringing the reader into a plural *nous* at the end of the argument. Or he has the Cartesian object to the author, addressing him in the second person.[15] The reader is often referred to Newton or to the evidence of experiments in order to arrive at the correct conclusion. The shift from *je* to *nous*, to *vous*, to *on*, to *ils* injects life into the work, which is a continual confrontation of the ideas Voltaire hopes to plant in the reader's mind and the error he assumes his reader accepts. Ask Descartes, he tells his reader; he will tell you so and so; now ask Malebranche; he will give you another hypothesis. Finally the reader is invited to consult Newton, and he learns the truth. Voltaire tries to develop in his reader a complete scepticism toward Descartes in order to bring him to belief in Newton's ability to perceive the truth. The same pattern is followed in almost every chapter of the *Eléments*

15. Chapter VII of 38A (pp. 90-109) offers good examples of these procedures.

de la philosophie de Newton.

Voltaire seems to have believed rather naively that, if he showed Descartes to have reached false conclusions, to have described with such convincing logic the universe in a way no longer corresponding to observable fact, then the whole Cartesian system would crumble, and the reader would have to accept Newtonism, which was proved by observation.

Descartes was not the only source of error. Voltaire put Newton's discoveries in a historical perspective, as he stated formally in a new passage added to the 1741 edition of the *Eléments de Newton*: "J'examinerai jusqu'où on a été avant lui, d'où il est parti, où il s'est arrêté, & quelquefois ce qu'on a encore trouvé après lui-même."[16] The story of scientific progress becomes also a long story of error, of Aristotle and the ancients, of a few monks in the middle ages, above all of Descartes and his disciples, of the failure of philosophic systems, the failure of common sense and reason. Only with Bacon and Galileo and Kepler did mankind begin to understand even dimly how to observe nature, how to unravel her truths. The *Eléments de la philosophie de Newton* is an anti-rationalist work, in that it attacks all philosophical systems. As long as Descartes and his followers believed empty space a rational impossibility, attraction at a distance a revival of occult qualities, as long as they insisted motion could be explained only by impulsion and that our senses deceived us, Voltaire knew he would not turn his Cartesian French readers into Newtonians. Voltaire's reader might well have expected to be convinced by reason, so Voltaire attempts to take him by surprise, to shake his confidence in rational truth.

In the first edition the *Eléments de Newton* began with fourteen chapters on light. For Descartes light was a fluid everywhere present in the universe, although concentrated in the sun and fixed stars. It was his first element. What we call light and colours is the result of pressure in our eyes caused by luminous bodies, which activate the element of light, communicating the pressure through the medium in all directions to all distances in

16. *Elémens de la philosophie de Neuton, contenant la métaphysique, la théorie de la lumiere, & celle du monde*, Londres [Paris], 1741, p. 74.

straight lines in an instant. Roemer had demonstrated the progression of light and had measured its speed. Was that not proof that Descartes was wrong about light and might be wrong about everything? Voltaire quotes Descartes himself as saying (38A, p. 18), "J'avoue que je ne sai rien en Philosophie si la lumiere du Soleil n'est pas transmise à nos yeux en un instant." In *Le Monde ou traité de la lumière* Descartes specified that no measurable amount of time is needed to transmit the light of the sun.[17] With a full page plate to show the eclipses of the moons of Jupiter, as Roemer observed them, Voltaire explains that light takes seven to eight minutes to travel from the sun to the earth. Then he concludes the section (38A, p. 22), "Il est donc démontré que Descartes s'est trompé & sur la nature de la lumiere & sur la maniere dont elle nous est transmise." Voltaire then tells his reader that the continued acceptance of Descartes's errors by authors that echo each other from book to book only shows how slowly truth can be established among men. If the reader has been convinced by Voltaire's arguments, he must feel superior in his new enlightenment.

Voltaire preaches scepticism toward all authority, whether based on reason, on revelation, on intuition, or in the case of Malebranche on meditation. The only authority is found in measurements, calculations, and experiments. At times Voltaire's scepticism extends to Newton himself, as when he raises the question of the ether (38A, p. 175):

"... il faut avouer que cette hypothèse rendroit raison de presque tous les mystères de la lumiere, & sur-tout de l'attraction & de la gravitation des corps; mais une hypothèse, quand même elle rendroit raison presque de tout, ne doit point être admise. Il ne suffit pas qu'un Systême soit possible pour mériter d'être cru, il faut qu'il soit prouvé...."

This is not always the case, however, since Voltaire finds it difficult to remain in doubt about everything science leaves unexplained. In the 1741 edition of the *Eléments* he is willing to turn most of the queries at the end of Newton's *Opticks* into

---

17. *Oeuvres*, C. Adam et P. Tannery, eds., Paris, 1897-1913, XI, p. 98.

statements of fact rather than propose them as unproved hypotheses, because he needs to know, and he has a clear prejudice in Newton's favour.

When Voltaire wrote the metaphysical section comparing Newton and Leibniz, he was not able to rely on measurements, calculations and experiments; he could not prove or disprove absolute time and space, as he could demonstrate the separation of sunlight into the colours of the spectrum. Voltaire sides with Newton against Leibniz for nine chapters and then says rather innocently to his reader (41, p. 73), "Voilà ce que pensoit Neuton sur la plûpart des questions qui tiennent à la Métaphysique; c'est à vous à juger entre lui & Leibnits."

Voltaire was not at all objective in his presentation of Leibniz, whose ideas he presents in order to attack them. What is at stake for Voltaire is his view of God, free-will, and the perfection of the universe. Voltaire felt that Leibniz's system, like Descartes', left no need for God, no room for attraction at a distance, none of the mystery and surprise already discussed in this article. Voltaire believed that the Leibnizian system denied free-will to both God and man.

There are prejudices of other sorts that Voltaire expected his readers to espouse and which are attacked in the *Eléments de Newton*, prejudices which would make them prefer Descartes to Newton. One was patriotic prejudice, which we could dismiss, if it were not so widespread. Newton was an Englishman and therefore much less likely to be right than a Frenchman. After all Descartes had freed mankind from the tyranny of Aristotle and from occult qualities. Descartes had won out over Gassendi in the dispute over empty space in the seventeenth century. Was it not a return to ignorance to reintroduce empty space into science? Such ideas might be expected from the barbaric English, but not from the French. Every patriotic Frenchman ought to hope Descartes was right and Newton wrong. Anyone who has read the periodicals for the first third of the eighteenth century has encountered these arguments. Even in the reviews of the *Principia*, which seem at first fair to Newton's ideas, the implication seems to be that Newton is all very well for the English; he is doubtless a great mathematician, but he has reintroduced occult qualities into science.[18]

More than once Voltaire complains that he has not been granted a *privilège* for the *Eléments de la philosophie de Newton* because he had dared attack Descartes. No Frenchman was permitted to do that.[19] He attacks patriotic prejudice several times in the *Eléments*. "Est-ce parce qu'on est né en France," he wrote (38A, p. 124), "qu'on rougit de recevoir la vérité d'un Anglais? Ce sentiment seroit bien indigne d'un Philosophe."

There is also religious prejudice on the part of Voltaire's readers to be combatted. Here Voltaire resorted to more subtle persuasion, no doubt because he hoped to receive his *privilège* from the censor. Nevertheless, even without the intended final chapter on God withheld from Ledet in Amsterdam, the first edition of the *Eléments* is a deistic work, in that it uses the order of the universe to argue for the existence of an intelligent creator and attraction at a distance across empty space to support a non-material cause for attraction, proved to exist in all matter, but unexplained by any impulsion. It depends directly on God (38A, p. 271). Voltaire attacks *abbé* Pluche, who argued against the progression of light, because it contradicted the order of creation in the book of Genesis, where God created light before he created the sun. This was quite possible in the Cartesian view, since light was everywhere present, even if not activated by the sun.

The chapter on the rainbow has its anti-scriptural overtones, without even mentioning the story of Noah. The rainbow is a necessary result of the refraction and reflection of light in drops of rain and therefore is not a miracle.

Voltaire is extremely discreet in speaking of the precession of the equinoxes (probably the subject of another of the chapters withheld from Ledet), described in the first edition (38A, p. 295) as a motion of the earth requiring almost 26,000 years. Voltaire knew perfectly well that many Christians, among them Bossuet,

---

18. For two examples see the *Journal des sçavans*, XXXVIII, October, 1707, pp. 137-49, and the *Journal de Trévoux*, LXVIII, February, 1718, p. 466. For a detailed account of French resistance to Newtonism see Pierre Brunet, *Introduction des théories de Newton en France au XVIIIe siècle*, Paris, 1931.

19. For example in Best. D 1423 and D 1436.

had believed less than 6,000 years had passed since the creation. How could one speak, then, of a movement that needed more than four times that time to complete? That is also the plausible reason for Voltaire to include in the original edition (38A, pp. 296-318) the digression on the period of 1,944,000 years recently discovered, to which Newton contributed nothing, but which, Voltaire says (p. 296), "sembleroit promettre au Genre Humain une durée que l'on n'oseroit concevoir." The anti-Christian aspect of Voltaire's Newtonism became clearer in the 1741 edition with the addition of the chapter on the precession of the equinoxes and above all with the publication, as part of the Eléments of the Métaphysique de Newton, in which he discussed openly God, the soul, free-will, atoms, monads, the conservation of energy, and the perfection of the universe.

This article has been concerned until now primarily with the first edition of the Eléments de la philosophie de Newton. That is only the beginning of the story. The changes made in the editions of 1741, 1748, 1751, 1752, and 1756 show that Voltaire transformed the work, so that its original purpose to bring Newton within the understanding of the common reader became less important. The additions and revisions make the Eléments as much a metaphysical as a scientific work. They show that Voltaire had new sorts of readers in mind. The additions of 1740 and 1741 are directed to madame Du Châtelet and against Leibniz, because she had turned to the philosophical views of the German philosopher and was using the principle of sufficient reason to attack attraction at a distance and empty space. A new dialogue is set up, as the subtitle to the separate printing of Part I in 1740 indicates: Parallèle des sentiments de Newton et de Leibniz. Only part of the dialogue, however, goes on within the Eléments, the rest taking place in madame Du Châtelet's Institutions de physique[20] and in the shorter works by both Voltaire and madame Du Châtelet on kinetic energy, etc.

In 1748 Voltaire published a new introduction to the Eléments de la philosophie de Newton in which he said farewell to science.[21] By then madame Du Châtelet was working on her

20. Paris, 1740. See also her Réponse à la lettre de Mr. Mairan, Bruxelles, 1741.
21. M. XXII, pp. 400-401.

translation of the *Principia*, and Voltaire had no reason to continue his attack on Leibniz, who had attracted few disciples in France. He presented no great threat for the Newtonians. Professor Barber has shown that 1736-1745, a period of eight years, marked the greatest interest in Leibnizianism in France.[22] Voltaire's additions attacking Leibniz fit neatly into this period. The additions made after 1745, as well as the many deletions, give the *Eléments* quite a different character.

The vision of a unified universe operated by attraction, in which man had his place, where the seven colours of the spectrum correspond to the seven notes of the tempered musical scale, where a whole series of laws operating according to the squares of the distance, or the time, or the velocity suggested a wise creator, this vision was qualified, then finally rejected. In 1748 Voltaire omitted the chapter on colours and music and qualified his discussion of attraction as the probable cause of the cohesion of matter, of magnetism, elasticity, and electricity. In 1756 he omitted the last three chapters of the *Eléments*, including all discussion of those parts of the solar system that lie beyond the earth. During these years he made many changes in the metaphysical section of the *Eléments*, adding two new chapters in 1752.[23]

These changes bring to mind the conversations between Micromégas and the Saturnian in Voltaire's *conte*. Although they try to discuss physics, they inevitably end up in metaphysical discussion. The properties of matter lead then to the question of the soul; gravitation sets them to discussing thought; the laws of nature raise the question of free-will. That suggests the pattern of Voltaire's own thought. There are occasions when he would like science to free itself of metaphysical speculation, but more often he turns back to metaphysics for answers science cannot give. Metaphysics in turn only increases his growing scepticism. As time went on, science, rather than giving Voltaire unshakable truths, led him back to the unanswered philosophic questions that obsess

22. W. H. Barber, *Leibniz in France, from Arnauld to Voltaire*, Oxford, 1955, p. 141.

23. Bibliographical descriptions of all these editions along with all textual variants will be published in *The Complete Works of Voltaire*, XV.

him.

There are copies of the 1741 edition of the *Eléments de la philosophie de Newton* issued with the date 1744, others with 1745. It would seem that Voltaire had asked his publisher to remove passages and insert cancels in their place, a new title page being added as well. One such cancel replaces two pages of text at the end of the chapter on God (Part I, Chapter I) and is found in some copies with the 1745 date. The chapter, as it appeared in 1740 and 1741, eloquently supports what Voltaire believes to be Newton's God, a God whose existence depends largely on the order of the universe. *Coeli enarrant gloriam Dei*: no better argument for the existence of God could be found (41, p. 10). In the cancel Voltaire, now on the defensive, tries to answer rationalists who seek clear proofs for God's existence. He argues that God cannot depend on syllogisms and *jeux d'esprit* and then reaffirms the arguments from the order of nature. In later editions Voltaire adds several long passages to this same chapter clearly directed against atheists for whom the presence of evil is an overwhelming argument against the existence of a beneficent God, and in fact of any God. Voltaire becomes harder and harder pressed to find satisfactory reasons to support a belief in God. In revising this chapter for the 1748 Dresden edition he resorts to arguments taken from his former enemy Leibniz and even uses Pascal's wager[24] to strengthen his argument. Clearly the atheist reader has replaced the Leibnizian one in importance, just as the Leibnizian replaced the Cartesian of the earlier editions of the *Eléments*.

In 1749 madame Du Châtelet died, and in 1750 Voltaire, having installed himself at the court of Frederick II, prepared a second edition of his complete works for Conrad Walther in Dresden. More additions to the chapter on God, plus two new chapters on free-will prove Voltaire to be even more involved with the arguments of the materialists and atheists. The first of the two new chapters, "Doutes sur la liberté,"[25] takes the form of a

24. M. XXII, pp. 403-407. Beuchot and Moland after him reprint the 1748 Dresden text of the *Eléments de la philosophie de Newton*. For the chapter on God they give no variants from earlier or later editions. It is interesting that Voltaire uses the same Leibnizian arguments to justify evil in *Memnon* (*Zadig*), published in 1747 (1748).

25. *Oeuvres de Mr de Voltaire, Nouvelle édition, revue, corrigée et considérable-*

dialogue with a sceptic who brings up the very arguments Voltaire had used in the *Discours en vers sur l'homme* to support his belief in a limited free-will. The argument arrives at an impasse. Voltaire admitted that in the past he was destined to believe in free-will; now he is destined to be sceptical of reaching any conclusion for or against free-will. In a sense two Voltaires face each other. Voltaire had been writing as much for Voltaire himself as to answer those materialists like La Mettrie, whom he encountered at Frederick's court. Whatever opinion one adopts, Voltaire admits at the end of this chapter, "le monde ira toujours comme il va," an idea to which Voltaire had given literary expression in the conte, *Le Monde comme il va*, first published in the 1748 Dresden edition to which we have referred.

It has been pointed out that science leads Voltaire to metaphysics, as it did Micromégas and his fellow traveller from Saturn. It also leads beyond metaphysics to literature. *Micromégas* is proof of that. It is probable that the earliest text of that *conte* is that published before the *Eléments de la philosophie de Newton* in volume V of that same second Dresden edition of *Oeuvres*.[26] Professor Wade has studied the steps that led Voltaire from science to this *conte*.[27] In the case of free-will the second of the two new chapters on that subject, published as part of the *Eléments* in 1752, is "Dialogue entre un bracmane et un jésuite sur la nécessité et l'enchaînement des choses."[28] The Brachmane in this dialogue is a determinist and denies man all free-will; the Jesuit gives man the maximum of free-will. After their conversation each goes his own way, the Brachmane destined to join his wife, the Jesuit free to give a lesson to a student, each firmly convinced of his own view.

No critic seems to have associated the *Dialogue* with the *Eléments de la philosophie de Newton*. It has been considered a separate work, first published in 1756. Yet for one edition it was part of the *Eléments*, and it has its place there in the development of Voltaire's thinking on free-will. Voltaire argued for a limited

---

ment augmentée par l'auteur, 8 vols, Dresde, 1752. I Partie, Chapitre V, Doutes sur la liberté, V, pp. 90-92.

26. *Ibid*, pp. 23-47.
27. *Voltaire's Micromégas*, pp. 3-88.
28. *Oeuvres*, V, 93-96.

sort of free-will in 1740 and 1741 in the face of strong objections against it from science. The arguments against free-will became more convincing, and Voltaire wrote a chapter, "Doutes sur la liberté," which almost repudiates the possibility of free-will. That is where science and metaphysics have taken him. Then he wrote a literary dialogue, which puts in more human terms the dilemma in which Voltaire found himself, believing in a limited free-will in spite of the many arguments against it.

Voltaire has come a long way from his original purpose in composing the *Eléments de la philosophie de Newton*. It became an attack on Leibniz, on atheism, a work of increasing scepticism even toward science. It became a very incomplete statement on Newtonism, with nothing to say in 1756, and later editions, on the moon, on comets, on Venus, Jupiter and Saturn, no attempt to use attraction to explain magnetism, electricity, chemical change, as was the case from 1741 to 1752. The chapter on colours and sounds, the harmonies of music and colour, that united man through his sense experiences to an external harmony operated by attraction and the law of inverse squares, was dropped in 1748. The vision began to crumble before Voltaire could piece it together. The Cartesian, Christian, worldly, patriotic French reader Voltaire had sought to convince of the Newtonian truth had long since disappeared.

One consistent element in the transformations of the *Eléments de la philosophie de Newton* is the dialogue. It is a polemic work, attacking in order to convince, protecting and defending truth. The ornaments are gone, but the influence of Fontenelle and Algarotti is quite evident. The great irony is that Voltaire himself introduced characters into the work with his Brachmane and Jesuit, not because he expected to amuse his readers, but because he was having a dialogue with himself, which had no conclusion.

"Mon principal but dans la recherche que je vais faire, est de me donner à moi-même, & peut-être à quelques Lecteurs, des idées nettes de ces loix primitives de la nature, que Neuton a trouvées," Voltaire explained in the 1741 edition of the *Eléments* (p. 74). Even at that date Voltaire placed his own goals before that of popularizing Newton. By writing a book about Newton he learned his Newtonism, as has already been suggested. It was by revising and rewriting, adding and deleting that he continued his education, that he finally came to a more just perspective regarding the new science. He discovered that science could not do what he hoped it had already done. By 1750 the *Eléments* remains a sounding board for Voltaire's ideas on metaphysics, but no longer has a role to play in converting Cartesians. The work still reflects Voltaire's intellectual activity in 1752 and also in 1756 in the first edition of his *Oeuvres* published by the Cramers in Geneva. That marks the end of the story. By then the *Eléments* had fulfilled its role in Voltaire's own personal intellectual development, not that he stopped carrying on intellectual dialogues with himself and with friends, enemies, and the reading public. He did it elsewhere, in *Candide* and the *Ingénu*, in the *Dictionnaire philosophique* and the *Questions sur l'Encyclopédie*, in the *Mélanges*, and, of course in his correspondence.

Part of Voltaire's most meaningful intellectual life seems to centre around Newtonism and especially around the *Eléments de la philosophie de Newton*. For a full twenty years, from the composition of the *Traité de métaphysique* in 1734, until his arrival in Geneva, Voltaire's intellectual preoccupations are remarkably well reflected in the different editions of the *Eléments*. The gardens of the mind he is most actively cultivating are those of physics, of metaphysics, and even of theology. That takes us to the events that lead to the composition of *Candide*, by which time Voltaire had discovered other gardens that needed tending.

R. L. Walters

Condillac's Influence
on French Scientific Thought

There is a widespread tendency among historians of science to look down upon the eighteenth century as a period of stagnation in scientific development, contrasting with the triumphant achievements of the great creative period which preceded it. Newton's towering personality is indeed such as to overshadow investigators of nature, who would otherwise have ranked as the foremost of their time and on a par with their great followers of the nineteenth century and of our own time. The main achievement of Newton, if we look at it in a wider historical perspective, is not what impressed so much the popularizers of his own time — his formulation of the law of universal gravitation, his experimental discoveries in optics, his vindication of a theological conception of the laws of nature. Above all, he initiated a new approach to nature, a new method of investigation of natural phenomena. This inductive method, starting from the direct observation of phenomena by painstaking, accurate experiments, and leading to a rational account of them, has since demonstrated its unfailing efficiency and power. It is the only method in human endeavour that leads to an unending accumulation of ever improved, ever expanding knowledge, which never suffers any set-back. This is not to say, of course, that it is the only way in which we establish relationships of lasting value with nature, but it is unique in this cumulative character, and the resulting certainty, of its acquisitions. For Newton, the source of such certainty was not in doubt: brought up in the Puritan ideology, with its deeply religious mode of expression, he naturally regarded the concept of a personal creator of the world as inherent in his natural philosophy, and saw in the divine origin of human reason the ultimate justification of the uncompromising rationalism that characterizes his whole approach.

From this point of view, one may say that the time of Newton, and above all Newton's own contribution, marks the birth of modern science, of science as we understand it, as the rational description of our experience of nature. No doubt Newton had a precursor in Galilei, who had a clear vision of the meaning of experiment as the source of our knowledge of natural phenomena, and of the power of human reason to discover the laws of these phenomena; but Galilei was still groping for the right way of experimenting, his mathematics had not the needed sophistication, and on both counts Newton was truly the innovator. As to Descartes' influence on Newton, deep as it was, it was more in the nature of an inspiration and a challenge than of a direct guidance. If any philosopher may be called a rationalist, it is certainly Descartes, but he lacked balance in his judgment: he tended to give rational thinking too large a part in the elaboration of a coherent view of the world, and to neglect the role of information derived from observation. As a result, his theoretical constructions about natural phenomena soon proved complete failures; the real point at issue, however, between Newton and the Cartesians was not, despite appearances, the contrast between their conceptions of the laws of nature, but above all the question of the method leading to the discovery and formulation of these laws.

With regard to the fundamental physical principle underlying the description of the world, there was no opposition between Newton and the followers of Descartes: all accepted the view that the material universe was a huge mechanism, a system of various kinds of particles moving in various ways and interacting only by direct contact. This mechanistic conception remained in fact unchallenged throughout the eighteenth and the nineteenth century, until it finally foundered against the problem of the nature of light, which was already puzzling Newton. About the necessarily hypothetical modalities of the mechanical world-picture there was much arbitrariness, and consequently much quarrelling: Newton dodged such fruitless speculations by his insistence on proceeding inductively to the stage which observation would lead to, and provisionally renouncing complete mechanical explanation rather than indulging in unverifiable hypotheses. It is on this methodical issue that Newton took his stand against the Cartesian advocacy of a purely rational construction of the mechanism underlying the phenomena. The paramount importance of this issue was keenly felt by Newton's contemporaries and those that upheld the Newtonian tradition in the eighteenth century. The latter were no mere epigones: their boundless admiration for Newton was perfectly genuine; it was prompted by a clear recognition of the superiority of his scientific method.

As to Newton's opponents, Cartesians in the broad sense of the word, special mention should be made of Leibnitz, whose mathematical conceptions, quite independently of the philosophy underlying them, proved even more successful than Newton's. The notorious clash between the two giants about the discovery of the calculus should not be judged on the basis of the superficial course that it took; if this conflict arose and took such proportions, it must have been more deeply motivated than by a mere quarrel of priority. Indeed, we again see that it did not really concern the facts of the case: the contestants and their supporters knew perfectly well that the two methods, the Newtonian method of fluxions and the Leibnitzian differential calculus, were essentially the same — otherwise, there would have been no question of possible plagiary. The real cause of the conflict is not difficult to establish, not by conjecture, but on the basis of actual documents, some of them only recently published: it was the opposition of two powerful temperaments, both of them imbued by the belief in rational thinking as the instrument of scientific inquiry, but disagreeing about the way in which this instrument should be handled in order to achieve a quantitative description of the phenomena. Newton was of the intuitive type: his whole conception of fluxion was derived from a visual picture of the motion of a particle on its trajectory, whereas Leibnitz was of the abstract logical type, laying the emphasis on the practical advantage of a neat formal representation of the various aspects of the phenomena by carefully chosen symbols, subject to precise mathematical and logical rules. The next generation, having assimilated these apparently conflicting approaches, was quite happy to use both of them and nobody would have dreamt of arguing which of the two was more fruitful or more powerful. But for the great pioneers, the issue was one aspect of the deep-lying questions of method, concerning which they held irreconcilably opposite views.

Thus was the scene set, at the beginning of the second quarter of the eighteenth century, for an exploration of nature stimulated by the impulse that Newton and Leibnitz had given to the development of adequate methods of investigation. The history of the following period may conveniently be divided into two stages. The second quarter of the century was a time of consolidation, so to speak, during which the natural philosophers learned to handle the new mathematical tools and refined them, while the experimental method opened up the new domains of electricity and "pneumatic" chemistry (the discovery of various kinds of gases, paving the way to a quantitative study of chemical reactions). Then, in the second half of the century, we see a new generation at work, fully trained in the use of the new methods, both as regards their technical aspects and their philosophical implications. There was no lack among them of powerful and original thinkers: the greatest perhaps was Euler, who came from the Leibnitzian school, but carried further, and systematized Newton's ideas: of comparable eminence were the French "geometers" who professed to be Newton's disciples – Clairaut and Alembert, followed by the latter's brilliant pupils Lagrange and Laplace – and the French chemists under Lavoisier's leadership. To get the measure of their achievements, one has only to compare Newton's *Principia* with the *Mécanique céleste* of Laplace, or the chemical ideas of Stahl with those of Lavoisier: the progress accomplished in those fifty or sixty years is quite comparable in importance and scope with the progress we have witnessed in the first half of our own century.

Against this background, Condillac is indeed a natural choice, for he is quite representative of the evolution of ideas about scientific method during the two stages that have been distinguished – the period of consolidation and the period of expansion and progress. Condillac is not a scientist in the modern sense of the term; he did not make any contribution to the scientific activity he was witnessing; but he did observe this activity with deep understanding, and managed in a masterly way to analyse and formulate the general methodical principles which guided his philosophical friends in their scientific endeavours.

The conceptions of Newton entered France rather late, because they had to overcome the formidable obstacle of the Cartesian tradition, whose influence was still so strong by the middle of the century that Voltaire himself, that knight errant of progressive ideas, had to champion the Newtonian philosophy in full armour. He was of course not alone in this fight, nor indeed the most influential. His role as a clever propagandist should not be underestimated, but cannot be compared with Clairaut's much weightier intervention: not only had Clairaut a hand in the French translation of the *Principia*, but he was the first to make a significant contribution to a problem discussed in the *Principia* – the problem of the shape of the earth – which went further than Newton's own treatment.

The Cartesians had one supporter of tremendous vitality, Fontenelle, who, as late as 1752, published a theory of the solar system based on an improved version of the Cartesian "tourbillons." Much more important, however, was the influence of Malebranche – I am not concerned here with Malebranche's theology, but with his scientific views, which are often underrated: he saw clearly the insufficiency of Descartes' physics and did his best to improve it, without abandoning its fundamental principles. Now, the Oratorian order, to which Malebranche belonged, introduced this better brand of Cartesianism into their schools, in which more place was given to the teaching of science than in most Jesuit colleges: this circumstance accounts for the prolonged hold of Cartesianism on French thought. Indeed, even such a staunch Newtonian as Alembert betrays in his philosophical attitude a greater influence of his Oratorian schooling than he would have liked to acknowledge: in the preface to his *Traité de Dynamique*, for instance, one perceives a distinct undercurrent of Cartesian rationalism.

The interest of the French "philosophes" in Newton was not purely scientific; of course, they were able to appreciate his scientific achievements, but (as clearly appears from Voltaire's *Lettres philosophiques*) they, above all, regarded his natural philosophy as a part of a wider intellectual and political movement that they had good reasons to contrast with the oppressive régime they were subjected to; hence their keenness in promoting Newtonian studies and Newton's natural philosophy. In the turbulent company of the "philosophes," Condillac, modest and retiring, stands out as a sharpsighted and acute thinker, grasping the essential points and expounding them with unequalled lucidity. His role in the philosophical debate was to discuss the epistemological issues raised by the Newtonian view of science. In England, this role had been fulfilled by Locke, whose *Treatise on Human Understanding* offered a systematic exposition of a theory of knowledge in harmony with Newton's conceptions. Condillac's first contribution, the *Exposition des origines des connaissances humaines*, had no other pretension than to introduce Locke to the French public – though it achieved much more. It was soon supplemented by a *Traité des systèmes*, which exposed the weaknesses of the metaphysical attitude common to Descartes and Leibnitz, and contrasted them with the firm guidance afforded by Newton's inductive method.

These two slender treatises, written with sharp precision and luminous simplicity, won him immediate recognition as the spokesman of the "philosophes" in matters of epistemology and psychology; but these qualities did not by far exhaust their significance. Locke had traced the origin of our knowledge of the laws of nature to sensations and abstract ideas, but he had left undecided the question of the nature of the latter; Condillac took this last step and showed that our abstract ideas could themselves be referred to sensations. This was a bold step indeed, which carried epistemology from what I called the stage of consolidation to that of innovation, implying as it did a definitive break with the idea of the divine origin of rational thinking, a possibility that Locke had still left open. Yet Condillac's thesis did not at first appeal to the materialists among the "philosophes": Diderot pointed out the danger implicit in it of bringing support to Berkeley's idealistic opposition to Newton. If, he argued, our ideas come from our sensations, they are somehow elaborated in our brain, and in this process become separated from the sensations and belong to our internal world; hence our rational thinking is a purely internal activity, without direct contact with the external world, as Berkeley asserted. It was this paradoxical conclusion that prompted Diderot to denounce idealism as the scandal of philosophy, because it was so difficult to prove its absurdity.

Condillac took up the challenge, and his answer to Diderot's query was the *Traité des sensations*, his masterpiece and a landmark in the history of epistemology. The argument he developed in this book is extremely remarkable, both by its logical subtlety and by the deep insight it reveals in an essential feature of the perceptive process. In a boldly dialectical way, he started by carrying Berkeley's thesis to the extreme, by means of his famous artifice – we would now say "Gedanken-experiment" – of the statue endowed with sensibility: beginning with the sensation of smell, and proceeding successively to the other senses, he showed that the statue could very well develop a kind of rational thinking, without being aware of any relation of this thinking to an external world. There is one exception, however: the sense of touch – we would speak of haptic sensations. The preceding argument holds only so long as the statue does not move, remains passive: this is its essential difference from a living being. As soon as we add the possibility of touching objects, which implies an active exploration of the environment, the spell of solipsism is broken: the thinking subject realizes that he is acting upon an external world. This tremendous intellectual achievement is all the more impressive when it is brought into relation with the modern development of genetic psychology: one of the fundamental features brought out by Piaget's studies of the mental development of children is precisely the inseparable union of the passive reception of a sensation and of the motor reaction it leads to, the building up of a sensory-motor scheme, which is the true unit with which our thinking, both concrete and abstract, operates.

The next work of Condillac was a direct continuation of the trend of argument by which he had established that there is nothing in our rational thinking that does not come from a purely material interaction with the external world. Buffon at the time had developed speculations about the evolution of the animal world, which seemed to suggest a separation of principle between animals and man, the animals being deprived of the power of building up abstract ideas. In his *Traité des animaux*, Condillac examines this question, and concludes, against Buffon, that there is no recognizable discontinuity between the behaviour of higher animals and that of man: it is in animals that the beginnings of consciousness and of our mental properties can be perceived. This was a contribution of great importance to the development of the materialistic view of the world, which Diderot and his friends were attempting, but from which Condillac himself kept aloof. In fact, Diderot's materialism remained rather ambiguous, since he was forced, as a result of Condillac's analysis, to extend the fundamental property of "sensibility" to all the constitutive elements of his material world.

In order to appreciate the scientific value of Condillac's psychology from the point of view of his own time, it is interesting to compare it with the views of one of the most powerful contemporary thinkers, Euler. As a mathematician and a theoretical physicist (as we would now call him), he dominates the eighteenth century in the same way as Newton dominated the second half of the seventeenth: the mathematical tools and the concepts of classical mechanics found in our textbooks and taught to students from generation to generation have the form that was given them by Euler. It is, therefore, important to know what opinions a man like Euler would have about the origin of the ideas he was so instrumental in shaping. We are fortunate in having from him a popular exposition of his view of the world, which he wrote in the form of letters, addressed to a German princess whose preceptor he was. Now, the psychology developed in these letters is very interesting, and certainly does not deserve the contempt which Alembert expresses about it. In fact, Euler goes even further than Condillac in trying to put psychology on a biological basis, by discussing the physiological processes underlying our thinking. Of course, such a discussion must remain very rudimentary and speculative, but at any rate he puts the question of the relation between our ideas and our nervous system. He fully accepts the thesis that our ideas have their origin in sensations which are located somewhere in the brain; he mentions the *corpus callosum* as the likely seat of sensations, the organ where they are collected and from which signals from motor reactions go out — thus he elaborates a physiology perhaps a bit primitive, but essentially correct (we might rather speak of the cerebellum, but this does not change the general picture). When he comes to the concept of *idea*, however, he is very embarrassed, because as a mathematician, he feels the need for a sharp definition; and since he has no basis for identifying any part of the nervous system with what we call *idea*, he introduces the abstract concept of "esprit" as an immaterial, individual element, whose role is to elaborate ideas and combine them according to the rules of thought. With mathematical rigour, he specified the properties which differentiate these "esprits" from matter – foremost among them being the impossibility of localizing them in space and time.

The dark point in this system was of course the problem of how the connection between "esprit" and sensations comes about. Euler plainly declares that the establishment of such a connection is a "miracle": this was the statement that aroused Alembert's wrath. What it amounts to, however, is just a confession of ignorance; unable to imagine any material way in which sensations could be related to ideas, Euler introduces "esprit" as a conceptual (not to say fictitious) representative of this necessary, but unknown link. What has Condillac to say about this problem, which he had also to face (even though he does not explicitly inquire about the processes going on in the brain)? He seems to dismiss it by the remark that talking about the "mind" is just confused thinking. This means, actually, that he felt as keenly as Euler the need for some clear conception of the relationship between sensations and ideas, and, like the latter, was at a loss as to what picture to imagine. Unlike Euler, he was reluctant to operate with such elusive concepts as "esprit" or "âme," which do not provide any picture at all. This difference of attitude illustrates once more the fundamental opposition between the Cartesian procedure which Euler followed when he introduced the purely ideal, but sharply defined, concept of "esprit," and the Newtonian method which Condillac favoured. At any rate, the comparison shows that the French philosopher was not unequal to the leading scientist of the time.

In the last quarter of the century, the intellectual movement inspired by the "philosophes" was on the wane, but a brilliant constellation of young scientists had taken over the tradition they had initiated, and was carrying on the exploration of nature with undiminished vigour. The impact of Condillac's theory of knowledge upon this new generation was profound, although it is not easy to document. They had little occasion to quote him (with one exception soon to be mentioned); but his influence is noticeable in their whole manner of thinking. In the field of psychology, in which he was a pioneer, Condillac had direct followers in the "idéologues" of the period of the Directoire and the Empire, but there was then hardly anything to add to his work. In fact, it is only in our own time that his views can be fruitfully taken up again in the light of increased knowledge of psychical phenomena derived from experimental investigation. Incomparably more significant, however, was the influence of Condillac's didactic writings – the course of instruction he wrote up for his pupil the duke of Parma. These volumes, in which he develops his epistemological considerations with the same wonderful simplicity, straightforwardness and clarity as in his original treatises, were the source from which the French scientists, all through the years of the Revolution, the Empire and the Restoration, received guidance and inspiration.

The most explicit evidence we have of an immediate application of Condillac's ideas to a scientific problem concerns Lavoisier's elaboration of a rational chemical nomenclature. This was a major advance in the development of chemistry, and was much more important than the analogy with Linne's system of classification of the three "reigns" of nature might suggest: for Linne's nomenclature was purely conventional, while Lavoisier's embodied his fundamental ideas – the precise definition of a chemical element and the theory of the acidifying principle, which mark the beginning of modern chemistry. It was quite natural for Lavoisier, faced with a chaotic mass of arbitrary denominations, to feel the need for a more orderly designation of the substances whose composition he was able to determine. Nevertheless, the emphasis he laid on the significance of this task, and the methodical way in which he accomplished it, are directly inspired by Condillac's teaching. Both in the preface to the *Méthode de Nomenclature chimique* and in the introduction to the *Traité de chimie*,

Lavoisier invokes the theory of the function of language, presented in Condillac's *Logique*, for a deeper justification of the characteristic features of the nomenclature he proposes. In the framework of Condillac's psychology, language occupies a prominent position. Emanating somehow from the sensations, the ideas and the relations between ideas have in turn to be represented by material signals: these constitute the language, which therefore provides us not only with a means of communication of our perceptions, but with an exquisitely flexible tool for the logical combination of ideas. Hence, it is a true analytical method, by means of which we proceed from the known to the unknown, just as mathematicians do. A language, describing a certain order of phenomena can even attain, ideally, the same precision as mathematics: it then becomes what we denote as the "science" of these phenomena − "a science is a well-contrived language." Mathematics itself is a language − "la langue des calculs," as Condillac calls it. When one realizes that his conception of language, with all its implications, was vividly present in Lavoisier's mind, one understands the full import of his concern with nomenclature, and his insistence on the active part it could play in the investigation of chemical processes.

There is in Lavoisier's considerations on the role of language a remark of striking modernity: the scientist, he says, is like a child. The child has also to learn the language, and how to use it. In this learning process, he makes mistakes, which he corrects by experience − let the scientist take a lesson from the child, and do the same. We know more, thanks to Piaget's studies, about the acquisition of language by the child, than Condillac and Lavoisier could imagine, and this more precise knowledge only goes to support Condillac's conception of the nature and function of language, and to strengthen the comparison of the scientist with the child. The learning of the language proceeds in two steps: in the first stage, the child has to learn the correspondence between the words and the sensory-motor schemes they symbolize; but the great discovery the child makes, in a second stage occurring at the average age of eleven, is that the word-symbols can be detached, so to speak, from the concrete representations of the sensory-motor schemes, and used by themselves in an infinity of logical combinations. This abstract mode of thinking pays for its tremendous increase in speed and scope with the danger of losing in the process the necessary contact with the sensory-motor experience — a danger to which children and scientists are indeed equally exposed. Lavoisier has a lapidary formula to summarize the profound insight into our thinking which he owed to Condillac and had made his own: "faits, idées, mots sont comme trois empreintes d'un même cachet." Facts, ideas, words — three imprints of the same seal: is this not the wisest legacy of the enlightenment?

L. Rosenfeld

La Fiction Autobiographique

Le but de cette communication est d'essayer de cerner, très rudimentairement encore, quelques problèmes qui se posent, pour le dix-huitiémiste notamment, dans l'étude de l'autobiographie et du roman à la première personne. Je dis *notamment*, car ils s'agit de difficultés qui ne tiennent pas essentiellement aux particularités historiques des oeuvres en question, mais aussi à la nature même de la littérature. Aussi serait-il vain d'en chercher la solution sans se munir d'outils théoriques, ce qui nous amènera inévitablement à déborder tout cadre historique précisément défini. Ces outils, en effet, ne peuvent être dégagés uniquement de l'étude empirique d'un *corpus* quelconque, mais doivent satisfaire aussi à des conditions d'intelligibilité générale; il en résulte que leur champ d'application n'est pas chronologiquement déterminé.

A mon sens, la façon dont les études littéraires sont structurées dans la majorité des universités ne favorise pas la juste perception de ces problèmes. Il y a de très bonnes raisons pour engager des professeurs à titre de médiéviste, seiziémiste, dix-septiémiste, etc., et pour faire figurer au programme de chaque étudiant un certain nombre de cours portant sur les diverses époques de la littérature. Là où cette pratique devient dangereuse, c'est lorsqu'on est tenté de croire que cette forme d'organisation dispense d'une réflexion plus poussée sur la méthodologie de notre recherche et de notre enseignement.

Il est permis en effet de se demander dans quel sens on peut dire qu'il existe une branche de la science qui s'appellerait, par exemple, "l'étude de la littérature du XVIIIe siècle," ou "l'étude du XVIIIe siècle." Prenons une comparaison: existe-t-il une science nommée "géologie du Canada"? Il est évident que les roches et les formations de terrain de ce pays sont objet d'étude, mais qu'il est impossible de s'y consacrer d'une façon un peu utile sans posséder à fond la théorie générale de la Terre, des minéraux, des formations géologiques, etc. De même, qui dit "littérature du XVIIIe siècle" dit "littérature," et se réfère donc, pour m'en tenir à une définition très grossière, à des productions de l'imagination dont le matériau est linguistique et qui servent à créer un rapport entre des hommes: essentiellement ceux qu'on a l'habitude de nommer "auteur" d'une part, "lecteurs, auditeurs, spectateurs" d'autre part. C'est dire que la littérature du XVIIIe siècle, si elle constitue un *corpus* d'oeuvres entretenant entre elles et avec le milieu qui les a vu naître des rapports particuliers, caractéristiques et uniques dans l'histoire, ne se soustrait pas non plus à ces conditions fondamentales d'existence du phénomène littéraire que je définissais tout à l'heure par trois mots clefs: imagination, langue, fonction sociale.

Il serait donc très hardi d'aborder cette littérature sans avoir réfléchi au phénomène littéraire en soi et sans avoir fait tout en son pouvoir pour se donner un outillage conceptuel suffisant, aussi explicite que possible. Cela vaut mieux, en tout cas, que de se fier uniquement à cet instrument peu sûr, pompeusement décoré du nom de *sens commun*, qui se révèle souvent à l'analyse ne pas être autre chose que la somme de ce qu'il y a de plus naïf, chez nos ancêtres et nous, en fait d'idées en l'air, de préjugés, de conclusions hâtives.

En plus d'être conforme à une certaine morale du critique, la réflexion sur les données fondamentales de la littérature peut sans doute ouvrir de nouveaux champs de travail à l'histoire littéraire proprement dite. C'est ce que je réussirai peut-être à faire entrevoir à propos de la fiction autobiographique au XVIIIe siècle.[1]

Je proposerai d'abord quelques observations sur deux textes.

Le premier livre des *Confessions* de Jean-Jacques Rousseau[2] raconte, après un préambule, les amours et le mariage des parents de l'auteur, puis le déroulement de sa vie jusqu'à sa fuite (mi-volontaire) de Genève, à l'âge de seize ans. Le récit respecte, avec quelques digressions, l'ordre chronologique, ne semble pas

---

1. Ce titre est volontairement ambigu. Il pourrait se gloser de plusieurs façons: "l'autobiographie considérée comme fiction," ou "la fiction considérée comme autobiographique," ou "la fiction sous forme d'autobiographie."

2. Jean-Jacques Rousseau, *Oeuvres complètes*, édition publiée sous la direction de Bernard Gagnebin et Marcel Raymond, Paris, 1959 suiv. Les *Confessions* sont au tome I. Reconnaissons notre dette envers cette édition magistrale, monument d'érudition et de pénétration critique.

contenir de graves inexactitudes et n'essaie pas de dissimuler le grand rôle du hasard dans l'enchaînement des faits. C'est un exemple tout à fait typique de récit autobiographique honnête. Mais n'est-ce que cela?

Si l'on examine le plan de ce livre,[3] on est immédiatement frappé par l'abondance des symétries. Au début, Jean-Jacques entre dans Genève en quittant, à demi mort, le sein de sa mère; à la fin, il est plus ou moins éjecté de la ville et s'enfuit; les réflexions qu'il fait à ce propos en écrivant les *Confessions* consistent en regrets sur la vie et la mort paisibles qu'il a manquées et qu'il aurait connues s'il était resté dans le "sein" de sa patrie (le mot revient deux fois, p. 43-44). — La première chose dont il nous parle après avoir décrit les conséquences de la mort de sa mère sont les lectures de romans galants et d'historiens antiques qu'il fit avec son père et qui remplirent son âme d'idéaux sentimentaux et héroïques; la dernière chose dont il est question avant la fuite sont les livres médiocres qu'il se procurait chez une loueuse et qui le lancèrent dans des rêveries sans fin, compensation à sa misère et à ses frustrations d'adolescent. — En poursuivant notre lecture en direction du centre, nous recontrons ensuite le personnage du frère de Jean-Jacques, apprenti polisson et libertin, mais fraternellement aimé, qui finit par prendre la clef des champs, et que nous retrouvons omniprésent, à la fin, sous les traits des voyous qui persécutent le cousin Bernard, les ouvriers pervertis que côtoie Jean-Jacques chez son maître et, bien entendu, de Jean-Jacques lui-même, avili, voleur et apprenti en rupture de ban. — Le thème de l'éducation est un leitmotiv; à chacune de ses réapparitions, il prend une couleur plus sombre, et "l'esclavage servile" des apprentis, à la fin, est présenté expressément comme le contraire de la "dépendance filiale" du début (p. 31). — Enfin, à la figure féminine de la première partie (tante Suzon) correspondent les deux objets d'amour de la troisième: Mlle de Vulson, adorée, courtisée, respectée, et une certaine petite Mlle Goton, dispensatrice de plaisirs masochistes clandestins.

Rousseau insiste longuement sur cette particularité de son caractère qui fait qu'il connaît "deux sortes d'amours très

---

3. Voir le schéma, p. 189.

distincts" (p. 27), et la relie aux expériences traumatisantes qui forment le noyau de l'épisode central, "Bossey." Mais aussi bien, c'est cet épisode qui donne son sens à tout le livre, et qui forme la charnière de cette structure en miroir que nous venons de décrire. Le temps me manque pour exposer en détail la profonde logique de cette composition. Qu'il suffise d'attirer l'attention sur les scènes de violence qui en occupent le centre.

Dans la première, lorsque Rousseau s'aperçoit que les fessées administrées par Mlle Lambercier, loin de remplir leur but punitif, lui procurent la volupté, c'est la loi fondamentale de son plaisir qui se révèle à lui: pour jouir, il faut qu'il commette un acte punissable, c'est-à-dire qu'il force l'être aimé à cesser de l'aimer — d'où ce dédoublement dans le comportement amoureux dont nous avons parlé: adoration galante et platonique pour Mlle de Vulson, voluptés perverses et clandestines avec Mlle Goton. Cet écartèlement de l'être, cette obligation de cacher toujours la moitié de soi-même sont à l'extrême opposé de la transparence et de l'authenticité qui régnaient dans les rapports entre l'enfant et sa tante, communication parfaite que signale, comme si souvent chez Rousseau, la présence de la musique.

Dans la deuxième scène, c'est toujours de châtiment corporel qu'il s'agit, mais sans résonance érotique cette fois. Sévèrement puni pour une faute qu'il n'a pas commise, l'enfant découvre l'écart qui sépare l'être du paraître, et se voit forcé de constater que les adultes aimés ne sont pas les dieux qu'il croyait, capables de lire dans son coeur, d'y aimer et d'y entretenir, par leur amour, l'innocence. Il perd confiance en eux et, du même coup, se trouve prêt à perdre confiance en soi.

C'est Rousseau lui-même qui, à propos du séjour à Bossey, parle de "paradis terrestre" (p. 20). La formule générale du récit s'impose à nous: il y eut une époque où j'étais bon, parce que j'étais entouré d'êtres bons et qu'il n'y avait pas d'obstacle à la communication entre les consciences. Puis vint non pas la faute, mais une inexplicable erreur d'aiguillage, et le mal entra dans ma vie avec la violence, le désir, l'incomprehension d'autrui. Ma vie avait perdu son sens, je fus ballotté ensuite au gré de l'intérêt et du vice, jusqu'au moment où je me procurai par la fuite hors de mon milieu naturel une fausse liberté, source de maux encore pires que les premiers. On voit tout de suite qu'il suffirait de remplacer dans ce récit la première personne par une généralisation, en disant "l'homme," pour retrouver le schéma fondamental de la pensée anthropologique de Rousseau. MM. Gagnebin et Raymond ont bien raison d'écrire: "Le récit de la catastrophe de Bossey, si proche soit-il de la vérité, a l'aspect d'un mythe" (p. 244). Et c'est là-dessus que je voudrais attirer l'attention: qu'est-ce que peut bien être l'autobiographie si, au moment même où elle respecte la vérité, elle obéit à des schémas qui sont les mêmes que ceux de la création philosophico-mythique? Où finit le produit de l'imagination et où commence le récit de la vie vécue?

Et, ajouterai-je, où finit le récit et où commence l'art? Le premier livre des *Confessions* est construit comme un diptyque, où chaque élément du premier volet se trouve répété dans le second, compte tenu de la loi d'inversion imposée par l'élément charnière; tout ce qui était clair et beau à gauche reparaît, noir et difforme, à droite. Un romancier qui aurait su composer de façon aussi solide — et voiler aussi habilement sa composition — passerait pour un grand artiste; mais s'il avait oublié de poser dans un des volets la tache de couleur appelée par l'autre, on le lui reprocherait. Or, c'est bien ce qu'avait fait Rousseau en 1765, comme nous le révèle le manuscrit de Neuchâtel. La construction était bancale, puisqu'aux amours dédoublées du second volet ne correspondait rien dans le premier; de tante Suzon et de ses chansons, du petit Jean-Jacques heureux à côté d'elle, pas un mot. O véracité! ô mensonge! Pourquoi tante Suzon paraît-elle maintenant dans le livre? Est-ce elle, est-ce son souvenir qui a insisté pour y entrer, ou est-ce le livre qui avait besoin d'elle? Est-ce la vie de Rousseau qui a produit les *Confessions*, ou sont-ce plutôt les *Confessions* qui ont produit cette chose, la seule que nous puissions dire exister vraiment, malgré le passage du temps, pour lui comme pour nous: la représentation mentale de la vie de Rousseau? Autant de questions que nous ne savons sans doute pas encore poser correctement.

J'ai devant moi un livre dont la couverture, la page de titre et les quelques premiers feuillets ont été arrachés. Le titre courant m'apprend cependant que cela s'appelle *Histoire de Gil Blas de Santillane*, et je constate dès les premières lignes qu'il s'agit d'une autobiographie, que tout rapproche du genre de romans qu'on appelle *picaresque*. Un personnage d'extraction modeste y passe par une longue série d'aventures qui lui font côtoyer des spécimens de toutes les professions et de tous les milieux et qui le mènent de déboire en déconvenue jusqu'au soir de la vie, où il jouit enfin d'une situation paisible et assurée. Le livre est amusant et extrêmement bien écrit, de sorte que je m'y intéresse et décide d'essayer d'en approfondir le sens.

Un petit détail frappe dès l'abord. Le mémorialiste prend soin de nous indiquer qu'il est né dix mois après le mariage de ses parents; ce n'est donc pas un héros typique de roman picaresque, puisque ces messieurs sont d'ordinaire des bâtards, ou du moins des enfants conçus avant les bénédictions de l'Eglise. Mais Gil Blas n'en est pas plus avantagé pour autant. Il n'a rien à nous dire au sujet de ses parents, si ce n'est que c'étaient des gens fort ordinaires, bien incapables de lui procurer une bonne éducation. Et, immédiatement, il se met à nous parler des maîtres qui l'ont formé.

Il faut entendre "maître" en deux sens: *magister* et *dominus*. Comme les héros picaresques auxquels nous l'avons déjà comparé, il est condamné aux positions subalternes, et les étapes de sa vie correspondent à des changements de sujétion. Mais ce qui est particulier chez lui, c'est le genre de dépendance affective et morale qui se greffe sur la dépendance économico-sociale. Le *pícaro* des romans espagnols est un être qui a compris une fois pour toutes l'inutilité de se rebeller contre la loi qui régit la société; elle se ramène à une alternative simple: je mange ou je suis mangé. L'homme qui veut survivre doit savoir qu'il est entouré de loups et se faire loup soi-même; cette règle vaut éminemment dans les rapports avec ceux que la Fortune a placés au-dessus de soi: les maîtres, *domini*. Le principe est affirmé avec force, dans l'auto-biographie que nous étudions en ce moment, par un ami du narrateur, Fabrice: "Un génie supérieur qui se met en condition ne fait pas son service matériellement comme un nigaud. Il entre dans une maison, pour commander plutôt que pour servir" (I, 17; I, 85).[4] Le *pícaro* est un être moralement seul, qui a renoncé à tout

4. Toutes les citations renvoient à l'édition Auguste Dupouy, Paris, 1935, 2 volumes. Je donne d'abord le livre et le chapitre, puis, au besoin, le tome et la page.

espoir de communication humaine, qui ne voit autour de soi que des dupes ou des ennemis, et se cramponne à un idéal d'orgueilleuse autarcie, à la fois parodie de stoïcisme et refuge angoissé contre une solitude et une vulnérabilité totales: "Il faut se consoler, mon enfant [déclare Fabrice à Gil Blas], de tous les malheurs de la vie. C'est par là qu'une ame forte et courageuse se distingue des ames foibles" (*ibid.*, p. 83).

Gil Blas n'est pas homme à entendre ces leçons. L'histoire de sa vie est celle de l'évanouissement de ses illusions, mais il ne perd jamais sa foi profonde en un idéal de succès matériel et social qui correspondrait à l'épanouissement de la bonté. Et, à la fin, il atteint bien quelque chose de cela. D'où le zèle de ceux qui se sont penchés sur sa vie à déterminer s'il y a bien dans son cas perfectionnement moral ou non. C'est, me semble-t-il, mal lire. Il ne s'agit pas de savoir si Gil Blas a fini par se rapprocher d'un idéal moral abstrait, mais de comprendre ce qu'il cherche et ce qui le fait agir. Or, ce qu'il cherche, c'est l'homme qui serait à la fois un maître, celui qui fait vivre et à qui on obéit, et un éducateur: une source de principes moraux, un exemple, une personne en qui on a foi, une règle de vie incarnée. Cette combinaison se trouve normalement réalisée pour l'enfant dans la figure des parents, qui sont des êtres nourriciers, des êtres aimés et puissants qui enseignent les lois de la vie en société et récompensent l'obéissance par l'amour. Les parents de Gil Blas ont doublement failli à leur tâche, puisque leur fils ne les aime ni ne les estime et que leur sagesse était vaine; ce qu'ils lui ont donné comme règle de conduite se révèle, à la première expérience, lamentablement insuffisant: "Loin de m'exhorter à ne tromper personne, ils devoient me recommander de ne pas me laisser dupper" (I, 2; t. I, p. 16).

Mais Gil Blas n'est pas un bâtard, résigné à l'isolement dans la jungle humaine. Sa vie ressemble à ce que Freud appelle un "roman familial," c'est-à-dire à ces fantaisies par lesquelles un sujet à tendances névrotiques essaie de se donner imaginairement des parents plus satisfaisants que ceux qu'il a réellement.[5] Il a envers ses maîtres une attitude qui ressemble bien peu à la férocité

5. Sigmund Freud, "Der Familienroman der Neurotiker," in *Gesammelte Werke*, Frankfurt am Main, tome VII, 1966, p. 227-231.

désespérée de ses pareils espagnols et au cynisme de son ami
Fabrice. En réalité, il ne demanderait qu'à se mettre à leur école; il
ne les dupe que dans la mesure où eux-mêmes font exprès pour l'y
inciter, et son attachement est en raison directe de leur valeur
humaine. Ceux dont il est le plus éloigné sont précisément ceux
qu'on pourrait appeler des êtres sans principes: qu'on compare le
ton sur lequel il parle de Don Bernard de Castil Blazo à qui il ne
pourrait reprocher qu'une chose: d'être absent et de ne pas
s'occuper de lui: (III, 1-3) et celui qu'il emprunte pour raconter la
mort de Don Mathias de Silva, le petit-maître: le duel, la mort du
maître, les réactions du valet nous parviennent comme le bruit que
feraient, à un grande distance, quelques boules de billard qui
s'entrechoquent sur une table au gré des lois de la mécanique (III,
8)

Le moment décisif de sa vie arrive lorsqu'il est mêlé aux
aventures d'un jeune homme qui avait toujours ignoré la vérité sur
sa naissance et qui se découvre fils de Don Cesar de Leyva (VI, 3).
On dirait que la réalisation du rêve de Gil Blas, qui est de trouver
un père idéal, même si elle se produit dans une autre personne, a
un effet magique: le voilà reçu avec toutes les marques possibles
d'estime et d'affection. C'est une sorte de nouvelle naissance;
comme le dit très justement M. Roger Laufer, il "va dès lors
connaître des aventures non plus en marge de la société mais en
son sein."[6] Le rang de ses maîtres s'élève; le dernier n'est rien
moins que le comte-duc d'Olivarès, premier ministre du roi
d'Espagne, et c'est presque un grand homme. En même temps, les
relations qui s'établissent entre le grand seigneur et son secrétaire
correspondent exactement à ce que celui-ci avait toujours sou-
haité: "le Comte-Duc [. . .] avoit un faible que je ne découvris pas
infrustueusement; c'étoit de vouloir être aimé. Dès qu'il s'apperce-
voit que quelqu'un s'attachoit à lui par inclination, il le prenoit en
amitié. Je n'êus garde de négliger cette observation. Je ne me
contentois pas de bien faire ce qu'il me commandoit, j'executois
ses ordres avec des démonstrations de zèle qui le ravissoient. [. . .]

---

6. Roger Laufer, *Lesage ou le métier de romancier*, Paris, 1971, p. 333. La hantise
paternelle de Gil Blas n'a pas échappé à cet excellent critique. Il a raison, à mon sens, de
l'envisager dans une perspective psychocritique, même si l'on peut estimer que la rigueur
de sa méthode n'est pas aussi en évidence que la finesse de ses intuitions.

je devins insensiblement le favori de mon Maître, qui de son côté, comme j'avois le même foible que lui, me gagna l'ame par les marques d'affection qu'il me donna" (XI, 8; t. II, p. 367).

On nous excusera de ne fournir dans ce cadre qu'une interprétation très sommaire de l'autobiographie de Gil Blas; Mais il ne s'agit ici que de soulever des interrogations sur la nature de l'autobiographie.

Qu'on me permette donc de poser, en renonçant à nuancer et à étayer cette affirmation par une analyse plus serrée du texte, que ce qui caractérise essentiellement la personnalité morale de Gil Blas, c'est le manque d'autonomie; entendons par là la faculté qu'aurait un être humain d'évoluer dans le monde en se guidant sur sa perception personnelle des choses, sur ses inclinations réelles et sur un système de valeurs qui découle de l'une et des autres. C'est le contraire qu'on observe chez notre homme, où ces trois principes de structuration présentent des caractères de faiblesse et de confusion remarquables. Sa vision du monde est un étrange assemblage de noir pessimisme et de candeur; ses affections sont entremêlées avec ses intérêts de telle sorte qu'il lui est presque impossible d'en sentir jamais l'authenticité et qu'elles sont toujours marquées d'une forte ambivalence; enfin, la recherche d'une règle morale implique pour lui le besoin d'une relation avec un être socialement supérieur, où l'on n'arrive plus à départager ce qui est clientèle, dépendance affective et ressentiment.

Il convient de compléter ce tableau en examinant l'attitude du mémorialiste envers les êtres qu'il côtoie au long de son aventureuse carrière. Je ne m'attarderai pas sur les pareils de Gil Blas, laquais, *pícaros* et brigands. Il ne s'est jamais senti à sa place parmieux, et il est normal, étant donné ce qu'il est, qu'il les rejette; si spirituel et si ironique que le personnage se montre à nous, c'est quand même un homme sérieux, ami du solide. Il veut arriver dans la société et non pas s'amuser en se faisant croire qu'il la domine; M. Laufer a sans doute raison de dire qu'il reproche avant tout aux Raphaël, Ambroise, Rolando, etc., d'être des *comédiens*.[7]

Les nobles, eux, bénéficient d'un préjugé favorable. Je crois

---

7. *Ibid.*, p. 325-326.

que l'on peut dire sans risque d'erreur que toutes les personnes tenues en haute estime par Gil Blas appartiennent à cette catégorie, et que celle qui brille de l'éclat le plus pur est un seigneur nommé Don Pompeyo de Castro, qu'il n'a vu qu'une fois et sans que cela ait la moindre suite, mais qui l'a suffisamment impressionné pour qu'il lui accorde deux chapitres dans le troisième livre de sa vie. La chose mérite attention; qu'y a-t-il de si extraordinaire dans cet homme pour que notre mémorialiste désabusé parle de lui pendant près de quinze pages sans que la moindre ironie vienne jeter une ombre sur le portrait?

Evidemment, Don Pompeyo incarne le succès. Espagnol transplanté en Pologne, il jouit de la faveur du roi; il est le gendre d'un des principaux seigneurs du pays; il se voit chargé de hautes missions diplomatiques. Mais ce n'est pas cela qui frappa le plus Gil Blas à l'époque où, valet d'un petit-maître, il put entrevoir le grand homme; c'était son "esprit solide et délié" (III, 6; t. I, p. 206). Et à quoi s'applique cet esprit dans les conversations qui nous sont rapportées? Au théâtre. Il est question du jeu des acteurs, et Don Pompeyo s'explique là-dessus d'une façon qui aurait transporté d'aise Molière ou Boileau; il ne daigne pas dire un mot de la pièce nouvelle qui vient d'être représentée, et adopte, pour juger les comédiens, des critères parfaitement Louis XIV. Cela n'a rien d'étonnant puisqu'on le dirait sorti lui-même d'un roman du XVIIe siècle ou d'une de ces nouvelles "historiques" ou "tragiques," pleines des beaux grands sentiments d'autrefois, qui eurent tant de faveur et dont les romanciers les plus légers parsemaient volontiers leurs ouvrages (on en trouve des exemples dans le livre qui nous occupe ici). Son histoire racontée par lui-même (III, 7) fait revivre cet univers: il y est question d'amours secrètes et passionnées, de rivaux odieux ramenés à la vertu par la générosité de leurs victimes, de l'honneur, du conflit entre le devoir de se venger et l'obéissance au roi, etc.

En un mot, l'être le plus parfait que Gil Blas semble avoir rencontré dans sa vie est le grand seigneur honnête homme du XVIIe siècle: homme d'armes et de gouvernement, galant, cultivé, d'un goût sûr, sévère et classique.

A l'opposé de Don Pompeyo, nous trouvons Fabrice. Il est présent, lui, du début jusqu'à la fin du livre; Gil Blas eut avec lui des rencontres très espacées, mais c'est le seul ami d'enfance qu'il ait revu à toutes les époques de sa vie. Leur situation de départ était identique, ils se trouvèrent souvent placés devant les mêmes choix; bref, si nous parlions d'un roman, nous dirions que Fabrice est un double du narrateur. Pouvons-nous définir l'attitude de Gil Blas face à lui?

Il faut distinguer entre les deux moitiés du livre. Dans la première, où Gil Blas, simple valet, oscille à la frontière entre le monde des nantis, où il voudrait avoir accès, et celui des délinquants, où se recrutent toutes ses connaissances, Fabrice est un initiateur, un entraîneur; nous avons vu plus haut quelles leçons de picarisme il dispense. Ensuite, leurs voies divergent. Gil Blas résout le problème de l'autonomie comme nous l'avons expliqué, c'est-à-dire en y renonçant dès que les circonstances le permettent; Fabrice, lui, opte pour l'une des formes de vie qui offrent les plus grandes possibilités de liberté intérieure à l'être humain: l'art; il devient écrivain (VII, 13). Mais quel écrivain! Son ambition n'est pas de produire une oeuvre qui soit sienne et qui affirme la vérité de son être: il cherche le succès. Or le public est à ses yeux composé d'imbéciles, dont il quête l'approbation sans s'illusionner sur leur bêtise. Inutile de dire qu'il donne dans le goût nouveau et n'a que dédain pour les grands auteurs du passé. La nécessité d'écrire en style gongoresque se justifie, d'après lui, par l'existence de classes sociales dont les unes méprisent les autres, barrières qui doivent se reproduire dans la littérature; bien loin d'échapper à sa condition servile, il n'a donc réussi qu'à ajouter une aliénation culturelle à son aliénation sociale. Ce malheureux goût de la littérature ne le mène évidemment qu'à des prospérités humiliantes et passagères ou à la misère (XI, 7 et 10; XII, 7). Gil Blas le traite avec le genre d'indulgence sermonneuse qu'on peut avoir pour des amis qui ont mal tourné, mais qu'on connaît depuis toujours, et le fond de son attitude envers lui est très certainement le mépris.

Le temps est venu de rassembler en faisceau toutes ces observations. Il suffira pour cela de renoncer à la fiction employée jusqu'ici et au nom de laquelle je feignais de croire que *Gil Blas* fût une autobiographie et non pas l'un des romans les plus célèbres de la littérature française, le chef-d'oeuvre de Lesage.

Roman, donc, fiction. Le temps n'est plus où l'on considérait les romans à la première personne comme des confessions et attribuait gaillardement à l'auteur les aventures et les sentiments du héros-narrateur. Loin de moi la pensée de déclarer, en me fondant sur *Gil Blas*, que Lesage ait été un mauvais fils, qu'il ait eu des démêlés avec la police dans sa jeunesse ou que nous sachions quelque chose sur son comportement envers les femmes. Ce roman est l'autobiographie d'un personnage fictif, Gil Blas, et de personne d'autre.

Et pourtant . . . Gil Blas doit être tenu responsable de chacune des phrases que nous lisons, de leur style, des jugements qu'elles expriment. Mais faut-il lui attribuer aussi l'identité de ses parents, le fait qu'il fut pris en captivité par les brigands du capitaine Rolando, la mort de sa femme, les aventures arrivées en Amérique à son valet Scipion, sa rencontre avec Laure après des années de séparation? C'est pour rester rigoureusement fidèle aux faits que nous refusons de prêter à l'auteur, personne réelle, ce qui appartient au personnage, être de fiction distinct de lui; mais ce serait être infidèle aux faits que d'attribuer le roman même à un être de fiction qui n'en est qu'une partie. Gil Blas n'a pas plus inventé Don Pompeyo de Castro que Rousseau n'a inventé Mlle Lambercier; si c'est Dieu le Père qui a créé Mlle Lambercier, Don Pompeyo est une créature de Lesage.

C'est dire que nous sommes en droit d'interroger le roman dans son ensemble pour savoir s'il nous dit quelque chose de la personne de son auteur. La réponse n'est pas sans intérêt. S'il s'agissait d'une autobiographie authentique, on s'étonnerait peut-être de la place qu'y occupe la littérature. Ce n'est pas le sujet qui revient le plus souvent dans le livre, mais je crois avoir montré que cet aspect quantitatif est de peu d'importance par rapport à la *position* du thème dans la structure. Le personnage qui a le plus de titres à être identifié comme un double du héros devient écrivain, et il est présenté comme digne tout au plus d'une indulgence méprisante;[8] le personnage le plus radieux de tout le livre est un

---

8. Je ne prétends pas avoir tout dit sur Fabrice; c'est un Hermès, psychagogue et faux, insaisissable. Je crois toutefois que, s'il représente une part de l'âme de Lesage, c'est une part peu estimée. M. Laufer l'embellit beaucoup lorsqu'il en fait une sorte de bohème fantaisiste et aimable; ce n'est pas ainsi, à non avis, que le montre le texte de Lesage.

seigneur à qui Lesage donne pendant un chapitre entier le loisir d'exposer la doctrine classique en matière d'art. Si l'on ajoute à cela qu'aucun écrivain vivant n'est présenté sous d'autres traits que ceux du ridicule ou de la bassesse, que le héros écrit lui aussi beaucoup et avec succès, mais des ouvrages de propagande commandés pour le fond et le style par ses maîtres, et qu'enfin, toute la vie de Gil Blas, non pas seulement telle qu'il la commente pour nous mais telle qu'elle s'organise réellement dans la succession de ses péripéties, démontre que le bonheur consiste à se faire aimer d'un maître puissant, nous en arriverons à des conclusions intéressantes à propos de cet homme, Lesage, à qui on accorde le titre de gloire d'avoir été le premier écrivain français à vivre de sa plume sans avoir de mécène et sans se prostituer. Le fin mot de son plus grand roman semble bien être qu'écrire n'est pas un métier honorable, que la liberté qu'on y trouve est fausse et qu'il faudrait être autre chose: un seigneur cultivé qui sait goûter, dans l'intervalle des travaux de gouvernment ou dans la paisible retraite d'un château campagnard, les oeuvres qui en valent la peine, c'est-à-dire celles qu'on n'écrit plus aujourd'hui.[9] Je ne sais pas si Lesage aurait dit cela dans ses mémoires; et pourtant, quelle confession nous introduirait plus avant dans l'intimité de la compréhension qu'il avait de sa propre vie?

Mon but aurait été atteint si ces rapides survols, en rappelant deux faits bien connus, avaient fait sentir l'urgence de se pencher sur le problème qu'ils soulèvent. Les faits sont, d'une part, que nous ne pouvons pas regarder un peu attentivement une autobiographie sans nous trouver face à face avec le roman; d'autre part, que, dans le roman à la première personne, l'interposition d'un héros-narrateur qui dit "je" sans être l'auteur n'empêche pas celui-ci de se dire dans l'oeuvre. Considérant au surplus que "le *je* du texte fictif est indiscernable du *je* de la narration autobiographique 'sincère,'"[10] on est conduit à se demander avec quelque effroi: mais alors, en quoi consiste donc la différence entre l'autobiographie et le roman à la première personne?

Il existe évidemment un critère externe de définition: "Les

9. A commencer par celles des Anciens. Voir Laufer, *op. cit.*, p. 354 sqq. et 361-362.

10. Jean Starobinski, *L'Oeil vivant II: la relation critique,* Paris, 1970, p. 86.

récits autobiographiques sont dits *autobiographies*, par opposition aux romans à la première personne, lorsqu'on sait qu'ils ont été écrits par la personne qui y raconte sa vie." Mais cette définition reste insatisfaisante à bien des points de vue. Son application pratique, d'abord, n'est pas toujours facile; au XVIIIe siècle, justement, fourmillent les romans "historiques," les pseudo-mémoires, et nous n'avons pas toujours les moyens d'identifier avec certitude le scripteur des textes que nous possédons. Ensuite, la définition nous placerait dans une situation délicate face aux autobiographies des menteurs et des mythomanes, qu'on a justement l'habitude d'appeler des "romans." Enfin elle nous laisse insatisfaits, nous, littéraires, puisqu'elle nous impose de recourir à un argument d'autorité pour déterminer le genre d'une oeuvre. Pour déclarer que nous avons affaire à un sonnet ou à une pièce de théâtre, nous ne demandons pas l'avis de l'auteur et de ceux qui l'ont fréquenté; lorsqu'il nous arrive d'hésiter entre deux désigna-tions, par exemple "drame" et "tragédie," ou "prose" et "poème en prose," l'avis de ces mêmes personnes n'a pour nous qu'une valeur d'indication, et c'est au texte d'une part, à notre idée des catégories littéraires d'autre part que nous demandons la lumière.

Qu'en est-il du texte des récits autobiographiques? Contient-il des éléments qui nous permettent de le rattacher avec certitude à un genre ou à l'autre? C'est la question que je voulais surtout poser ici. Mais pour savoir s'il est possible d'y répondre, il convient de réfléchir un moment sur ce que c'est qu'un récit et sur la façon dont s'établit le contact entre son auteur et nous. Un schéma très grossier du processus de la communication en littérature nous aidera peut-être.[11]

Il est légitime de poser au départ un individu historique réel, un homme de chair et d'os, qui écrit. Mais ce serait une illusion de croire qu'on ait par là défini l'auteur. En effet, dans le rapport que ce personnage établit avec le destinataire de son oeuvre, ce n'est pas le tout de sa personne qui est en jeu. Il n'est plus simplement ce qu'il est, il est celui qui veut dire quelque chose, celui qui veut être compris d'une certaine façon. Pour désigner cet aspect de l'auteur — l'auteur tel qu'il veut, consciemment ou incon-

11. Voir p. 188.

sciemment, être compris — la critique anglo-saxonne a introduit le terme excellent de *second self*, de "moi second." Si ce moi second était perçu exactement comme il veut l'être, la communication serait parfaitement réussie. Mais cela est tout à fait impossible. Le moi historique joue parfois de bien mauvais tours au moi second, le lecteur met beaucoup du sien dans sa lecture et, enfin, il est illusoire de penser qu'aucune oeuvre puisse jamais être un verre parfaitement transparent, pur non seulement de tout défaut, mais ne possédant pas non plus d'indice de réfraction. Le moi second n'est donc connu que d'une façon approchée, sous la forme de ce que les critiques évoqués plus haut appellent le "moi induit," l'*implied author* reconstitué à partir de l'oeuvre. (Ces réserves, déjà, feront comprendre pourquoi le schéma proposé est qualifié d'*idéal* et de *simplifié*.)

Entre l'auteur et l'oeuvre se situe un écart qui peut, parfois, avoir l'air d'une insignifiante fissure, mais qui n'en reste pas moins infranchissable. Dans l'énoncé meurt celui qui le produit. Pour se communiquer, la pensée doit devenir langage, et le récit, au moment même où il se forme, expulse son auteur et le rend inutile. Je ne peux rien dire de moi sans me ramener immédiatement au statut de pronom personnel, d'un impertinent *je* qui, bien loin de me servir fidèlement, est prêt à se passer de moi dès que je l'ai engendré; il se substitue à moi et continue à faire sa fonction même si je quitte le royaume des vivants. Dans le récit, donc, ce n'est jamais la voix de l'auteur que nous entendons; le plus souvent, d'ailleurs, il est mort ou loin de nous. Les phrases se présentent à nous comme des phrases de quelqu'un; mais d'un *quelqu'un* qui n'est pas l'auteur, que nous avons tendance à imaginer comme distinct du récit mais qui est entièrement contenu en lui et sans qui il n'y aurait pas de texte. Je l'appelle le *narrateur.*

On est parfois tenté d'oublier son existence, tellement il sait se déguiser sous des dehors d'objectivité ou de discrétion. Mais il constitue quand même l'élément le plus solide et le plus immédiatement concret du récit. Comme le disait déjà magistralement Käte Friedemann au début de ce siècle: "'Wirklich' im dramatischen Sinne ist ein Vorgang, der eben jetzt geschieht [. . .] 'Wirklich' im epischen Sinne aber ist zunächst überhaupt nicht der erzählte Vorgang, sondern das Erzählen selbst."[12]

Il convient de signaler rapidement deux axes en fonction desquels se définit le narrateur; l'un est celui de la représentation, l'autre celui de la proximité par rapport au moi second:

(1) Le narrateur peut chercher à se dissimuler au maximum en évitant toute manifestation voyante de sa présence. On écrira: "Un homme entra dans le bar et demanda une bière," et croira peut-être, naïvement, avoir laissé l'histoire se raconter toute seule; pourtant, quelqu'un a dit: "Un homme entra." A l'autre **extrême**, le texte lui-même représente avec tellement de force cette action de raconter qu'il en naît un simulacre d'être humain complet, qui dit "je" et parle de soi, et qui est ce qu'on appelle communément le narrateur, ou le héros-narrateur quand on traite du roman à la première personne.

(2) Que le narrateur soit représenté dans le texte ou demeure implicite, l'auteur peut à son gré faire en sorte qu'il lui ressemble plus ou moins. Il est évident que le narrateur d'un roman de Balzac ressemble beaucoup à Balzac lui-même et que Faulkner n'est pas l'idiot de *The Sound and the Fury*. Il est donc loisible au moi second de se masquer plus ou moins, de se rendre plus ou moins difficile d'accès, de tendre plus ou moins de pièges au lecteur.[13]

Il est temps que nous parlions de celui-ci, car il est, à son insu, un élément actif dans la production de l'oeuvre. Nous avons défini le moi second comme l'auteur dans la mesure où il entre dans un processus de communication. Avec qui? Pas plus que le moi second ne peut exister sans le support d'un moi historique, la communication ne peut s'adresser à autre chose qu'à des êtres réels, des lecteurs réels; mais pas plus que le moi historique ne se confond avec le moi second, les individus qui abordent un roman ne sont ses vrais destinataires. Ce n'est pas à eux tout simplement qu'il s'adresse, mais à eux dans la mesure où ils le comprennent. C'est ce qu'on veut faire entendre quand on dit que les livres *font* leurs lecteurs.

12. Käte Friedemann, *Die Rolle des Erzählers in der Epik*, Berlin, 1910, reproduction photomécanique, Darmstadt, p. 25. Traduction: "Ce qui est 'réel' au sens du drame, c'est l'événement qui se produit maintenant devant nous. Ce qui est 'réel' au sens de la narration, ce n'est absolument pas d'abord l'événement raconté, mais bien le fait même de raconter."

13. Cf. Wayne C. Booth, *The Rhetoric of Fiction*, Chicago, 1961.

On écrit donc pour être compris; pour être compris, il faut être compréhensible; et être compréhensible n'est pas une notion définissable dans l'abstrait; c'est toujours être compréhensible pour quelqu'un. C'est dire que l'auteur est obligé de tenir compte de l'outillage mental de son lecteur; il n'a pas entière liberté de moyens dans la constitution de son moi second ni dans la composition de son oeuvre. Il lui faut, sous peine de cesser d'écrire ou de ne produire que des enchaînements de mots dépourvus de sens, utiliser non seulement les structures du langage, mais aussi les structures mentales (affectives, imaginaires, intellectuelles) de l'homme en général et des hommes de son temps en particulier.

On appelle *vraisemblable* une oeuvre qui obéit à ces conditions. En effet, il serait vain de croire que la vraisemblance désigne un rapport direct entre le contenu du discours et la réalité; la complexité et du discours, et de la réalité, ainsi que leur hétérogénéité radicale, mettent des obstacles extrêmement puissants à leur comparaison. Cela est particulièrement vrai d'un récit un peu étendu. On doit donc considérer le sentiment de la vraisemblance comme résultant de la concordance entre un récit et la conception que ses lecteurs se font de la réalité, c'est-à-dire la façon dont ils l'imaginent.

D'où les quelques propositions que je voudrais soumettre en terminant.

Il ressort, selon moi, de ce qui vient d'être dit que les autobiographies se distinguent des romans non pas en ce qu'elles rejettent la fiction et s'en tiennent à la réalité, mais en ce qu'elles ajoutent à la fiction romanesque un degré de plus, en feignant de croire à l'identité de l'auteur et du narrateur. Elles n'échappent pas plus que les ouvrages d'imagination aux lois générales qui régissent le langage, elles sont aussi des livres, mais n'avouent ce caractère qu'à moitié, ou pas du tout.

Elles masquent leur véritable nature en mettant en avant leur caractère de véracité (sur le plan des faits ou de la psychologie). Or l'adéquation entre un discours et une réalité (surtout aussi complexe qu'une personne et qu'une vie) est la chose la plus problématique du monde. Si le mémorialiste veut être cru, il faut qu'il soit lui aussi vraisemblable, c'est-à-dire qu'il s'arrange pour se donner une conception de son destin qui soit pensable avec les catégories mentales de ses lecteurs.[14] C'est-à-dire que l'acte même de raconter sa vie est un biais par lequel la pensée d'autrui se glisse dans la sienne. Si le mémorialiste refusait de se plier à cette loi, si, par un attachement irréductible à son unicité, il s'obstinait à écarter les schémas stéréotypés qui peuvent seuls devenir les éléments porteurs d'un message intelligible, il deviendrait entièrement désordonné et incohérent; il détruirait son image au moment de se peindre. Rien ne donne moins l'impression de la vie qu'une énumération de faits vrais, sans les liens qu'y ajoute l'esprit.

De là découle qu'il est impossible, absolument, de parler de soi. Une conclusion aussi abstraite ne nous mène cependant pas très loin. Il vaut mieux revenir à des réalités plus concrètes: il est constant qu'il existe des autobiographies, c'est-à-dire des textes dont les auteurs, liés consciemment et inconsciemment à des schémas linguistiques et mentaux préétablis, ont quand même voulu prendre pour fil d'Ariane non pas le "vraisemblable," mais le "vrai." Sans vouloir nier l'intérêt des études nombreuses, et parfois excellentes, sur les techniques employées pas les auteurs de romans à la première personne (au XVIIIe siècle notamment) pour donner à leurs fictions l'allure d'authentiques autobiographies, il faut bien admettre que ces recherches mettent entre parenthèses le problème le plus ardu. En réalité, que les romans soient vraisemblables n'est pas surprenant: ils sont faits pour cela. Ils s'adressent à notre imagination en utilisant son langage, qu'ils peuvent parler purement et correctement puisqu'ils ne sont pas tenus de respecter l'enchaînement de faits réellement arrivés. Beaucoup plus mystérieuse est la vraisemblance des récits qui ne se donnent pas pour fictifs. Tout l'art de l'autobiographie consiste peut-être à combiner, en les infléchissant imperceptiblement, des schémas narratifs qui ne doivent rien à la vie du mémorialiste.

Il semble donc que l'étude de l'autobiographie à une époque donnée ait pour préalable celle des fictions qui avaient cours à la même époque. Plutôt que de comparer les autobiographies, morceau par morceau, aux fragments de réalité objective que nous croyons connaître à propos de leurs auteurs, il faudrait sans doute

---

14. L'exemple le plus clair de ce que je veux dire est sans doute fourni par l'abondance des autobiographies qui reprennent la structure du roman picaresque (par exemple les premiers livres des *Confessions* de Rousseau).

les envisager très exactement comme ce qu'elles sont, à savoir des livres. Plutôt que de faire comme si leur cohérence et leurs incohérences étaient dues tout entières à l'auteur et à sa vie (leur logique provenant de l'unité de la personne et de la continuité de son évolution, les incohérences venant des hasards de la vie, et la mauvaise foi brochant sur le tout), il faudrait tâcher d'en dégager la structure comme on le fait pour des romans. Cela procurerait deux avantages: d'abord, on découvrirait peut-être qu'il y a des lois structurales qui jouent dans les premières et non dans les seconds, et on trouverait peut-être une réponse à la question posée plus haut, à savoir s'il y a *dans le texte* des critères qui nous permettent de départager les autobiographies authentiques et les fictions; et surtout, une telle méthode nous révélerait des choses plus intimes et plus certaines sur le fonctionnement de l'esprit de l'auteur, donc sur sa personne, que l'éternelle et vaine supputation des degrés et des nuances de sa sincérité.

R. Joly

SCHEMA IDEAL SIMPLIFIE
DE LA COMMUNICATION EN LITTERATURE

(appliqué au genre narratif)

AUTEUR	OEUVRE	LECTEUR
Moi historique	Narrateur	Lecteur réel
⇩ Moi second	⇧ Narré ⇧	⇩ Lecteur souhaité

LE PREMIER LIVRE DES *CONFESSIONS* DE JEAN–JACQUES ROUSSEAU

Préambule
Les parents de Jean-Jacques

GENEVE I

Naissance, mort de la mère
Lectures, rêves héroïques
Le frère de Jean-Jacques
Education en liberté
Tante Suzon

BOSSEY

La nature, l'amitié;
éducation disciplinée,
mais libre
La violence;
Les fessées de Mlle Lambercier
Le peigne cassé
Epilogue et intermezzo; le
noyer de la terrasse

GENEVE II

Chez l'oncle Bernard: éducation
négligée
Les deux amours: Mlle de Vulson
et Mlle Goton
L'apprentissage: la tyrannie,
l'avilissement
Lectures, rêveries
Fuite de Genève

*Medal by John Croker to commemorate the arrival
of George I in Britain*

From the Library of Thames & Hudson

George I as an English & a European Figure

Georg Ludwig, Elector of Hanover from 1689 until his death in 1727, but better known by the name and title which came to him in 1714 when he — by virtue of the Act of Settlement — was proclaimed George I of Great Britain is in need of a fresh evaluation. Indeed, in my *Europe in the Age of Louis XIV*[1] I put George on a list of "biographies wanted," fully conscious that the great gains of recent research in the English speaking countries and in Germany[2] had not yet been worked into "accepted history," but little expecting to be talked into undertaking the project myself, I did this with some hesitation, for, though such great gains had been made, and though I myself had worked long and hard on

1. London and New York, 1968, p. 244.
2. On the English and North American side mention must be made of: J. H. Plumb, *The Growth of Political Stability, 1675-1725*, London, 1967; J. M. Beattie, *The English Court in the Reign of George I*, Cambridge, 1967; A. S. Foord, *His Majesty's Opposition, 1715-1830*, Oxford, 1964; J. J. Murray, *George I, The Baltic and the Whig Split*, Chicago and London, 1969; G. C. Gibbs, "Britain and the Alliance of Hanover, April 1725 — February 1726," *English Historical Review* 73, 1958; G. C. Gibbs, "Parliament and Foreign Policy in the Age of Stanhope and Walpole," *English Historical Review* 77, 1962; G. C. Gibbs, "Laying Treaties Before Parliament in the Eighteenth Century," in *Studies in Diplomatic History. Essays in Memory of David Bayne Horn*, Ragnhild Hatton and M. S. Anderson, eds., London, 1970; C. G. Gibbs, "Parliament and the Treaty of Quadruple Alliance," in *William III and Louis XIV: Essays by and for Mark A. Thomson*, Ragnhild Hatton and J. S. Bromley, eds., Liverpool and Toronto, 1968.
On the German side Professor Georg Schnath has been prolific beyond belief. In 1938 vol. I of his *Geschichte Hannovers* was published. A vast tome of over 800 pages, it ends with the establishment of the Electorate in 1692. Although now retired he is hard at work on a second volume that will end in 1714. In the interim he has published 17 books and more than 80 essays and articles. For a full bibliography see: "Verzeichnis der Veröffentlichungen von Georg Schnath" in George Schnath, *Ausgewählte Beiträge zur Landesgeschichte Niedersachsens*, Hildesheim, 1968, a volume of selected essays in honour of his 70th birthday. In addition to this one might mention: Joachim Lampe, *Aristokratie, Hofadel und Staaspatriziat in Kurhannover. Die Lebenskreise der höheren Beamten an den Kurhannoverssch. Zentral -u. Hofbehörden 1714-1760*, Hildesheim, 1963, 2 vols.; Mathilde Knoop, *Kurfürstin Sophie von Hannover*, Hildesheim, 1964; W. Mediger, *Mecklenburg, Russland und England-Hanover, 1706-1721*, Hildesheim, 1967; Jürger Prüser, *Die Göhrde*, Hildesheim, 1969.

George's foreign policy,[3] I was aware that the masses of official correspondence and documents in Hanover and England was counter-balanced by a dearth of material on the personal side. How might one tell George's share from that of his ministers in the policies pursued? How might one deduce his motives and objectives? How might one learn sufficiently about the private person to assess what effect it had on the public person and the way in which George carried out his *métier* as a ruler? For George left no memoirs for us to analyse, in contrast to Louis XIV who purposely, and with great care for content and style, composed some for at least parts of his reign to explain himself "before history."[4]

Circumstances did not oblige George — as they did William III after 1688, in respect of Heinsius, the Dutch Raadpensionaris — to correspond regularly with a trusted collaborator for the better part of each year.[5] Before 1714 George lived in so close a proximity to his Hanoverian ministers and advisers that he could dispense with letter-writing; after 1714 he took a German Chancery (the *Deutsche Kanzlei*) with him to London, and when he visited his Electorate — as he did for several months at a time in 1716, 1719, 1720, 1723[6] — not only did his Hanoverian ministers go with him, but also one or more of his English ministers on whom the task of keeping in touch with their colleagues at home devolved. The ministers, English as well as German, were in their turn kept too busy — or felt the need for discretion sufficiently — not to pen memoirs of political significance.[7] If they wrote *aide-mémoires* (in

3. See my *Diplomatic Relations Between Great Britain and the Dutch Republic 1714-1721*, London, 1959, and *Charles XII of Sweden*, London, 1968, New York, 1969, pp. 369 ff.

4. See the Introduction by Paul Sonnino to his translation of Louis XIV's *Mémoires for the Instruction of the Dauphin*, New York and London, 1970; my *Louis XIV and his World*, London and New York, 1972, pp. 91-92.

5. This correspondence is in *Archives de la Maison d'Orange-Nassau*, 3rd series, 3 vols., Leiden 1907-9, F. J. L. Krämer, ed.; selected letters translated into English are in P. Grimblot, *Letters of William III and Louis XIV and of their Ministers 1697-1700*, London, 2 vols., 1848.

6. He was on his way to Hanover in 1727 for a fifth visit when he was taken ill and died at Osnabrück on the night of 21-22 June.

7. We have those of Bothmer for his early youth only: *Aus den Erinnerungen des Hans Kaspar von Bothmer. Lehr- und Wanderjahre eines hannoversch-englischen Staatsmannes um 1700*, Karl Freiherr von Bothmer and G. Schnath, eds., Hildesheim, 1936.

the manner of Robert Harley),[8] or notes of conversations and discussions on controversial issues, these have not survived and may well have been destroyed on purpose.[9] Nothing is more striking to the scholar who obtains access to the Stanhope papers than the riches before 1714 and the dearth of material after Stanhope becomes one of George I's principal ministers, unless it is the neat piles of the Bernstorff correspondence at Gartow which contain letters from numerous correspondents to Bernstorff throughout the period when he was in the confidence of George, both as Elector and as King, but never a draft reply or even a marginal comment.

It would seem as if the struggle for office and power was strong enough both in the Electorate (where there was an anti-Bernstorff faction round F. W. von Görtz which had considerable influence)[10] and in England to have an inhibiting effect: these were the statesmen who were well aware of the spynets of factions and parties, of the bribes which were offered to servants and secretaries, no less than of the opening and decoding of letters on the international level.[11] Hanover, indeed, was, since the days of the anti-French alliance between William III and Duke Georg Wilhelm of Celle (the uncle of our George), the chief centre for such a service,[12] an alliance which Duke Ernst August of Calenberg (George's father) joined during the Nine Years War.[13]

It is necessary therefore, to search for substitute material or sources. These are of three kinds. First and most important are the draft despatches to Hanoverian diplomats in the *Deutsche Kanzlei.* George took a strong interest in these as in the incoming letters from diplomats abroad, whether in Hanoverian or English service,

---

8. In the Harley papers, Portland Loan, deposited in the British Museum.

9. Professor Plumb found among the Cholmondeley papers jottings of headings for Robert Walpole's discussions with George I, but 90% or more dealt with patronage.

10. W. Mediger, *op. cit.* I, p. 231 and the same author's "Die Gewinnung Bremens und Verdens," *Nieders. Jahrb. für Landesg.*, 1971, pp. 37-56.

11. See K. L. Ellis, *The Post Office in the Eighteenth Century*, London, 1958, pp. 74 ff.

12. See S. P. Oakley, "The Interception of Posts in Celle 1694-1700," in *William III and Louis XIV*, pp. 95 ff.; Bengt Peterson, "The Correspondent in Paris: en engelsk informationskälle under 1700-talet," *Scandia*, 1961, pp. 387-99.

13. Janine Fayard, "Les Tentatives de Constitution d'un 'Tiers Party' en Allemagne du Nord (1690-94)," *Revue d'Histoire Diplomatique*, 1965.

and by studying additions and changes and in whose hand these
are made (e.g. if in the hand of the King's private secretary,
Hattorf), much can be learned not only about the debate on
foreign policy issues but of the King's share in it. Second, a close
study of the Journals of the House of Lords and of the House of
Commons and of English manuscript material, makes it possible to
assess, with some certainty, the English components of George's
policy after 1714. Third, letters between English statesmen in
Hanover and colleagues or friends in England, where they touch
upon policy debates or royal decisions, are at times significant.
They are, of course, not safe to use unless the correspondents were
on good terms and trusted each other: to give you an example,
what Stanhope writes to Townshend and Walpole in the autumn
of 1716 can not help us since Stanhope and Sunderland were at
that time committed to ousting their two colleagues. Finally, but
in exceptional cases only, foreign diplomats can be seen to possess
inside information: e.g. an Austrian diplomat to St. James's in the
early years of George's reign was in the confidence of the German
ministers in London and from his despatches a good deal of light is
thrown on how policy decisions were arrived at.

Letters from George to individuals close to him in a private
capacity are nearly as scarce as letters to ministers. Those he wrote
to his wife, Sophie Dorothea, between the marriage (in 1682) and
the divorce (of 1694) — and we do know that he wrote some —
have been destroyed or lost, as have those to his brothers. Those
to his daughter Sophie Dorothea (b. 1687; better known as the
mother of Frederick the Great), after her marriage to the Hohenzollern heir, Frederick William in 1706, have survived to the number
of 45 in the Brandenburg-Preussisches Hausarchiv, but they throw
light only on facets of the personality, not on motivation of
policy. They were evaluated as far back as 1937 by Mrs. R. L.
Arkell and show George as a fond father with concern also for the
health and upbringing of his grandchildren, and, incidentally — if
not unexpectedly — as critical of the behaviour of the Prince of
Wales after 1717.[14] Thanks to the stimulus of seeing two letters

14. R. L. Arkell, "George I's letters to his Daughter," *English Historical Review* 52,
1937, pp. 492-499.

of 1703 from George to his mother, mentioned in the Knoop biography, the discovery was made of a small but important series of 31 letters (some in French, some in German) addressed to his mother between 1685 and 1706.[15] These illuminate his whole personality and character and I shall have occasion to mention them again. These are all the personal letters which have so far come to light.

We can, however, utilize the letters of others and, in particular, the vast published correspondence of the Electress Sophia with her relatives and with Leibniz. Read with specific questions in respect of George in mind these, as other German and also English correspondence and memoirs,[16] yield more significant results than one might expect.

That George was so circumspect in respect of personal letters was due not only to the lessons taught during the divorce investigations of 1694 (when some letters from Königsmarck to Sophie Dorothea were found in playing-card boxes and behind curtain-hangings),[17] but also to George's desire – after the international scandal of the divorce and the many rumours connected with Königsmarck's disappearance – to avoid gossip about his family life. His mistress of long standing (from some time in the late 1680s or early 90s), Ehrengard Melusine von Schulenburg – who bore him three daughters (in 1692, 1693 and 1701)[18] – went with him to England, where in 1716 she was

---

15. Now deposited in the Niedersächsisches Staatsarchiv, Hanover.

16. E. Bodemann has edited Sophia's letters to the following: her brother (1885); his children (by the Raugräfin Luise von Degenfeld) whom Sophia regarded as her nephews and nieces (1888); to her Oberhofmeisterin A. K. von Harling (1895); and also those from Liselotte to Sophia (2 vols. 1891); Sophia's letters to Liselotte have been lost. O. Klopp has edited the correspondence between Sophia and Leibniz in vols. VII, VIII and IX of *Die Werke von G. W. Leibniz*, 1873 ff. G. Schnath has edited Sophia's correspondence with the Hohenzollern family into which both her daughter and her granddaughter married (1927). A selection from Sophia's correspondence, translated into German, is in Robert Geerds, *Die Mutter der Könige von Preussen und England*, Ebenhausen-Munich and Leipzig, 1913. The most important memoirs on the personal side are those by Bothmer (see note 7 above); by the Countess of Cowper (see note 25 below) and those by Fabrice who became George's Kammerherr in 1719 (see note 19 below).

17. See G. Schnath, "Eleonore von Knesebeck, die Gefangene von Scharzfells," *Ausgewählte Beiträge*, p. 135.

18. Luise Anna (who married Count Delitz) and Petronella Melusine (created Lady Walsingham in the English peerage) who in 1733 married Philip Dormer Stanhope, Lord

created Duchess of Munster in the Irish peerage and in 1719 Duchess of Kendal in the English peerage. So did the two youngest girls (the eldest was already married by 1714), but all three were, as in Hanover, presented to the world as her nieces. They were part of the close family circle, present at supper parties, driving with the King. They appeared with George and their mother at court, at the opera and at concerts, but though we know a good deal about George's concern for them (thanks to a fairly recently published series of letters from Johanne Sophie zu Schaumburg-Lippe, of the Household of the Princess of Wales, who in 1721 became the mother-in-law of George's favourite, "die schöne Gertrud"),[19] no letters either to them or to the Duchess of Kendal from the King have ever been discovered. In the Duchess' case this could be explained by the fact that she was hardly ever parted from George after 1694, but deliberate destruction of letters and documents would seem the more likely explanation if we take into account the more open relationship of George's father Ernst August with his *maîtresse en titre*, the Countess of Platen, wife of his *premier ministre*.

It might be worth mentioning that the daughter of this relationship, the Sophie Charlotte von Platen who married Baron von Kielmansegg, was a half-sister of George I's and acknowledged as such, since in English historiography the Baroness Kielmansegg is usually identified as a mistress of George, the rival of Schulenburg. I dare say you remember the stock picture of George of the older textbooks and biographies: inarticulate, insensitive, boorish, cold and even cruel, of unprepossessing looks, with rapacious and comic mistresses, one tall and thin, the other short and fat – the Giraffe and the Elephant.[20] There is, of course, no

---

Chesterfield, were given out to be the children of Friedrich Achaz von der Schulenburg and his wife Margarethe Gertrud; the youngest, Margarethe Gertrud, was given out to be the daughter of Rabe Christoph von Oeyenhausen and his wife Sophia Juliana von der Schulenburg. She married in 1721 Count Albrecht Wolfgang zu Schaumburg-Lippe with whom she had two sons; she died in 1726.

19. F. W. Schaer, ed., Hanover, 1968. For "die schöne Gertrud" (or "Trudchen") see also *Die Memoiren des Kammerherrn Friedrich Ernst von Fabrice (1683-1750)*, Rudolph Grieser, ed., Hildesheim, 1956, pp. 125 ff.

20. Even Wolfgang Michael, *Englische Geschichte im 18. Jahrh.*, 4 vols., 1895-1937, relied on English memoir material and failed to discover the blood relationship between George I and Kielmansegg.

reason why a half-sister should not be a mistress; but incest was never imputed to George by anyone who came close to the royal circle. Indeed, the veiled hints of a physical relationship between them voiced by a confectioner of the royal household were regarded as scandalous by household officials who found nothing scandalous in the common talk about Schulenburg as George's mistress. They wished the man punished: George – who thought him a good pastry-cook and was fond of his food – just gave him the sack.[21] When Kielmansegg (after her husband's death) was naturalised and created Countess of Darlington in the English peerage it was stressed that she was of the *consanguineam nostram* (of our royal blood).[22] She was a lively and learned lady, a good conversationalist, and much liked at court. From the private accounts of George's – kept by his Turkish-born official Mehemet, a naturalised Hanoverian, a baptised Christian, ennobled as Ludwig Maximilian von Königstreu in 1716 – in the Hanover family archives,[23] I have noted that it was to his half-sister that George entrusted the task of buying presents for his daughter Sophie Dorothea, a task which it might have been indelicate to ask Schulenburg to undertake.

It seems likely that George entered into a morganatic marriage with Schulenburg, though there is no direct evidence of this. It is of little importance whether they were married or not, but the stable relationship with her was clearly beneficial, making George content and giving him balance in his emotional life. Contemporary memoirs and letters depict them as a settled couple, rather like Louis XIV and Maintenon – spending a great deal of time together, where the fact that the mistress was a morganatic wife was accepted even without proof in an inner circle of family and ministers, since she was honoured in the family circle and was present at working sessions between the King and his ministers,

21. Beattie, *op. cit.*, p. 136, note 1.
22. *Briefe des Herzog Ernst August zu Braunschweig-Lüneburg an Johann Franz Friedrich von Wendt aus den Jahren 1703 bis 1726*, Erich Graf Kielsmansegg, ed., Hanover and Leipzig, 1902, pp. 64 ff.
23. I am grateful for permission from Prince Ernst August of Hanover, Herzog zu Braunschweig und Lüneburg, to use these archives, deposited in the Niedersächsisches Staatsarchiv, Hanover.

singly or in small groups.[24] There is a telling remark of Robert Walpole's, noted by Mary Countess of Cowper in her diary for 1720, to the effect that he regarded the Duchess of Kendal "as much Queen of England as ever anyone was."[25] Her ennoblement by the Emperor in 1719 (as Reichsfürstin Eberstein) and her correspondence with the Empress also point in the direction of a morganatic marriage. Of some significance also is the fact that Hanover in 1694 insisted vis-à-vis Celle that there should be a *divorce*, as opposed to a *separation* between George and Sophie Dorothea: in the terms finally agreed upon the former was permitted to marry again, while the latter (as the guilty party who had refused to return to live with her husband in spite of attempts by a court to effect reconciliation) was not.[26]

Since most of Königsmarck's letters to Sophie Dorothea had been returned to him for safer keeping, and none of hers to him had been intercepted, George may have been spared the cruel comments of both on himself. He could not have been blind to her indifference which amounted to dislike: her lady-in-waiting, Eleonore von Knesebeck, in 1694 testified that as early as 1686 Sophie Dorothea had wished to end her marriage to George. The two spouses differed in temperament. George was, moreover, absent on campaign for long periods of time — in 1683, in 1684-5, in 1690-3. It is also possible that he may have contributed to her disappointment either by keeping one or more mistresses from his bachelor days or by taking new ones. Unlike her mother-in-law (who in a similar situation had learned to hide her emotional distress and hurt pride and remain a good wife),[27] Sophie Dorothea felt a passionate need to break out of a loveless marriage. Once she had fallen in love with Königsmarck, she pleaded, unsuccessfully, with her parents to help her obtain a

24. See my *Louis XIV and his World*, pp. 55-57.

25. *Diary of Mary Countess of Cowper 1714-1720*, London, 1864, p. 132 (in index erroneously given as remark by Horatio Walpole).

26. G. Schnath, "Die Prinzessin in Ahlden: Sophie Dorotheas Gefangenschaft 1694-1726," in *Ausgewählte Beiträge*, pp. 174 ff.

27. For George's having a mistress as early as 1676-7 see *Correspondance de la Duchesse Sophia de Hanover avec son frère Charles Louis*, E. Bodemann, ed., Leipzig-Paris, 1886, pp. 177-92; for Sophia's attitude when her husband took a mistress see her *Mémoires*, Adolf Köcher, ed., Leipzig, 1879.

divorce from George. She, as well as Königsmarck, gave vent to hatred and contempt for George in their correspondence. If those letters of his which Sophie Dorothea kept by her in the Leineschloss contained sentences even faintly reminiscent of those which increasingly pepper the bulk of their correspondence — discovered, much later, in Sweden and elsewhere[28] — and if they were shown to George on his return from Berlin, he must indeed have been hurt to the quick.

The last paragraph contains two speculative *ifs* (if the letters contained . . . and if they were shown to George), and I wish now to return to safer ground — but grounds which are not well trodden in English historiography. The estrangement of George I from the Prince of Wales looms large between 1717 and 1720, but is usually interpreted either as a natural antipathy between ruler and heir, or as an attribute of George's (largely unexplained) dislike of his son.[29] Once more, as in the case of George I's careful avoidance of personal correspondence, we need to have recourse to pre-1714 experiences. George was, in a very important sense, doubly the victim of family circumstances. His father, Ernst August, the youngest of four sons, with only the prospect of becoming Prince-Bishop of Osnabrück on the death of the present incumbent, was ambitious. So was his mother, Sophia, the granddaughter of James I who lived at the court of her brother, the Count Palatine, at Heidelberg and had reached the age of 27 without a marriage being contracted for her. She noted frankly in her memoirs that she was anxious to get "well settled" and accepted with some alacrity the offer of Georg Ludwig, Ernst August's elder brother (the second of four sons), who ruled the Calenberg duchy. The marriage contract was already signed when Georg Wilhelm in 1658 changed his mind and entered (to save the family honour) into an agreement with Ernst August that in return

28. See G. Schnath's introduction to *Der Königsmarck-Briefwechsel*, Hildesheim, 1952.
29. Michael, *op. cit.*, II, pp. 49 ff. is the fullest, printing pp. 625-6 Appendix I, from copies in the Vienna Archives, the Prince's letters of 30 Nov. and 1 and 2 Dec. 1717; J. H. Plumb, *Sir Robert Walpole*, I, London, 1956, p. 260 prints for the first time the letter from George to his Vice-Chamberlain (from the Panshanger MSS in the Hertfordshire Record Office) demanding that the Prince of Wales and his wife should ask permission to see their daughters and that visits should be limited to once a week.

for his taking Sophia as a bride, he, Georg Wilhelm, would swear never to marry so that his lands would eventually devolve on Ernst and his male issue — a succession that might, of course, be distant (in the event Georg Wilhelm outlived Ernst August), but seemed safe.[30]

Luck did, to some extent, come the way of the couple. Osnabrück became theirs in 1661 and enabled them to have an independent household (they had at first shared with Georg Wilhelm); the death of the eldest brother (Christian Ludwig) without issue in 1665 gave Georg Ludwig the chance to move to Celle, reckoned more prestigious than the Calenberg duchy, which went to the third brother, Johann Friedrich; and when the latter died in 1679, leaving no sons, Ernst August became ruler of Calenberg. From that time onwards Ernst and Sophia — knowing that by the 1658 arrangement Celle would eventually be united to Calenberg — conceived the idea of creating an Electorate of Brunswick-Lüneburg or, as it was called for short, Hanover. The first step was to have primogeniture introduced in Calenberg and this was done by 1682 (and approved by the Emperor in 1683). Its consequence, however, was a most violent and tragic family quarrel. Sophia had borne her husband six sons and a daughter,[31] and in turn the brothers closest to George in age rebelled against the primogeniture decision since it robbed them of what they considered their rightful share of the family inheritance. Friedrich August in 1684 and Maximilian Wilhelm in 1691 plotted with foreign powers to restore the pre-1682 situation, and Sophia's desperate but vain attempts to reconcile them to Ernst August are mirrored in a selection of 55 letters (published by Anna Wendland in 1937).[32] Both sons were driven into exile and Sophia never saw the elder again. Their lack of prospects at home made some of her sons become Catholics to further their careers in the Imperial

---

30. See my "The Beggarly Electorate," *History of the English Speaking Peoples* 5, (Purnell part publications), pp. 2094 ff.; for fuller treatment see G. Schnath's *Geschichte Hannovers.*

31. Georg Ludwig 1660-1727; Friedrich August 1660-1690; Maximilian Wilhelm 1668-1726 (a male twin was stillborn); Sophie Charlotte 1668-1705; Karl Philip 1669-1690; Christian Heinrich 1671-1703; Ernst Augustus 1674-1728.

32. *Prinzenbriefe zur Primogeniturstreit 1685-1701*, vol. 46 of "Quellen und Darstellungen," Hildesheim, 1937, *passim.*

army (another cause of grief for the Protestant Sophia) and three died in action (two in 1690, one in 1703). After 1703 there was only George and the youngest, Ernst August (b. 1674), left.

Sophia's and Ernst's plans next seemed threatened by Georg Wilhelm. He fell in love with a young French woman, Eleonore d'Olbreuse, and wished to marry her, but under pressure he desisted from a legal union and confirmed the 1658 arrangement. When a daughter, Sophie Dorothea, was born to them, however, he, to improve her social standing, and to ensure that she would inherit his personal estates and fortune, in 1679 obtained Imperial permission to enter into a church marriage with Eleonore. Sophie Dorothea was thus legitimized and became the greatest catch on the North German marriage market. She seemed destined for the elder Brunswick-Wolfenbüttel line (at odds with Ernst, Sophia and their ambitions) and was engaged successively to two sons of Duke Anton Ulrich. To undo this engagement now became for George's parents a complementary aim to that of achieving the Electorate: for if the girl was married to anyone else but George there was a risk that her husband – backed by the rich dowry that came his way – would, on Georg Wilhelm's death, try by force to upset the 1658 agreement. Ruthless pressure on Georg Wilhelm brought his consent to the marriage of George with Sophie Dorothea in 1682 when she was fifteen years old. Two children were born to the young couple, the boy George in 1683 and the daughter Sophie Dorothea in 1687, but – as we have seen – the marriage foundered.

Against the background of the revolts of his brothers, Friedrich August and Maximilian Wilhelm, we can now take a fresh look at the estrangement between George and the Prince of Wales in 1717. As Electoral Prince after 1698 he had caused anxiety to his father and grandmother. Sophia's correspondence with Berlin charts the ups and downs: now he is less rash and truculant; perhaps his service in the War of the Spanish Succession and possibly his marriage (he was permitted to choose his own bride) has improved him; now he gives new cause for worry. George's decision to take him and his wife and daughters to England with him, while leaving their only boy, Friedrich Ludwig, behind in Hanover may well have been prompted by a feeling that he had to keep an eye on his son. Certainly, on George's first return visit to Hanover in 1716 the Prince of Wales' powers within the regency council were circumscribed and he was allowed no influence or patronage. Tension within the royal family and the ministry rose when he managed to build up a Parliamentary following of his own during his father's absence and George I was forced to return to England earlier than planned. The King had welcomed the social life centred round the younger couple at St. James's since it freed him from many duties which he was glad to escape; but the wilful political independence of the Prince — secure in his grant from Parliament — caused the break of 1717. The facts of the quarrel are too well-known to need repetition here except in the barest outline. On the birth of a second son, the Prince wished to nominate godparents of his own choosing; the King insisted, reasonably enough, that he must not offend by excluding the Lord Chamberlain (the Duke of Newcastle) who by English custom had to be one of them; the Prince gave in but vented his anger on the Duke at the christening. The Duke's report that the Prince had threatened him at the ceremony was not maliciously intended; the King's demand that the Prince apologize to the Duke was meant to smooth matters over; but the Prince's refusal led to his expulsion from St. James's, and his insult to the King, in visiting his children without calling on his father — though he was in residence — was a studied one. Yet a significant break could not have occurred but for the Prince's attempt to form an opposition to his father's ministry in Parliament.[33] Phrases in the correspondence between father and son are illuminating. George thunders that "c'est le Monde renversé quand le Fils veut préscrire au Père quel Pouvoir il doit lay donner;" the Prince justifies his actions by (and I quote his very words) "his right as an English subject."[34] The whole Hanoverian family had, as you may remember, been naturalized before the death of Queen Anne.[35]

33. See e.g. George I's letter printed in *Diary of Mary Countess of Cowper*, p. 191: "Je voudrois scavoir quel Droit vous aviez de faire des Messages à la Chambre contre mon Intention"; cp. Beattie, *op. cit.*, pp. 262 ff.

34. The Prince's letter is in the Stanhope (Chevening) papers and I am grateful for permission to quote from them; the quotation from George is in *Diary of Mary Countess of Cowper*, p. 191.

35. It is worth noting that the naturalisation process was after 1714 extended to

This was explosive material, a challenge to the King's power, and reminiscent of the revolts within the family at Hanover. It is clear from George's letters to his daughter in Berlin in 1720 that he resented the fact that the Prince finally submitted to him not of his own initiative, but because Walpole and Townshend forced him to do so;[36] to make this resentment, however, the cause of George's making a will which stipulated the separation of Hanover from England is, in my view, an over-simplification. The will had, as we shall see, much wider roots than a desire − as is usually wrongly assumed − to rob the Prince of Wales of part of his inheritance.

So far I have been concerned to demonstrate that George's youthful experiences influenced his behaviour and reactions as a ruler, and would also seem to have had an effect on his mature personality and his style of life. He was outwardly reserved − English witnesses agree here with his mother, the Electress Sophia, who characterised him in a letter to her granddaughter as "somewhat forbidding." But Sophia went on to explain how deep and real his feelings were, even if he tried to hide them.[37] We know that he could be gay and affectionate in private, though the "spatial distance" between King and subjects which has been so finely analysed by Hugh Murray Baillie as typical of the English court (in contrast to the French where the distance was one of "timing"),[38] naturally limited intimacy to the chosen few in England. Coming to the country as late in middle age as he did (he was 54 in 1714) and without a command of English (it is worth noting that his mother left her English books to the youngest son Ernst August − later created Duke of York − who was of a more

George's closest circle: Schulenburg in 1716, her middle daughter (created Lady Walsingham) in 1722.

36. *E.H.R.* 53, 1937, p. 495, extract of letter of 9 July 1720: "la soumission . . . auroit eue melleieure grace sy elle auroit etté faitte plus tot et sens ettre induit par le party quy sest reconcilié."

37. Sophia's letter to her granddaughter of 16 December, 1706: *Briefwechsel der Kurfürstin Sophie von Hannover mit dem Preussischen, Königshaus,* G. Schnath, ed., Berlin and Leipzig, 1927, p. 105.

38. Hugh Murray Baillie, "Etiquette and the Planning of the State Apartments in Baroque Palaces," *Archeologica* CI, Oxford, 1967, pp. 169-199, especially pp. 175 ff; cp. César de Saussure, *A Foreign View of England in the Reigns of George I and George II,* London 1902, pp. 39 ff.

intellectual bent than George), he naturally found it easier to converse with those in England who spoke French and/or German well whether they were men or women. Some of his pleasantries to women, noted in French by Mary Countess of Cowper from 1714 to 1716, are not as bad as such remarks usually are when read in cold print. With the men he would clearly have most in common with those who knew Europe well and were interested in European problems: Cadogan, Townshend, Stanhope, Sunderland, Carteret.

Here again his Hanoverian heritage played a large part. So much had been sacrificed for the Electoral hat, in terms of family happiness and in terms of money – it has been estimated that it cost 2 million *Thaler* before 1692 and a good deal more in that military expenditure during the Nine Years War which was a *quid-pro-quo* for receiving the Electoral hat.[39] Further investment, in the form of participation on the allied side in the War of the Spanish Succession, was also necessary before formal investiture and admission to the Electoral College of the Diet was obtained. George, who had happily accompanied his father in the field at the age of fifteen, and had soon proved himself a brave officer, learnt to become a reluctant and wily commander – now threatening to withdraw his troops, now being more forward till these objectives had been gained by 1708. Shrewdness, reluctance to squander the resources of the Electorate, intense persistence in achieving foreign policy goals with skill and guile amounting to downright deceit, remains typical of George for the rest of his life as Elector and as King. The chief Hanoverian objective between 1710 and 1720 was the absorption of the duchies of Bremen and Verden: not first and foremost because they would add to the resources of the Electorate (though they did),[40] but to deny them to Denmark which had conquered the Bremen duchy in 1710 and thus provoked the counter-occupation by Hanover in 1712 of Verden – nominally on behalf of Hanover's old ally Sweden.

After the Swedish defeat at Poltava (1709), Charles XII's enemies multiplied. Not only did Denmark-Norway and Augustus

---

39. See G. Schnath, *Geschichte Hannovers*, pp. 650 ff.
40. This is clear from an examination of the accounts of state kept in the Niedersächsisches Staatsarchiv, Hanover.

of Saxony-Poland renew their alliance with Russia, but Prussia and Hanover — freer in the West now that the War of the Spanish Succession was coming to an end — decided to claim their share if the Swedish possessions in the Empire were to be redistributed.[41] The Emperor hoped to gain Wismar, but was diverted by a war with Turkey which left the North German princes freer. On its own Hanover could never have got the terms George wanted from the enlarged anti-Swedish coalition. He could play for high stakes after he became George I in the summer of 1714 because of a trump card: the British navy could be sent to the Baltic, positioned so as to help Sweden's enemies greatly, though not as openly or directly as individual allies might desire or be led to believe would happen.

The cost to Britain was large.[42] To stress these incontestible facts is not to make common cause with the contemporary opposition in Parliament which argued that British resources were squandered for the sake of Hanover. There were important British interests involved in conveying trade safely to those Russian-held Baltic ports of the Swedish empire which Charles XII had declared strictly blockaded in 1715: and British fears that Sweden might help the cause of the Pretender (having a good excuse since George as Elector had formally declared war on Charles in 1715 as soon as Denmark had let the duchy of Bremen be occupied by Hanoverian troops) were genuine. And when in the end the settlement was made with Sweden in 1719, the price for a promise of naval help against Russia was not only Bremen and Verden for Hanover but trade advantages for Britain. The very size of the squadrons, the extra cost of the sailors not being paid off in the winter (that the ships might be got ready all the sooner for the next season), the Hanoverians' insistence to allies that trade protection was a "mere pretext" for the use of the British navy in the interests of the anti-Swedish coalition, the skilful exploitation of any Swedish contact with the Jacobites even when it was known to ministers that Charles XII refused to take up the cause of the Pretender, the propaganda which showed the advantages which would accrue to

41. See my *Charles XII*, p. 369 ff.
42. See for the sums involved James Postlethwayt, *The History of the Public Revenue*, London 1759, pp. 100 ff.

Britain from Hanover's possession of Bremen and Verden — all this must be given some weight. It may justify a conclusion that the balance of interests was weighted on the Hanoverian side before 1719 and on the British side in the 1723-27 period when fears of the Emperor Charles VI's upsetting the European balance of power (becoming an "exorbitant state" through his advantageous treaty with Spain) moved the ministry as much as the anti-Spanish majority in Parliament, where fear was endemic that Philip V would cheat Britain out of the advantages gained by the Peace of Utrecht. The Hanover alliance of 1725 — as Gibbs has shown — put Hanover at risk for Britain's sake.

In many ways George I (as William III before him) became British — if not in accent — then outlook. The very resources of their British kingdom enabled George, as William, to play greater roles as European rulers. In the process both learnt to take care of British interests and susceptibilities. (I have been pondering, apropos accents, whether George did not learn to speak some English as well as to understand some: it seems significant to me that the Countess of Cowper who in 1714-17 always quotes George in French, in 1720 quotes him in English with a grammatical error which precludes her having translated his remark on the Townshend-Walpole split, "What did they go away for? It was their own Faults."[43]

There is, of course, contrast in the roles the two foreign-born kings sought to play due to the changed European circumstances. William was a war leader (as well as a skilled diplomat). George was a ruler whose chief aim was to avoid war and to wage it more by diplomacy than by military action if the declaration of war became necessary. William spoke of the "indivisibility of the peace," but he could not forget 1672 and meant that if France could not be stopped by moral solidarity, then war would have to be waged energetically by Grand Alliances united against Louis XIV. George was in his turn the product of his own generation — a generation that had had enough of large-scale war — and took his clue from the old Louis (that is the post-1697 Louis) in supporting attempts to solve European problems before they led to war.

43. *Diary*, p. 146.

Compromise was necessary; advantages all around and sacrifices all around in order to maintain a European balance. He allied with France in 1716 and backed Stanhope against Bernstorff in 1718-19. The latter was forced to drop his anti-Prussian stance to facilitate the "Peace Plan of the North,"[44] which had as its aim the disgorging by Russia of some of her Baltic conquests. For the same reason George accepted the French demand that Sweden be permitted to retain a foothold in the Empire. These were sacrifices of purely Hanoverian objectives: Bernstorff looked upon Prussia as a dangerous future exorbitant which would swallow Hanover, and all the North German states wished to throw Sweden out of the Empire lock, stock and barrel. Similarly George (and Stanhope) would have been willing, for the sake of the "Peace Plan of the South"[45] being adopted without recourse to arms, to sacrifice Gibraltar: Minorca was to them a sufficient base in the Mediterranean. But for Parliament Gibraltar was non-negotiable, and luck was with George and Stanhope that Philip V had to be coerced by Britain and France into the Quadruple Alliance. Once force (even minimum force) had been used they were able to hide behind the formula "provided Parliament agrees."[46]

The Peace Plan of the North was only partially successful. Russia had by joint Anglo-Hanoverian diplomatic efforts been driven out of the Empire by the summer of 1717. Tsar Peter gave up his pet project of making Mecklenburg a client state, one that via a canal would make it possible for Russian ships to bypass the Sound and go straight into the North Sea. But in the unsettled period of the South Sea Bubble crash in England and Law's crash in France there was not enough energy to spare from home affairs in George's British ministry to force Russia to return to Sweden any part of her former East Baltic provinces.

The Peace Plan of the South was on the whole successful, and established the important principle of congresses to be held to find solutions to European problems before they led to war: all

44. For this plan see my *Charles XII*, pp. 511 ff. and my *War and Peace 1680-1720*, London, 1969, p. 22.

45. *Ibid.*, pp. 21 ff. and see my *Diplomatic Relations between Great Britain and the Dutch Republic*, pp. 159 ff.

46. See my *War and Peace 1680-1720*, p. 21, note 57; and Stetson Conn, *Gibraltar in British Diplomacy*, New Haven, 1942, pp. 31 ff.

signatories of the Quadruple Alliance bound themselves to submit their differences to such congresses. That of Cambrai met from 1722 to 1725 and — once the show of strength of the Hanover alliance and the skill of Fleury's diplomacy had dissipated the danger of war 1725-1726 — that of Soissons was arranged before George's death. Most books of the period regard these two congresses as "useless," but in my view they served to ventilate problems and to make it easier to come to terms even when limited wars did break out (as over the Polish succession in 1733).[47] It should be noted that they were European congresses since not only the signatories of the Quadruple Alliances attended: any ruler or state who wished, could participate.

In all this George showed himself in tune with the rationalist spirit of the age. He was not an intellectual and did not read widely, but he learned by talking and by discussion: his mother writes to Leibniz, in 1710, recapitulating with some pride George's argument in a dispute about philosophy with the famous Molanus. And it was with some delight (I must admit) that in one of the letters to his mother, which I came across in the Hanover archives, I found George well aware of the battle between ancients and moderns, ranging himself firmly on the side of the moderns. His tone is slightly teasing with echoes of past conversations. More seriously, it is typical of him that he refused, as had William, to touch for the King's evil, though Queen Anne had done so.

George's rationalism is also evident in his soon becoming convinced that it would be best for Britain and Hanover to part. The price of the dynastic union was high: tension between British and German ministers at times; Hanoverian families being split and not sure whether they wanted to settle in England for good; the inconvenience attendant on his own absences in Hanover with their danger of producing feuds and factions among British advisers; the conviction that Hanover risked becoming a mere dependency, a province. He realized that a dissolution of the dynastic union would necessitate consent by Parliament and by the Emperor and he did not visualize the separation coming until

47. See my *War and Peace 1680-1720*, pp. 22 ff. and my *Europe in the Age of Louis XIV*, pp. 208-209.

the 4th generation. He had no wish to interfere with the rights of anyone living, neither his son the Prince of Wales nor his elder grandson Friedrich Ludwig must suffer. In his will he laid down that if Frederick (who was 20 at the time of his grandfather's death, but not yet married) should have more than one son, the elder should become King of Britain and the second Elector of Hanover. If he had only one son (sufficient for Britain but not for Hanover), Hanover should go to the Wolfenbüttel cousins. A copy of the will was left with the Wolfenbüttel Duke, another with the Archbishop of Canterbury, a third with the grandson Frederick. In the event Frederick had four sons, but as his father George II suppressed the will (and Frederick himself died before his father), he had no chance to follow George I's lead. Frederick admired his grandfather tremendously ("the kindest man, a good and great king," he said of him), and in the instructions he left for his elder son he urged the adoption of George I's will.

Few would share Frederick's total admiration for George I. Nor can we take seriously the panegyric of court odes.[48] The older biographies – by Melville[49] and Imbert Terry[50] – were written long before modern research illuminated the period. Anyone who works on the reign in depth will learn, however, to respect George's toleration, his concern for the *via media*, for moderation and for rational solutions. It is noticeable that Wolfgang Michael – who worked mainly from English source material – in his volume I of 1895 of the *Englische Geschichte in 18. Jahrhundert* painted an unsympathetic picture of George and that his summing up in volume III, published in 1934, is more positive, stressing George's concern for Britain's welfare, for justice and the law.[51] Schnath admits that George was able (*tüchtig*), but finds him cold and selfish.[52] Perhaps what our generation of historians might add is a touch of sympathy as well as respect.

R. M. Hatton

48. For these see Rosamond McGuiness, *English Court Odes 1680-1820*, Oxford, 1971, pp. 148 ff.

49. Lewis Melville, *The First George in Hanover and England*, 2 vols., London, 1908.

50. H. M. Imbert Terry, *A Constitutional King, George the First*, London, 1927.

51. Compare Michael, I, 1895, and sec. ed., unchanged, 1921, pp. 408 ff. and III, pp. 501-09.

52. G. Schnath, *Geschichte Hannovers*, pp. 156 ff.

Archdeacon William Coxe (1747-1828)

Archdeacon William Coxe
as Political Biographer

No other English political biographer of the eighteenth century has been so unjustly underestimated as has Archdeacon William Coxe (1747-1828). Contemporaries and later generations have had but little praise for either him or his works. Jeremy Bentham recorded one of the milder verdicts when he declared in a letter to his brother, Samuel Bentham, that:

His subjects and materials are highly interesting: but he is but a so so writer.[1]

Bentham's correspondent pronounced, however, the more common view of him. He declared that he was viewed as a great bore who spent most of his time asking "unconnected and frivolous questions."[2] Archdeacon Coxe's love of pedantry and technical knowledge, in an age which abhorred it, led one rhymester to pen these lines about him:

In a club of choice chaps, says one Joseph Knox
Who of peers was not economical,
Since you're greeted by all as comical Cox,
'Tis plain that you must be Cox-comical.[3]

This unfavourable view was echoed in the nineteenth century. G. P. Gooch in his *History and Historians in the Nineteenth Century* claimed that the sole value of his works was that they provided a "quarry from which abler men would draw."[4] And in this century

---

1. J. H. Burns, ed., *The Collected Works of Jeremy Bentham*, London, 1968. *Correspondence*, II, p. 513.

2. *Ibid.*, p. 513.

3. Lines penned in the frontispiece of Coxe's *Account of the Russian Discoveries Between Asia and America*, London, 1787, found in the copy in the National Library, Ottawa.

4. G. P. Gooch, *History and HIstorians in the Nineteenth Century*, 1959, p. 288. For a favourable view of Archdeacon Coxe and his works see the long essay by John Adolphus in the *Quarterly Review*, October 1833, pp. 88-121.

T. P. Peardon expressed a like assessment.[5] Not until some sixteen years ago did he receive his first strong advocate when Mark Thomson in his inaugural lecture at University College, London, pointed out that not only was Coxe a most distinguished biographer but that:

> more of the accepted version of English history in the first half of the eighteenth century goes back to Coxe, and is buttressed by documents he published, than is always realized.[6]

His reference was to his four main political biographies. The first of these, *The Life and Administration of Robert Walpole, Earl of Orford*, was published in 1789, the year of the fall of the Bastille. In 1802 his *Memoirs of Horatio, Lord Walpole* was published and it was not until seventeen years later, the year of the Peterloo Massacre, that his *Memoirs of the Duke of Marlborough* was offered for sale. In 1829, the year of Catholic Emancipation, there appeared posthumously his *Memoirs of the Pelham Administration*. Although these are not his only biographical works[7] they have been selected as the basis for providing a re-evaluation of his particular contribution to the writing of historical biography.

Before turning to his writings, what may we say of the biographer himself, for E. H. Carr's injunction to "study the historian before you begin to study the facts" applies equally to the historian as biographer.[8] The task is not an easy one in the case of Archdeacon Coxe. His own manuscripts, although carefully preserved in the British Museum, contain but little reference to him as a personality and are largely his research notes, first drafts etc., for his various histories and biographies. Although little survives of his own personal correspondence certain facets of both his career and personality may be established.

Born in 1747 as the son of a London physician he listed

5. T. P. Peardon, *The Transition in English Historical Writing, 1760 – 1830,* New York, 1933, p. 193.
6. M. A. Thomson, *Some Developments in English Historiography During the Eighteenth Century,* London, 1957, p. 15.
7. He also wrote: *Literary Life and Select Works of Benjamin Stillingfleet,* 1811, and *Private and Original Correspondence of Charles Talbot, Duke of Shrewsbury,* 1821.
8. E. H. Carr, *What is History?,* Penguin, 1964, p. 23.

among his contemporaries Edward Gibbon, Josiah Wedgewood, Fanny Burney, James Boswell and Joseph Priestly. His earliest years were spent in that great metropolitan centre of London that was in these years experiencing one of the most profound series of social and economic changes since the middle ages. It was not until the mid-1750s that he left his father's house in Piccadilly and the Marleybone grammar school to begin that process of education that was to take him from Eton to King's College, Cambridge, and to his election as a fellow of that college in 1768. From this point, until his death in 1829, he had three main preoccupations: church preferment, travel and writing.

Under the patronage of Lord Pembroke he received two of his main preferments. In 1788 he became rector of Bemerton and in 1811 rector of Fovant, both in Wiltshire. In addition, on the recommendation of Sir Richard Colt Hoare, he received the rectorship of Stourton and since 1791 he had been prebend of Salisbury. In 1804 he was appointed by Bishop Douglas to the highest office he was to hold in his lifetime — the Archdeaconry of Wiltshire.

Association with members of the upper class did not only bring him church preferment, however, for it was his cultivation of two of them, the Duke of Marlborough and Lord Pembroke, that led to his involvement in a good deal of foreign travel. Each of them asked him, in due course, to accompany their sons on the Grand Tour as their tutor. These travels took him to Switzerland, Poland, France, Russia, Sweden and Denmark. His observations were duly recorded and published upon his return. So closely identified was he with travel that he became known to a host of his friends as "the travelling Archdeacon." Foreign travel did not, however, have a broadening impact upon him. Quite the reverse. It served only to bring to the surface his strong anti-French, anti-Dutch, and anti-German prejudices. These were well articulated in his monthly letters to Lord Herbert on his son's progress. From France he wrote:

I am not at all surprised, that his Lordship is not over-whelmed to like the French. . . . He sees at once that all their compliments mean nothing, and that when they seem your greatest friends, they care little about you.[9]

And from Holland he wrote:

I cannot say I should like to be an inhabitant of Holland; the inhabitants have mostly a sallow look, and both men and women in general very bad teeth, which I should think a proof of their unhealthiness.[10]

So, too, with Germany. While in this latter country he had been persuaded to participate in German folk dances. Even though he admitted that he was very awkward and "danced like a cat upon hot irons" it mattered but little for he would have no use for that sort of thing when he returned.[11] Foreign travel served but to cement ever more firmly Archdeacon Coxe's conviction that everything that was English was superior. He wrote Lord Herbert:

I would always wish his Lordship to retain his attachment to Old England, and when he returns to be altogether an Englishman. He sees plainly the superiority of our government and of our religion; and as I am an enthusiast for the love of my country, I shall endeavour to cultivate rather than extinguish this rational, as I may call it, amiable affection, which he has for England.[12]

It was this overpowering nationalistic bias, reinforced by foreign travel, that was to be so strongly reflected in his writings. This bias was undoubtedly one of the contributing factors that led him to write a biography of Marlborough, for in the preface to that life he lamented the fact that "as an Englishman ... no biographical monument had been raised to the memory of so great a general and statesman."[13]

In his political beliefs the Archdeacon was a staunch Whig partisan and as testimony to this he has left a superb document. The sermon preached by the Reverend Richard Price, the dissenting minister, at the Old Jewry in 1789 brought as a direct

9. Lord Herbert, ed., *The Pembroke Papers 1734-1780. Letters and Diaries of Henry, Tenth Earl of Pembroke and His Circle*, London, 1939, p. 66.

10. *Ibid.*, p. 104.

11. *Ibid.*, p. 67.

12. *Ibid.*, p. 66.

13. Coxe, *Memoirs of the Duke of Marlborough*, London, 1893, p. ix.

response more than Edmund Burke's *Reflections on the Revolution in France*. In addition Dr. Price was pilloried in a forty-six page published letter by Archdeacon Coxe.[14] He expressed their opposing views of the Revolution of 1688 in this vein. "What I had long considered as a most glorious work, you look upon as imperfect; what I held to be a free constitution, you estimate as little better than slavery."[15] Rather than attacking in any way the present civil and religious establishment Coxe speaks of it with the utmost of reverence:

> Feeling, as I do, these inestimable blessings of a free constitution, I look back, almost with adoration, to the character of William the Third, our great deliverer, and recollect with enthusiasm, the memory of those among our forefathers, who assisted in establishing that revolution, which rescued us from arbitrary power, reduced within proper limits the prerogatives of the crown, and established on the firmest basis the rights of the people. No language can be too warm. no expressions too strong, no panegyric too animated, in commemorating that glorious era.[16]

Archdeacon Coxe supported wholeheartedly William Paley's view of the constitution as one shaped by "occasion and emergency" and in form resembling that of:

> those old mansions, which, instead of being built all at once, after a regular plan, and according to the rules of architecture at present established, has been reared in different ages of the art, has been altered from time to time, and has been continually receiving alterations and repairs, suited to the taste, fortune or conveniency of its successive proprietors.[17]

Quite unlike Price, who had expressed a strong approbation for what was happening in France, Coxe had nothing but contempt. He was convinced that the national assembly was "undermining, overturning, or annihilating the whole of the civil and ecclesiastical

14. Coxe, *A Letter to the Reverend Richard Price*, London, 1790.
15. *Ibid.*, p. 6.
16. *Ibid.*, p. 5.
17. William Paley, *The Principles of Moral and Political Philosophy*, II, London, 1824, p. 325.

polity." The result could only be anarchy. On this note he concluded his letter:

> I am bold to avow, that the English constitution is of all others, that, in which the true principles of liberty are best understood and practised, and that I have visited no country, in which persons of all ranks and denominations possess such solid comforts, such real and substantial happiness.[18]

A profound respect, approaching reverence and awe, for the British constitution, a deep admiration for the values of mixed government, an unbridled enthusiasm for the accomplishments of the revolution of 1688 — these attributes well qualify Coxe as one of the foremost exponents of Whig political values. These, together with his strong nationalistic bias and his favoured position within the state church, are central elements in explaining why he singled out for full-scale biographical treatment four of the leading Whig politicians of the eighteenth century — Robert Walpole, Horatio Walpole, the Duke of Marlborough and Henry Pelham.

These latter features do not explain fully, however, his choice of individuals. His view of what constituted the subject matter of history does. Historical content for Archdeacon Coxe was politics, international diplomacy and war. In each of these specific areas a great man controlled and shaped events. As he wrote in the preface to one of his histories:

> Unfortunately for man, it is the sword which decides the fate of nations, secures their tranquility, and promotes their aggrandisement; — it is the sword alone which is the guardian of national honour, and the protector of public and private happiness. Commerce may enrich, the arts may civilise, science may illuminate a people; but these blessings can only owe their safety and stability to military force. War, therefore, to the regret of every milder virtue, must form the principal subject of history.[19]

Robert Walpole and Henry Pelham became, therefore, the outstanding examples of the great man in politics; Horatio Walpole his

---

18. Coxe, *Letter to the Reverend Richard Price*, p. 45.
19. Coxe, *History of the House of Austria*, London, 1877, p. v.

choice of the great man in diplomacy; the Duke of Marlborough the leading example of the great man in war. His view of history and all of his strong personal prejudices are blatantly trumpeted in this passage from his life of Marlborough:

> More than any individual, [he] contributed to consolidate the great work of the Revolution, to baffle the hopes and machinations of the Stuarts and their adherents, and to smite that great colossus of power, which threatened the destruction of civil and religious liberty, and on which they placed their hopes of effecting a counter-revolution.[20]

His view of the great man theory of history is well expressed in his account of the South Sea Bubble disaster and of Robert Walpole's part in it. Of his role he wrote:

> When the public distress was arrived to a most alarming height, and despair pervaded all ranks of people, to Walpole every eye was directed, as the only person capable of affording assistance, under the pressure of immediate necessity.[21]

He further adds:

> Fortunately, in this moment of suspense and agitation, the public voice called forth Walpole, as the only man calculated to save the nation from impending destruction.[22]

Yet another feature that pervades Coxe's political biographies and tends to make his character portrayals one dimensional is his strong belief in what one writer has called the eighteenth century biographer's conviction that a man's career was dominated by a single "ruling passion."[23] For Archdeacon Coxe that single unifying force within that shaped the whole of Robert Walpole's career was the desire for peace. He expressed it in this way:

> The portrait of a Minister is to be traced from the history of

20. Coxe, *Marlborough*, I, p. 76.
21. Coxe, *Memoirs of the Life and Administration of Robert Walpole*, I, London, 1798, p. 135.
22. *Ibid.*, p. 138.
23. Donald A. Stauffer, *The Art of Biography in Eighteenth Century England*, Princeton, 1941, p. 323.

his whole administration. Candour therefore requires that we should not judge by the selection of detached parts, but combine the whole in a connective series, and referring his conduct to one grand principle of action, judge of it as critics do of an epic poem, by comprehending, in one point of view, the beginning, the middle, and the end.

Did the administration of Walpole present any uniform principle, which may be traced in every part, and gave combination and consistency to the whole? — Yes. — And that principle was THE LOVE OF PEACE.[24]

Such are the obvious limitations of Archdeacon William Coxe's political biographies. The real significance of his contribution to the writing of historical biography lies, however, in an examination of what constituted for him the aims and the method of historical biography.

The prime objective of the historian as biographer was the absolute necessity for him to establish the accuracy of his information. Neither eulogy, invective, anecdote or hearsay were to be given positions of any significance. Nor was carelessness or slipshod research to be tolerated. The sole object of the biographer must be the establishment of historical fact. In delineating the character of Marlborough he made it clear that he had:

> endeavoured to avoid an error, too common with biographers, who often hold forth the subject of their memoirs as a perfect being, like a hero of a romance, without frailty or blemish.[25]

How could this best be achieved? In the first instance the biographer must avoid the errors of others who had relied solely on accounts of those opposed to the individuals he had singled out for full-scale biographical treatment. In his particular case he was convinced that far too many writers had been "dazzled by the eloquence of Pulteney, seduced by the sophistry of Bolingbroke, or deluded by the speciousness of Chesterfield."[26] Accounts by contemporary writers and observers, of whatever political persua-

24. Coxe, *Walpole*, I, p. 744.
25. Coxe, *Marlborough*, I, p. x.
26. Coxe, *Walpole*, I, p. xviii.

sion, must be weighed carefully. In the preface to his life of Walpole he states that he has been most anxious to avoid yet another error of biographers; namely, "that of considering only one side of the question."[27] Therefore, he saw it as absolutely essential for the biographer to procure the papers of those who opposed as well as those who supported the administration and from a "scrupulous comparison of both to extract the truth."[28] And not only must contemporary accounts be used with caution but the works of other historians must be regarded with equal suspicion. The works of Tobias Smollett and Henry Belsham he singled out for special attack, for as Tory partisans he saw them as in no way sympathetic to Whig administrators. They had, he said, "stigmatized the whole administration of Robert Walpole as a uniform mass of corruption and depravity." Tindal's continuation of Rapin de Thoyras' *History of England* he saw as a much more balanced account. Although Dr. Birch had written a large part of it and was, like the Archdeacon, a staunch Whig, Coxe was convinced that political convictions had not seriously — as in the case of Smollett and Belsham — allowed him to forget his duty as an historian. "He has not garbled or falsified debates, or mis-stated facts," declared Coxe.[29]

An essential part of Coxe's method involved the collection of as much data as possible about his subject. In this respect he surpassed all previous political biographers both in the range and the quality of the materials he consulted. After carefully working his way through all the published materials — journals, newspapers, pamphlets, parliamentary debates, etc. — he then turned to the exhaustive and time consuming examination of as many private collections of papers as he could gain access to. Coxe is the first of the English political biographers to make extensive use of private manuscript collections. Especially important to him were the subject's own letters, for these, he felt, would reveal his true character and motives in a way that nothing else could, since they were "neither expected nor intended to meet the public eye."[30]

27. *Ibid.*, p. xvii.
28. *Ibid.*, p. xx.
29. *Ibid.*, p. xix.
30. Coxe, *Marlborough*, I, p. x.

For his life of Walpole he read and took transcripts of several thousand items. In all, some twenty-one private manuscript collections were carefully worked through, among them those of Horatio Walpole, the Earl of Orford, the Countess Waldegrave, the Earl of Harrington, Lord Onslow and Lord Middleton. Often weary to the point of exhaustion he turned the task of copying correspondence over to one of his trusted amanuenses. The information gleaned from the written record was supplemented by oral interviews with individuals either closely or directly involved in the events he wrote about, or the descendants of those individuals. Also he called on the specialized knowledge of others wherever he felt it necessary to do so. For his life of Marlborough, for example, he drew heavily on the knowledge of Major Charles Hamilton Smith for all aspects of military operations.[31] His boundless energy and drive for accuracy of detail often enabled him to recreate an historical situation of considerable vividness. He has, for example, left us this account of the death of George I:

> The king eat some melons after supper, which probably caused the indigestion of which he died. He returned that evening to Delden, and set out early the next morning, after having breakfasted on a cup of hot chocolate. On his arrival at Bentheim, the king felt himself indisposed, but continued his journey in opposition to the repeated entreaties of his suite. His indisposition increased, and when he arrived at Ippenburen, he was quite lethargic; his hand fell down as lifeless, and his tongue hung out of his mouth. He gave, however, signs of life, by continually crying out, as well as he could articulate, Osnabrug, Osnabrug. . . . But it was too late. The exact time and place of his death cannot be ascertained; but it is most probable, that he expired as the carriage was ascending the hill near Ippenburen, or on the summit.[32]

In the case of his life of Walpole the end product was three large quarto volumes running to well over two thousand pages of close

---

31. Coxe, *Marlborough*, I, p. xiv. According to the account in the *Dictionary of National Biography* XVIII, p. 433, Charles Hamilton Smith (1776-1859) "wrote the military part of Coxe's 'Life of the Duke of Marlborough,' and the plans of the battles and campaigns were mainly under his inspection."

32. Coxe, *Walpole*, I, p. 266.

print. The first volume comprised the life study and the last two the supporting documentation. Such a luxury was not allowed him, however, when he came to write his life of Horatio Walpole for, as he himself admitted, there would not have been sufficient sales to warrant the expense of putting forth such an effort. Besides this he saw the latter biography of nearly five hundred pages as but a "companion and supplement" to his life of Robert Walpole.

It must be pointed out that Coxe's use of private manuscript collections did not always allow him the degree of freedom he might have wished. Like all biographers, whether of the eighteenth or the twentieth century, he was faced with the question of how much should the biographer tell?[33] Because he had been allowed access to so many private collections of papers Archdeacon Coxe felt he had a moral duty to their owners. That consisted of an obligation to report as favourably on his subject as possible. This conviction of his is well substantiated by one of Coxe's contemporaries, Thomas Somerville, the Scottish historian.[34] Coxe had allowed him to use transcripts of his taken from private collections but with the proviso that it would be "gratifying to the proprietors if he could see his way clear to justify the Whig ministry for rejecting the terms of the peace proposed by Louis XIV in 1707-9." Somerville could not do so from his reading of the documents and therefore was not allowed to print his version, since Coxe felt "it would be indelicate and offensive to criminate them upon evidence furnished by themselves." He also knew full well that an unfavourable account might well deny him access to other collections.

To aim for objectivity, to strive to overcome one's own political bias, to report only true facts, to maintain what he called "a manly intergrity" and a "candid temperance" — these were, in Archdeacon Coxe's view, the main aims of the biographer. He is the first of the eighteenth century English historians to demand

33. For a discussion of this problem see: James L. Clifford, "How Much Should the Biographer Tell?" in *Essays in Eighteenth Century Biography*, P. B. Daghlian, ed., Bloomington, 1968.
34. Thomas Somerville, *My Own Life and Times 1741-1814*, Edingurgh, 1861, p. 289.

that the standards set by the enlightenment historians in the matter of method and approach should also be the prime prerequisites for the historian as biographer.[35] Literary style (which he lacked in abundance) was to be no substitute for accuracy and detailed research. His injunction that this object could best be achieved through the wide use of and careful scrutiny of manuscript materials marks a significant departure in the writing of political biography. Those biographies that predate Coxe's are of quite a different character. Almost all are eulogies, are largely undocumented and are highly praiseworthy of their subject. They read more as fiction than as fact and the reader ploughs through page after page of the most empty-sounding passages about the biographer's subject. A few examples will illustrate this. The biographer William Hamilton writing of his subject James Bonnell at the beginning of the century declared:

> Equal to his Justice was his Charity, which like that of Heaven, Rejoic'd in doing Good to All. He had a true Concern for the Souls of Men; He Contemplated, so constantly, the amazing Love of our Saviour to Mankind, with his Bitter Sufferings to Redeem their Souls; that he was Acted, with some Degree of his Infinite Love, and Burn'd with his Heavenly Flame.[36]

Or, Robert Nelson in his life of Dr. George Bull wrote:

> I think it may be fairly inferred from his early Dedication of himself to the Service of the Altar, in a Time when Rebellion and Sacrilege rid Triumphant, that in his Youth and Flower of his Days, he had a true Relish for Piety, and a Zeal for the Salvation of Souls.[37]

Robert Campbell in his *Life of the Duke of Argyle* published in 1745 wrote:

---

35. R. N. Stromberg, "History in the Eighteenth Century," *Journal of the History of Ideas*, 1951, pp. 297, 299; J. H. Brumfitt, *Voltaire. Historian*, Oxford, 1958, pp. 95 ff.

36. William Hamilton, *The Life and Character of James Bonnell, Esq., Late Accountant General of Ireland*, London, 1707, pp. 212-13.

37. Robert Nelson, *The Life of Dr. George Bull, late Lord Bishop of St. David's*, London, 1714, p. 27.

Were it possible for us to represent that great Man really as he was, in this venal Age, the Relation would appear a Romance; that steady Attachment to the Interest of his Country, in the worst of Times; the uniform Zeal he express'd for the Honour and Liberty of these Nations, . . . , and his unwearied Endeavours to promote the Good of the people, directed by the most consumate Wisdom, and temper'd by the most unshaken Loyalty to his Sovereign; are Virtues so uncommon, they rather seem what we would wish, than what existed in real Life: . . .; At such a Period of Time, amidst such a Torrent of Corruption and Barefaced Veniality, such a Character as That of the late Duke of Argyle must appear fictitious.[38]

The same hollowness and the same fictitious qualities characterize the bulk of English political biographies in these years. As has been already demonstrated such was not the character of those written by Archdeacon William Coxe. The nature of the bias that permeates his biographies prevents them from falling within that category that Harold Nicolson, in his outline of *The Development of English Biography*, entitled "pure biography."[39] The techniques he followed and the standards he set well qualify the Archdeacon, however, for the position of the first of the "modern" English political biographers.

P. *Fritz*

---

38. Campbell, *Life of the Duke of Argyle*, London, 1745, p. 2.
39. Harold Nicolson, *The Development of English Biography*, London, 1968, Chapter 1.

Boswell:
The Cautious Empiricist

Boswell learned much of his art as a biographer from Johnson; he often acknowledged his indebtedness, most conspicuously at the beginning of his *Life of Johnson* by quoting an extended passage from *Rambler* no. 60, which deals with the subject. Johnson, who loved the "biographical part of literature" best, was not only an assiduous practitioner of that art but also a critical theorist who steered its development into new channels more congenial to eighteenth-century thought. Among other good advice, he urged Boswell to collect anecdotes, by which he meant tid-bits of unpublished "secret history," as he defined the word in his *Dictionary*.[1] He was stressing the basic principle of eighteenth-century empiricism that valid general statements may be founded only on masses of verifiable facts. Boswell took him at his word. His book is massive, and it is crammed with facts – names, dates, letters, the conversations of Johnson and his associates, and narratives, all checked and double checked, the process itself of checking often being traced in either the text or the footnotes. As he wrote in the "Advertisement," his *Life* "consists of innumerable detached particulars, all which, even the most minute, I have spared no pains to ascertain with a scrupulous authenticity."[2] He faithfully built his biographical structure out of the best bricks of empirical fact.

Nevertheless Johnson was of two minds about biography. Though he never ceased writing it, he often spoke of the difficulty of doing it properly, especially of the difficulty of collecting

1. He disliked using the word to mean insignificant particulars, as in French, though he added such a sense in the fourth edition of the *Dictionary*. Cf: *Letters of James Boswell*, C. B. Tinker, ed., Oxford, 1924, p. 382.
2. All citations of Boswell are to *Boswell's Life of Johnson*, George Birkbeck Hill and L. F. Powell, eds., Oxford, 6 volumes, 1934-50, cited as *Life*. This quotation is from *Life* I, pp. 6-7.

anecdotes. There were two problems: few people remembered anecdotes about their friends and acquaintances, and those they did produce were often fabulous. His own experience had led him to that conclusion. Early in his life he had thought of writing a biography of Dryden and had sent Samuel Derrick to gather materials for it from Dryden's relations. But he gave the project up when he saw how inadequate the materials were. "It was nothing," he said.[3] All his life he kept commenting on the amount of falsehood there was in circulation in the world, and on the willingness of people to believe and to repeat marvels whose falsity should have been apparent to them. He warned Mrs. Thrale about it particularly, knowing how fond that lively lady was of repeating gossip.[4] His works are full of similar comments. Boswell quoted the following one from an essay in the *Literary Magazine* in 1756:

> Nothing but experience could evince the frequency of false information, or enable any man to conceive that so many groundless reports should be propagated, as every man of eminence may hear of himself. Some men relate what they think, as what they know; some men of confused memories and habitual inaccuracy, ascribe to one man what belongs to another; and some talk on, without thought or care. A few men are sufficient to broach falsehoods, which are afterwards innocently diffused by successive relaters.[5]

Similar remarks occur in Johnson's lives of Congreve, Cowley, and Pope. The implication for the biographer is serious and obvious. He must be sceptical. As early as 1742 Johnson wrote: "distrust is a necessary qualification of a student in history. Distrust quickens his discernment of different degrees of probability, animates his search after evidence, and, perhaps heightens his pleasure at the discovery of truth."[6] Johnson's scepticism was so intense that it cast a shadow over the very possibility of reliable biography.

Though he continued to write biographies, his scepticism made him often prefer autobiography. I have commented previously on his own half-hearted pursuit of anecdotes, first in a paper published many years ago entitled "Johnson and the Art of Anecdote,"[7] and again in the "Introduction" to my recent edition of Johnson's *Life of Savage*;[8] and everybody remembers Johnson's reluctance to hear whatever Lord Marchmount might have to say about Pope: "If it rained knowledge," he declared, "I'd hold out my hand; but I would not give myself the trouble to go in quest of it."[9] What would be the use of going in quest of it, if all one could hope for was the sort of thing that Derrick had got about Dryden? Though he never entirely rejected the anecdote in either theory or practice, from the start he felt confident only about anecdotes that came from the subject himself, that were, in other words, autobiographical ones. In the early essay in which he recommended distrust to the student of history, he went on to say that truth was nowhere "more likely to be found than in private memoirs." Later his preference for autobiography over biography was the subject of *Idler* no. 84. "The writer of his own life," he wrote in that essay, "has at least the first qualification of an historian, the knowledge of the truth." In these post-Freudian days, aware as we all are that man is a maze of conscious, subconscious, and unconscious motives constantly battered by delusions and obsessions, Johnson's statement seems strange, especially when he compounded it with the curious declaration that no man is a hero to himself. Usually, we will say, Johnson was more on his guard against the treachery of the human heart. But in an article published ten years ago, Anthony Tillinghast examined this part of Johnson's thinking and made it more acceptable by placing it in its intellectual context.[10] After showing that

7. *UTQ* 15, 1945, pp. 86-93.
8. Oxford, 1971, pp. xii-xiv.
9. *Life* III, p. 344. Cf: *Boswell in Extremes, 1776-1778*, Charles McC. Weis and Frederick A. Pottle, eds., New York, 1970, p. 338.
10. Anthony J. Tillinghast, "The Moral and Philosophical Basis of Johnson's and Boswell's Idea of Biography," in *Johnsonian Studies*, Magdi Wahba, ed., Cairo, 1962, pp. 115-31. While I agree with the greater part of Mr. Tillinghast's paper, I am unable to accept his thesis that Johnson's views altered between the date of the *Rambler* (1750) and that of the *Idler* (1759). Johnson's scepticism may have darkened as he grew older, but it existed from the start, and yet he went on writing biography and planning to write it until the end of his life. David L. Passler, *Time, Form, and Style in Boswell's* Life of

Johnson's scepticism was in agreement with the views of numerous empirical philosophers of the eighteenth century, such as Adam Smith, David Hume, and Lord Kames, he went on to explain that the sort of autobiography that Johnson believed in was not the public one, like the *Autobiography* of Lord Herbert of Cherbury, written as an outlet for his lordship's egotism, but the private one, written for the eyes of the author alone. He conceived of such a work as the product of the duty every Christian should feel of constant self-examination, carried out rigorously and prayerfully as under the eye of God. In such a work, he must have felt, there would be no motive for either bias or concealment. His own *Prayers and Meditations* as well as the journals he mainly destroyed before his death are examples of what he must have had in mind. Moreover, when he recommended to Boswell that he keep a journal and encouraged him in doing so, he must have been thinking of the same sort of private memoir. He kept urging Boswell to record the states of his mind. Consequently, according to this view, when Boswell got down volume after volume of his journal to read to himself during the long winter evenings in Edinburgh, he was not necessarily indulging in narcissism but, at least in theory, carrying out a religious duty that may often have been painful, but which was a necessary preliminary to repentance and absolution. Both his work and Johnson's seem to us remarkably truthful, though only God can judge, and go far to support Johnson's high valuation of autobiography.

But Johnson's *Idler* argument leaves Boswell's *Life of Johnson* out on a limb. Though much of it was torn out of the bowels of Boswell's journals, it was undeniably biography, not autobiography. True, he followed the implications of Johnson's argument so far as he could by making Johnson write, or appear to write, much of his own story. He included reports of Johnson's conversations as well as more intimate anecdotes told him by Johnson in private, and he got as much as he could from *Prayers and Meditations* and such of Johnson's other private diaries as he had been able to get

Johnson, New Haven, 1971, p. 36, writes that the motive for Boswell's journal was "self-improvement" rather than a desire to follow what he calls "the Puritan practice." That may be true, but one must remember Boswell's Calvinist background. In any case the actual difference is not very significant.

his hands on. He also printed, generally in their entirety, all of Johnson's letters that he had either received himself or had been able to collect from Johnson's other correspondents. These autobiographical materials form the core of the *Life of Johnson*. But Boswell clearly felt that he had got less from those sources than what he needed for doing justice to the personality and achievements of his eminent friend. So he also collected as much else as he could, including anecdotes from Johnson's other friends. In the opening pages of the *Life* he expressed the wish that they had been "as diligent and ardent" as he had been so that Johnson "might have been almost entirely preserved."[11] In a recent volume in the Research Edition of Boswell's Private Papers published at Yale, Marshall Waingrow has gathered together all of Boswell's correspondence with Johnson's other friends concerning their possible contributions to his book and has studied his use of what they provided. His estimate is that materials from such sources comprise more than half of the *Life of Johnson*.[12] By no stretch of the imagination might this additional material be called autobiographical; much of it, in fact, consists of exactly the sort of anecdote that Johnson distrusted, and if the other friends had lived up to Boswell's expectations the bulk of the enormous work that would have resulted would have been of the same kind.

Moreover, it is a question how reliable even the autobiographical materials are, according to Johnson's rigorous criteria of judgment. Much of it, for example, consists of letters, and Johnson was wary about letters as biographical evidence. "It has been so long said as to be commonly believed," he wrote in his *Life of Pope*, "that the true characters of men may be found in their letters, and that he who writes to his friend lays his heart open before him. But the truth is that such were simple friendships of the *Golden Age*, and are now the friendships only of children. Very few can boast of hearts which they dare lay open to themselves, and of which, by whatever accident exposed, they do not shun a distinct and continued view; and certainly what we hide from ourselves we do not shew to our friends. There is,

11. *Life* I, p. 30.
12. Marshall Waingrow, *The Correspondence and other Papers of James Boswell Relating to the Making of* The Life of Johnson, New York and Toronto, 1968, p. xxiii.

indeed, no transaction which offers stronger temptations to fallacy and sophistication than epistolary intercourse."[13] Even stronger objections might be made to the conversations. As Boswell admitted, Johnson often talked for victory and nobody could be sure which side of an argument he would espouse, and it was remarked that it was difficult to be certain of Johnson's real opinion on any subject merely on the basis of what he said about it in company. As a conversationist Johnson was an "intellectual gladiator," to use a phrase he himself first employed to describe the personages in Congreve's comedies,[14] rather than a man humbly and sincerely laying open his heart. Even what Johnson told Boswell privately, especially when Boswell had him to himself in the Highlands, at Ashbourne, or at Oxford, is a far cry from the conscientious self-examination recommended by the theologians from whom Johnson derived his idea of autobiography. In fact, there is none of that kind of material in the *Life* except for the brief extracts from *Prayers and Meditations* and the Johnsonian journals; the rest of it is all either extraneous to Johnson's mind or matter produced by him under circumstances that permitted bias, concealment, and other ulterior motives. The *Life*, in short, is a biography, and was put together mainly from the sort of materials Johnson had declared unreliable.

The book that Boswell produced, often described as the greatest biography in the language, is a work *sui generis*, many of whose special characteristics seem to have been given it as responses to the problems just mentioned. Although he seldom alluded to any of the theoretical principles underlying biography, and was in no sense of the word a philosopher, he often wrote about his methods of work, which he thought the best yet used by any biographer, and drew attention to the care with which he verified his facts, sometimes running half way across London to check a date. He took special pains, for example, with his account of Johnson's interview with George III, a section of his work of which he was justly proud, and which cost him unusual trouble

13. *Lives of the English Poets*, George Birkbeck Hill, ed., Oxford, 1903, III, pp. 206-7.
14. *Ibid.*, II, p. 228. Boswell himself first turned the gladiator image to Johnson. *Life* II, p. 106.

because he himself was not only not present at the interview but far away in Edinburgh. The only person present in addition to Johnson and the king was Mr. Barnard, the royal librarian. Nevertheless Boswell collated five versions of the story, all of which originated with either Johnson or Barnard, and he had the final draft submitted to the king, who examined it and gave it his imprimatur.[15] He was unable to take equal care over every part, and without doubt he made mistakes, but he did the best he could and he set a new standard of accuracy in biographical research.

His concern for detail became the basis of his style, making him careless of what Johnson once called "preparation and connexion and illustration and all those arts by which a big book is made."[16] Except for such special occasions as the interview in the royal library and the Wilkes dinner, he preferred to give his readers a discontinuous series of short episodes, each leading up to a pronouncement or a *mot* by Johnson, often made the more striking, or even alarming, by being stripped of most of its original context. It was as if Democritus's atoms had lost their hooks. Apart from normally following chronological order, he seemed reluctant to impose any structural pattern on his materials, stringing his facts together as they came and disregarding transitions. Occasionally he took liberties with the flow of time, as when he reminded his readers close to Johnson's death of his hero's possible youthful sins of the flesh or when he referred to various other examples of Johnson's fearlessness in the context of Macpherson's threat of physical violence – every biographer will do that – but generally he avoided any topical arrangement. Even chronology had little meaning for him except as a convenient rack to lay his facts on; his Johnson did not evolve with time. He obviously wanted his facts to speak for themselves and he left the sorting out for his readers to do. Many of them over the years have consequently read *in* his book oftener than they have read it through, using the index as the most appropriate way in, like the

---

15. *Life* II, p. 34. n. 1. Cf: Frank Taylor, "Johnsoniana from the Bagshawe Muniments in the John Rylands Library," *Bulletin of the John Rylands Library* 35, 1952-53, pp. 235-47. Reprinted in *Twentieth Century Interpretations of Boswell's* Life of Johnson, J. L. Clifford, ed., Englewood Cliffs, 1970, pp. 40-44.

16. *Boswell's Journal of a Tour to the Hebrides*, Frederick A. Pottle and Charles H. Bennett, eds., New York, 1961, p. 22.

back door in a Nova Scotia farm house. His style is aphoristic, to use Johnson's term for it, and though his book is big in physical bulk it is not formidable like an elaborate treatise. It is chatty, companionable, intimate, informal, and essentially shapeless.

He was thus not only a cautious empiricist but in some respects an inadequate one. He did not induce significant general conclusions from the facts he had accumulated. Many an early biography had been wound up with what was called a *character*, a short pithy summation of the character of the man whose career had been chronicled in the earlier pages. Unfortunately in most of those biographies little significant relationship was established between the character and the chronicle, so that the character appeared to rest only on the writer's *a priori* judgment. But in Johnson's best lives, like that of Pope, the character is brilliantly induced from the facts Johnson had at his disposal, so that the loose ends of the previous narrative are tied together and broad conclusions drawn about Pope's character and genius. Boswell honoured the old custom too with a character of Johnson, but it is a failure. The reader has had the main lines of the personality drilled into him so often in the preceding 1500 pages that the six pages of character are otiose — they add nothing to what he knows already — and he feels that Boswell's heart was not in it. Boswell's gift was for collecting facts. Moreover, unlike Johnson, who knew when he had enough facts, Boswell's thirst for them seemed unquenchable. He added new ones to the second edition, some of them having come to hand while the work was printing, and had he lived he would have gone on adding facts. After his death more were added in the third edition by Edmund Malone. Ever since, scholars have been making their contributions in footnotes and appendices to successive editions, so that now the work looks like one of those giant laminated snowballs that Canadian schoolboys start by rolling little fistfulls of snow across the neighbours' lawns. If Boswell's wish had come true that all Johnson's other friends had done as he did, what an immense mass of facts there would have been! But even so, would Johnson have been "almost entirely preserved?" Certainly not, in any final sense, for in Boswell the process was additive. The structure of his book seems capable of almost infinite expansion, until the world itself would be unable to hold all that might be written.

The part of biography, however, that gave most concern to Johnson and the philosophers quoted by Mr. Tillinghast was not that of finding and organizing historical facts, difficult as it was, but rather that of understanding motives and beliefs. The biographer has no way of knowing what went on inside the mind of his subject other than through the use of his sympathetic imagination:

> As we have no immediate experience of what other men feel [wrote Adam Smith], we can form no idea of the manner in which they are affected, but by conceiving what we ourselves should feel in the like situation. . . . Our senses . . . never did, and never can, carry us beyond our own person, and it is by the imagination only that we can form any conception of what are his [i.e. another's] sensations.[17]

Johnson said much the same thing in *Idler* no. 84, adding that the conjectures made by biographers about "another's motives and sentiments" are "easily modified by fancy or desire." In other words, unless he is bold enough to plunge into the dangerous waters of subjective judgment, he must be content with external and verifiable facts. To an extraordinary extent Boswell seems to have accepted this self-denying ordinance, and refrained from analyses of either Johnson's personality, his opinions, his literary works, or his friendships. As a result his book may seem to a reader of modern biography superficial in spite of its richness of material.

Obviously Boswell had a tremendous admiration for Johnson, consulting him about his law cases, seeking his advice on personal, especially religious, problems, and keeping his image constantly before him as a shining example. "Be Johnson," he used to say to himself whenever he felt he needed bucking up. He obviously thought of Johnson as a man of powerful personality, who was also possessed of a keenly analytical mind, strong religious faith, and a charitable disposition. Though he was aware of Johnson's

17. Adam Smith, "The Theory of Moral Sentiments," 1759, rpt. *Essays*, London, 1869, p. 9. Quoted by Tillinghast, p. 122.

oddities and weaknesses — his contentiousness, his nervous tics, his compulsive laughing, his voracity, and his inconsistencies — he seemed unwilling to get behind any of them in order to study Johnson's strength in the context of his weaknesses. He offered no explanation, for example, of Johnson's motives for espousing the cause of the Reverend Dr. Dodd, the fashionable preacher "in the French style" — as Walpole described him —who was the idol of titled ladies thronging the chapel of the Magdalens to hear and weep with him over their sins, and who was eventually hanged at Tyburn for forging Lord Chesterfield's name to a bond in spite of a petition to the king for his pardon signed by thousands of people, and written by Johnson. Dodd was clearly guilty, and the hysterical mob who backed him was behaving in a way that ordinarily filled Johnson with contempt. Boswell gave Johnson's support of Dodd merely as an example of his kindness to a man in trouble, and many pages later hinted that his main motive had been his objection to capital punishment. But Boswell seems to have been unaware of the inconsistency in Johnson's behaviour that was apparent to Sir John Hawkins.[18] His treatment of Johnson's marriage is a far more serious example of his refusal to go beneath the surface. He romanticized it, largely ignoring the evidence he himself presented that it had not been an entire success. In fact, Boswell was inadequate in his treatment of all Johnson's relations with women. Even without accepting Katharine Balderston's sensational theories about the nature of Johnson's attachment to Hester Thrale,[19] we can see that she satisfied much deeper needs in him than Boswell seemed aware of. His reverence for Johnson, indeed, may have blinded him to the deep-seated weaknesses in Johnson's personality that made it impossible for him to establish a satisfactory relationship with any woman.

The same thing is true of Boswell's treatment of Johnson's oral

---

18. The phrase quoted from Horace Walpole occurs in a letter written to George Montagu, dated 28 January 1760. *Letters of Horace Walpole*, Mrs. Paget Toynbee, ed., Oxford, 1903, IV, p. 347. For Boswell's account see *Life* III, pp. 139 *et seq.*, and *Life* IV, pp. 207-8. Cf: Sir John Hawkins, *The Life of Samuel Johnson*, Bertram H. Davis, ed., New York, 1961, p. 235.

19. "Johnson's Vile Melancholy," in *The Age of Johnson: Essays Presented to Chauncey Brewster Tinker*, New Haven, 1949, pp. 3-14.

pronouncements. He quoted all that he could remember, even when he disagreed with them, and when he disagreed, he almost never attempted to account for Johnson's opinions by connecting them to his basic intellectual convictions, to his experience, or to his deep psychological needs. Instead, he simply disagreed with them, and not only set forth his own contradictory views at length but also gave himself the last word. A number of examples might be found, but one will have to suffice.[20] Under date of 1768 he alluded to Johnson's preference for the novels of Richardson over those of Fielding. "In comparing the two writers," he wrote, "he used this expression: 'that there was as great a difference between them as between a man who knew how a watch was made, and a man who could tell the hour by looking on the dialplate.' This was a short and figurative statement of the distinction between drawing characters of nature and characters only of manners. But I cannot help being of opinion . . . ." And he went on to fill the rest of a long paragraph with his own refutation of Johnson. Modern readers will mostly agree with Boswell rather than with Johnson, but not many of them read the *Life of Johnson* for the sake of learning about Boswell's opinions on the relative merits of Richardson and Fielding. Although Boswell was under no obligation to support Johnson's views, even if he had agreed with them, one would have expected him to try to account for them on some grounds that he as biographer understood better than we: such as Johnson's friendship for Richardson, his deep interest in feminine character, some prejudice against Fielding, some misconception of Fielding's intentions. Yet one must admit that Boswell did put his cards on the table. His posthumous talking back to Johnson was an intrusion of his personal views less liable to the

---

20. A few of the many conversations that might be chosen to illustrate this habit are the ones about predestination (*Life* II, p. 104), fornication in a clergyman (*Life* II, pp. 171-2), the merits of Mr. Francis Osborn (*Life* II, pp. 193-4), action in public speaking (*Life* II, p. 211), the introduction of scriptural phrases into secular discourse (*Life* II, p. 213), the merits of Robertson's historical works (*Life* II, pp. 237-8), the non-jurors (*Life* II, pp. 321-2), the morality of the *Beggar's Opera* (*Life* II, pp. 367-8), conjugal infidelity (*Life* III, pp. 406-7), and the neglect of genius (*Life* IV, p. 172). The conversation about Fielding and Richardson will be found in *Life* II, p. 49; they returned to the subject in *Life* II, pp. 173-4. In his "Boswell's Control of Aesthetic Distance" (*UTQ* 38, 1969, pp. 174-91), Paul Alkon defends Boswell on this score interestingly but on different grounds from mine.

objections raised by Johnson and Adam Smith than the sort of analysis common in critical biographies today. Boswell gave us only what he knew and avoided tricky subjective judgments about Johnson's beliefs and motives.

Most other biographers of men of letters, moreover, see in the literary works of their subjects an index to their personalities and analyse them for the sake of throwing light on their author's thinking. Johnson was good at this marrying of biography with literary criticism. But Boswell's comments on Johnson's publications almost always leave the reader unsatisfied. They are almost invariably favourable, indeed enthusiastically so, but when they are not merely general they are peripheral and often inconsequential. His comments on the *Rambler* are typical.[21] He first gave the basic bibliographical facts, commented on the choice of title, quoted the prayer Johnson composed when he began writing it, and mentioned Johnson's rapidity in composition. He then quoted at some length from one of Johnson's preliminary sketches, partly to illustrate Johnson's methods and partly for the pleasure of contradicting Sir John Hawkins. Afterwards he went on to comment on the paper's reception, which gave him an opportunity to introduce two letters from James Elphinston, the Edinburgh bookseller who published the *Rambler* in Scotland. Finally he wrote two or three paragraphs of general comment on the moral subject-matter of the essays, but he dropped that theme in order to defend Johnson's literary style against its detractors, which occupied him for a longer time than anything else. His failure to make full use of the content of the *Rambler* essays, philosophical, religious, moral, and literary, as a means of unlocking Johnson's personality and of connecting his thought with various traditions in both classical and contemporary thought is the more remarkable in light of the fact that he had almost no other information about Johnson to fill up his pages for that particular year, 1750. One feels the same disappointment with respect to his treatment of all Johnson's works. He spoke of the preface to Shakespeare as a fine essay, but he devoted most of his space to the attacks made on it by Kenrick and Voltaire.[22] Similarly most of the space he

21. *Life* I, pp. 201-26.
22. *Life* I, pp. 496-500.

gave to the *Lives of the Poets* is taken up with variant readings,[23] and a conspicuous part of his commentary on the *Life of Savage* has to do with Johnson's prejudice against actors![24] Apparently Boswell felt that his duty as a biographer forbade him to impose on the reader his own judgments and required him to confine himself to such crumbs of biographical and bibliographical fact as could be verified.

Finally, in spite of all the materials he received from contributors, Boswell made little attempt to present those aspects of Johnson's personality that he showed to other friends or to see him through their eyes. In fact, Boswell's Johnson himself seems to exist, like characters in a Defoe novel, only when he is on stage. We read in the extracts that Boswell included from his own letters complaints that Johnson had not written to him, and when Johnson did write, we get in his letters some information about what he has been doing and suffering. Otherwise we tend to forget that time has been going on during Boswell's absence, as Boswell perhaps intended that we should. But Johnson went on living during those intervals, had occupations to carry on, and other friendships to keep in repair. Even though many of those other friends were not so much concerned as he was with recording Johnson's sayings, and a few were uncooperative, he might have asked himself what they all meant to Johnson, what sides of him they drew out, and what he might have been doing in their company in his own absence. Instead they were merely quarried for anecdotes. William Gerard Hamilton, for example, though only partially cooperative, had been in Boswell's words an "eminent friend" with whom Johnson had maintained a "long intimacy,"[25] and who during his last illness touched him deeply by offering to

23. *Life* IV, pp. 34-65. Sometimes one wonders how well Boswell understood Johnson's mind. His remark that "if digested and arranged in one system . . . [Johnson's critical comments in the *Lives of the Poets*], might form a code upon that subject" (*Life* IV, pp. 35-6), suggests a misunderstanding of the pragmatic character of his critical thinking. Cf: *Rambler* no. 93: "The beauties of writing have been observed to be often such as cannot in the present state of human knowledge be evinced by evidence, or drawn out into demonstrations: they are therefore wholly subject to the imagination, and do not force their effects upon a mind preoccupied by unfavourable sentiments, nor overcome the counteraction of a false principle or of stubborn partiality." Also *Rambler* no. 158: "Criticism . . . has not yet attained the certainty and stability of science."

24. *Life* I, pp. 165-74.

25. *Life* II, p. 317; IV, p. 111.

lend him money. Boswell mentioned Hamilton only a few times, usually anonymously, and there is nothing in any of those references to explain the basis of the friendship. An even more intimate friend was the Reverend Dr. John Taylor of Ashbourne, whose connection with Johnson extended back to their school days and with whom Johnson spent his summers. Mrs. Thrale described him as Johnson's "truest friend," and Johnson himself said that Taylor was "better acquainted with my heart than any man or woman now alive."[26] He was fully cooperative, but if Boswell's picture of him is accurate it is difficult to understand what could have attracted Johnson to him year after year. Boswell evidently found Taylor uncongenial, and when he was at Ashbourne he seemed to have really enjoyed himself only when Taylor was in bed or busy with his crops and his bullocks leaving Boswell alone with Johnson. In the *Life*, Boswell conveyed something of his own distaste for Taylor but little if anything of Johnson's liking. Another friend about whom I should like to know more was the Reverend Dr. William Maxwell, for some years preacher at the Inner Temple, from whom Boswell got a bulky collection of anecdotes that he lumped together under date 1770. Maxwell must have meant a great deal to Johnson, because when his mother died in 1759 it was to him that he turned in his distress for comfort and spiritual advice.[27]

There were others from whom no anecdotes could be expected, but about whom and from whom much might have been learned that would illuminate aspects of Johnson. One such person was Mrs. Francis Abington, the actress, whose benefit Johnson attended in spite of his bad hearing and eyesight and with whom he supped some days afterwards. He enjoyed her jelly, which he declared better than Mrs. Thrale's. Boswell told us that Johnson was proud of having been a part of the gay and elegant world, but it is a side of Johnson that he failed to develop.[28] And what about George Psalmanazar, the literary impostor, whose opinions Johnson said he respected as much as he did a bishop's and who was

26. Quoted from James Gray, "Dr. Johnson and the King of Ashbourne," *UTQ* 23, 1954, p. 242, notes 1-2.

27. *Life* II, pp. 116-33.

28. *Life* II, pp. 321, 324, 330, 349.

one of the few men whose company he had ever "sought after?"[29] Finally, from the life and personality of Richard Savage Boswell might also have learned a great deal about Johnson's early London years, about which he had only scanty information. Although he had Johnson's biography of Savage on his table, he did not mention Savage until after his death in 1743, and then only in connection with the publication of Johnson's book. But Savage and Johnson had been remarkably intimate in 1738 and 1739, enjoying that close comradeship that only two very poor men can feel who have to roam the streets together and sleep in ash heaps, and it seems probable that at first Savage, who was older, more knowing, much better acquainted, a good talker, and in his tatterdemalion way brilliant, was the dominant member of the pair. Boswell did mention the possibility that Johnson might have been led by Savage into sexual irregularities for which he felt remorse on his deathbed, but whatever the truth about that may have been — Professor Pottle rejects the charge for want of evidence[30] — Savage had had a lot more influence on Johnson than Boswell understood. Boswell might have read between the lines of Johnson's book how Johnson's first close friendship for Savage gradually grew more and more detached and finally turned, after Savage left London in 1739, into that mood of ironic but compassionate concern in which the *Life of Savage* was written five years later. But to have done so would have meant using the eyes of his imagination. The multiple point of view with which Boswell is often credited is then an illusion. He got materials from various sources, but he did not turn those sources into living, breathing human beings. They all spoke with the same voice and from the same point in space, as in a monaural recording.

Such was Boswell's answer to the difficulties raised by Johnson against biography: stick as close as you can to facts. But, as has often been observed before, when you throw apriorism out the window it often comes back in through the door. That is what happened with Boswell. His obsessive purpose was not merely to preserve the facts about Johnson but to perpetuate Johnson

29. *Life* III, p. 314; IV, p. 274.
30. Frederick A. Pottle, "The Dark Hints of Sir John Hawkins and Boswell," *MLN* 56, 1941, pp. 325-29. Reprinted in a revised form in *New Light on Dr. Johnson*, F. W.

himself. It is agreed by the most scholarly and perceptive modern students, such as Frederick Pottle, Ralph Rader, and Marshall Waingrow,[31] that Boswell was essentially a creative artist and that the Johnson of the *Life* was Boswell's Johnson, a creation of his imagination. By saying imagination, they do not mean to say, with Bernard Shaw, that Boswell "created" Johnson in the same way as Shakespeare created Falstaff and Hamlet.[32] The difference is that whereas Shakespeare drew his inspiration from his experience and knowledge of human nature in general, Boswell drew his mainly from his knowledge of a particular person. For behind Boswell's Johnson lay more than twenty years of intimate association with Johnson, during which time he had saturated himself in the Johnsonian aether. By common consent he could imitate Johnson's mannerisms and style of speaking better than anybody else. His imagination not only had hard facts to feed upon but was to a large extent controlled by them. His image of Johnson was not the product of a free-wheeling imagination like Shakespeare's but one disciplined and restrained by contingent facts. Nevertheless, the image was imaginary. The same must be true of all great biographers. All attempts to recreate any portion of the past, as Ernst Cassirer has said, are exercises of the productive imagination.[33]

The way Boswell's mind worked can be traced both in the way he edited the anecdotes furnished him by others and in the various stages through which Johnson's conversations went under his hand, through rough notes and written-up journal entries to their final form in the *Life* itself. Of the instances of editing presented by Professor Waingrow I must confine myself to one: his toning down of the statement made by Dr. Brocklesby, one of the

Hilles, ed., New Haven, 1959, pp. 153-62.

31. Frederick A. Pottle, "The *Life of Johnson*: Art and Authenticity," in *Twentieth Century Interpretations of Boswell's* Life of Johnson, J. L. Clifford, ed., pp. 66-73. Ralph W. Rader, "Literary Form in Factual Narrative: The Example of Boswell's Johnson," in *Essays in Eighteenth-Century Biography*, Philip B. Daghlian, ed., Bloomington and London, 1968, pp. 3-42. Marshall Waingrow, "Introduction" to his *Correspondence . . . Relating to the Making of the* Life of Johnson.

32. Hesketh Pearson, *Ventilations: being Biographical Asides*, Philadelphia and London, 1930, p. 14.

33. Ernst Cassirer, *An Essay on Man*, 1944, rpd. Garden City, New York, N.D., pp. 257-8.

physicians attending Johnson during his last illness, that Johnson's reason was in conflict with his religious faith.[34] Boswell rejected that view as inconsistent with his own view of the truth, and one must admit that he had at least as much right to his opinion as Dr. Brocklesby had to his. But he was suppressing a piece of weighty evidence, and it may be argued that his view was the product not merely of twenty years of intimacy with Johnson but also of deep psychological needs in himself that had partially blinded him to the truth. The evidence provided by his treatment of other material leads to much the same conclusion. Being convinced that Johnson had achieved in his own personality that synthesis of faith and reason that he himself was painfully aware of lacking, in one passage in the *Life* he edited away the greater part of a revealing "philosophical" discussion on the efficacy of prayer,[35] and in another context omitted altogether Johnson's categorical denial that one may have "the same conviction of the truth of Religion that one has in the common affairs of life."[36] Moreover, feeling, perhaps, that it made Johnson look too much like a Methodist, he omitted a clause from Johnson's last prayer that is our strongest evidence for the religious conversion that he experienced before his death.[37] In politics, too, Boswell tended to present Johnson clothed in the robes of his own romantic toryism, as Donald Greene has made very clear, rather than in those of the toryism of Johnson's own time.[38] Boswell's Johnson, then, is neither the Johnson of Fanny Burney, Hester Thrale, or Sir John Hawkins, nor the Johnson of the letters and the works. He is not the Johnson that any of us would construct if we could work with the same materials and under the same circumstances. But he is Boswell's friend, his spiritual advisor, and his ideal, a man of

34. *Correspondence . . . Relating to the Making of* The Life of Johnson, pp. xli-xlii, 31-32.
35. Compare *Life* II, p. 178 with *Boswell for the Defence*, W. K. Wimsatt and Frederick A. Pottle, eds., New York, 1959, p. 102.
36. *The Private Papers of James Boswell*, Geoffrey Scott and Frederick A. Pottle, eds., XIV, 1932, p. 245. There is no corresponding entry in the *Life*.
37. *Life* IV, p. 417. Cf: Samuel Johnson, *Diaries, Prayers, and Annals*, E. L. McAdam with Donald and Mary Hyde, eds., New Haven, 1958, pp. 417-8. Cf: Donald J. Greene, "Dr. Johnson's 'Late Conversion': a Reconsideration," in *Johnsonian Studies*, Magdi Wahba, ed., pp. 61-92.
38. Donald J. Greene, *The Politics of Samuel Johnson*, New Haven, 1960.

strong personality who had fought his way triumphantly through problems in religion and morality that constantly baffled Boswell, a man able to stand staunchly on his own feet, and a man so great that he could not be dishonoured by an account of his little oddities and occasional absurdities. To a very large extent that is the real Johnson, no doubt, but blended with an indeterminate number of subjective ingredients originating in Boswell's own psyche.

It would be wrong, then, to think of Boswell exclusively as either a collector of facts or a creative artist. For he was both. If the synthesis was not perfect in him, the reason may only be that such a synthesis is always hard to make in a strabismic art such as that of biography. The tendency now prevailing among critics is to emphasize his creative side, and critical principles relating to the rhetoric of the novel are being applied to the *Life of Johnson*. I have no quarrel with these proceedings. But I think it would be unwise to forget that Boswell's art was founded on empiricism and that much of the success of his book came from the same source. Indeed, one of the strongest traditions in the eighteenth-century novel itself was the pretence that it was not fiction at all, but collections of letters, or memoirs, or history, or biography. The demand in both biography and the novel was for the reassuring appearance of factual accuracy. I should not go so far as to say that Boswell made of his empirical techniques the same sort of pretence that we find in Defoe and Richardson; his facts were real facts and he took pains to authenticate them. But the effect on readers was nevertheless much the same. They gave them confidence in his reliability. Moreover, it is not at all clear that Boswell thought of them as techniques. The view that Boswell was a supremely self-confident creative artist is founded on the curious argument that whereas he spoke repeatedly about his methods and about his doubts over his own moral stamina, he was quite silent over his powers as an imaginative writer. Certainly he was aware that he had many gifts, such as his ability to recreate conversations that were essentially accurate if not literally so, his mastery of the Johnsonian idiom, and his flair for lucid and informal prose. But was he aware that his Johnson was the objective correlative of his own needs and ideals, a picture of himself as much as it was a picture of Johnson? There is, of course, no evidence. But his silence on these matters may serve as a useful hint that we should not forget those empirical principles that he did often speak about and that he often discussed with Johnson as the operative basis of his work.

They do give us confidence in him. The very lumpiness of his style draws attention to the care with which he collected and checked his facts. The diversity of his sources seems to be a guarantee of the fairness and completeness of his picture. Even the haphazard arrangement of his materials gives us a strong impression of existential reality, for it is the haphazard plan of life itself, adding greatly to the conviction with which we accept his view of Johnson. The very superficiality of his comments on Johnson's personality and literary works, though a weakness, has a similar result. We are reassured by the spectacle of Boswell's humility, his unwillingness to obtrude himself and his explanations upon us his readers. What a Roman holiday some biographers would have had over the sensational affair of Dr. Dodd, and how lean and almost ascetic by contrast was Boswell's handling of it! Most of all the book succeeds by its actuality. "For James Boswell," wrote Sir Harold Nicolson, "invented actuality."[39] It was Boswell's facts that led his readers to imagine themselves right there participating in the nights and feasts of the Johnsonian gods. They said to themselves as they read: "There is Johnson; there is Goldsmith; that man shading his eyes is Reynolds; those are his tables and chairs; his orange peels are on the mantle shelf; Hodge is eating his oysters." So the whole drama enacted itself before their eyes.

C. Tracy

39. Harold Nicolson, *The Development of English Biography*, London, 1928, pp. 87 ff.

Benjamin Constant (1767-1830)

Benjamin Constant
& Restoration Liberalism

In a preface to a collection of his essays published in 1829, Benjamin Constant wrote: "j'ai défendu quarante ans le même principe, liberté en tout, en religion, en philosophie, en littérature, en industrie, en politique. . . ."[1] The matter of consistency has remained paramount in any discussion of his political life. In fact, although he was the theoretician of Restoration liberalism and played a key role in the liberal opposition, especially in the first crucial decade of that era, Constant has seldom been accorded the recognition due to him. A cursory glance at Restoration liberalism and at his behaviour during that decade may indicate some of the reasons for this neglect.

The political career of Constant falls into two phases; the first (1795-1802) culminated in his expulsion from the Tribunate by Napoleon. In those years, like all those who feared a return of either the Bourbons or the Jacobins, Constant sought some form of constitutional government, but Napoleon had only contempt for "idéalogues" who wished to raise an English form of constitutional opposition. So Constant as a faithful acolyte of Madame de Staël followed her into exile to continue their opposition. During the period, 1802-1813, he published no political tracts, but the tumultuous events of 1814-1815 that culminated in the second return of the Bourbons, evoked from him his major political works on which his reputation as a political theorist is based. Until the end of his career in December 1830, his pamphlets and his parliamentary activities were responses to day-to-day issues and they elaborated his essentially middle-class, Natural Rights liberalism, the credo that feared the despotism of both the absolute monarch and of the masses. Restoration

---

1. B. Constant, *Oeuvres*, A. Roulin, ed., Paris, 1957, p. 801.

liberalism[2] was conditioned philosophically by the Revolution and practically by the behaviour, in 1814-15, of Constant and of many of those who were to be leading opposition Liberals.

In 1813 Constant first appeared on the scene in the baggage train of Bernadotte, former Marshal of the Empire and heir designate, on whose hopes of replacing Napoleon he had attached his ambition. Bernadotte never reached Paris, as Constant had already noted in the *Journaux intimes* "son propre terrain est mourant. Ma cabane bâtie le-dessus serait du sable sur du sable."[3] But on 31 December 1813, Constant published his first political tract since his exile, the famous anti-Napoleon philippic, *De l'Esprit de conquête et de l'usurpation dans leurs rapports avec la civilisation européenne*. In it, he expressed a liberal optimistic view of man and a belief in human perfectibility. He did not see Liberty and Pacifism as natural predispositions of man, but rather as the fruit of civilisation and progress that are always threatened by despotism and the spirit of conquest. War was now an anachronism and the important new forces in the world, trade and commerce, tend to peace and liberty. He made direct attacks on Napoleon, the usurper, and argued that legitimacy could be conferred on a ruler only by free elections or by heredity. Unlike legitimate rulers "un usurpateur siège avec effroi sur un trône illégitime, comme sur une pyramide solitaire. Aucun assentiment ne l'appuie."[4]

Although by June 1814 the *Esprit* had gone through four editions, Constant played no part in what was to be seen as the beginning of Restoration liberalism, the fruitless effort by the Imperial Senate to impose terms on the returning Bourbons in April 1814. Contractual monarchy was one of the precepts of Liberals who throughout the Restoration argued that a contract, implied if not explicit, had taken place between the nation and the returning Bourbons. The pre-eminence of Talleyrand as vice-President of the Senate and as a friend of the Russian Tsar was at

---

2. E. Cappadocia, "The Nature of French Liberalism During the Restoration," *Historical Papers, The Canadian Historical Association*, 1961, J. Heisler and P. Dumas eds., pp. 132-141.

3. 11 November, 1813. "Journaux intimes," *Oeuvres*, p. 685.

4. *Ibid.*, p. 1061.

first cause for despair, but: "La liberté n'est pas perdue. Tâchons de nous faire une place commode dans un système paisible. Essayer vaut la peine."[5] He soon consoled himself: "Tâchons d'être désiré,"[6] and once in Paris he felt that, "il y a de la ressource pour la liberté."[7] ... "Servons la bonne cause et servons-nous."[8]

In the summer of 1814 all those who during the Restoration were to be spokesmen of liberalism gave the Bourbons their good will.[9] Lafayette, who had never compromised with Napoleon and who was to become the flag of the Liberals, informed Jefferson that he and his friends were striving to make the Bourbon throne as rational and as liberal as possible.[10] Constant even claimed that the French restoration of 1814 combined the advantages of the English restoration of 1660 and of the Revolution of 1688.

Constant continued to elaborate liberal principles and to hope in vain for a place in the new political world: "Les éloges sans résultat me font plus de peine que de plaisir."[11] The praises he was receiving came for a major pamphlet,[12] published in May 1814, on political theory. To the traditional three powers dear to liberal writers since Montesquieu, he added a fourth, the neutral power of the Crown. He stressed the inviolability of the Crown and the responsibility of ministers as the two fundamental principles of a constitutional system.

At a time when the government began to consider the limitations to the freedom of the press, Constant wrote the first of his many pamphlets on that subject. In it he presented the classical liberal argument that only through a free press can the authorities know public opinion, and that "ce que la nation voulait en 1789,

5. 7 April, 1814, *ibid.*, p. 695.
6. 11 April, *ibid.*, p. 695.
7. 15 April, *ibid.*, p. 695.
8. 16 April, *ibid.*, p. 695.
9. E. Cappadocia, "The Liberals and the Crisis of the First Restoration in France," *Historical Papers, The Canadian Historical Association*, 1966, J. Heisler and F. Ouellet eds., pp. 141-154.
10. Lafayette to Jefferson, 14 August, 1814, in *Général Lafayette, Mémoires, correspondance et manuscrits du général Lafayette publiés par sa famille* V, 6 vols., Paris, 1837-48, pp. 486-489.
11. 28 May, 1814. "Journaux intimes," *Oeuvres*, p. 699.
12. *Réflexions sur les constitutions, la distribution et les garanties dans une monarchie constitionnelle*, Paris, 1814.

c'est à dire une liberté raisonnable, elle le veut encore aujourd'hui."[13] After six months of emotional chaos over Madame Récamier's failure to return his love, Constant re-entered the political world with another pamphlet on the responsibility of ministers.[14] But by that time, February 1815, future Liberals were in despair over the follies of the *émigrés*. Constant wrote to Lafayette: "L'avenir est bien incertain. Il n'y a de sûr qu'une chose, c'est que les purs ne veulent pas de nous. Ils se perdront et nous perdront."[15]

The return of Napoleon from the island of Elba in March 1815 was to be an important factor in determining the fate of Restoration liberalism. Lafayette and Constant at first cast aside recent doubts and rallied to the Bourbons who now made frantic last-minute efforts to identify the Crown with constitutionalism. The Chamber of Representatives characterized the Bourbon Charter of June 1814 as the development of the principles of 1789. Constant wrote on 11 March a bitter anti-Napoleon article which he feared might endanger his life: "Vogue la galère. S'il faut périr, périssons bien."[16] And although he was being approached by Bonapartists, "ils m'amadouent,"[17] on the 18th he wrote the famous diatribe against Napoleon which appeared in the *Journal des débats* the following day. The unequivocal attacks on "the Corsican," on whose side he saw only slavery, anarchy, and war, was accompanied by a spirited defence of the Bourbons, the ensurers of constitutional liberty, safety, and peace, and included the well-known sentence: "Je n'irais pas, misérable transfuge, me traîner, d'un pouvoir à l'autre, couvrir l'infamie par le sophisme et balbutier des mots profanés pour racheter une vie honteuse."[18] Yet by 14 April he rallied to Napoleon, became a member of the Council of State and, as most future Restoration Liberals, convinced himself that Napoleon could become a constitutional monarch.

13. *De La Liberté des brochures, des pamphlets et des journaux considérée sous le rapport de l'intérêt du gouvernement*, Paris, 1814, *Oeuvres*, p. 1243.

14. *De La Responsabilité des ministres*, Paris, 1815.

15. 20 February, 1815, "Journaux intimes," *op. cit.*, p. 739.

16. *Ibid.*, p. 742.

17. 12 March, 1815, p. 742.

18. *Journal des débats*, 19 March, 1815.

Napoleon entered Paris on 22 March, two days after Louis XVIII had left it. Since his landing he had voiced the language of constitutional monarchy and of liberalism. He proclaimed freedom of the press and on the 25th the Council of State declared: "La souveraineté réside dans le peuple, il est la source lègitime du pouvoir."[19] After an absence of six days, Constant returned on the 27th and by the 31st he was noting in his *Journaux*: "Les intentions sont libérales: la pratique sera despotique. N'importe."[20] On 9 April, Lafayette wrote to Constant that the Emperor's whole career made him inimical to guarantees of liberty, but though Napoleon and liberty were irreconcilable, in comparison with the *émigrés* the emperor's government represented the lesser of the two evils.[21] Meanwhile Constant on 14 April met Napoleon who persuaded him, his opponent since 1800, and his recent detractor, to draw up a constitution. On 7 June, Napoleon told the newly elected Chamber that he was beginning his "monarchie constitutionnelle."

In May 1815, Constant was to see not only the acceptance of his constitution, *L'Acte Additionnel aux Constitutions de L'Empire*, also known as "la Benjamine," but also, and perhaps even more important, a significant book on political theory which he had completed on 13 April.[22] The *Benjamine* was more liberal than the Bourbon Charter, but the plebiscite on it attracted fewer voters than Napoleon's earlier efforts to ascertain popular will. The experiment in Bonapartist constitutionalism never took place because Waterloo rescued the anti-Bourbon Liberals from the dismaying illusion of totalitarian liberalism.

Throughout the Restoration, Liberals had to explain their conduct during the Hundred Days. Constant's defence[23] centred

---

19. *Moniteur*, 25 March, 1815.
20. 31 March, 1815. "Journaux intimes," *op. cit.*, p. 744.
21. Lafayette V, p. 416.
22. *Principes de politique applicables à tous les gouvernements réprésentatifs et particulièrement à la constitution actuelle de la France, Oeuvres*, pp. 1065-1215. Constant did not believe that one should talk in the abstract about "sovereignty of the people," although he accepts it as a principle, because such talk does not enhance the liberty of the individual. To him Natural Rights come first. Law is the expression of "la volonté de tous" which becomes "la volonté générale" if one accepts the power of a few when sanctioned by all. He devotes key chapters on the inviolability of property, on press and religious freedom and above all on individual liberty.
23. *Mémoires sur les Cent-Jours*, Paris, 1829.

on his claim that his first duty was the defence of liberal principle and that political organisation was merely a means to guarantee specific ends: liberty, order and the happiness of the people. Moreover on 20 March, he had raised his eyes and saw that, though the king had disappeared, France was still there. The fact that France was at war was an additional reason for supporting Napoleon. He had also been convinced that the way was then clear to surround Napoleon with constitutional barriers. Moreover, in his major study on political principles which he finished in April 1815, Constant argued that the English people became free when James II fled from England and his flight was declared to be an abdication. He concluded this important work with the justification:

> "Alors, après avoir, pendant 20 ans, réclamé les droits de l'espèce humaine, la sûreté des individus, la liberté de la penseé, la garantie des propriétés, l'abolition de tout arbitraire, j'oserai me féliciter de m'être réuni, avant la victoire, aux institutions qui consacrent tous ces droits. J'avais accompli l'ouvrage de ma vie."[24]

In April 1814, Liberalism had consisted of the futile efforts to impose terms on Louis XVIII; the following year it had centred on surrounding Napoleon with constitutional limitations, and after his defeat it meant the engineering of his second abdication. Constant played no important part after Waterloo neither with regard to the succession nor to the Chamber of Representatives' futile debate on the fundamentals of a liberal constitution — the distillation of the principles of 1789 as understood in 1815.[25]

By the time of the second return of the Bourbons, Constant's reappearance in the political arena had been less than successful. Although he had had a glimpse at fleeting glory in the resplendent

---

24. *Principes, op. cit.*, p. 1215.
25. L. Duguit et H. Monnier, *Déclaration des droits des Français et des principes fondamentaux de leurs institutions votés par la chambre des représentants le 5 juillet 1815*, pp. 198-199. This document is important not so much for the stress on liberty and equality, on the demand for the abolition of the nobility, of privilege, but rather for its last article (XIII) which unequivocally declared that no prince could rule until he had taken the oath to observe the present declaration. The restatement of the principles of 1789 were combined with the belief in the contract theory of government — a recurrent theme of Liberals who finally achieved their goal in the Revolution of 1830.

uniform of Councillor of State, and he was to wait until the Revolution of 1830 to be again amongst those with political power, he had made more meaningful contributions to liberalism by his writings. But the frantic desire for recognition, the restless ambition for honours and office, the passionate need for acceptance drove him to foolish opportunism. On 31 May, 1814, he confided to his *Journaux*:

> "Folies d'imagination. Je me crois dédaigné de tout le monde et personne n'y pense. C'est moi qui ne prends pas ma place, et je crois qu'on me la refuse."[26]

One need not share Henri Guillemin's[27] sardonic view of Constant to recognize that ambition and opportunism went side-by-side with a brilliant intellect and facile pen.

The return of the Bourbons meant that for over two years the Liberals played no part in French politics. They had to depend on Liberalism by princely grace and rejoiced when Louis XVIII followed a policy of reconciliation between the old and the new France. In September 1816, he dissolved the reactionary "Chambre introuvable" elected the previous year, even though this action outraged the Ultras, his more reactionary supporters who followed the leadership of his brother, the future Charles X. Until the murder of the heir to the throne, the Duc de Berri, in February 1820, Louis XVIII encouraged the moderation of the Centre group in the Chamber of Deputies. By 1818 this group split into the Right Centre under the Duc de Richelieu, who did not want the policy of moderation to antagonise the Right, and into Left Centre under Elie Decazes who was willing to rely on the Liberals.

This royal moderation was supported by liberal-minded people who hailed the "coup" of September 1816, and who greeted with enthusiasm the election law of the following year. It was under that law with its restricted franchise (about 90,000 voters in a nation of over thirty million people), that the Liberals were to make their reappearance in the Chamber of Deputies in the partial renewal of that body in the elections of 1817, 1818, and 1819.

26. "Journaux intimes," *op. cit.*, p. 699.
27. H. Guillemin, *Mme de Staël, Benjamin Constant et Napoléon*, Paris, 1959.

Constant, Lafayette and other "Independent"[28] candidates for the partial renewal of 1817 were suspected as the men of the Hundred Days and were considered "anti-dynastic." Constant sought to allay fears aroused by their candidacy in a pamphlet in which he saw the choice presented for the electorate as one among the partisans of the *ancien régime* (the Ultras), those who accepted the new regime but who insisted that, for a while yet, exceptional laws must be maintained (the Centrists), and those who were loyal to the Charter but who wanted to see the constitutional monarchy go forward only with the assistance of "constitutional liberty" (the Independents).[29] Although Lafayette and Constant were not elected, the Independents did make substantial gains.

The Liberals gave only grudging and uncertain support to Decazes and the Left Centre, the only group that could help them realize their hopes for liberal reforms. One of these reforms, the press laws of 1818, led to the appearance of more newspapers, one of the most important of which was to be the Liberal journal *Minerve*, brilliantly edited by Constant. In it he carried out the constitutional education of France.[30] His main theme was stated repeatedly: the purpose of the State is to guarantee personal liberty, that is to free the individual from all restraints that limit his growth. By liberty he meant the guarantee of individual rights for the masses of the common people. Moreover, he argued that this liberty could be established only by wise combination of monarchical power and the rights of the people. He feared the "revolutionary" policy of the Ultras, who, he felt, wanted to undermine the system of government by the Charter:

C'est parce que je crains les bouleversements, c'est parce que je hais les révolutions, c'est parce que je veux la stabilité de la monarchie constitutionnelle, que je crois qu'il est urgent de repousser les projets qui favorisent tout ce que je crains de

---

28. In 1817 and 1818 the Liberals called themselves Independents to disassociate themselves from the Centrist followers of the Richelieu-Decazes ministry. To their enemies they were known also as Jacobins, Radicals, Revolutionaries, and the Left.

29. *Journal général de France*, 19 September, 1817.

30. For the aims of the *Minerve*, see I, February, 1818, III, August, 1818, p. 159; IV, November, 1818, p. 100; IX, February, 1820, p. 107.

voir reparaître, et qui mettent en péril tout ce que je voudrais qui fût conservé.[31]

In the midst of the turmoils of 1821 Constant was to declare in the Chamber that, "la stabilité est bonne en toutes choses," and that to conserve that which exists in order to profit from it, is better than to look for hazardous new things.[32] Revolution was justified only when the rights of the individual could not be attained within the framework of the existing form of government, whatever its nature might be. He spoke of the aristocratic basis of English liberty and praised the English aristocracy which, unlike the French, had never been the enemy of the people. The realization of the liberty of the individual was the paramount issue in the writings of Constant, whose erudite lectures on constitutionalism, the biting sarcasm that characterized the *Minerve's* attacks on the Ultras and on the government, were to make that journal popular both in France and abroad.

An event equal in significance for Restoration liberalism as the appearance of the *Minerve* was the posthumous publication in 1818 of Madame de Staël's study of the Revolution. This book[33] represented one of the first systematic defences of the Revolution and set the pattern for the interpretation of those momentous years that was to be followed by the Liberals, whose leaders, such as Lafayette and Constant, had been her personal friends and admirers. In the second half of the *Considérations* written in 1816, which was directed towards the existing political situation in France, Madame de Staël was aware of the dangers which liberalism would encounter in France if it identified itself with Bonapartism. She admonished "les amis de la liberté" to separate their cause from that of the Bonapartists and cautioned them not to confound "les principes de la Révolution" with those of Napoleon.[34]

31. *Ibid.* VIII, December, 1819, p. 295.
32. *Discours de Benjamin Constant à la chambre des députés*, 2 vols., Paris, 1827-28. I, p. 416.
33. Staël-Holstein, Anne-Louise-Germaine Necker, Madame la baronne de, *Considérations sur les principaux événements de la Révolution française, ouvrage posthume de madame la baronne de Staël*, Duc de Broglie and Baron de Staël, eds., 3 vols., Paris, 1818.
34. *Ibid.* III, p. 169.

Constant gave the *Considérations* a surprisingly lukewarm reception, and he failed to make any references to her views on Bonapartism and on the danger of identifying it with liberalism. He and writers in other Liberal journals[35] wanted to de-emphasize the inherent contradiction between Liberalism and Bonapartism, because they realized that Bonapartism was popular among the masses.

The Bonapartist issue remained a divisive force between the Liberals and the ministry, and it emerged over the issue whether or not the regicides and those who, because of their activities during the Hundred Days, had been banished temporarily by the law of 1816, should be allowed to return. When a parliamentary committee recommended that the petitions on behalf of the banished be disregarded, and the decision as to who should return to France be left to the king, only twenty votes, all Liberals, were cast against them.

The Liberal press gave little direct attention to Napoleon himself, but Napoleonic military anniversaries were recalled and the songs of Pierre-Jean de Béranger, the famous and popular songster of the Liberal and Bonapartist opposition, were given prominence. The *Indépendant* was disturbed because the memories of Napoleon's triumphs served to worry even certain Liberals about "le destin de la liberté."[36] The identification of Liberalism with Bonapartism was to become more marked after the death of Napoleon in 1821. The Liberals, who no longer had to fear his return, now expected to recruit more followers. Even Lafayette, who had never been a Bonapartist, was relieved by the death because he foresaw that "many Bonapartists" would now attach themselves to the "patriotic" party, as he then called the Liberals.[37]

In the election campaigns of 1818 and 1819, and throughout the stormy events following the assassination of the Duc de Berri the following year, the Liberals stressed the theme that they were

35. E. Cappadocia, "The Liberals and Madame de Staël in 1818," in R. Herr and H. Parker, eds., *Ideas in History, Essays Presented to Louis Gottschalk by his former students*, Durham, 1965.
36. *Indépendant*, 23 June, 1819.
37. Lafayette VI, p. 128.

the preservers of the *status-quo* because they, unlike the Ultras, wanted no radical change but wished to preserve the gains of the Revolution. They emphasized the need to follow the "strict application" of the Charter. Constant presented his colleagues in 1817 as the true conservatives, the representatives of the peaceful element of the nation whose "true strength" could be found in the middle-class, the defenders of stability in all things.[38]

The Liberal gains in 1818 when, among others, Lafayette was elected, dismayed the Duc de Richelieu who resigned as president of the council of ministers. He had been shocked by the "alliance monstreuse"[39] between the Liberals and the Bonapartists. Decazes, the man responsible for the liberal measures of the previous two years, became more important in the new ministry nominally headed by General Dessoles. But the Liberals, for whom the year 1819 was "une époque d'espérance," gave the new ministry little support, because they were expecting greater gains in the elections of 1819. The Bonapartist undercurrent and the important Liberal success that did materialize convinced Decazes and Louis XVIII, the architect and supporter of the moderate Centrist position, that the time had come to modify their policy. They had presupposed acquiescence, if not positive support, from those who saw themselves as the defenders of the new France. But before Decazes could give a new orientation to his policy, the Duc de Berri was murdered by a young fanatic, on 13 February 1820. This event was fraught with disastrous consequences for French Restoration Liberalism. Although Decazes introduced bills to revise the election law of 1817, to suspend individual liberty and to re-establish press censorship, Louis XVIII bowed to pressure from the Ultras, led by his brother, and dismissed him. The return of the Duc de Richelieu to head the ministry ended the era of Left-Centre moderation.

The new government's measures to reverse the Left-Centre policies evoked from the Liberals a spirited defence of the *status-quo*. They took refuge in the Charter which now became

38. *Minerve* III, August, 1818, pp. 433-446.
39. Cited in E. Daudet, *Louis XVIII et le duc Decazes 1815-1820, d'après des documents inédits*, Paris, 1899, p. 281.

the palladium of Liberalism. To the *Indépendant* the Revolution of 1789 and the Charter were now synonomous. By 1822 the Liberals spoke of the Charter as superior to the king himself and insisted that only a constitutional convention representing the "nation" could revise it.

The Liberals and Constant gave a classic defence of individual liberty and of freedom of the press when bills to curb both were debated in the Chamber of Deputies. In his lecture on individual liberty Constant insisted that all arbitrary governments want to rule by exceptional measures and any law to limit individual freedom attacks not only liberty, justice, and morals, but also the credit system in finance, industry, and the prosperity of France. He accused the government of wanting the powers enjoyed by Napoleon, of wishing to return to absolutism and of overthrowing the Charter. In the measures proposed, he saw the return of 1788 and with it the doom of liberalism.[40]

The Liberals fought tenaciously and eloquently, if to no avail, against changes in the election law of 1817, which had made their success possible. Parliamentary speeches became effective appeals to agitate public opinion, especially students, in the streets. Since the proposed system of the double vote and indirect elections gave the richest electors more power, the Liberals centred their attacks on the aristocracy. They identified the mass of the people with the middle-class and saw the changes as an attack on the Charter. When an Ultra spoke of the Liberals as the men responsible for the march of the women on Versailles on 5 and 6 October 1789, for the September 1792 massacres, for the murder of Louis XVI, and for the return of Napoleon on 20 March 1815, Constant re-interpreted the French Revolution. To him the Liberals were the constitutionalists of 1789 who had defended the throne in 1792, had been the victims of the Terror and the enemies of Napoleon. In 1814 they had warned the king's government of its perilous situation, and who, if listened to, could have saved the Bourbons in March 1815. He now wanted "les Bourbons, rien que les Bourbons avec la Charte, toute la Charte sous les Bourbons."[41] The events of the Revolution and of the 1814 and 1815

40. *Archives parlementaires*, 2nd series, XXVI, 1820, p. 354.
41. *Ibid*. XXVIII, pp. 57-61.

restorations were constantly re-examined by speakers on both sides of the Chamber of Deputies. In 1820 Constant began to publish the defence of his actions during the Hundred Days.[42]

In 1820 the Liberals sought comfort from events abroad, the revolution in Naples and, even more important, that in Spain. These revolutions, undertaken in the name of liberalism, were hailed by the Liberals who contrasted the twilight of liberalism at home with the dawn of a new era abroad. Since they feared the intervention of Austria, Prussia, and Russia, the Liberals advocated a policy of open diplomacy and non-intervention. When the Congress of Verona (1822) led to the French invasion of Spain to crush the rebellion, the Liberals saw the invasion as a "hypocriso-politico-religious" war on liberalism.[43] The easy victory in Spain brought prestige to the Ultras and despondency to the Liberals. Their decline, already visible in the partial renewals of 1821 and 1822, was to be confirmed in the crushing defeat they suffered in the general elections of the following year. As Lafayette admitted to Jefferson, the mass of the people in Italy and Spain had been indifferent to liberalism. Only the "less ignorant part" had been alert, the rest were still under the influence of "prejudice and superstition."[44]

Although Constant had been a vigorous debater in the Chamber, and was to be the cause of demonstrations on the part of his supporters and opponents both in Paris and in his constituency of the Sarthe, unlike Lafayette and many other Liberals, he took no part in the military conspiracies of 1820 and 1822. He was essentially a political theorist anxious to lecture France on constitutionalism. In 1818-1819 he published four volumes[45] of his writings to serve as a course on constitutional politics. In 1821 in the Chamber he returned to the theme of the responsibility of ministers, on which he had published a pamphlet six years before. He again based himself on the English practice and insisted that

42. *Mémoires sur les Cent-Jours.*
43. *A. P.* XXXVIII, 1823, p. 380.
44. Lafayette to Jefferson, 20 December, 1823, *Massachusetts Historical Society* (Louis Gottschalk photostats).
45. *Collection complète des ouvrages publiés sur le gouvernement représentatif et la constitution actuelle de la France, formant une espèce de cours de politique constitutionnelle*, 4 vols., Paris, 1818-1819.

the ministry should lead the defence of, and always uphold, a measure it presented to the Chamber of Deputies. He did not, however, believe that a defeat in that body should lead to the resignation of the government. Constant could not face the logic of responsible parliamentary government, such as was to develop in England after the Reform Bill of 1832, whereby the ministry has to resign when it no longer commands a majority in the House of Commons. To accept such a practice in France in 1821 would have meant an Ultra ministry. To him, a ministry should resign only if it sees no immediate prospects of obtaining a majority.[46]

Constant remained the voice of middle-class liberalism.[47] Unlike such Liberals as the pamphleteer Paul-Louis Courier or the songwriter Béranger, he feared the "mob" and could not appeal to the mass of the "people." Throughout the stormy and angry debates of 1820-1822, unlike many of his colleagues, he believed that it was still possible to convince the Right-Centre and even the Right, if not the extreme Ultras, that their path would lead to the perdition of the monarchy. To him the Charter had consecrated the Revolution, i.e. the political and civil gains of the middle-class. Therefore he wanted some accommodation to maintain the Charter and avoid another revolution. The only "people" he would trust were the educated and the property owners.

Constant, though defeated in 1822, was re-elected in 1824 and for the next six years played an important part in the opposition to the policies of Charles X. Until the crisis of 1829-1830, he devoted most of his energies to gambling and to his study of religion, his major non-political interest. In August 1827 he made a triumphal trip to Alsace and, with Lafayette, became a symbol of opposition to Charles X. During the July Revolution of 1830, which to Constant and to the Liberals became their version of 1688 in England, he wrote the important declaration in favour of the future King Louis-Philippe. By that time Constant and Lafayette were symbols. Power was in the hands of younger men

---

46. *A. P.* XXXI, 1821, pp. 672-673.

47. Baron Pasquier, who became minister for foreign affairs in 1820, declared that at that time the youth in the schools, the army, big businessmen, big industrialists, rich capitalists, capable, esteemed, highly considered men were nearly all "partisans des ideés plus ou moins libérales." Pasquier, *Mémoires du chancelier Pasquier*, 5 vols., Paris, 1892-95, IV, p. 356.

such as Guizot and Thiers. A month later, Constant was named president of a section of the Council of State and the king gave him the large sum of 200,000 francs to pay his debts.

It is important to note that Constant's last speech in the Chamber was in favour of printers and booksellers, but his motion for more liberal measures were defeated. In September he had written to the Duchesse de Broglie:

> Nous avons tous les éléments de la liberté il y a prodige dans les biens. Mais il ya moyen de gâter ce prodige.[48]

When he died in December 1830, his funeral was the occasion of popular demonstration. He finally achieved the popularity for which he had so often yearned.

Louis-Philippe's generosity (or was it repayment?) raises again the question of opportunism in Constant. Was his behaviour during the Hundred Days merely a personal demarche, a clumsy interplay of personal ambition and principles or a benediction of Bonapartism by liberalism? At first it was the one and then became the other. But personal vicissitudes, obvious contradictions, turncoat accusations cannot vitiate the importance of Constant's writings. They are relevant not only to the issues of his day, but to the understanding of Restoration Liberalism and of the Nineteenth-Century Natural Rights school of continental Liberalism.

E. Cappadocia

---

48. Comtesse Jean de Pange, "Quelques lettres inédites de Benjamin Constant à Auguste et Albertine de Staël entre 1815 et 1830," pp. 119-125, in *Benjamin Constant, actes du congrès de Lausanne*, October, 1967, P. Cordey et J. L. Seylaz eds., Geneva, 1968, p. 125.

Goethe's Dichtung und Wahrheit: The Emergence of a Poet

Just one month before his death, Goethe spoke of his life as a process of collecting and using all that had confronted his senses. His life work was that of a collective being and this work bears the name of Goethe.[1] These rather prosaic observations from one of the world's supreme poets convey the most important characteristic of his personality, which lies in his intense awareness of the world about him and furthermore, his need to interpret it. His works are, as he remarks in his autobiography, fragments of one great confession.[2] With Goethe, poetic expression in Germany achieved a new depth by purposely assuming the function of a personal confession. The personality of a poet took on startlingly different proportions, for it really assumed now the primary role in a work of art: it demanded that subject matter and its form of expression reflect the unique nature of a personality and his poetic genius. To explore briefly how this came about will be the subject of this paper.

If all of Goethe's literary output is confessional in nature, then it follows that his autobiography, *Dichtung und Wahrheit*, is the most thorough-going of all his confessions. Among his autobiographical writings it is recognized as the richest in revelation of personality and the most intimate in its relationship to the reader.[3] The title is immediately tantalizing: *Poetry and Truth*. "Dichtung" is hard to render precisely into English: "Poetry" must be understood in the widest possible sense, embracing the entire scope of imaginative writing, and not just verse form. It is Goethe's intention to devote half of his autobiography to it. We

1. Friedrich Soret, *Zehn Jahre bei Goethe Erinnerungen an Weimars klassische Zeit 1822-32*, Leipzig, 1929, p. 630.
2. *Goethes Werke*, E. Trunz, ed., vol. IX, Hamburg, 1955, p. 283; hereafter cited as *Werke*.
3. Roy Pascal, *Die Autobiographie Gehalt und Gestalt*, Stuttgart, 1965, p. 25.

must, therefore, approach this self-portrait of the artist as a young man with this in mind. For Goethe intends "poetic" or "inner" truth which is, to be sure, built upon the consultation of historical sources. The list of reference works used by Goethe in order to reconstruct his youth is staggering. But it is simply the necessary point of departure for a permanent recording of a significant personality and the spirit of the times in which he lived.

The idea of writing an autobiography was first noted by Goethe in October of 1809. As he so delightfully puts it, he is beginning to become historical.[4] Looking back upon the past half century, he sees the need for a durable monument to the period of transition from the sweet reasonableness of the Enlightenment to the exuberant realism of Storm and Stress, for which he is in part responsible.

A basic motive for this autobiography is, then, to record the critical beginnings of a new era of self-consciousness and, subsequently, self-expression. The poet now comes of age as the dominant personality in Germany; he proclaims himself a genius, whether he is one or not. More important for Goethe at the age of sixty-two is the need to fulfill his genius. For despite the impressive list of accomplishments in literature, science, and affairs of state, it is quite apparent that he is becoming increasingly dissatisfied with the small and fragmentary nature of his creative output.[5] The works he has written, taken together, appear hardly to be the work of one author;[6] as opposed to the writings of Shakespeare, Racine, and Klopstock, they display no unity. He is now seeking to "fill in the gaps" and to realize an inner coherence of what he has experienced and thought. For Goethe, the main object of biography is to exhibit the man in relation to the features of his time and to show what view of mankind and the world he, the poet, has formed from them. The individual must know himself and his age and for Goethe the relationship is so close that, to quote him directly:

4. *Werke*, IX, p. 559. See also Ursula Wertheim "Zu Problemen von Biographie und Autobiographie in Goethe's *Asthetik*" in *Goethe-Studien*, Berlin, 1968, and Hans Pyritz "Selbstschau des alten Goethe" in *Goethe-Studien*, Köln, 1962, as valuable studies of this aspect of Goethe's creative career.

5. *Ibid.*, p. 7.

6. *Ibid.*, p. 7.

Any person born ten years earlier or later would have been quite a different being, both as regards his own attitude and his influence upon others.[7]

Before starting his autobiography, Goethe had occupied himself considerably with this genre. His reaction was one of almost total dissatisfaction with the writing of biography in the eighteenth century. Pedantic compilations of factual detail had, so far as he was concerned, simply destroyed numerous interesting personalities whom he had come across;[8] they did not provide the sense of unity necessary to satisfy his artistic impulses. And for Goethe, autobiography belonged rightfully to the genre of poetry. In a letter to Schiller in 1802, he spoke of the interest that could be derived from the perspective of old age, for it was the maturity and wisdom that comes with age which would provide the interpretation, that is, the indispensable "Dichtung" of the work.[9]

Seven years elapsed before Goethe made note of an outline for an autobiography, two more before he actually began work upon it. It deals only with the first twenty-five years of his life, from his birth in 1749 till his departure under dramatic circumstances for Weimar in 1775. The situation is that of an elderly epic writer trying to objectify, with irony and distance at his disposal, a period of intensely subjective, lyrical expression. The work is divided into twenty books and four parts, each part containing five books and a maxim to provide a moral. It reveals a basic pattern of interweaving the personal joys and tribulations of the narrator with those of his nation and the century in which destiny has placed him. The subject matter constantly shifts between the practical and the specific on the one hand, the abstract and the general on the other. The simplest details of everyday life are closely associated with crucial intellectual issues of the day. Sometimes Goethe speaks for himself, at other times for his nation. What unfolds before us then, are the emotional conflicts of a poet bound up with those of a young, vibrant but amorphous nation struggling to regain its self-expression. The intimate

7. *Ibid.*, p. 9.
8. *Ibid.*, p. 600.
9. *Ibid.*, p. 604.

relationship between the poet and his nation is repeatedly underscored; both come of age simultaneously, which would appear to be a unique phenomenon in the history of literature. A most charming feature of this work is that it is spiritual autobiography and spiritual biography, as well.

Let us now consider the four parts of *Dichtung und Wahrheit* in order to see what kind of personality Goethe has wished to leave with us, and how it was fashioned by the world about him.

The writing of Part I occupied Goethe the better part of the year 1811;[10] in it he tells us of the first fifteen years of his life, taking us up to 1764. They are spent entirely in Frankfurt and its surroundings, which Goethe describes here with the love and pride of a native son. He is much more a citizen of Frankfurt than he is a German. Frankfurt is a veritable macrocosm which provides a relief from the occasional tension in his home. It serves as the dominant poetic symbol throughout the first five books, recalling the past splendor of the Holy Roman Empire and appearing not to be appreciably changed from the Germany of the sixteenth century. The portrait culminates with an impressive portrayal of the coronation of Joseph II as King of Rome, an event which Goethe was privileged to witness and record for his father.

Fond recollections of relatives, illnesses and doubts as to the effectiveness of inoculation, an education that smacks of dilettantism despite a watchful father, a strong desire to write verse — these are the dominant impressions and issues of the first six years of Goethe's life. The earthquake in Lisbon in 1755 disturbs the basic peace and happiness of earliest childhood; a sense of harmony is lost that is not to return for the remainder of the autobiography. Belief in God as a benevolent Creator is severely shaken. The first of several religious crises is upon Goethe; in retrospect, he speaks respectfully of the growing movement of Separatists in opposition to Orthodox Protestantism during his boyhood, and in this unique manner symbolizes what were his first feelings of uneasiness about dogmatic religion and his need for spiritual depth. This is highly characteristic of him and furthermore it reveals an important source of his poetic inspira-

10. *Ibid.*, pp. 604-7.

tion. He plays the role of boy-priest, worshipping at an altar which he has constructed in his room. It is the earliest demonstration of his need for a direct, personal relationship with God.

The boy-priest however, usually gives way to the boy-poet. Goethe speaks of a vague feeling early in life that he was going to do something extraordinary; a bit later, he sees himself wearing the laurel wreath of the poet. A mission in life has been realized, but the obstacles to complete fulfilment are to be numerous.

The sense of external peace is further shattered in 1756 with the outbreak of the Seven Year's War. For Frankfurt it means occupation by French troops. For Goethe, it means withdrawal into the home and subsequently into the realm of his rapidly developing imagination. Political differences within the family, brought on by the war, destroy a previous sense of harmony in this sphere. A French count quarters himself in the Goethe household, and while the father detests his presence, the son can only admire his personal behaviour and artistic taste.

A very positive image of France, derived from many influences, impresses itself upon the ten year old. It is the first great culture to make itself felt in his life. He passionately attends the theatre and is captivated by the art of Marivaux, Racine, and Molière. He makes the acquaintance of French travelling players, imitates French forms of drama, and begins to study the theories of Corneille. Rich as his experience with French culture is, his intellectual horizon expands in other directions at this time: the English language, the Books of Moses, mythology, geography all capture his attention. Klopstock has brought alive the figures of the Old Testament, yet the Anacreontic poets also charm with their wit and grace. The impressive library of Goethe's father, with its encyclopaedias of 17th century learning and its histories, is at his disposal and avidly used.

With the Treaty of Hubertusburg, the war is concluded and Goethe experiences life in the outside world once more. Frequently sent on errands by his father, he acquires a healthy respect for the artisan and the lower middle class and too, he learns of the seamier side of life. He makes friends easily for he can tell a good tale. Because of his poetic gifts, he becomes an object of hero-worship, but due to his youthful naivety and his comfortable circumstances, he is a target for schemers as well. At fifteen he falls in love with a girl named Gretchen, but she returns his affection with merely an amiable, polite condescension befitting an older sister. He becomes slightly involved in a scandal; the disgrace arising therefrom causes a physical breakdown. Part I ends on a note of despair, with Goethe in extreme mental anguish about the fate of Gretchen; he is clearly a victim of his imagination. The maxim: "Man is educated through disgrace," would indicate that sorrow is necessary for the understanding and mastery of life. It is a theme that is to assume profound importance for Goethe's poetry.

The personality of a would-be poet has emerged, one of intense sensibility and fantasy, one who is both gregarious and intellectually curious. He is highly aware of his poetic gift, but he is not certain of its implication. Furthermore, there is a father who is most sympathetic to the development of his son's talent, a rather happy exception in Germany at this time, one would suspect. In fact, he expects an annual volume of poetic works! The conditions for development are both promising and ominous.

Part II records the last year and a half spent in Frankfurt as a child, three rather unsatisfying yet valuable years in Leipzig, the subsequent need for a second physical and mental recuperation at home, and the start of an exciting new emotional and intellectual life in Strassburg. It is a span of six years, from 1765-71, and it records a breath-taking development. In order to recover from the affair with Gretchen, Goethe seeks in nature and in study emotional relief. Nature does provide this, study does not. Nature is able to convey a sense of the sublime and awaken in his artistic temperament the impulse to sketch rather than to write poetry. The conflict in Goethe, whether to express himself poetically or pictorially, is dwelt upon frequently. His eye now becomes aware of the universe, whereas previously it had been restricted either to his immediate surroundings or to paintings at home. The quest for learning, however, so necessary for Goethe's poetry, leads merely to frustration; philosophy and religion as dogmatical discourse have no appeal and the occupation with encyclopaedias, once a happy introduction to this world, now tends only to confuse.

It is with a feeling of liberation and high expectancy that

Goethe departs for Leipzig in October, 1765 to experience university life. For an aspiring poet, the atmosphere could hardly be more discouraging. The conflict, whether to pursue legal studies or belles-lettres, is serious; his counsellor has little use for the latter, and the professors whom he does hear on most any subject are hardly enlightening. He gives us a charming account of his experiences in the lecture hall:

> I here mention . . . another evil by which students are much embarrassed. Professors . . . cannot all be of the same age, but when the younger ones teach . . . only that they may learn, and moreover, if they have any talent, and anticipate their age, they acquire their own cultivation . . . at the cost of their hearers, since these are not instructed in what they really need but in that which the professor finds it neccesary to elaborate for himself. Among the oldest professors, on the contrary, many are for a long time stationary, they deliver on the whole only fixed views, and, in the details much that time has already condemned as useless and false. Between the two arises a sad conflict . . . which can scarcely be set right by the middle-aged professors who, though sufficiently instructed and cultivated, always feel within themselves an active endeavour after knowledge and reflection.[11]

The sense of alienation is deep; Goethe feels both intellectually and socially completely misplaced in this "small Paris." His precocity borders on the arrogant; his Frankfurt dialect and his odd clothing help to discourage any sense of belonging. The fragmentary nature of the German nation and its intellectual fabric is tellingly portrayed here. Critical analyses of the Bible disturb Goethe, for this is a work which has been the basis of his moral education and is, furthermore, an expression of poetic genius. Even with those professors who do instruct literature, there is little rapport. Gellert has no sympathy whatever for his verse and little for his prose. There is no supreme principle of art to follow, the standard of literary criticism is much lower than in

11. *The Autobiography of Johann Wolfgang von Goethe (Dichtung und Wahrheit).* Translated by John Oxenford, introduction by Gregor Sebba, London, 1971, p. 266.

other fields of learning, and there is a desperate need for a substantial subject matter of national significance. Goethe observes that Lessing's comedy, *Minna von Barnhelm*, has provided precisely this, for in its portrayal of a reconciliation between Prussia and Saxony it is a symbol of a national ideal. Perhaps poetry, by its example in the realm of art, can point to the solution of problems in the realm of life. Goethe would appear to become aware at this point of a highly important aspect of his chosen profession. It will become the basis of his mature work.

His own poetry takes an important step forward. Convinced by now that he is not a descriptive poet, he learns to turn each event or object, as a source either of joy or sorrow, into a symbol. This will have profound implications for the development of German literature. As a re-creator of nature he can now more adequately come to grips with the world and can begin to produce his great confession. What Goethe has now to confess about his life is consistently negative: he behaves moodily, even nastily in his second love affair with Käthe Schönkopf; this subsequently takes poetic form in his first play, *The Lover's Caprice*. Daily life is tedious and thus filled with pranks. Religious doubts increase and encourage hypochondria. Figures of authority, be they Frederick the Great or Gellert, lose stature and his only friend, Behrisch, is an eccentric whose greatest talent lies in caricature and sarcasm. After two years in Leipzig, Goethe's hopes for a new sense of fulfillment fade; he realizes that as a writer and a person he lacks considerable experience, which for him is indispensable for the creative process. The only benefit he has derived has been from visits to art galleries in Leipzig and Dresden. He is acquainted with the criticism of Lessing and Winckelmann and is able better to establish the relationship of painting to literature, and of art to nature. Goethe does not write outstanding poetry while at Leipzig; in fact, he burns all his works and projects in a moment of despair. But he appears to have become aware of new directions that poetry, his own and that of his nation, must take.

In September, 1768, Goethe returns home with the feeling of being shipwrecked. The ensuing months are ones of intensive soul-searching. Within a short space of time he falls ill twice and seeks healing both in alchemy and in a world of Neo-Platonic, cabbalistic, and mystical thought which, he tells us, looked strange enough. He re-reads letters written from Leipzig, which serve to impress upon him the superficial state of his heart and mind.

By the spring of 1770, his mental and physical health is finally restored. With a desire to step into life once more, Goethe leaves for Strassburg to resume his study of law. What was so negative in Leipzig is now depicted at his second university in a positive, even exuberant light; friendship, intellectual and artistic experience, self-confidence, and love all deepen and grow. His world becomes expanded through stimulating discussions with medical students and through his experience of the Cathedral; he begins to forsake the occult for the world of natural science. Marie Antoinette appears personally and impresses with the grandeur and importance of political power. Instead of a Behrisch for a friend, he now confides in an upright young man such as Jung Stilling. He is more consciously aware of the power and merit of human passion as the key to understanding the nature of man; even his occupation with the law, up to now an incoherent mass of encyclopaedic knowledge, assumes new meaning through the practical nature of that study and its application in Strassburg. He meets Herder, who opens his eyes to profoundly different functions of poetry, for it expresses the feelings not of the educated, but rather of the people. Recalling these joyful, enriching experiences in 1812, Goethe sees the present re-awakening of interest in German medieval art as a splendid fulfillment of youthful desires and impressions in Strassburg; hence the motto of Part II is: "Whatever one wishes in youth one has in abundance in old age."

Books 11 through 15, comprising Part III, reveal the full emergence of the poet and his nation as independent entities. The German genius, individual and national, comes of age. The years covered are 1771-4, in which Goethe concludes his stay in Strassburg and experiences the Imperial Court of Justice at Wetzlar briefly; the time spent at home in Frankfurt rapidly diminishes, for frequent side-trips to the region of the Rhine bring him increasingly in contact with the world of the court and encouraging prospects for a future career. The early seventies are a period of immense creativity; Goethe develops his own lyrical style. He deals with a range of human passion considerably beyond that of Klopstock, not to mention his predecessors. A more direct relationship between the poet and his surroundings is expressed. These are possibly his two most significant contributions to German poetry. In *Götz von Berlichingen* and *The Sorrows of Young Werther* he has revolutionized the drama and novel as well. The over-riding power of sentiment now makes its presence felt; love becomes the dominant sentiment. The affair with Friederike Brion evokes joy and a subsequent confession of guilt which is reflected in his lyric and in the dramas *Götz von Berlichingen* and *Clavigo*. The agonies in parting from Friederike are soon to be followed by those of an unanswered love for Charlotte Buff; this precipitates his departure from Wetzlar and the subsequent resolution to write *Werther* in order to prevent suicide. It is a powerful example of Goethe's ability through the poetic process to achieve mental equilibrium and thus avoid a personal catastrophe.

The ever-present concern with intellectual inquiry — be it in history, mythology, law, religion or natural history — occupies much of his time and energy without providing any ultimate spiritual fulfillment. Goethe obtains his degree in jurisprudence and his dissertation is cautiously approved, but the chances for realizing a soul-satisfying practice of the law appear remote. This deeply frustrating situation is expressed in two ways: first, in a portrayal of his father's increasing dissatisfaction with the political structure of his native city; we see him as one completely alienated from the political process and therefore seeking consolation in cultural interests. Consequently, he distrusts court life in general. Second, Goethe makes the legal machinery at Wetzlar into a convincing poetic symbol of all that is decadent and inefficient in the Holy Roman Empire. It stands out in dramatic contrast to the past splendour envisaged in the imagery of Frankfurt in Part I.

The conflict of a creative genius trying to reconcile himself with the world of practical affairs now appears in a new form in Germany. For Goethe is more concerned with creativity than a Hagedorn or a Gellert, and he is more occupied with practical matters than a Klopstock. With the double success of *Götz* and *Werther*, he is the acknowledged leader of a group of uninhibited poets that is about to declare war on all forms of social and political injustice. Yet he admits that he and his friends have no inclination to deal directly with these issues; they prefer instead to study the nature of man. The narrator is no longer "I," it is now "we." Pride in German tradition expresses itself in numerous ways; *Götz* dramatizes the German as great, vibrant, and honest, the Strassburg Cathedral is German, not Gothic architecture. Klopstock revives the heroes of Germanic mythology to replace those of classical antiquity in his poetry. A feeling of youthful German vigour is about to unleash itself but there is, strangely enough, no natural channel into which to direct it, for the generally peaceful political temper of the times serves to deter rather than encourage the poetic imagination and budding intellectual spirit. Yet the fierce cultural patriotism of the day does lead an attack on French culture, for Strassburg has awakened feelings of political suppression by the French; their intellectual and social arrogance is underscored. It is a nation and culture old in spirit. Goethe is no longer concerned with Marivaux; he prefers to denounce Holbach. Moreover, with the composition of *Werther*, he now favours the English mind as a literary example; he particularly admires its ability to portray so convincingly the world of melancholia and, we must remember, it is the genius of Shakespeare that has provided the poetic inspiration for *Götz von Berlichingen*.

The search for an emotionally satisfying religion continues to plague Goethe; once more he tries to construct his own theology. Personal acquaintance with Lavater, Basedow, and the circle of Storm and Stress provides only limited insight. The *Ethics* of Spinoza, with its unselfish love of God, gives considerably more peace of mind. The self-portrait is that of a child of the world, a poet convinced of his calling in life yet still very uncertain as to how to realize it. Can a poet be a creator, can he be totally adjusted to his surroundings and furthermore, what can he really do to improve them? These are the problems presently confronting Goethe. He becomes pre-occupied with the divine qualities in man; he attempts to deal artistically with various religious figures such as Mahomet, the Wandering Jew, and Prometheus, but all these works remain fragments. Even if he had completed them, he would have satisfied only the creative and not the practical side of his personality. Frankfurt provides no sense of fulfillment in law and business; its medieval splendor now gives way to a symbol of physical, social, and intellectual confinement. The only feeling of accomplishment is derived from work on a journal of literary criticism.

All the more appealing, then, is the prospect of life in a culturally active duchy. Such a notion does not meet with the approval of his father. Whether to travel, to pursue a profession, or to marry — these are the questions facing a successful poet and rather unsuccessful human being and, on a note of bewilderment, the third part of the autobiography concludes. In retrospect, Goethe realizes that there are limits to the aspiration of youthful genius; he applies accordingly to Part III the following maxim: "It is provided for that trees do not grow in Heaven."

In marked contrast to the first three parts, Part IV (Books 16–20) is considerably shorter. Its writing was frequently interrupted and for lengthy intervals, extending to March, 1831, just one year before Goethe's death.[12] The structure is much looser, and the epic narrative gives way to brief commentaries upon both personalities and general conditions encountered during the years 1774-5. The issue of physiognomy is in particular dwelt upon. The parallel treatment of poet and nation recedes and the tone is decidedly aphoristic and all too fragmentary. The motto of this section: "There is no one against God, unless it be God himself," reflects further the poet's basic concern with divine laws and the proper adjustment to them. The feeling of uncertainty, dominant since the very opening pages, continues to prevail. As Goethe becomes increasingly at odds with the world, the awareness of his natural gifts crystallizes into the form of a daimon, which he can only hope will guide him to a happy destiny.

The problem of how a poet adjusts to society is even more pressing than how he comes to satisfactory terms with the universe. The practice of law remains no more than a routine function. Yet another love affair, now with Lili Schönemann, shows Goethe's characteristic lack of resolution in dealing with young ladies. Socially he feels inferior to Lili, and it is only through the initiative of an eager matchmaker that he finds

12. *Werke*, X, pp. 615-17.

himself engaged to the talented beauty. The joys of being a fiancé are but momentary and, confronted with reality, a sense of crisis and indecision prevails. The incompatibility of religion and family background turns Goethe away from an alliance or any firm commitment; he seeks refuge instead in his own genius and exaggerated sense of independence. A trip to Switzerland provides a momentary respite from immediate problems; upon his return, he resolves his dilemma characteristically by creating the tragic figure of Count Egmont and accepting the call to Weimar. On the paradoxical note of the beginning rather than the end of a brilliant career, the autobiography closes. The sense of the demonic has now fully taken hold which Goethe, identifying himself with Egmont, graphically portrays in one of the most breath-taking poetic images in the literature of Storm and Stress:

> Child! Child! no more! The coursers of time, lashed, as it were, by invisible spirits, hurry on the light car of our destiny, and all that we can do in cool self-possession is to hold the reins with a firm hand, and to guide the wheels, now to the left, now to the right, avoiding a stone here, or a precipice there. Whither it is hurrying who can tell? and who, indeed, can remember the point from which it started?[13]

What has Goethe revealed of himself personally, and how does he appear as a German personality of the 18th century? It is a personality mercurial rather than strong; genius creates more problems than it solves. The variety of emotion and situation presented in this self-revelation is stunning; Goethe gives us the widest possible spectrum – he is morally earnest and yet also impish, he is a frustrated theologian, but he does enjoy cards and outings; he is not too good a dancer or a painter, but his powers of combination and his quickness of comprehension are remarkable. He enjoys ice-skating and swimming in the nude with his fellow geniuses. He is a fickle lover but a dutiful son and a devoted brother. He is aware that assertion of self must be counter-balanced by renunciation of that same self in order to be at peace with laws and forces that guide the universe. He balances his

13. *The Autobiography of Goethe*, Vol. II, London, 1882, p. 168.

virtues with his vices; in marked contrast, he is consistently generous when speaking of others and in portraying his relationship to them, be they great or insignificant personalities. He tends to portray men realistically and women idealistically. His father is a perfectly delightful figure, for he is convincingly human. His mother, on the other hand, seems idealized, indeed almost infallible. When portraying men, Goethe presents the world in which he must live — one of error, frailty, and limitation; when portraying women, he gives us the world in which he would like to live — one of moral order, preservation, and stability. It is characteristic of him and his century that a woman Pietist and "Beautiful Soul," Susanna von Klettenberg, should give him the proper advice to seek wider horizons in Weimar.

He is above all a poet — a victim of his imagination yet, paradoxically, dependent upon it for mental equilibrium and survival. Basically, a universal nature of poet and personality is revealed. One is astounded at the variety of verse form and genre contemplated and attempted, if not mastered, before Goethe's twenty-fifth year. It has been well observed that for a clue to the mystery of the creative process, Goethe's autobiography provides the best possible source.[14] For Goethe concerns himself constantly with the catalysts necessary to revive German literature: experience, emotion, learning, faith, reverence for one's own cultural tradition and those of other civilizations — he used all of these elements to produce a great confession.

Goethe's autobiography was intended to record the struggle, individual and national in scope, for self-realization. Fortunately, the outcome was successful. For Goethe, this meant being a poet, one who exists for his own sake; it reflects a driving need to turn reality into poetry. In the first twenty-five years of Goethe's life, the poet had made spectacular advances in intellectual and social stature.[15] He became a prophet, an educator, a leader;[16] he began to assume a dignity half-divine and unassailable. He could become

14. James Fenton, review of *The Autobiography of Goethe*, John Oxenford, transl., in the *New Statesman*, 10 Dec. 1971.

15. W. H. Bruford, *Germany in the 18th Century: The Social Background to the Literary Revival*, Pt. IV, Chs. I & II, Cambridge, 1959.

16. Max Kommerell, *Der Dichter als Führer in der deutschen Klassik*, Berlin, 1928.

a great man, and in Germany, this is precisely what happened. By 1775, the most eminent figures in Germany were men of letters who had exalted their subject above other branches of learning. Poetry was the fount of knowledge, not religion or philosophy; this is what Goethe was beginning to feel at Leipzig.[17] He entered that university in 1765 with the modest hope of becoming a professor, a skilled versifier, and a useful member of upper middle-class society. Ten years later, he was at the mercy of his genius, advising a duke how to govern his duchy and helping him to create a new nobility of mind and spirit to replace a nobility of social class that had fallen into ill repute. It is interesting to note that in his search for a new nobility of the 18th century how frequently he returned in his imagination to that of the 16th century, with its spirit of "Nobilitas Litteraria" and its sense of freedom. Such diverse figures as Gotz von Berlichingen, Martin Luther, Ulrich von Hutten, and Hans Sachs are objects of admiration in the autobiography. It would appear to be time for a second Reformation in Germany

The sense of order and optimism into which Goethe was born at mid-century had been, as we have seen, severely challenged. But with the destruction of one teleological order a new one, aesthetically conceived, took its place. The artistic vision of the whole became for Goethe a fundamental guide; to realize it was the basis for his poetry. The autobiography abounds with images and even direct statements reflecting this principle. An important aspect of his personality was this deep desire for totality and a fear of fragmentation.[18] Being in agreement with his surroundings is one way of expressing it. He has been hailed as the living example of the integrated personality, whereas Schiller merely put forth the ideal.[19] One would like to ask: how often did Goethe feel integrated, that is, really in harmony with the universe that he so incessantly explored? Probably only when directly engaged in the poetic process, for it is in this act that he can fully realize his

17. *Werke*, IX, Bks. VI - VIII.
18. E. M. Butler, *The Tyranny of Greece over Germany*, Boston, 1958, pp. 85-154. This is a most valuable commentary on this aspect of Goethe's artistic personality.
19. E. M. Wilkinson and L. A. Willoughby, *Goethe Poet and Thinker*, New York, 1962, p. 17.

deepest impulse, which is to build a world in which he can live. This is a world not of realism, but rather of poetic realism.

Dichtung und Wahrheit is hardly the work of a self-satisfied poet enjoying world acclamation. It is rather the attempt to fully identify a personality with the spirit of his times — the spirit of passion, introspection, empiricism, patriotism, sentimentalism, pantheism, the sublime, humane ideals, and moral fervor. This spirit also reflected itself in national and historical consciousness, the search for a precise definition of art, and a new awareness of the potential conflict between art and life. Goethe did not create these values nor these issues, but he shared them with the age of his youth in full measure. He was, in retrospect, in total agreement with the times, which had called for profound spiritual unrest and change. This had to be recorded for posterity. The autobiography reveals a sense of spiritual fulfillment for a nation, but hardly for its poet. This it must provide — an aesthetic and psychological experience that will relieve Goethe of a sense of fragmentation. There must be a feeling of unity in his work, and therefore in his life. He was at one time in accord with his century; is he now? Underlying this work of mature artistry is the need to create a poetic symbol that can provide a convincing justification of a life, for the abundance of old age has clearly not been realized. While *Faust* is rightfully recognized to be the supreme expression of Goethe's intellectual and emotional strivings, one should pay considerable tribute to *Dichtung und Wahrheit* as a unique confession of a brilliant early maturity and the need to fulfill those promising beginnings. It provides a magnificent cultural portrait and it helps greatly to explain the problems confronting an 18th century poet and his personality.

R. Van Dusen

Popular Protest
in 18th Century Europe

Internal conflict was a feature of the eighteenth century, as it was of any other. Historically, of course, the most significant conflicts were those for the control of the State; the conflicts between monarchy and privileged orders, and those of the "rising" bourgeoisie either as an ally of one or the other or in opposition to both. But there was also a fourth type of conflict, which also tended to assume greater dimensions and a greater momentum as the century went on. This was the challenge to authority by peasants, industrial workers and the urban and rural poor, struggling for an element of social justice or a place in the sun. There were occasions when such movements became harnessed to those of the aristocracy or middle class and contributed, in consequence, to the power-struggle of other contending groups. More often, however, they had an identity of their own and were concerned with more limited aims which aroused little or no sympathy among the "middling" or upper classes. It is for this reason, no doubt, that historians have largely ignored them or treated them with mild disdain or condescension. (G. M. Trevelyan, for example, decided that English riots of the time, though frequent, were merely blind explosions of anger behind which there lay "little or no social discontent."[1]

These popular protests assumed a variety of forms, depending on the classes engaged in them and the geography or social development of the regions and countries in which they took place. They varied between the peasant rebellions in Eastern Europe and the food riots that were more common in the West; between wages' and consumers' movements, and city riots in which social and political issues were often blended. Yet, for all their variety, they had certain qualities in common which,

---

1. G. M. Trevelyan, *England in the Age of Johnson*, London, 1920, p. 7.

broadly, distinguished them from popular disturbances in the century that followed. For one thing, they tended to take the form of direct action and the destruction of property rather than of petitions or peaceful marches or demonstrations; and this was as true of peasant rebellion as it was of industrial machine-breaking, the imposition of a "just" price in food riots or the "pulling-down" of houses or the burning of their victims in effigy in city outbreaks. Yet such targets were generally carefully selected and destruction was rarely wanton or indiscriminate. Such movements tended to be spontaneous, to grow from small beginnings and to have a minimum of organisation; they tended, too, to be led by leaders from "outside" or, if from "inside," by men whose authority was limited to the occasion. They were generally defensive, conservative and "backward-looking," more concerned to restore what had been lost from a "golden" past than to blaze a trail for something new; and, accordingly, such political ideas as they expressed were more often conservative than radical and they tended (with some notable though rare excep-tions) to be borrowed from conservative rather than radical groups. Theirs, in short, was the typical pattern of protest of a "pre-industrial" age.[2]

Let us look more closely at the various forms that protest took. The old-style peasant rebellion was now – for the time being, at least – largely confined to countries in Eastern and South-eastern Europe, where feudal tenures and obligations were more than mere survivals, where agricultural "improvement" had made little progress, and where the taxes levied by the absolute, bureaucratic state were an increasing burden on peasants and small owners of land. Russia was such a case and here, since Peter I's time and more particularly in the reign of the Empress Elizabeth and the first dozen years of Catherine the Great, peasant risings were almost endemic. There were 73 risings in 1762-9 alone; and these take no account of the innumerable disputes of the indentured peasant workers engaged in the Urals foundries and mines.[3] Risings were generally directed against officials and

2. See G. Rudé, *London and Paris in the 18th Century. Studies in Popular Protest*, London, 1970, pp. 17-34.
3. R. Portal, *L'Oural au XVIIIe siècle. Etude d'histoire économique et sociale*,

landlords — over taxes, land, feudal obligations, army recruiting, or simply poverty and the high price of bread — but rarely (if ever) against the person of the Tsar or Empress herself. The greatest of them — in fact, it was the greatest peasant rebellion of the century whether in Russia or anywhere else — was that led by Emelyan Pugachev, an illiterate Don Cossack soldier, in September 1773 to December 1774. Pugachev turned up in September in the district of Yaik in the south Urals, where the Cossacks were already in open revolt against the government over the loss of traditional privileges. Like a dozen other pretenders before him, he claimed to be the murdered Peter III, "the protector of the people," whose decrees of 1762 (shortly before his assassination) had raised hopes of a general peasant liberation;[4] and he promised to restore their liberties to the Cossacks, freedom to the serfs and independence to the Bashkir people to the east. So, with an army of Bashkirs and Cossacks swelling to one of 20,000 men, he marched up the Volga, recruiting peasants on the way and urging the serfs on the nobles' domains and the peasant-workers in the Urals foundries to revolt against their masters. He captured Kazan; a serf revolt followed at Nijni; and such of the Urals foundries as were not burned to the ground by the Bashkirs went on strike. Pugachev was now expected to march on Moscow and there was near-panic at St. Petersburg. So Russia's topmost generals, including Panin and Suvorov, were ordered to the Volga to head him off. But Pugachev, to avoid a frontal engagement, now turned south. He captured Saratov and nearly took Tsaritzin; yet he was defeated at Sarepta and his support was dwindling, as the Cossacks refused to take part in any general peasant rising. So, losing faith in his cause, his lieutenants handed him over to the army who brought him to Moscow in a cage for execution. Once the government had bestirred itself, the rebellion had been crushed with comparative ease; moreover, it was, in a sense, only the last of a long series of peasant disturbances that had gone on for the last twenty years. Yet it had distinguishing features that set it apart and caused intense alarm among the governing classes. It had spread over a

Paris, 1950, pp. 315-29.

4. Marc Raeff, "Pugachev's Rebellion," in *Pre-conditions of Revolution in Early Modern Europe*, R. Forster and C. P. Greene, eds, New York, 1970, pp. 169-72.

vast region, enclosing the middle Volga valley and the plains lying between the southern slopes of the Urals and the Caspian Sea. It had won support among such disparate elements as Cossacks, Old Believers, Urals foundry-workers and the serfs of the Volga domains; and it had shaken the throne itself with its widely believed imposture of a "people's Tsar." So it stirred up a violent backlash and, while leaving potent memories to later generations, more immediately contributed to the speed with which Catherine abandoned all further thoughts of a general peasant reform.

Outside Russia, the most sustained of the peasant rebellions in the East were those in the Austrian dominions. Broadly, they fall into two main periods: those preceding (or anticipating) the Emperor Joseph II's agrarian reforms, and those following in their wake. Among the first was a peasant rebellion in Silesia, directed against the *Robot*, or compulsory labour service, in 1767. Four years later, the first of the *Robot* Patents, imposing a standard form of service, was applied to Silesia. But it was not yet applied elsewhere, though rumours were rife that Joseph, who had been co-ruler with his mother, Maria Theresa, since 1765, was already planning a general charter of peasant "liberties." Fed by this rumour, an uprising took place in Bohemia in 1775, when 15,000 peasants marched on Prague; they were led by a young man who bore a striking likeness to the Emperor himself, and they demanded that the landlords should immediately put into effect the charter which they mistakenly believed had already been proclaimed at Vienna. So the demonstration was clearly one of support for and not one of hostility to the Imperial government; and, to justify the peasants' confidence, the standard *corvée* was now applied in Bohemia as it had been in Silesia before, while Maria Theresa ordered that the old manual *Robot* should be commuted to a monetary payment on her private estates. Joseph's reforms of the 1780s, as is well known, went considerably further. The Emancipation Patent of 1781 ended personal bondage by giving the peasant freedom to leave his village and to marry without his lord's consent; and the Taxation Patent of 1789 extended Maria Theresa's earlier and more limited reform by allowing the peasants throughout the Austrian dominions to discharge their labour-service obligations by making a payment in money instead of in kind. But there were two important reservations: the reform applied only to peasants on "rustical" (that is, non-domain) lands and those paying an annual land tax of two florins or more. So perhaps half the peasants were excluded. Moreover, there was the usual delay in enforcing the law. So there were rebellions both by peasants excluded by the law, by those impatient to enjoy its provisions, and by others to whom the new method appeared a greater burden than the old. For these and other reasons, peasant revolts broke out in Transylvania in 1784, in Moravia in 1786 and in Austria in 1789. A more despairing outcry was caused by the repeal of Joseph's law of 1789 a year after it had been passed: many peasants had, meanwhile, sold their teams of oxen and felt, with some justification, that they had been badly let down. So there was a widespread refusal to render *Robot* in either form; but peasant spirits, elated by the hope of a better life to come, had been crushed and no overt rebellion followed.[5]

Elsewhere, the eastern-style of peasant rebellion appeared to be a thing of the past; yet in those countries where feudal, or seigneurial, relations still survived — as in France, Spain and Germany — it needed only a new general convulsion like that stirred by the revolution in France to bring it back to life. France herself was, in this respect, an interesting case. The peasant *jacquerie*, or direct confrontation with the landlord or government (the latter being, at this stage, far more common than the former), had been a frequent occurrence in the century before. In Richelieu's time, in the 1620s to 1640s, there had been the rebellions of the *Croquants* (or "poor countrymen") and the anti-taxation riots of the *Jean-va-nu-pieds* in Normandy. Under Louis XIV, peasant rebellions had flared up again in the great rising over the salt tax around Bordeaux in the 1670s, which had extended over ten provinces in the south and west. In the 1680s and 'nineties, there had been the revolt of the *Camisards* in

5. For the above, see E. M. Link, *The Emancipation of the Austrian Peasant 1740-1798*, New York, 1949, pp. 105-65; R. J. Kerner, *Bohemia in the Eighteenth Century*, New York, 1932, pp. 278-83; E. Denis, *La Bohème depuis la Montagne-Blanche*, 2 vols., Paris, 1903, I, pp. 550-558; P. F. Sugar, "The Influence of the Enlightenment and the French Revolution in Eighteenth Century Hungary," *Journal of Central European Affairs*, 17, 1958, pp. 342-3.

Calvinist Languedoc and other revolts in Catholic Quercy and Périgord over *corvée*, taxes and tithe; while the reign ended in a final outburst of peasant riots over the disastrous harvest and famine of 1709 and the exactions of the tax collectors for the War of the Spanish Succession. After which (apart from a widespread outbreak of rural hunger-rioting during the Regency in the 1720s), peasant rebellion came to a stop and only revived in anything like its earlier form in the early months of 1789; while, in the intervening sixty-five years, such peasant protest as occurred took the form of intermittent food-rioting, which, as we shall presently see, involved not only peasants but other small consumers as well. It is a strange phenomenon, as the more fundamental peasant grievances – over tithe, taxes and seigneurial obligations – had by no means been solved, as would become amply evident when the Revolution broke out. The explanation must lie in the evidence brought forward by the researches of Edouard Labrousse: they convincingly show that a great part of these intervening years (more particularly those of 1733 to 1778) were years of steadily advancing prices and prosperity for rural proprietors and tenant farmers, or for any one else in the countryside whose holding was large enough for him to produce for sale in the market.[6] So the rest – the *parcellaires*, the *métayers*, the landless and the small consumers – vented their anger in food riots when occasion demanded; while the underlying grievances of the peasant community as a whole lay dormant and would only explode again, with renewed vigour and dramatic suddenness, in the economic catastrophe that began to face them all in the great crisis of 1787-8.

England's case was quite a different one. Here there was virtually no trace of that feudal or semi-feudal system of landlord-tenant relations that still existed in France; and here the agricultural revolution was affecting a far more thorough social transformation than in any other part of Europe. One of its characteristic forms was the enclosure of the old "open" field, the displacement of the small peasant freeholder (or his conversion

---

6. C. E. Labrousse, *Esquisse du mouvement des prix et des revenues en France au XVIIIe siècle*, 2 vols., Paris, 1933; *La crise de l'économie française à la fin de l'Ancien Régime et au début de la Révolution*, Paris, 1944, pp. ix-xli, 625.

into a hired labourer) and the growth in the size of properties and farms; while, as a further sign of the times, turnpikes were set up to levy tolls on the new roads that brought the growing loads of grain to market. So the destruction of turnpikes and fences became a frequent occurrence in the English countryside. There were riots against turnpikes around Hereford and Worcester in 1735-6; around Bristol in 1727 and again in 1753; and, in June of that year, every turnpike was pulled down near Leeds, Wakefield and Beeston in the West Riding of Yorkshire. Enclosure riots, though most frequent after the first General Enclosure Act was passed in 1760, were scattered throughout the century: in Northampton in 1710, in Wiltshire and Norwich in 1758, Northampton and Oxford in 1765, Boston in 1771, Worcester in 1772, Sheffield in 1791, and in the Northampton district in 1798.

The Scandinavian experience was a different one again. Sweden and Norway (though not Denmark) were countries of small peasant proprietors enjoying a relatively dignified and independent status: in Sweden, the peasants even had their own parliamentary representation. Moreover, as in France, the greater part of the century was a period of rural prosperity; nor had the small peasants, as in England, been depleted by enclosure or an agricultural revolution. After 1760, however, the peasants began to face a double threat: first, the tax collector; and, second, an acute economic depression in the 1780s. They reacted vigorously to each in turn. In 1762, Denmark (which then included Norway) nearly went to war with Russia over Schleswig-Holstein, and the consequent exactions of the tax collectors provoked the peasants in the south of Norway to engage in the so-called "Strilars' War." In Sweden, too, in the 1770s, the peasants fought tax collectors — in Finland, Holland and Skåne — and royal officials attempting to enforce a government monopoly in brandy.[7]

More serious disturbances followed the economic depression of the 1780s, first in Sweden and later in Norway. The most protracted and the most significant of these was the Lofthuus affair that spread through the south-western districts of Norway in

---

7. See B. J. Hovde, *The Scandinavian Countries, 1720-1865*, New York, 1948, pp. 191-9; and H. Koht, *Les luttes des paysans en Norvège du XVIe au XIXe siècle*, Paris, 1929, pp. 236-52.

1786 and 1787. As in all the Scandinavian countries, it was a period of crop failures and shortage that threatened the peasants and small consumers as a whole. But the Norwegian rural population – cultivators, fishermen and foresters alike – had other grievances besides: the Danes held a monopoly in the sale of grain (revived after the fall of the "enlightened" Dr. Struensee in 1772); the high prices of imported wheat were a boon to merchants but a threat to farmers; and rich merchants were buying up forests that came up for sale at knock-down prices. So a movement developed, involving fishermen, foresters and farmers; its targets were government officials and the wealthy bourgeoisie – but not the King, whom the peasants saw, as they did in Austria and Russia, as "the father of his people." The movement found a spokesman in Christian Lofthuus, a one-time prosperous farmer who had been ruined by business failures during the American War. In June 1786, Lofthuus took what was at first a purely private petition, addressed to the King, to the capital city, Copenhagen. He was received by the Crown Prince who asked him if he also spoke on behalf of others. Thus encouraged, Lofthuus returned to Norway and began to round up the peasants to support a collective petition to the King. Its terms were: an end of the Danish monopoly; a reduction in the large number of taxes (said to be thirty-six) that the peasants had to pay; and, most radical and novel of them all, "that the King shall give us as our superiors natives of Norway who understand our needs." The peasants responded with enthusiasm; and when local officials attempted to arrest Lofthuus (collective petitions had been made illegal in 1765), they prevented it; and the Intendant was forced to grant him and thirty others a permit to travel to Copenhagen to lay their petition before the King. However, on landing in Denmark, they found that their permit had been cancelled and returned to their homeland to muster further support. Meanwhile, a commission had been set up in Copenhagen to look into the peasants' grievances, which found eventually that most of them were justified; redress was ordered and over-zealous officials were punished. Lofthuus, however, was not spared. A warrant was issued for his arrest; he was hunted down, condemned to a life sentence, and locked up in the fortress of Akershus, where he died, ten years later, in 1797. Yet the affair was an important one and, like Pugachev's very different style of revolt in Russia, had considerable repercussions. It had actively involved two provinces and touched seven more. It had had a remarkable success: most of the grievances had been met by 1795; and though Lofthuus died in the event, the legend of the great peasant leader lingered on for generations. Moreover, it was an unusual movement of its kind which, in its type of leadership, its precise demands and its organisation and peaceful petitioning, looked forward to the movements of the century that followed.[8]

Meanwhile, with the advance of industrialisation, there developed in several European countries a growing rift between the masters and their employees. As the old guild system disintegrated and as the guild became more and more the sole preserve of the master craftsmen, the wage-earners and journeymen found themselves increasingly thrown on their own resources and sought protection in organisations or "combinations" of their own. In England, trade unions of hatters, tailors and woolcombers, though strictly illegal, were already in evidence in the early years of the century; and, in London, strikes were conducted by committees of tailors from 1719 on and there were committees of sailors and weavers in the great wave of industrial disputes in the 1760s. In France, organisation (though never quite as sophisticated as in England) took two main forms. These were the (legal) *confréries* of the trades which, although ostensibly benevolent societies – like the Box Clubs and Goose Clubs in England – also raised money for the conduct of industrial disputes. There were, besides, the more exclusive, illegal and secret journeymen's associations, or *compagnonnages*, organised on masonic lines, which, in addition to lodging apprentices at ports of call during the Tour de France, set standards of work and rates of pay and organised strikes. There were two main confederations among the *compagnonnages*: the Enfants de Solomon and the Compagnons de Devoir; and these, in turn, were further divided into "gavots" and "dévorants," who were often at daggers drawn.

Strikes, then as now, were generally fought over workers'

8. Koht, *op. cit.*, pp. 258-78; Hvode, *op. cit.*, pp. 199-202.

wages and conditions: to increase or maintain wages, and to shorten hours which were inordinately long (the Paris book-binders, for example, struck in 1776 for a fourteen-hour day). Or they might, as they were increasingly after the 1770s, be directed against the use of machinery; or, again, against the employment of wage-cutting or unwelcome intruders: in London, weavers and building workers rioted against cheap Irish labour in 1736 and the "single-handed" weavers fought it out with the "engine-loom" weavers in 1768; while, in France, "gavots" and "dévorants" were continually at each others' throats. In both countries, there were three main waves of strikes in the three-quarters of a century preceding the French Revolution. In France, up to the late 1720s, it was paper workers, the most highly organised and most militant of all French industrial workers of the time, who appear to have been most frequently engaged. There was a lull in the 1730s to 1760s, only broken by a great strike of Lyons silk weavers in 1744. After 1770, strikes became generally more frequent: with paper workers involved again in 1772 and 1780, Paris bookbinders and printers in 1776, and Beauvais textile workers in 1778. The biggest wave of all was in the years of economic crisis leading up to revolution: Lyons silk weavers again in 1786, miners in 1788, and a simultaneous movement of trades in Paris, Nîmes and St. Etienne between 1786 and 1789. In England, it was not paper workers but miners, woolcombers, tailors and London's Spitalfields weavers that were most commonly to the fore. Early in the century, there were the weavers' "calico" riots and tailors' strikes in London between 1719 and 1722. In 1768-9, there was a great wave of strikes of London weavers and coalheavers and half-a-dozen other trades, similar to that in Paris twenty years later; while, in the 1780s, with the advent of an industrial revolution, disputes tended to become more frequent and to spread more widely over the industrial centres of the Midlands and the north.

While the purpose of strikes were broadly similar to those of today, their timing and the forms they took were different. As trade unions were illegal, short-lived and local, or few and far between, disputes tended to take place when labour was scarce rather than in plentiful supply, that is, on the crest of a boom rather than in the trough of a slump. As to methods, these were sometimes peaceful, taking the form of raising money, marches and petitions: there were a number of this kind in the London strikes of the 1760s. But these were more often the exception than the rule.[9] More typically, strikes developed into riots and attacks on property, attended by the destruction of the employer's house, machinery or mill. This machine-breaking (or "Luddism"), as Dr. Hobsbawn has pointed out, was of two kinds. On the one hand, it might be a form of "collective bargaining by riot," where the intention was purely to bring an uncooperative employer to heel; this was the more typical and traditional of the two, going back in both France and England to the sixteenth century, at least. The other — the more recent kind — was directed against machines that put, or were believed to be putting, men out of work.[10] This was the case in a sawyers' riot in London in 1768; but it became more frequent, as the industrial revolution gathered momentum, in the 1780s. In France, it was first seen on a large scale in the machine-breaking that followed the importation of the new "English machines" into the textile mills of Normandy and Picardy in 1788-9.[11]

But strikes, whether violent or peaceful, were, until the last two decades of the century, a comparatively rare occurrence even in the West. Far more frequent and more typical of the age, and embracing far larger numbers, were the movements of small consumers of town and countryside that generally took the form of food riots. Of 275 disturbances that I have noted in England between 1735 and 1800 (and there were certainly many more than these), 175 were disturbances of this kind; and Daniel Mornet records 100 food riots occurring in France between 1724 and 1789, of which more than half took place in the twenty-five years immediately preceding the Revolution.[12] They were so frequent both because bread (which was generally the main item involved)

9. E. Labrousse *et al.*, *Histoire économique et sociale de la France*, 2 vols., Paris, 1970, I, pp. 682-6.

10. E. J. Hobsbawm, "The Machine-Breakers," *Past and Present*, Feb. 1952, pp. 57-70.

11. F. E. Manuel, "The Luddite Movement in France," *Journal of Modern History*, 10, 1938, p. 183.

12 D. Mornet, *Les origines intellectuelles de la Révolution française*, Paris, 1933, pp. 444-8.

was the staple diet of the poor, accounting for a large part of the poor man's weekly budget; and because its price was subject to frequent and violent fluctuations. M. Labrousse has estimated that in France, between the 1720s and 1780s, the average wage earner would spend, even in times of relative plenty, about half of his income on bread;[13] in England the proportion was probably not quite so high. These proportions would, of course, rise significantly in times of shortage and rising prices, which, in both France and England, became more frequent after the early 1760s. This was due to a number of factors, including the subsidies paid to exporters (thus depleting stocks available for home consumption); speculation, "forestalling" and the "cornering" of supplies by dealers; the poorness of communications, which hindered a more effective distribution from "producing" to "consuming" districts; the progressive abandonment of government-sponsored controls and regulations; and a series of bad harvests which, irrespective of all other considerations, depleted stocks, forced up prices and provoked waves of panic buying. And it was, not surprisingly, in such years of shortage and fear of famine (rather than of famine itself) that food rioting most characteristically developed. In England, there were provincial riots in 1727, sporadically in the 1730s, in 1740, 1756-7, 1766 (the worst year of all), 1772-3, 1783, 1790 and 1795. For France, Mornet has recorded them in forty separate years between 1724 and 1789 and in all but three of the twenty-five years following 1763.[14] In both countries, rioting occurred mainly in country districts and market and provincial towns. The capital cities went relatively unscathed, though this was more true of London than of Paris. In Paris, serious bread-rioting before 1789 occurred in 1725, 1740, 1752, and 1775, with minor outbreaks in 1771 and 1778; while, in London, if we except a few handbills and slogans in 1768, no single food riot took place until the lean war-years of 1795 and 1800. This relative immunity may have been largely due to the special measures taken by governments, for sound political reasons, to provision and police the largest centres of population.

13. Labrousse, *Esquisse*, II, pp. 597-608.
14. Mornet, *loc. cit.*

In the case of London, there were probably other reasons as well. For one thing, the London poor were never at any time exposed to the same fear of famine as the poor in Paris. In addition, London had a protective shield that other cities lacked: the shield of the near-urban county of Middlesex, which, to the north and west, could serve as a shock-absorber to this type of riot on its most vulnerable flank. (Paris, on the other hand, lay dangerously exposed to "contagion" from the villages round about).[15]

Food riots drew in a variety of participants and assumed a variety of forms.[16] In towns, the small consumers taking part in them were a cross-section of the urban *menu peuple*; in villages, they were, typically, peasants, cottagers, rural craftsmen and industrial workers: miners, tinners, woodcutters, weavers, spinners and the like. Their object might be to stop grain being shipped overseas or from being taken from a producing to a non-producing district; or, in both types of district, to force the merchants, millers or bakers to reduce the current market price. In the first case, they might loot the stocks of grain or prevent the departure of the ships, barges or waggons transporting them elsewhere; in the second, they might invade the market, flour-mill, barn or baker's shop and loot or destroy stocks or demand that the price come down. In the latter (the more frequent) case, it was generally a mixture of all three; but the most characteristic form of protest and that reflecting most closely what Edward Thompson has called "the moral economy of the Poor,"[17] was, having demanded that prices be reduced and received an unsatisfactory response, to impose a reduction of their own (the French *taxation populaire*). This is what frequently happened in the two largest outbreaks of food-rioting in the century: that of July-October 1766 in England and of April-May 1775 in France.

In the first, riots broke out, at intervals, in four or five separate regions of the Midlands and west, beginning in Devon and spreading, in a series of disconnected and uncoordinated leaps, to

---

15. G. Rudé, *op. cit.*, pp. 55-6.
16. For France, see Louise A. Tilly, "The Food Riot as a Form of Political Conflict in France," *The Journal of Interdisciplinary History*, 2 (1), 1971, pp. 23-51.
17. E. P. Thompson, "The Moral Economy of the English Crowd in the Eighteenth Century," *Past and Present*, May 1971, pp. 71-136.

Gloucester and Wolverhampton in the west, to Norwich in the east, to Derby and Nottingham in the north and Leicester in the centre. Those taking part in them were, according to newspaper reports, most commonly weavers, tinners, colliers, bargemen, disbanded servicemen, or merely "poor" — in short, the typical participants in English rural riots of the day; and, in nearly every district, they invaded markets, flour-mills, and bakers' and enforced the sale of wheat and flour at 5s. a bushel, bread at 1d or 2d, butter at 6d or 7d, meat at 2 1/2d and cheese at 2-1/2d or 3d a pound. The French riots — the so-called *guerre des farines*, or "flour-war," of Turgot's day — took a somewhat different form. They were a single "snow-ball" movement, starting at Beaumont-sur-Oise, to the north of Paris, on 27 April and, fed by rumour and example, spreading eastwards, northwards and westwards in a series of consecutive and closely related eruptions from one market or village to the next, and petering out near Fontainebleau a fortnight later. In this time, they had gripped the Ile de France, the capital itself and four of its bordering provinces. The rioters (except in Paris and at Beaumont) were predominantly peasants: wine-growers, farm labourers, small farmers and village craftsmen, but with a sprinkling of village priests and the better-to-do; and everywhere they imposed a similar pattern of prices, with wheat most commonly fixed at 2 1/2 francs a bushel, flour at 20 *sous* and bread at 2 *sous* a pound. So there were significant variations between the two movements: they followed a different pattern of progression; they involved different sets of people; and, in England, their targets were not only grain and bread but butter, meat and cheese besides. But the similarities were more striking. In both, the riots were provoked by a sharp rise in prices following bad harvests and shortage. In both, an appeal was made to authority to revive the old custom of "setting the price" at a "just" or traditional level; and when authority (in most, though not in all, cases) refused to intervene, the people stepped in and "set" it themselves. In neither case was there any substantial political intrusion from outside: even Turgot's numerous enemies at court have been exonerated from the charge.[18] In short, in both countries, this was the typical rural riot in its predominantly spontaneous and undiluted form.

Urban riots, on the other hand, were not so simple and were more frequently touched by political ideas. They arose over a variety of issues. It might be the price of bread or the shortage of food; rarely in Paris and London (as we have seen), but more often perhaps in such cities as Naples, Vienna, Palermo or Constantinople.[19] At Edinburgh, in 1736, the riots that led to the lynching of Captain Porteous arose from the sentencing of two smugglers to death. At Oporto, there were riots in 1757 against the enforcement of a government monopoly in the sale of spirits. In Madrid, the riots of 1766 were directed (ostensibly, at least) against an Italian, Squillace, who, as Minister of Finance, had banned the wearing of wide hats and long capes. Parisians rioted against John Law, the Scottish banker, in 1720; against the militia ballot in 1743 and 1752; against the suspected abduction of children to the colonies in 1720 and 1750; against the Church's so-called *billets de confession* in 1752; and, from 1753 onwards, on behalf of the Parlement in its numerous contests with the ministers of the Crown. Londoners, meanwhile, rioted against Protestant Nonconformists in 1709 and 1715, against Sir Robert Walpole's Excise in 1733, and against the Gin Bill and the Irish in 1736. In 1753, there were "commotions" (though hardly riots) against a government Bill to grant easier naturalisation to alien Jews. On a larger scale altogether were the riots on behalf of John Wilkes in the 1760s and 1770s and against Roman Catholics and their supporters in the summer of 1780. The last of these were the wildest and most destructive and most extensive in the whole of London's history. They lasted for a week during which £100,000 of damage was done, 32 private houses were destroyed, and Newgate and other prisons went up in flames: on the night of 7 June, Horace Walpole counted thirty-six fires raging on both sides

18. For a discussion of the evidence on this point, see Edgar Faure, *La disgrâce de Turgot*, Paris, 1961, pp. 293-318. In the case of the English riots of 1766, I am persuaded by the new evidence brought forward by Dr. Walter Shelton in his recent doctoral dissertation on the subject (Waterloo Lutheran University, 1971) that the hostility of local gentry to grainmerchants served to prolong them. I am grateful to Dr. Shelton for allowing me to consult this work.

19. E. J. Hobsbawm, *Primitive Rebels*, Manchester, 1959, pp. 114-16.

of the Thames.[20] Nearly 300 people were shot dead in the streets or died of wounds and, of more than 450 persons arrested, twenty-five were hanged and fifty others sent to prison. "The destruction of property," writes M. Godechot, "was ten times that done in Paris during the whole period of the Revolution."[21] While the scale of the violence done to property was exceptional, the methods used were not. Both on this and on other occasions — and this was as true of other cities as it was of London — houses marked for destruction were "pulled down" and their contents flung into the streets and burned. Yet targets were carefully selected and not left to chance or momentary excitement. Moreover, the violence to property was not matched by a similar violence to persons. In the Gordon Riots not one of the 285 people killed in the streets was a victim of the crowd; and the murder of Captain Porteous in the Grassmarket at Edinburgh was a quite exceptional case.

Apart from the ostensible issues, why did such rioting take place? It may be argued that the very structure of old cities — with their tortuous alleys and closely packed tenements — lent itself to disturbance. Others have argued that "urbanisation," or the rapid growth of cities, inevitably brought in its train not only overcrowding, crime and destitution, but also periodic social protest.[22] Such explanations, however, tend to beg all sorts of other questions and, even where they are not entirely misleading, do not take us far. Among such other questions, the economic factor clearly played a part. Wages, taxes and food prices were matters of constant popular concern; and these often obtruded even where other issues were more immediately apparent. Food prices, for example, were high at the time of the London anti-Irish riots and the Edinburgh Porteous riots of 1736, as they were in the Wilkite disturbances of 1768-9 and 1771-2 and the Paris riots accompanying the "aristocratic revolt" of 1787-8; and they were more obtrusive still (if they were not the primary cause) in the

20. *The Letters of Horace Walpole, Earl of Orford*, P. Cunningham, ed., 9 vols., London, 1891, VII, p. 388.

21. J. Godechot, *The Taking of the Bastille*, London, 1970, p. 18.

22. See, e.g., Louis Chevalier, *Classes laborieuses et classes dangereuses à Paris dans la première moitié du dix-neuvième siècle*, Paris, 1958.

Madrid riots of 1766. Yet there were other riotous occasions — as in London in 1763, 1774 and 1780 — when prices were stable or comparatively low; so this, too, cannot serve as a universal explanation. In some disturbances, a religious element played a part: notably so in the *billets de confessions* agitation in Paris and the London outbreaks against Protestant Nonconformists in 1709 and 1715 and against Roman Catholics in 1780. In others, there were evident signs of national prejudice or of hostility to foreigners. Thus there were anti-English feelings engaged in the Edinburgh riots of 1736, while the Wilkite movement, conversely, was in part directed against the Scots; as the Madrid riots were directed against Italians and the Gordon Riots found targets among a variety of foreigners, including Irishmen, Italians, Frenchmen and Spaniards.

But a more distinctive feature of the eighteenth century urban riot was its liability to have political undertones; this broadly sets it apart from the other types of disturbance we considered earlier. This political intrusion generally came from outside and from "above." Thus in Paris, it was the Parlement that served as the initiator, if not actually the instigator, of the riots over John Law in 1720, over the *billets de confession* in 1752, and in practically every disturbance that was not directly concerned with wages or food between 1753 and 1788. In London, a similar impetus was given by the City's Court of Common Council or its Common Hall to the disturbances that broke out over Excise in 1733, gin in 1736 and the ill-fated "Jew Bill" of 1753; and, again, over Wilkes on various occasions between 1763 and 1774 and over the Catholics in 1780. (On the latter occasion, the Common Council protested against the relief being granted to Catholics on the eve of the riots and repeated their protest when the riots were at their height.) This is not to say that in either city the crowds had no interests of their own and were merely slavishly obeying the orders given them by others; but it does suggest that there was, in both, a certain collusion between the rioters and the city authorities in which the Parlement in the one case and the Common Council in the other served as a kind of political mentor to the people in the streets.[23] Yet there was a significant distinction between the two.

23. For a discussion of this "collusion" in London, see my "Collusion and

In Paris the mentor was an aristocratic group; in London, it was what the Webbs have called a "rate-payers' democracy." The distinction, as we shall see shortly, might be of some importance.

For the politics of urban riots – where such issues intruded – tended to be conservative rather than radical; that is, they reflected causes that were aristocratic, clerical or monarchic rather than those promoting middle-class liberal or democratic reform. In Madrid, the riots of 1766, while concerned with food-prices, Italians and broad-brimmed hats, were strongly suspected (though possibly erroneously) of having been provoked by the Jesuits to unseat the reforming anticlerical ministers of Charles III. In Naples, the *lazzeroni*, like the *popolino* in Rome and Palermo, were, in spite of their frequent riots, staunch upholders of Church and King.[24] In Stockholm, it was with the aid of the people in the streets that Gustavus III carried out his "enlightened-monarchist" *coup d'état* against the aristocracy in 1772. In Tuscan cities in 1790, crowds rioted against Archduke Leopold's measures to curb the influence of the Church. In Brussels, they attacked the houses of the Vonckist democrats in March 1789, disarmed them, beat them up and drove them out of town. In Vienna, they welcomed Pope Pius VI when he came to remonstrate with Joseph II over his Church reforms, as they would later against General Bernadotte when he hoisted the tricolour flag over the French Embassy in 1798. Parisians, as we have seen were rioting on behalf of the aristocratic Parlement up to the very eve of the Revolution. In London, too, the crowd's allies in the Common Council were Tories or Jacobites and King and Church men until the 1750s; but when William Pitt, the Great Commoner, arrived on the scene, the Common Council changed its colours and became radical, and the crowd followed suit. This new political complexion was clear enough for all to see in the Wilkite riots of the 1760s and 'seventies, though it was not quite so obvious in the "No Popery" riots of 1780. On the one hand, they showed no regard for religious toleration and their outcome strengthened the Court party and Lord North at the expense of the old Whig opposition:

Convergence in Eighteenth-Century Political Action," in *Paris and London in the 18th Century*, pp. 319-40.

24. Hobsbawm, *op. cit.*, p. 115.

to that extent they clearly served the established order. On the other hand, hostility to Popery was part of a long-standing Whig and radical tradition; and it was City radicals like Wilkes's friend Frederick Bull (and at first they included Wilkes himself) who had protested most loudly against Catholic relief. So it was not simply a return to the old-style Church and King movements of the early years of George I. Moreover, when English city crowds turned right again — as they did in the Birmingham and Manchester riots of 1791 and 1792 — it was not for long; and popular radicalism, nourished by the writings of Tom Paine, returned soon after to London and the north.

So the "lower orders" of London, partly because they had middle-class and not aristocratic mentors, were the first to make a decisive turn to the left; they were followed in the early and mid-1780s by those of Geneva and of certain large cities in Holland like Amsterdam and Utrecht. Elsewhere, the turning-point came with the French Revolution. In Paris, the crowd switched sharply to the bourgeois-radical cause after September 1788, when the Parlement, by insisting that the Estates-General should be constituted as it had been early in the century before, disappointed all hopes that it might serve as an instrument of radical reform. So the crowd, having abandoned one ally and attached itself to another, moved left. Other cities followed after a shorter or longer lapse of time, depending on what their bourgeoisie had to offer or on their proximity to France. The lapse was shorter in Belgium, Switzerland, the German Rhineland and the north of Italy, and longer (as we should expect) in central and southern Italy, most of Germany, Scandinavia, Austria and Spain.

One further question remains: it is really a kind of addendum to what I have said already. We have seen that popular movements, like those of the aristocracy and bourgeoisie, assumed a greater frequency and intensity after the 1760s: the Pugachev rebellion in Russia, the peasant revolts in Austria, the Lofthuus affair in Norway, the Wilkite and "No Popery" riots in London, the *guerre des farines* in France, the popular uprising in Geneva (in 1782), all took place in the last twenty or thirty years before the French Revolution. M. Jacques Godechot, the distinguished French historian, has argued that all of them — including the Boston riots of 1773, but excluding the Wilkite and Lofthuus movements with which he is not concerned – should be treated in a common context of industrial and agrarian change, of rising prices and falling wages and of a rapid growth in population; moreover (he adds) they all reflect the consequent development of a common "revolutionary mentality."[25] Thus, in his view, there are substantial connecting links between these riots and rebellions breaking out from the early 1770s onwards "from the Urals to the Alleghanies."[26] It is a view that has, most recently, been endorsed by Dr. Paul Dukes, a historian of Russia, who has argued that the Pugachev rebellion must be firmly placed within the context of the "Atlantic" or "Democratic" revolution of the West.[27]

I am willing to concede that this "common-context" argument has a good deal to recommend it. It is certain that the great changes in population, in industrialisation, the growing exactions of the bureaucratic State, the spread of the Enlightenment and the lag of wages behind prices were features of the later rather than of the earlier half of the century. Thus, the 1760s may be seen as a kind of watershed of social and political change; and this, in turn, helps to explain why so many riots and disturbances of every sort occurred in the last two or three decades of the Old Régime. In this sense, even if we insist that in some countries these factors were far more potent than in others, we may agree that there is a broad common context, reaching beyond the boundaries of individual countries, in which they may all be placed; and it is perhaps more than a pure coincidence that so many of these events – in France, Bohemia, Russia and America – happened almost simultaneously about 1775. But to argue further (as M. Godechot does) that they were all expressions of a generally developing revolution of the West is surely to distort the picture and to overstate the case. For even if the Genevan events of 1781-2 and the Dutch events of 1783-7 may be seen as a prelude to later revolution, the same can hardly, without outrageously

25. Godechot, *op. cit.*, pp. 5 ff.
26. J. Godechot, *France and the Atlantic Revolution of the Eighteenth Century*, New York, 1965, p. 3.
27. P. Dukes, "Russia and the Eighteenth Century Revolution," *History*, no. 118, Oct. 1971, pp. 371-86.

stretching the limits of credulity, be said of the Gordon Riots, the Pugachev rebellion, or even of the grain riots of 1775 in France. The distortion perhaps arises from a failure to look through the telescope at both ends; for each of these events can only be brought into proper historical focus by seeing it in its national as well as in its international context. In short, when it really comes to the point — and I hope this won't seem too insulting a question — don't England's and Russia's earlier history and their current stage of development tell us much more about the Gordon Riots and the Pugachev rebellion than the demographic "explosion" or what happened at Boston in 1773?

G. Rudé

Towards a Study of Crime
in 18th Century England:
A Note on Indictments

Throughout the eighteenth century Englishmen were convinced that crime was increasing. From the anonymous pamphlet
Hanging Not Punishment Enough (1701) at the beginning of the
century to the long and detailed analysis of London crime by
Patrick Colquhoun at the end,[1] there was a stream of alarmed
comment about the danger of the rising tide of criminality,
analyses of its causes and prescriptions for its solution. The stream
broadened with the century, not only because the alarm increased,
but because the growth of newspapers and magazines of all kinds
made available the means of bringing crime before the public in a
way never before possible. And the public was obviously both
insatiably curious and appalled and alarmed at the same time.

Most of the contemporary comment was directed against
violent crime and violent crime in London in particular. The
danger of travelling in and around the capital, the likelihood of
being beaten and robbed not only on the highways but in the very
streets of the city itself was repeated and embroidered throughout
the century. The anonymous author mentioned above thought
that highway robbery had reached such proportions in the recent
past that some deterrent more frightening than hanging would
have to be found to check it. The death penalty unadorned was
clearly too mild: "Were it not so," he argued,

> Our Roads would not be so pester'd with that wicked
> Generation of Men, nor our Sessions-Paper Monthly, and the
> Publick News daily full of so many Relations of Robberies

* I would like to thank the Canada Council for the financial support that made the
research for this article possible.
1. Patrick Colquhoun, *A Treatise on the Police of the Metropolis*, (1796).

and Murthers, and all the Pleasure and Satisfaction of Travelling destroyed, as it is now, by being so dangerous and unsafe. . . . If some Remedy be not found to stop this growing Evil, we will shortly not dare to travel in England, unless, as in the Desarts of Arabia, it be in large Companies, and Arm'd.[2]

The particular dangers of London were at the centre of concern throughout the century, but the conviction that crime was rising out of control was more general than that. There was an increasing sense not only of the growth of crime but of its pervasiveness, a fear that society was in danger of being engulfed. It is this that lies behind the increasing harshness of the criminal law. The progressive extension of the death penalty – a process that began in the sixteenth century but which accelerated rapidly in the eighteenth[3] – was most frequently justified in the multiplying statutes by a declaration that the crime in question had in late years much increased and new rigour was called for. It is perhaps true that the harshness of the law was to a considerable extent offset in practice,[4] but the fact remains that members of parliament wanted capital punishment to be more extensively employed because they thought the country gripped by increasing lawlessness.

In commenting on the growth of crime in this period – in default of anything resembling criminal statistics – historians have most commonly reported this contemporary opinion. Some have detected evidence of a reduction of violent crime in London in the second half of the century,[5] but on the whole, if any view can be said to hold, it is the contemporary belief in rising crime rates, and especially for crimes against property. But no very clear picture emerges in the historical literature. One searches in vain for a precise discussion of the nature of these trends: when did the rise

2. *Hanging Not Punishment Enough for Murtherers, Highway-men and House-breakers*, 1701, reprinted by Basil Montagu, 1812, pp. 7-8.
3. Leon Radzinowicz, *A History of the English Criminal Law and its Administration since 1750* I, 1948, p. 4.
4. *Ibid.*, pp. 25-28.
5. Dorothy George, *London Life in the Eighteenth Century*, 1925, pp. 16-17; W. E. H. Lecky, *History of England in the Eighteenth Century* VII, 1892, pp. 335-8; George Rudé, *Hanoverian London, 1714-1808*, 1971, p. 97.

begin; was it a rural as well as urban phenomenon; was it largely professional or necessitous crime; was violent crime in fact on the wane, and if so when did the decline begin; were other kinds of crime besides larceny increasing? These are not the only questions that can be asked about crime in this or any other period. But they lie half-formed behind much of the work that touches on crime in the century; half-formed and even less investigated. And it is hard to see how they could be investigated on the basis of the contemporary verbal evidence which, however indispensable it is for many questions, cannot give much help with these. If they are to be satisfactorily investigated we will have to find some new source of evidence. It is the contention of this paper that such a source exists in the judicial records, and in particular in indictments. Though they require careful handling — for there are numerous difficulties surrounding their use as 'criminal statistics' and, indeed, surrounding the whole question of the measurement of crime — the data that can be derived from indictments does provide us with a way of measuring trends in various kinds of crimes and in various parts of the country over the course of the eighteenth century.

II

Formal charges for the vast majority of crimes in the eighteenth century were laid by way of indictment in the court of quarter sessions and at the assizes.[6] The bill of indictment, which

6. Most of the criminal business arising in a county was dealt with by the county quarter sessions and the assizes. By the late seventeenth century, the relationship between these two courts was clear. The quarter sessions confined itself almost entirely to petty crimes — assaults, petty larceny, misdemeanors of various kinds — and left the major offences to the assizes. It was the principal task of the professional judges who came on circuit twice a year to clear the gaols: they tried the serious felonies, especially those that brought the death penalty. Quarter sessions were also held in many boroughs, but it would seem that the criminal jurisdiction of most of these courts was very limited in practice. In Surrey, for example, quarter sessions were held four times a year for the Borough of Southwark at which, in the second half of the eighteenth century at least, a number of petty thefts and other crimes were dealt with. But this was unusual. It is likely that Guildford and Kingston-upon-Thames are more representative of the normal situations of boroughs. In both towns quarter sessions were regularly held by the mayor and aldermen but they were principally concerned with nuisances and administrative disputes of various kinds. Occasionally they heard an assault case, but the normal criminal business of the towns was left to the county quarter sessions and to the assizes.

was drawn by the clerk of the court on parchment (and, before 1732, in Latin) provides the following information: the name, residence and occupation of the accused; the date, place and nature of the crime; the name of the victim; the names of witnesses; and frequently, though not invariably, the plea of the accused, the verdict of the jury and the sentence of the court. Though indictments have some serious deficiencies as sources for the study of crime,[7] they do provide a good deal of information and, where they survive in consistent series,[8] they enable us to reconstruct the principal criminal business conducted in a county from year to year. The important question, however, is whether the trends revealed in this criminal business reflect changes in actual crime or in something else. Before plunging ahead to count indictments we must ask how trustworthy they are as guides to criminality.

The general problem of the validity of criminal statistics has been debated in criminological circles since the subject was first opened up in the second quarter of the nineteenth century. There are a number of crucial problems, mostly centering around the so-called "dark figure" of unknown crime — crime that never appears in any statistics, however carefully collected and sophisticated they may be. There are many stages between the commission of a crime and the appearance of an accused person before the courts: the crime has to be detected and reported; the accused has to be identified; the authorities have to pursue and apprehend him; and he has to be committed to trial. But not all crime is in

7. The most important is that the charge against the accused is legally defined and categorized; and it is in the nature of the indictment to subsume variety under the legal definition and make it fit an appropriate legal niche. To the law one robbery was much like another. A clumsy and impulsive hold-up by a half-starved amateur, netting him a few pennies-worth of food would be described in an indictment in the same terms as a planned heist of several hundred pounds worth of goods by a professional gang. The nature and value of the goods stolen would, however, be included in the indictment and this is some help, but generally speaking indictments are at their weakest as sources for the historian of crime when what is required is knowledge of motives and the actual nature of an event. The information that would allow crimes to be categorized by other than legal criteria — motive, for example, or the degree of violence employed — cannot be derived from the formal charge laid before the court.

8. Assizes indictments for the eighteenth century are preserved for the Oxford, Northern and Home Circuits only; county quarter sessions indictments are available for most counties.

fact detected; not all detected crime is reported; and not all criminals are identified; and so on. All criminal statistics represent a sample of the crime actually committed and the sample is either larger or smaller depending on the point along the chain of administrative procedure it is drawn from; at every stage it is further reduced. Most modern criminologists support the view that the best sample is drawn from a point as close as possible to the actual commission of the crime; that is to say that the number of reported crimes (crimes "known to the police") is a better guide to criminality than the number of people committed to trial and that this in turn is better than the number convicted.[9]

In the eighteenth century there is no possibility of recovering an equivalent of "crimes known" to the authorities and the best sample, according to this dictum, is provided by the number of accused sent to trial, that is by the number of indictments. There is no doubt, however, that this gives only the most fragile guide to actual criminality. Even in modern societies with fully developed and professional police forces, the "dark figure" of unknown crime is thought to be very large indeed.[10] It is likely, given the comparative haphazardness and inefficiency of the administrative system, that an even smaller proportion of the crime committed in the eighteenth century found its way to the courts. It is impossible to know how much crime in fact went unreported. Patrick Colquhoun guessed that it might be ninety per cent in the 1790s and considering modern estimates this might not be too far off.[11] There is the further problem of differential selection: it is likely that certain kinds of crimes would be more reported than others, certain kinds of offenders than others, and that a higher proportion of crimes committed in a rural area would get to court than those committed in London. The weakness of indictments as reliable indicators of the crime actually committed is evident and, though a comparison of crime reported in the press with the amount of crime indicted in the same period might give us some rough insight into the dimension of the problem, the "dark figure"

9. Thorsten Sellin and Marvin E. Wolfgang, *The Measurement of Delinquency*, 1964, p. 19.
10 *Ibid.*, pp. 36-40.
11. Colquhoun, *Treatise*, p. 223.

will remain as a permanent difficulty.

On the other hand, if one could be sure that the "dark figure" remains stable, that the relationship between actual and known crime remains constant over a long period, then changes in the level of indictments for various crimes could be taken to indicate trends in those crimes. The question is whether this relationship does remain constant. If it does not, if at one point a larger or smaller proportion of actual crime is getting into the courts than at another, the changing levels of indictments will clearly not reflect trends in crimes, but something else. For, as has been said, the number of indictments tried before the courts mirrors social attitudes and administrative processes as well as the amount of crime in the community. Public attitudes towards the law and towards punishments, the trouble and expense involved in a prosecution, the nature and efficiency of the magistrates and the police and of the judicial system in general – all this and more is reflected in the number of accused persons who appear in court. And it is clear that a significant change in any of these elements could produce a change in the number of indictments coming to trial without there being any change at all in crime actually committed. If indictments are to be used to indicate trends in crime over the course of the eighteenth century, therefore, it is necessary to see if there were any significant changes that might seriously affect that proportion of actual crime that found its way into the courts. The most important elements that must be examined are the reporting of crime and the nature of the administrative system.

Concerning the reporting of crime, there is some evidence to suggest that public attitudes towards the law did indeed change over the course of the eighteenth century in such a way as to decrease the number of prosecutions undertaken – that as the law became increasingly harsh, men became more reluctant to invoke it. It was the burden of two generations of law reformers after 1780 that the changes in the criminal code had become self-defeating and that a very large number of crimes were being committed with impunity every year because the public was unwilling to bring men to justice for a relatively minor crime if capital punishment was the likely outcome. In addition to an increasing public reluctance to prosecute, the reformers also argued that magistrates were less willing to commit criminals to trial, that clerks of the peace were less anxious to draw indictments that would lead to capital punishment on conviction, that grand and petty juries were less willing to convict in such cases. The whole burden of the reformers' case was that the extension of capital punishment had encouraged crime by making punishment uncertain. A great deal of evidence was gathered to support this contention.[12]

On the other hand, there is evidence to suggest that neither the reluctance to prosecute nor the discretionary toning down of charges by magistrates and others were entirely new in the late eighteenth and early nineteenth centuries. In 1701, for example, the author of *Hanging Not Punishment Enough* spoke of the public's reluctance to prosecute as a reason to make the punishment of those who did come before the courts as terrifying as possible. Henry Fielding complained in the middle of the century about the remissness of prosecutors who are "tender-hearted and cannot take away the life of a man." And Blackstone, too, noted that the result of a large number of lesser crimes being subject to capital punishment meant that "the injured, through compassion, will often forbear to prosecute."[13] And there is evidence that administrative discretion too was working in favour of leniency earlier in the eighteenth century. Between 1736 and 1739 in Surrey, for example, thirty-one men were committed to gaol on capital charges ranging from theft from a dwelling house to burglary who were in fact actually tried for simple grand larceny and were thereby saved from the gallows.[14] And both in this period and earlier, juries were as anxious as those later — perhaps even more anxious — to take advantage of the possibility of "pious perjury," that is finding a man guilty of a lesser crime than that with which he was charged.

It is unwise to be dogmatic about such a subject. It would

12. See, for example, the *Report from the Select Committee on the Criminal Laws. Parliamentary Papers* VIII, 1819.
13. *Hanging Not Punishment Enough*, 1701, reprinted 1812, pp. 15-16; Radzinowicz, *English Criminal Law* I, p. 414; Colquhoun, *Treatise*, p. 6.
14. Surrey Assize files: Asz 35/176-179 (Home Circuit indictments).

seem reasonable to suppose that the reform campaign of the late eighteenth century did in fact rest on an increasingly wide base of popular disapproval and revulsion against the bloodiness of the criminal code and that that disapproval manifested itself in one way by discouraging victims of crimes against property not involving violence either to refrain from prosecution altogether or to prosecute on a lesser charge.[15] But the change in public attitudes towards the law was not perhaps as sharp as the evidence collected by the criminal law reformers of the early nineteenth century suggests. Similar reluctance to prosecute can be found earlier in the century and though the feelings of revulsion against the law perhaps intensified towards the end and though we undoubtedly must be prepared to take some downward influence on the number of indictments into account, it would not appear to have been such a massive swing nor to have had such a striking influence on the number of charges laid as to make comparisons over time entirely out of the question.

Apart from the affect on the number of prosecutions of changes in public attitudes, other influences could also determine the number of indictments coming before the courts. The most obvious are changes in the administrative system. Such changes might, for example, affect the trouble and expense involved in

15. Fewer and fewer crimes against property which did not involve violence or the threat of violence but which carried the death penalty on conviction — like theft from a dwelling house to the value of 40s. or more, shoplifting, picking-pockets, sheep-stealing and horse-theft — were indicted as time went on. There was never a very large number of pickpockets caught and indicted in Surrey, so a decline from an annual average of four in the 1720s is not startling; but it is striking that not a single person was indicted for picking pockets in Surrey between 1780 and 1784. The fall in the number of indictments for shop-lifting or stealing from a dwelling house or warehouse or ship is just as obvious, from an average of fourteen in the 1720s to nine in the 1750s to four in the 1780s. Housebreaking shows a similar trend, but other crimes which involved violence or in which violence was threatened, like burglary and highway robbery, do not change significantly over the period, except in relation to the growth of the population.

All of this gives apparent support to the views of the criminal law reformers that victims of these crimes were increasingly reluctant in the eighteenth century to see the law take its course. And it means that indictments provide little guide to the incidence of a large number of particular crimes against property. But it does not mean necessarily that fewer and fewer larcenies were being reported, for as indictments for these crimes declined in number there was an increase in the number of crimes prosecuted as simple grand larceny. This suggests that if attitudes to the law were changing the result was a fudging of the evidence, a holding back of the real nature of the crime by the victim or the magistrate in order to prevent the danger of capital punishment, rather than an outright refusal to indict at all.

undertaking a prosecution. These could be important considerations influencing a victim's decision to undertake a prosecution or not. For this involved an initial appearance before a magistrate and then attendance at the trial and a possible wait of several days before the case came on. It must have imposed an even greater burden in the country than in London. In the countryside a man might have to go several miles to find a J.P. in the first place and attendance at the quarter sessions or the assizes would almost certainly involve him in another and longer journey. Apart from these expenses and those of his witnesses he would have the additional burden of legal fees payable for the issuance of warrants and the drawing of the indictment. The time and the expense must have been a considerable discouragement, especially to the poor. In London the expenses involved in journeys and being away from home was probably a little less burdensome. At least in London magistrates were more readily available and some kept regular hours; and the courts also sat more frequently and closer at hand. Even in London, however, the expense and the loss of time involved in a prosecution were seen as discouragements, especially since the chances of recovering lost property were slim. Henry Fielding thought it so serious indeed that he recommended that the public bear the expenses of prosecutors and witnesses; and shortly thereafter, in 1752 and 1754, two Acts authorized the courts to do so if the accused were convicted. In 1778 another Act allowed such expenses to be paid regardless of the outcome of the trial.[16] It is possible that such inducements encouraged more prosecutions, though in the 1790s Patrick Colquhoun was still concerned about it and argued that prosecutions should not be left to the private citizen because too many could not afford either the time or the money involved in undertaking them.[17]

Of great potential significance, then, are changes in the effectiveness of the system of judicial administration. If there were changes in the numbers of J.P.'s or of the officers charged with apprehending and bringing offenders to court, this in itself could significantly increase or diminish the number of indictments tried.

16. 25 Geo II, c. 36, s 11, 1752; 27 Geo II, c. 3, s 3, 1754; 18 Geo III, c. 13, 1778.
17. Colquhoun, *Treatise*, pp. 24-5.

And there were such changes in the eighteenth century. The number of J.P.'s, for example, increased strikingly, as these figures for Surrey and Sussex indicate:[18]

	1680	1702	1715	1742	1761
Surrey	78	118	202	346	468
Sussex	73	88	103	—	163

In Sussex the Commission doubled between 1680 and 1761, while in Surrey it increased six-fold in the same period. However, before conclusions can be drawn about the likely effects of such increases on the number of offenders being brought to trial, we need to know both the distribution — the places of residence — of the new J.P.'s in their counties and also, and even more important, their degree of activity. For many men were in the Commission in a purely formal way, their membership being a matter of social or political rather than administrative significance. A large number of J.P.'s did not even bother to take out their *dedimus potestatem*, which empowered them to act. But beyond that, there were recurring complaints throughout the century that even those qualified to act were unwilling to take their duties seriously. Hardwicke, the Lord Chancellor, complained that "Gentlemen are apt to be very pressing to get into the Commission of the Peace, and when they are appointed, to be very backward in Acting." He went on to say that it was a problem in many counties that "tho' great Numbers are in the Commission, yet there are not acting Justices enough to do the ordinary Business of the Country."[19] Men wanted to be justices for many reasons other than a zeal for local administration and, equally, the political importance of such appointments was not lost on the government. An increase in the number of J.P.'s does not therefore mean too much in itself. Indeed, there is some evidence to suggest that the expansion of the Commission of the Peace did little more than maintain the level of activity of the magistracy. This is suggested by figures from Surrey for the number of J.P.'s committing men to gaol and the house of correction. Between 1720 and 1750, for example, the Surrey

18. *ex inf.*, Miss Norma Landau.
19. Add Mss 35870, f. 242 (I owe this reference to Miss Norma Landau).

Commission of the Peace more than doubled but the number of magistrates making commitments remained the same, as the following table indicates:[20]

1720

1	J.P.	committed	89	prisoners	
1	"	"	23	"	
1	"	"	7	"	
3	"	"	5	"	each
2	"	"	3	"	"
2	"	"	2	"	"
8	"	"	1	"	"
18	"	"	152	"	in total

1750

1	J.P.	committed	53	prisoners	
1	"	"	40	"	
1	"	"	8	"	
1	"	"	6	"	
1	"	"	4	"	
2	"	"	3	"	each
3	"	"	2	"	"
6	"	"	1	"	"
16	"	"	129	"	in total

The number of magistrates making commitments to the county gaol and the house of correction in Southwark remains remarkably constant despite the fact that the Surrey bench more than doubled during this period. And the distribution of the work remained constant too: two men in each period carried the bulk of the load, making between them 74% of the commitments in 1720 and 70% in 1750. A number of others were moderately active but most of the J.P.'s who appear in this list only very occasionally committed someone for trial or to the house of correction. Behind them there is the vast bulk of the magistracy who never apparently committed anyone ever.

20. Surrey Quarter Sessions Papers, 1720 and 1750.

It was this inactivity and the fact that most of the work in the London area was being left to trading justices who had acquired an unsavoury reputation for corruption and acquisitiveness, that lay behind the demand for properly professional magistrates. A start was made by the Fieldings at Bow Street in the middle of the century and soon thereafter several "rotation offices" were established at which magistrates sat daily from 10 a.m. until 3 p.m.[21] In 1792 seven "public offices" were established in addition to the one at Bow Street, each of which was staffed by three professional magistrates and six constables. The salaried magistracy perhaps cleared up some of the abuses associated with trading justices for unlike their predecessors they did not depend on fees for a living. Perhaps they discouraged malicious prosecutions, but it is also possible that by keeping regular hours and having at their disposal a small force of professional constables they encouraged more real prosecutions and were also able to bring more men to trial. But it is difficult to believe that the improvement they brought was on such a scale as to have a massive impact on the number of indictments for serious crimes in the London area. This is true even in the 1790s. Before that there do not seem to have been any changes in the magistracy that might in themselves affect the indictment totals very significantly. And I would say at the moment that this includes the number of J.P.'s in the Commission of the Peace, though a lot more needs to be known about the impact of the expansion of the bench, especially in the countryside.

There may well have been some improvement in the London area in the lower administration, the constables and other officers charged with the apprehension of suspects. Beginning in the 1750s a number of full-time constables were engaged and attached to the "public office" at Bow Street and these were increased in 1792. But these men did not supplant the existing parochial system of scores of independent bodies of watchmen and constables, many of whom were serving for a pittance as a deputy for a wealthier citizen, and all of whom even if they were not old and decrepit, were amateurish and untrained. In the 1820s, on the eve of the

21. Dorothy George, *London Life*, p. 7.

establishment of a professional police force in the metropolis, the overwhelming majority of the officers devoted to keeping the peace and apprehending suspects were still under parochial direction; and despite the improvements brought by the stipendiary magistrates and by the efforts of reforming vestries to improve the quality of the watch in their parishes, "the weaknesses in the structure of the machinery for keeping the peace" in Professor Radzinowicz's words, "remained at the beginning of the nineteenth century as fundamental as they had been half a century earlier."[22] There is even less reason to think that before 1790 the changes that can be observed in the lower administration in the metropolis had a really significant effect on the number of accused brought to trial; and in rural parishes there were no structural changes before the nineteenth century.

I am not arguing here that the improvements in the magistracy or in the parochial administration in London in the second half of the century had no effect at all on the nature or the amount of crime committed in the capital. It may well be, as Dorothy George said, that there was a gradual improvement in the quality of life in London after 1750 and that this brought with it a decline of violence and of crime in general.[23] What I am arguing, rather, is that the changes in the administrative system were not so sudden or so massive as to alter fundamentally the sample of crime represented by indictments, to alter it in such a way, that is, as to make indictment totals an invalid guide to changes in criminality.

The characteristic device used in the eighteenth century to bring offenders to trial was not in any case the improvement of the machinery of law enforcement, but the stimulation of the private enterprise of the citizen.[24] Beginning in the late seventeenth century, the rewards accruing to the individual who successfully prosecuted an offender were gradually extended. Rewards were paid under statute upon the conviction of men accused of certain of the most serious crimes and in addition monetary rewards were more and more frequently offered in the eighteenth century by departments of the government, by local

22. Radzinowicz, *History* II, pp. 178-9.
23. Dorothy George, *London Life*, Introduction.
24. The following paragraph is based on Radzinowicz, *History* II, part I.

authorities and by private citizens. Associations for the prosecution of felons were established all over the country to raise money for just such a purpose. Other rewards were available too. Accomplices were offered pardons for giving evidence leading to the conviction of their colleagues, for example; and the successful prosecution of some crimes brought the informer either a share in the fine, or the award of an exemption from the obligation to serve in local offices. Such rewards lay behind the activities of both the unofficial "thief-takers" like Jonathan Wild and the official work of the "Bow Street Runners" and their successors, for such professionals depended very largely for their living on the fees they earned. This system of financial and other encouragements to prosecution depended on the availability of information concerning both the commission of a crime and the offer of a reward and it is surely no coincidence that it developed along with newspapers and that it became employed more and more extensively as the century progressed and as newspapers developed in both numbers and scope.

How effective it was in stimulating prosecutions is extremely difficult to know. As more and more rewards were offered and as the means of disseminating the information became more readily available, were men brought to court who otherwise would have gone free and, more to the point for my purposes, did it lead to a higher proportion of crimes committed coming to court? It is possible, though the evidence I have at the moment suggests that statutory rewards were not very effective in stimulating successful prosecutions. Substantial rewards were offered, for example, for the conviction of robbers, burglars, pick-pockets and those who stole from shops and houses to the value of five shillings or more — just those crimes, that is, that seem in Surrey at least, to decline in number or remain stagnant over the course of the century.[25] In these cases at least, rewards do not seem to have been effective in stimulating prosecutions when punishments seemed excessively harsh to the public. The same might be said for the granting of an absolute pardon to an accomplice upon the conviction of his companions, for such a temptation was available to the highway

25. See above, note 15.

robber, the burglar and the housebreaker. But this only begins to touch on the problem. There is no really conclusive evidence either way about the effects of monetary rewards and other inducements on the number of indictments brought to trial over the course of the period and it must remain to some extent an open question.

We can have more confidence about the effects of one other change in the judicial system that could easily produce complications for the comparison of indictments over time: changes in jurisdiction among the various courts and levels of administration. Fortunately this is not a great problem in this period or at least its effect is limited. The central problem concerns the growth of summary jurisdiction, the power of magistrates acting alone or at petty sessions to deal with certain crimes. If a significant amount of criminal business had been transferred from higher courts to the jurisdiction of magistrates over the course of the period a serious problem would arise, for it is simply not possible to assemble a consistent record of magistrates' activities over time and on a county-wide basis. There was some such transfer and it does create something of a problem. But it is a minor problem. In the nineteenth century more and more petty crimes – including assaults and larcenies without violence – were transferred from the higher courts to the jurisdiction of magistrates. But this process did not begin in a massive and significant way until 1827. Before that date summary jurisdiction, though constantly expanding, was more limited. Magistrates had the power to deal with infringements of the customs and excise laws and of the game laws; in addition they had wide-ranging powers to regulate pawnbrokers, hawkers, peddlars, as well as alehouses, weights and measures and a whole host of nuisances forbidden by statute. The higher courts could still deal with these matters too, but it is clear that nothing of any significance can be learned about the trend in these offences from the number of indictments tried before the assizes and quarter sessions. But summary jurisdiction did not in the eighteenth century extend significantly to major crimes, and the judicial data is not therefore seriously affected in this period by the kind of transfer of cases from one level of courts to another that must complicate the criminal statistics of the nineteenth century.

III

It is not possible to come to any firm conclusions about the extent to which trends in the level of indictments are likely to be a reflection of changes in social attitudes or in the administrative system rather than changes in criminality. Many variables come into play and the affects of few of them can be measured precisely. Much more needs to be learned about the affects of the enlarged magistracy and the payment of rewards for the conviction of offenders. Perhaps, too, something more precise could be learned about changing public attitudes towards the law and the administration of justice by a study of the reporting of crime in newspapers. It would seem to me at the moment, however, that none of these is likely to have had a really serious, certainly not a sharp, affect on the indictment level. The question is by no means closed, but I would argue that the influences discussed in this paper are much more likely to have slightly retarded or exaggerated changes in the number of indictments coming before the courts than to have caused them. This is not to say that changing indictment levels is a very sensitive guide to changes in criminality. Over the long-term especially, the comparison of indictment totals is fraught with difficulty. But so long as we can be satisfied that factors other than crime itself are not having a massive affect on the data, comparisons even over the long-term are hazardous rather than invalid. We should at least be able to establish the general direction and the nature of changes in crime over the course of the century. And over the shorter-term we can have even more confidence that data derived from indictments reflects changes in criminality. In sum, then, the judicial records, and especially the sessions rolls of the assize courts and of the quarter sessions, provide us with a body of data which, carefully handled, will enable us to make some judgements about changes in the pattern of crime in eighteenth century England. At the very least it will usefully supplement the contemporary guesses and estimates upon which we are now so dependent.

J. M. Beattie

The Deerfield Massacre of 1704 & Local Historical Writing in the United States

The massacre in the small, frontier town of Deerfield, Massachusetts, on February 29, 1704, and the subsequent captivity of many of its inhabitants in Quebec is one of the most famous incidents in the history of American towns — almost as famous as the Salem withcraft trials. The basic facts of the incident have long been agreed upon, but when simply and clearly put, rob the story of its inherent drama. Deerfield was attacked, not simply because it was "a menace to the French," not because "there would be any military profit in its destruction," but because, as the French commander explained, "we must keep things astir in the direction of Boston else the Abenakis will declare for the English."[1] The Abenaki Indians wished to avenge the deaths of those in their tribe who had been killed in an attack on settlements in Maine. The expedition against Deerfield was organized at the insistence of the Abenakis to show the Indians the French were their friends and to remove the possibility of the Abenakis and the English making a peace treaty. Two hundred French soldiers accompanied a force of one hundred and forty Indians, who were the active party in the assault on the garrison in the center of the village. The French objective, apparently, was simply to capture the town's minister, Rev. John Williams, so that he could be held in exchange for Captain Baptiste, a prisoner of the English in Boston. During

1. *The Proceedings of the Pocumtuck Valley Memorial Association* 4, 1904, pp. 477-478. Henceforth cited as *PVMA*. Also, *PVMA* 4, 1899, pp. 12-13; George Shedon, *History of Deerfield, Massachusetts; The Times When and the People By Whom It Was Settled, Unsettled, and Resettled; With a Special Study of the Indian Wars in the Connecticut Valley, with Genealogies*, 2 volumes, Deerfield, 1895-1896, I, pp. 293-294.

the attack, the Indians killed forty-nine and took one hundred and eleven as captives back to Canada with them so that they could be rewarded with ransom money from the colonial government in Boston. Most of the captives were ransomed within a year or two after the attack.[2]

Those are the facts. The question is, why did the incident become so famous? After all, there were other attacks by the French and their Indian allies on English frontier villages, and the taking of prisoners for ransom was a common occurrence in the warfare of this period. Why, whenever this writer mentions his hometown is Deerfield, Massachusetts, do those who have no possible reason for knowing of the town's existence reply, "Oh, you mean the town that had the massacre?"

One reason for the massacre's popularity, surely, is that it is a good story, a vivid human drama of hostility, violence, death, hardship, separation, and alienation. But many good stories fail to become famous historical incidents. Why this one? Of immeasurable importance was the memorable and popular account of the event penned by the Rev. John Williams shortly after his ransom, an account which became a kind of colonial best-seller. In this way, what would have been remembered only around the Deerfield area, became something people all over New England heard about, indeed, learned about in William's religious tract as another instance of the mysterious and wondrous ways God made his will known in the affairs of man. But, why the continued popularity of the massacre, long *after* the time literate Americans turned to writings of a religious orientation for an explanation of their life on earth? Again, it was a great story, the kind of story that was easily utilized by those who wrote Sunday school lessons, adventure stories, historical novels, children's stories, biographies, or even, as in the case of Francis Parkman, narrative history of great sweep and scope.

At the same time, certain Deerfield families have been notably persistent in their efforts to preserve the historical character of the physical setting for the incident. For instance, the house whose inhabitants held off the Indian attack the longest stood until

2. *Ibid.* I, pp. 283-384.

1847, when the earliest recorded organized attempt in the United States to preserve a house of historical significance failed. The battered, tomahawk-chopped door of that house *still* stands in the town's museum. Members of the local historical society contributed numerous essays on various aspects of the event. The society's long-term president devoted over one-hundred pages (out of fourteen hundred) to it in his massive, two-volume history of the town, published at the end of the nineteenth century. The gravestone in the "Old Burying Ground" for those who died in the massacre is well maintained, and in the museum there are mural tablets bearing the names of the victims. Indeed, the local historical society was founded largely because it was felt the massacre and captivity ought to be suitably commemorated in some way.[3] Even the society's annual meeting is held on the anniversary of the great event.

So, this famous incident in local history — again, like the Salem witch-craft trials — has remained in the public mind through several, complementary means. You can read about it, and, if you are really curious, you can, to some extent, see it and touch it.

The massacre at Deerfield is also an instance of what J. H. Plumb has called the "uses of the past," that is, it has been used by writers and descendants of the participants for some purpose other than to understand the event on its own terms. That purpose has varied widely: explaining God's will in human affairs, showing the heroism of one's ancestors, telling a rousing adventure story in fictive terms. By contrast, this writer should fit Plumb's definition of the historian, that is one who tries to "bring to the human story both the detachment and insight and intellectual comprehension that natural philosophers have brought to their study of the external world."[4] Perhaps I can "try to understand what happened, purely in its own terms, and not in the service of religion or national destiny, or morality, or the sanctity of institutions."[5] But, can I escape personal involvement? After all, its *my* town. Can an historian be objective — leaving out nagging

3. *PVMA* 2, 1884, pp. 160-163.
4. J. H. Plumb, *The Death of the Past*, Boston, 1970, p. 13.
5. *Ibid*.

questions involving personality, bias, perspective, and philosophy — if he writes about something that provided the immediate setting for his own life during its most impressionable and formative years? This problem becomes important when one seeks — as I do — to write the history of his hometown.

Personal matters aside, the most interesting and important aspect of the well-known Deerfield massacre is that the innumerable accounts of it reflect, pretty accurately, the changing character of historical writing, broadly defined, in the United States from the eighteenth century to the present day. It must be stressed that historical writing in the United States did not always have the national perspective that we so naturally associate with it. There was no nation before 1776, of course. And, as Daniel J. Boorstin makes clear in his *The Americans: the National Experience*, even in the half-century after Independence, "the history of states and regions seemed primary; the history of the United States contrived and derivative. Many years would pass before Americans would see their history the other way around. . . . Not until after the Civil War would a national perspective on American history seem normal."[6]

During the mid- and late-nineteenth century a line of great synthesizers wrote multi-volume histories that forced a rather large reading public to conceive of their history from a national perspective. In this century, text-book writers have maintained that perspective, even as a growing army of scholars writes more and more about less and less.

In the last several years, however, a number of scholars have offered generalizations about town life that suggest, I believe, a new scheme for American history. Since colonial society was comprised of semi-autonomous, semi-isolated villages and had a rural population who lived in and around those villages, the story of the Americans should focus on the question of how this society was transformed into a modern society whose life is organized on a nation-wide, not village-wide, basis, and whose people live in and around cities. Under this scheme, a national perspective would

6. Daniel J. Boorstin, *The Americans: the National Experience*, paperback edition; New York, 1967, pp. 363, 367.

become appropriate only when life became, in fact, nationalized, which was largely in this century. In any case, whether or not this last-mentioned scheme finds acceptance, there was local history in what is now the United States long before there was a national history.

In the colonial period, at least in New England, historical writing was characterized by what Peter Gay, in his *A Loss of Mastery: Puritan Historians in Colonial America*[7] calls "a modernized, Protestant, Anglicized theology of history developed more than a thousand years before by Orosius and St. Augustine. . . . [This scheme] clarified the religious experience and organized the historical knowledge of Christian Englishmen. It gave God his glory, man his place, events their meaning — and England its due."[8] This Christian view of history was used by each religious group against the others: Anglican against Puritan; Puritan against Anglican; and both against Rome. The great histories of Puritan New England — William Bradford's *Of Plymouth Plantation*, Cotton Mather's *Magnalia Christi Americana*, Jonathan Edward's *History of the Work of Redemption* — all fit the old mold, with, of course, a Puritan twist, even as the historical craft was elsewhere assuming its modern form.

Cotton Mather, the most influential minister of his time in New England, was excited when some of the Deerfield captives were ransomed and returned to Boston. Certain that it was a Providential deliverance, Mather invited them to his church, where "we gave thanks together, and I preached unto them a sermon, on the great things done by the Lord for them."[9] The captives came armed with a pastoral letter written by Williams for their benefit, in which he said the massacre was punishment for sins, followed by a divine testing of the captives' faith, something that should lead to a renewal of faith because God had not forsaken them. The day after the sermon Mather decided to publish what he called "a collection of memorables relating to the captives: the marvellous displays of the divine power and goodness, towards many of them,

7. Berkeley and Los Angeles, 1966.
8. *Ibid.*, pp. 9-10.
9. *The Diary of Cotton Mather*, New York, 1957, 2 vols., I, p. 567.

especially in the deliverances, the means of their constancy under temptations of Popery. . . ."[10] In a week, the printer had sold off a thousand copies, making it what we would call an instant best-seller. Obviously, readers were interested in the massacre and captivity, or, at least, in its religious meaning.

When Williams himself was ransomed and returned to Boston, Mather — who was a cousin of the Deerfield minister's wife Eunice — "satt with him; and studied and contrived and unitted councils with him, how the Lord might have revenues of glory from his experience; and I particularly employ'd him, to preach my lecture, unto a great auditory (the general assembly then also sitting) and directed him to show how great things God had done unto him."[11]

Williams did more than preach. During the following year he wrote and had printed an account of the massacre and captivity, entitled *The Redeemed Captive Returning to Zion, or the Captivity and Deliverance of the Rev. John Williams of Deerfield.*[12] *The Redeemed Captive* is a fine example of Puritanical historical writing. It obviously does not have the sweep and breadth of Bradford's or Mather's more general accounts. But it has much more depth: Williams takes a single incident whose nature was tailor-made for the classic, Puritan historical treatment and explores at length the religious meaning of human travail, not that of a whole colony, but that of a small group of survivor-captives following a massacre in a single village.

His account of the massacre itself is sometimes funny, if taken literally. When the Indians burst into the minister's house we are told: "I reached up my hands to the bed-tester for my pistol, uttering a short petition to God, for everlasting mercies for me and mine on the account of the merits of our glorified redeemer; saying in myself as Isaiah 38: 10,11, I said, in cutting off my days, I shall go to the gates of the grave; I am deprived of the residue of my years. I said, I shall not see the Lord, even the Lord, in the lands of the living: I shall behold man no more with the inhabitants of the world." — all this while reaching for a pistol.[13]

10. *Ibid.*
11. *Ibid.*, I, p. 575.
12. Boston, 1707.
13. Rev. John Williams, *The Redeemed Captive Returning to Zion*, 5th edition,

But there are also statements that capture what must have been something close to the true feeling of the moment: "Who can tell what sorrows pierced our souls, when we saw ourselves carried away from God's sanctuary, to go unto a strange land, exposed to so many trials; the journey being at least three hundred miles we were to travel; the snow up to the knees, and we never inured to such hardships and fatigues; the place we were carried to a Popish country."[14]

The account of William's parting with his wife contains an amalgam of genuine emotion, melodrama, and, inevitably, religious meaning: "My wife told me, her strength of body began to fail, and that I might expect to part with her; saying, she hoped God would preserve my life, and the life of some, if not all our children, with us; and commended me, under God, the care of them. She never spake of any discontented word as to what had befallen us. Both with suitable expressions, justified God, in what had befallen us. We soon made an halt, in which time my chief surviving master came up, upon which I was put upon marching with the foremost, and so made to take my farewell of my dear wife, the desire of my eyes, and companion of many mercies and afflictions. Upon our separation from each other, we asked for each other, grace sufficient for what God should call us to. After our parting from one another, she spent the few remaining minutes of her stay, in reading holy scriptures. . . ."[15] She was slain with a single blow of an Indian's hatchet.

Williams prayed fervently to God to remove the afflictions that befell his sinful but loyal subject, and his prayers were sometimes answered: "When we entered on the lake, the ice was very rough and uneven, which was very grevious to my feet, that could scarce endure to set down on smooth ice, on the river. I lifted up my cry to God in ejaculatory requests, that he would take notice of my state and some way or other relieve [me]. I had not marched above a half a mile, before there fell a moist snow, about an inch and a half deep, that made it very soft for my feet, to pass over the lake, to the place where my master's family was.

Boston, 1774, p. 6.
   14. *Ibid.*, p. 7.
   15. *Ibid.*, pp. 8-9.

Wonderful favours in the midst of trying afflictions."[16]

During the trip to Quebec, the Abenakis allowed their captives "to join together in worship of God, and encourage one another to a patient bearing [of] the indignation of the Lord, till he should plead our cause." On one Sabbath Williams was allowed to preach and chose as his text: "The Lord is righteous, for I have rebelled against his commandment: *Hear, I pray you, all people, and behold my sorrow. My virgins and my young men are gone into captivity*" — not *completely* appropriate, though close enough.[17]

But when the captives reached Quebec, all this ended abruptly. The Jesuits would not allow it. John Foxe's "Book of Martyrs" has nothing on this last segment of Williams' *Redeemed Captive*. Time and again the Jesuits are depicted as unscrupulous proseletizers who used any means at their disposal — deception, fabrication, brainwashing of all kinds — to convert their Protestant captors. Time and again, the captives steadfastly resisted, maintaining their loyalty to their Puritan God — or at least most of them did. Williams himself, subjected to the full treatment, would not budge at all. It was a particularly cruel irony for him, therefore, that one of his own daughters was not only persuaded to become a Papist but refused to leave her Indian hosts, staying on as an adopted Indian as well.

The Redeemed Captive thus contains all the right elements for the Puritan version of the Christian theology of history: punishment, banishment, deliverance, and, above all, loyalty in the face of Popish attempts to lead God's children astray. Williams dedicated the book to the Governor of his province, "to preserve the memory of these [events], it has been thought adviseable to publish a short account of some of those signal appearances of divine power and goodness for us; hoping it may serve to excite the praise, faith, and hope of all that loved God...."[18] In his opening statement, he elaborated somewhat: "The history I am going to write, proves, that days of fasting and prayer, without reformation, will not avail to turn away the anger of God from a professing people; and yet witnesseth, how very advantageous,

16. *Ibid.*, p. 14.
17. *Ibid.*, p. 11.
18. *Ibid.*, p. 3.

gracious supplications are, to prepare particular Christians, patient-
ly to suffer the will of God, in very trying publick calamities."[19]

The Redeemed Captive was quite popular. Williams undoubtedly knew it would be, and Cotton Mather probably
encouraged him to write the account. After all, Mather's own,
preliminary collection had sold well. Editions of The Redeemed
Captive were printed in 1707, 1720, 1758, 1773, 1774, 1776,
1793, 1795, and 1800, with additions in the form of sermons on
the religious meaning of the story being appended from time to
time.

The 1793 edition was printed in Greenfield and contained an
essay by Deerfield's minister, Rev. John Taylor, that must be
called the earliest history of the town. Taylor was quite sensitive
to the timing of his effort. "Most of the facts mentioned," he
wrote, "I have taken from some gentlemen, who kept them, only
for their own satisfaction, and were not particular; and now, the
distance of time, precludes the possibility of obtaining such an
account of circumstances, as may be depended on." Indeed, the
religious meaning of Williams' narrative was only one of the
reasons it was republished in 1793. Rev. Taylor was anxious to
satisfy any who were "desirous that the narrative should be
reprinted, especially the descendants of those who were either
killed, wounded, or captured; and for this reason I have been
careful also to mention the names of such. . . . [Furthermore], I
think that every vestige of history which reflects the early
settlement of a country, should be preserved, for the satisfaction
of future generations."[20] What had been good Puritan history was,
by the 1790s, being reduced to a local story, something of interest
mainly to those who lived in its afterglow. Indeed, in the course of
the next century, local history became the property of writers
who sought to memorialize the lives of their own ancestors, the
early settlers of their communities. It was as Harvard's Albert
Bushnell Hart unabashedly put it, "the worship of ancestry."[21]

In Deerfield, this was largely the work of one man, George
Sheldon. Sheldon was one of the more notable of the antiquarian-

19. *Ibid.*, p. 5.
20. Sixth edition, Boston, 1795, p. 113.
21. *PVMA* 6, 1911, p. 519.

town historians who were keepers of the past during the late nineteenth century. He certainly looked the part. He was a "handsome, tall, and large man, with brilliant eyes deep set under bushy brows, a hawk nose," and a long, pointed white beard. His head was bald and he often wore either a skull cap or a round wire screen bound with metal, the latter to protect his head from flies and for ventilation as well.[22] Long-time President of the local historical society, curator of its museum, and author of a two-volume history of Deerfield, he dominated the historical activities of his fellow townsmen to an unusual extent. These were impressive achievements for a man who had no education beyond that of the local academy, who had no long-term occupation other than that of a farmer, and whose only public office beyond one term was that of justice of the peace.

Though largely self educated, and initially without economic or social prominence, Sheldon recognized his own family was every bit as prominent as any other, if viewed *historically*. It may have been a Williams who was the most prominent survivor and captive, but it was a Sheldon who led them out of captivity. The story was incomplete without either; Sheldon made sure it was complete. In his *History*, he wrote of his ancestor: "In the efforts for the recovery and redemption of the captives from Canada, Ensign John Sheldon was a central figure. To his tenderness of heart, to his unflagging faith, is due in large measure, the success which followed."[23] It was Ensign Sheldon who built the "Old Indian House," where the stiffest defense against the attackers during the massacre had been made.

Sheldon's dedication through half of his ninety-eight year life to the task of preserving the past of family and town was what one associate called simply, "a labor of love."[24] His second wife, Jennie Arms, had a more elaborate explanation. Sheldon, she thought, had been driven on by a vision: "In one word it was a MEMORIAL. A memorial of the men, women, and children of early New England, especially of the valley of the Pocumtuck. The

22. Margaret Whiting, "Recollections of George Sheldon," p. 3. Sheldon Papers, *PVMA* Library.
23. Sheldon, *History of Deerfield*, I, pp. 324-325.
24. *PVMA* 4, 1901, pp. 241-242.

lives and deeds of these people should not perish from the earth, but should live on in their records of stone and iron, of wood and manuscript page. These records should be snatched from destruction, gathered together and reverently preserved. The babe unborn to remote generations should know of the brave beginnings of New England in this frontier of our old Commonwealth." How did he come to that vision? "He had seen, as a child, through the eyes of his grandmother, the early inhabitants whom we call Indians, peeking at eventide through the windows of the Old Indian House. He had felt through his grandmother's stories the frightfulness of Indian captivity. As a mature man he had lived, in thought, with the white pioneers until, in very truth, he had become one of them, not only in blood but in spirit. Loyalty had changed to love — then the vision was born. Pondering alone in the firelight, the love-passion and the vision developed into an all-controlling purpose."[25]

Sheldon's interest in the past was, from the beginning, an interest in both the written record and surviving artifact — the two meshed, became inseparable in his historical imagination. He was upset when the Old Indian House was torn down in 1847, belonged to the Deerfield Society for Rural Improvement in the 1850s and helped "to improve the streets and public grounds of the village,"[26] was on the committee that had a monument built right after the Civil War and managed to dedicate it to both the dead of that war and the early settlers as well, and, in 1870, was founder of the Pocumtuck Valley Memorial Association, whose purpose was "the collecting and preserving of such memorials, books, papers and curiosities, as may tend to illustrate and perpetuate the history of the early settlers of this region, and of the race which vanished before them. . . ."

The PVMA, was founded when Sheldon and others talked in 1869 about the desirability of marking the site where Eunice Williams was slain and of providing a monument in the Old Burying Ground for those who died in the Massacre of 1704.[27] In

25. *PVMA* 7, 1921, p. 60.

26. Constitution of the Deerfield Society for Rural Improvement, Deerfield Society for Rural Improvement Papers. *PVMA* Library.

27. *PVMA* 2, 1884, p. 160.

his public call for an initial meeting, Sheldon invited all to "lay aside your business for one short day; leave your farms and your merchandise . . . Let us consult together how best to honor the times and lives of those, through whose trials and hardships we, under Providence, are this day in possession of these broad fields and these blooming hillsides."[28]

The PVMA was a very successful antiquarian society if judged solely in terms of its stated objectives. Over the half-century of Sheldon's leadership, it came into possession of the town's academy's building and converted it into a "Memorial Hall"; it amassed a large collection of furnishings from the colonial period, including the battered door from the Old Indian House, as well as Indian artifacts, and opened its hall for public inspection; its President put together an impressive collection of family papers, tracts, pamphlets, brochures, and books dealing with local history; it had annual meetings indoors and field meetings outside at various places around the valley, both of which were addressed by antiquarians of widely varying capacity and ability; and it commemorated many events, persons, and families, and in doing so, left a trail of memorial tablets strewn throughout the village and surrounding county.[29]

Several of the "field meetings" dealt with the massacre. These meetings had long programs including such things as hymns, prayers, dedicatory addresses, chorales, dirges, audience marches, basket lunches, music by a band, open singing, historical addresses, odes and other poems, and "miscellaneous speaking interspersed with music." Though they had the atmosphere of an outing, these meetings gave members and guests an opportunity to reflect on their view of the past and on the meaning of the important events in their town's history.

Appropriately enough, Sheldon's own, most balanced statement on the meaning of Deerfield's past came in an address on the bi-centennial of the massacre: "We honor our ancestors for their bravery and their steadfastness; we sympathize with them in their sufferings, and are grateful to them for the results — which are

28. *PVMA* 1, 1870, p. 8.
29. *PVMA* 1, 1880, pp. 434-442; 6, 1920, pp. 554-565.

ours. They filled that measure which the world of today demands as the pride of its homage — they were successful. . . . We meet today in vain if we are not stronger for their strength, and more faithful, perservering, industrious and economical for their example." Sheldon readily admitted the Puritans were bigotted, self-centered, superstitious, and intolerant, "but speaking broadly in the perspective of the centuries, this other fact remains: we see in them a people sifted out from the deeper darkness and despotism which they left behind them in Old England: we see them as the pioneers and the vanguard of civil and religious freedom for the nations."[30]

The people who were active with Sheldon in the PVMA were, typically, prominent in their own communities. Indeed, the roster of the Association's membership reads like a "Who's Who" of Franklin County. What Sheldon provided in his role as historical impressario — cajoling, persuading, hinting, planning, scheduling, and generally keeping up enthusiasm for an undertaking beyond the unassisted talent of most of his associates — was a much needed focus for those whose families had lived in the area for a long time and who shared his view of the past. What is most remarkable, in a social sense, about all this is that Sheldon — largely by virtue of his fame as an antiquarian-local historian — became, by all accounts, one of the most prominent persons in his own community. It is quite revealing that social prominence in a small town at the turn of the century could come to a farmer who happened to become interested in the past and had some talent in writing about it and in collecting its artifacts. To be sure, his marriage in 1897 to Jennie Arms, who was from a family of some wealth, helped. But his prominence appears to have been based primarily on his anitquarian activities far more than on his wife's wealth. He was prominent before he ever married her.

Sheldon's own historical writings tower above those of his associates in the PVMA. His persistence, dedication, and seriousness of purpose were distinctive. All lauded his efforts, but no one could emulate him. Though largely self-trained, he had a brief, but significant partnership with Rev. J. H. Temple. Both the scope and

30. *PVMA* 4, 1903, pp. 385-386.

scale of his own *History* are clearly foreshadowed in their
collaborative history of the nearby town of Northfield, published
in 1875, a decade before his own work on Deerfield was serialized
in the local newspaper. Sheldon and Temple were certain they
were expanding what had hitherto constituted "local history."
"The field of these researches," they wrote, "is to a great extent
new ground." Theirs was a work based consistently on "manuscript documents," which they listed: (1) town and church
records, (2) county records, (3) state archives, (4) family papers,
(5) memories of aged persons, and (6) tradition.[31]

How Sheldon appears to have revelled in the accumulation,
preservation, and close reading of the great array of materials he
used for his own history, worked on for at least a decade. In his
preface he "thanks the owners of the hundreds of garretts, closets,
and trunks which I have ransacked at will. . . ."[32] He used the same

31. It is clear that Sheldon and Temple had something approaching a grand scheme
for the whole upper Connecticut Valley in Massachusetts. Sylvester Judd's earlier history
of Hadley, Massachusetts, was regarded as having covered the territory the Norwottucks
Indians occupied, their history of Northfield covered the territory of the Sguakheags,
and Sheldon was already planning a history of Deerfield covering the territory of the
Pocumtucks. Thus, the authors of the early history of Hadley, Northfield, and Deerfield
were also dealing with great Indian districts extending over a large area of western
Massachusetts, districts that roughly corresponded to the boundaries of these "mother"
towns of the valley. Viewed in this manner the ultimate purpose of their histories made
perfect sense: "It is the hope of the authors that these pages furnish sufficient facts to
enable the careful student to understand how civilized life here came into contact with
and finally displaced savage life; how and why, after two unsuccessful attempts, the
whites held permanent possession of the place; and then pushed on up the Connecticut
Valley." George Sheldon and Rev. J. H. Temple, *A History of the Town of Northfield,
Mass.*, Albany, 1875.
It is also clear Judd was the pioneer, his work the model for Sheldon's and
Temple's. That Sheldon owed a lot to Judd is indicated in his preface to a new edition of
Judd's history, published in 1905. Arguing its rareness and indispensibility "to any
well-equipped library of Americana" made a new edition a necessity, Sheldon revealed
"how more than thirty years ago, I bought the only copy I could find on sale in
Boston." The esteem with which he held Judd is evident throughout his introduction:
"Judd's *History* has been known as a standard work ever since it was issued. . . . Those
who have seen the mass of his accumulated papers are surprized at the extent and
diversity of his research. . . . [This] work was . . . and is, and always will be, a rich mine
for the delver after family history in the valley of the Connecticut. . . . Mr. Judd must
always be looked up to as a sound historical authority of the highest rank." Sylvester
Judd, *History of Hadley*, Springfield Mass., 1905; Reprint.
32. A colleague later described his research in the following manner: "The attics of
old homesteads were searched, and old newspapers, old diaries, family letters, account
books of businessmen and miscellaneous papers of all kinds were sought out and
examined. . . . The records of the town, the courts, the churches, and the voluminous

kinds of sources he and Temple had listed earlier with one, simple aim in mind: ". . . [To] write as far as [possible] from original sources of information."[33]

Sheldon's massive, sprawling *History of Deerfield* goes on and on for 1401 pages. Hailed as a "triumphant model of local historical writing" by an awed colleague,[34] Sheldon's *History* was, in fact, a good example of late nineteenth century town history, a version that greatly expanded upon earlier efforts in the pre-Civil War years. These earlier efforts usually reflected their author's particular interests — whether genealogical, biographical, military, or religious — or whatever records the writer happened to come upon. But Sheldon and others who shared his approach tried to utilize *in a systematic fashion* the whole array of town, court, church, and even family papers no one had bothered to investigate before.

The result was *not* the comprehensive history we expect to find, given the means adopted. True, Sheldon expanded upon such established areas within local historical writing, such as genealogy and war history. He also added considerably to the scope of what had been included in earlier town histories. A great array of subjects[35] receive at least brief attention. But there is no attempt at analysis and interpretation. Great chunks of information are lifted, in undigested form, from the mass of material he examined so closely. The result is more a catalogue or chronicle than what we would call historical writing.

Thus, Sheldon, though he expanded what was already developed in local history, significantly failed to develop other areas of town life beyond the mere listing of information.

archives of the state were examined and transcribed with wonderous fidelity." *PVMA* 4, 1901, p. 241.

33. Sheldon, *History of Deerfield*, I, p. iv.

34. *PVMA* 6, 1917, p. 369. Some simply threw up their hands with comments like: "No more complete, well-balanced and trustworthy record can be conceived." *PVMA* 5, 1905, p. 149.

35. A listing of those topics includes: town origins, topography, layout of the town street, local place names, graveyards, town clock and bell, biographical sketches of important people, various ministries, meeting houses, town officials, town meetings, municipal affairs, houses, roads, canals, river travel, bridges, common fields and fences, farmlands, home industries, mills, cultural-intellectual-economic associations of various kinds, libraries, schools, reform movements, and the establishment of new towns carved out of Deerfield.

Mesmerized by the sources he labored over for so long, he did not have the capacity to analyze them. Local historical writing, in his hands, thus expanded in length and scope, but did not significantly alter in character.

Sheldon's account of the massacre shows him off at his best. Still the most important event in the history of the town, in his judgment, the massacre and captivity receive one-hundred pages of detailed investigation. All the relevant sources — town records, correspondence of commanders and ministers and government officials, legislative debates and resolutions, petitions to the legislature, and, of course, Williams' *Redeemed Captive* — are examined separately for their authenticity and accuracy and the information they reveal. Only then is the reader given an account of the incident as understood by Sheldon himself. It is a thorough treatment presented in Sheldon's rather fact-laden prose, which can, nevertheless, sketch word pictures and create vivid, dramatic situations when he forces it to.

To Sheldon, the story had little religious significance. To him, it was the supreme example of the essential heroism of the original settlers of the town: "We usually speak of the catastrophe of February 29, 1704, as the 'destruction of Deerfield,' and rightly too. For twenty years, the persistent settlers had struggled bravely, but not only against the inevitable hardships of a new plantation, but against the plague of worms, frost, and drought, against war, pestilence, and almost famine. But the end had now come. The ground could be held no longer. . . . More than half the population, including their loved minister, were being swept over the snow to Popish Canada, or laid underneath it, in one wide grave hard by in their own God's acre. . . . [This] speck of civilization became once more a waste place in the wilderness. . . ."[36] Of course, the town was rebuilt; Deerfield endured.

From the perspective of the late twentieth century, how *narrow* does Sheldon's view of history appear. Indeed, how constricted a view of his own community he had. In the very years he and his associates were most active, great migrations of Irish, French Canadians, and Poles moved into the Connecticut Valley

36. Sheldon, *History of Deerfield*, I, p. 316.

and, in particular, into the southern part of the township of Deerfield. This influx of Catholic immigrants and the development of industry and technology would transform the rural, agricultural, cohesive, Yankee small town Sheldon so fondly remembered. And yet there is not the slightest hint of any of this in his *History*. His view of the past precluded his paying any attention to such things — at least as part of his town's *History*. Sheldon's interest all but ends with the Revolution. The short portion of his *History* dealing with the nineteenth century is highly fragmentary. The only genealogies he prepared on his own initative were those for families living in the town *before* the Revolution.[37] At times, in the last section, he almost seems bored with it all, as if fulfilling some obligation to bring the story into his own time. The account does not end; it just stops; the reader does not know where he has been left. For Sheldon, the great drama and adventure of his heroic ancestors ended with the great triumph of liberty over tyranny, the Revolution. Thereafter, his view of historical time became vague and misty. The New England town had been established, through great effort during the colonial period and had placed itself under a national government dedicated to human freedom as a result of a successful revolution. That was all one really needed to know; that is all George Sheldon cared to know. Nor did his successors in the PVMA want to know any more. In all the years after his death that the Association published addresses and articles, not one word was ever printed about the nineteenth century, about industrialization, about the Irish or the Poles, in short, about the changing character of the community they lived in.

An incident such as the massacre of 1704 takes on a quite

37. The original, newspaper edition of the history contained "a notice of every family and every man known to have settled here before the close of the Revolutionary War. Their ancestry in America, so far as it could be discovered, was given and all their descendants remaining here, for a hundred years later." Sheldon was, by his own admission, interested only in the families "who laid the foundations of our town." And, even though, in the published version, the "scheme has been enlarged to some extent, and many later coming families included, . . . this added matter has been mainly the result of contributions from interested parties instead of original research by the author. Hence it follows that of this class, families the most fully represented are those whose members showed the most interest in this undertaking by furnishing material." Sheldon, *History of Deerfield* II, part 2, p. 4.

different meaning from Sheldon's to the local historian of the late twentieth century. Of course, it was, as he thought, an example of frontier life during colonial wars. But it was not the most important event in the town's history, though perhaps the most dramatic. The story of Deerfield is important *in its totality* because it is the story of a small town, and most Americans lived in small towns until our century.

Even if the massacre is offered as an example of a certain kind of human conflict, it is clearly only one of many such incidents that *could* be cited. In the perspective of time it can be seen that what divided a continent now divides a nation within that continent. In the seventeenth and eighteenth centuries — in the colonial context of New England and New France — the hostility of English and French, of Protestant and Catholic was a continental phenomenon. In the nineteenth and twentieth centuries, such hostility has been largely confined to what has become Canada.

J. H. Plumb was right. Both Williams and Sheldon used the past for their own ends, whether they be for the glory of God or their own ancestors. The modern historian presumably knows better. He has methodological tools by which he can, with a significant degree of accuracy, study the past for its own sake. But does he really want to? Should not the study of history, at bottom, be an intensely personal undertaking, an extension of one's own understanding of life and change and death. Should a "scientific methodology" empty historical inquiry of its sense of curiosity and wonderment, turn it into something other than a quest having a personal meaning. In the broadest sense, of course, the history of anything recognizeably human can be of personal interest to the historian. Why should he study anything he can not relate to his own evolving understanding of life, his *own* life.

Certainly such musings are pertinent to the modern scholar who would write the history of his hometown. Armed with the methodology of his discipline, he deals with material whose significance reaches directly into his own life. Can he react as a historian should when childhood memories jostle with new feelings and both with scholarly thoughts? The answer, surely, is, Yes, if he wills it. The two interests — historical and personal —

reinforce one another. True, dangers abound. Will he turn the outsiders and newcomers into heroes the way Sheldon did the original settlers: Will he present those with significant power in the community less favorably than those without it? Awareness of such questions helps. Biases must be dealt with and neutralized.

And yet the "personal" element of the undertaking must not be. The modern historian from Deerfield looks upon the massacre differently from the antiquarian-historian of the late nineteenth century from Deerfield did. But, like Sheldon, he grew up on childhood stories of it, saw its remains in the old burying ground, pushed his finger through the hole in the battered door of the old Indian house, and "experienced" an historical incident the way everyone who grows up in Deerfield does. Can *that* kind of history ever be made a fit subject for analysis in that historian's mind? The answer, again, is Yes, if he wills it.

For him, history is personal *and* something to be presented to others, is a blend of the subjective *and* objective. But is not that what all history is — or should be?

D. J. Russo

The 18th Century Economic Analysis of the Decline of Spain

In 1786, Léon de Arroyal wrote a series of letters to the Count of Lerena urging the adoption of extensive political reforms in Spain. Arroyal is not a well-known figure. He was a minor poet whose satires were censured in 1785 for the bitterness of their attack on the privileged orders in society. Despite this official disapprobation of his opinions he managed to gain an office in the Spanish exchequer.[1] It was while occupying this position that he wrote the *Political-Economic Letters to the Count of Lerena*, a work attributed until recently to more noteworthy authors.[2] Arroyal's letters made a significant contribution to the reform literature produced in Spain during the second half of the eighteenth century. They were based on two assumptions generally shared by all reformers of the period — first that Spain had recently suffered a grave national decline, and secondly, that "a happy revolution," engineered from above, could restore the nation to health. Nevertheless, they represent an important departure from the main current of reform literature; and the principal difference centred on Arroyal's analysis of Spanish decadence.

Throughout the eighteenth century, Spanish intellectuals interpreted the decline experienced by their country almost entirely in economic terms.[3] Oppressed by the skeletal remains of

* I extend my thanks to McMaster University for a summer research stipend helping to finance the research for this paper.

1. Léon de Arroyal, *Cartas Político-Económicas al Conde de Llerena*, Antonio Elorza, ed., Madrid, 1968, p. 19.

2. *Ibid.*, p. 11. The most important recent study of eighteenth century Spain in English, Richard Herr, *The Eighteenth-Century Revolution in Spain*, Princeton, 1958, attributes the letters to Campomanes. The other author frequently mentioned is Cabarrús, a French immigrant to Spain and founder of the National Bank of San Carlos.

3. Vicente Palacio Atard, *Derrota, Agotamiento, Decadencia, en La España del Siglo XVII*, 3rd ed., Madrid, 1966, pp. 170-174. Also by the same author *Los Españoles de la Illustratión*, Madrid, 1964, p. 19 and pp. 33-34.

once populous and industrious cities, such as Toledo and Burgos,
writers like don Gaspar de Jovellanos and the Count of Campomanes, both reforming ministers in the government of Charles III
(1759-1788) concentrated their attention on proving the causal
relationship existing between specific laws, institutions, and social
customs and the collapse of the Spanish economy.[4] Their
economic analysis of decline was used to support a programme of
primarily economic reform. In contrast, Arroyal moved from the
specific to the general, and from the economic to the political. "It
is an incontrovertible truth," he wrote:

> that the happiness or unhappiness of a kingdom arises from its
> good or bad constitution. Upon this also depends the quality
> of its government and the ... measures [adopted] which
> immediately influence the growth or decline of agriculture,
> industry, and commerce, which in themselves constitute the
> temporal felicity or infelicity of men.[5]

Adopting this theoretical position, he dated the decline of Spain
from the emergence in the early sixteenth century of an absolutist
monarchy.[6] This development he considered to have destroyed the
potential balance inherent in the medieval constitution between
the Crown, the aristocracy, and the people. Hence, from his
viewpoint, the regeneration of Spain was a political problem
demanding constitutional reform.

Historians have tended to regard the ideas expressed by
eighteenth century Spanish reformers as being the product of
opinions imported into Spain from abroad. The doctrines of men
like Jovellanos and Campomanes have been linked to the
Enlightenment in France, and the more radical doctrines of men
like Arroyal to the revolutionary fervour of the French

---

4. The numerous works of Jovellanos have been gathered together in the *Biblioteca de Autores Españoles*. . ., Madrid, 1956-63, XLVI, L, LXXXV, LXXXVI, and LXXXVII. The literature produced by Campomanes is less accessible, but a good secondary source based on an intensive study of his work is R. Krebs Wilckens, *El Pensamiento Histórico, Político, y Económico del Conde de Campomanes*, Santiago, Chile, 1960.
5. Léon de Arroyal, *op. cit.*, p. 72.
6. Arroyal devoted the whole of his second letter to a synoptic history of Spain from the reign of Alfonso XI. Cardinal Ximenes bore the blame for destroying the liberties of his Castilian subjects by creating a militia, and the defeat of the rebellious towns at the beginning of the reign of Charles V was, for Arroyal, "the last sight of Castilian liberty."

Revolution.[7] This interpretation has a certain validity. Spanish intellectuals kept abreast of foreign literature, and even books prohibited by the Inquisition were widely circulated and read. To place an inordinate stress on this dependence, however, oversimplifies the complexities of Spanish intellectual life and distorts its character. Arroyal, like most reformers, openly acknowledged his debt to foreign writers, and borrowed, in particular, from Montesquieu. Yet of greater importance than tracing the lineage of the political ideas championed by him and others is the task of understanding why these opinions became increasingly popular in Spain from the late 1780s; why they provided the basis for a new theory of Spanish decadence; and why this theory became the one eventually embraced by nineteenth century Spanish liberals.[8]

In attempting to solve these problems, it is essential to keep in mind one obvious point. The ideas borrowed by Spaniards from abroad were adapted to meet the demands of their own situation; and central to their particular situation was the need to account for the decline of Spain. This was a pre-occupation apparent in practically all forms of literature.[9] Indeed, the topic was of universal concern. The causes of Spain's debility were analyzed by most European writers interested in politics and economics. Montesquieu, for example, exploited to the full its potential to illustrate what impeded the development of human prosperity and happiness.[10] But for Spaniards the topic possessed more than

7. See in particular Paul Merimée, *L'Influence Français en Espagne au Dix-huitième Siècle*, Paris, 1936. More recent studies also emphasizing French influence on eighteenth century Spain are Jean Sarrailh, *L'Espagne Eclairée de la Seconde Moitié du XVIIIe Siècle*, Paris, 1964, M. Deforneaux, *L'Inquisition Espagnole et les Livres Français au XVIIIe Siècle*, Paris, 1963, and R. Herr, *op. cit.*

8. Luis Sánchez-Agesta, *Historia del Constitucionalismo Español*, 2nd ed., Madrid, 1964, pp. 26-29. By the early nineteenth century, the tendency to condemn the entire political system, viewing it as the primary cause of the decline of Spain, was shared by both liberals and Carlists.

9. For the literature on this subject see in particular Pedro Saínz y Rodríguez, *Evolución de las Ideas Sobre la Decadencia Española y Otros Estudios de Crítica Literia*, Madrid, 1962, Vicente Palacio Atard, *Derrota, Agotamiento, Decadencia. . . .*, and also the fascinating study by María Teresa Perez Picazo, *La Publicista Española en la Guerra de Sucesión*, Madrid, 1966.

10. P. Barrière, "Montesquieu et L'Espagne," *Bulletin Hispanique* XLIX, 1947, pp. 299-310. An indication of the extensive interest shown in Spain's economic collapse by foreign writers is provided by E. Heckscher, *Mercantilism*, 2 vols., London, 1934, II, p. 315.

purely academic interest. The debate over the causes of their national decline penetrated to the roots of their cultural and political values, laying bare their prejudices and their political inclinations. It was one of the most crucial and divisive issues confronting their society.

For this reason, the shift from an economic to a political and constitutional analysis of Spanish decadence represented a major change in the intellectual climate of Spain. To account for the gradual acceptance of an interpretation of decline which could be and was employed to support demands for drastic constitutional reforms, it is insufficient to concentrate on the rather obvious relationship between Spanish radicalism and political radicalism abroad. It is also necessary to determine why the earlier economic interpretation, employed to support demands primarily for economic reforms, lost its credibility and its general appeal.

The specific economic analysis of the decline of Spain emerging during the second half of the eighteenth century was shaped by a variety of influences. It reflected, in the first instance, the desire of reformers to discover by rational and empirical means solutions to the problems besetting their nation, and to evolve a programme of reforms which would serve to enhance the power and prestige of the monarchy. It characterized, in other words, the political philosophy of "enlightened despotism." It also reflected the constant interplay of two more specific influences – the literature on the subject of decline produced in Spain during the seventeenth and early eighteenth centuries, and the new science of political economics being developed in Northern Europe. The interaction of these two influences helped to mold the character and to determine the limitations of the eighteenth century economic interpretation of Spanish decadence.

During the 1770s and 1780s Spaniards began to display a growing interest in the earliest attempts made by their countrymen to comprehend the phenomenon of their national decline. They recovered from the past an extensive literature on the subject, employing it to serve a variety of immediately useful functions.[11] It provided them with a point of reference from

11. One of the most interesting of numerous studies of these seventeenth century

which old theories on the topic could be revised, or new and contradictory theories advanced. Also, it established proof of the existence in Spain of a long and continuous movement for economic reform, thereby clearly delineating a political tradition into which they could place their own thought.

This anchorage was especially important given the propensity of reformers to borrow ideas from abroad. They enthusiastically embraced all the new sciences developing in Northern Europe, opening their minds especially to the science of political economics as represented by such commanding figures as Richard Cantillon and Adam Smith.[12] The works of these men they translated and avidly discussed. In the process, they made the economic panaceas of France and England, notably freedom of trade, the abolition of monopolies, and the removal of restrictions on the economic freedom of individuals, the economic panaceas of Spain as well. This tendency to imitate exposed them to the charge, repeated subsequently by numerous historians, of sacrificing Spanish traditions to foreign gods.[13] Few reformers, however, can be completely identified with the intellectual leaders of the European Enlightenment. They remained intensely Spanish and somewhat aloof from those foreign writers who, even when they exemplified the wisdom available from the new sciences, often propagated in their works a satirical anti-Spanish polemic. The "black legend" was inextricably woven into the fabric of the European Enlightenment, much to the chagrin of progressive Spaniards.[14] The irrational nature of the polemic threw them into

Spanish *arbitristas* is Pierre Vilar, "Los primitivos españoles del pensamiento económico: 'Cuantitativismo' y 'bullionismo,'" *Crecimiento y Desarrollo: Economía e Historia: Reflexiones Sobre el Caso Español*, Barcelona, 1964, pp. 175-208. A good bibliography of their writings is M. Colmeiro, *Biblioteca de los Economistas Españoles de los Siglos XVI, XVII, y XVIII*, Madrid, 1880.

12. The influence of Adam Smith has been examined by R. S. Smith, "The Wealth of Nations in Spain and Hispanic America, 1780-1830," *Journal of Political Economy* 65, 1957, pp. 104-125.

13. The most famous of the accusers is Don Marcelino Menéndez y Pelayo, *Historia de los Heterodoxos Españoles*, D. Miguel Artigas, ed., 2nd ed., 7 vols., Madrid, 1930, VI.

14. There is an extensive literature on the black legend, starting with Julián Juderiás y Loyot, *La Leyenda Negra, Estudios Acerca del Concepto de España en el Extranjero*, 14 ed., Madrid, 1960. See also Pablo Alvarez Rubiano, *La Historia y el Problemo de España*, Valladolid, 1962, Sebastián Quesada Marco, *La Leyenda Antiespañola*, Madrid, 1967, and Julio Caro Baroja, *El Mito del Carácter Nacional, Meditaciones a Contrapelo*, Madrid, 1970.

a quandry, perhaps best illustrated by José Cadalso's response to Montesquieu's famous caricature of Spain in the *Persian Letters*. Writing as a father addressing a somewhat rebellious son, he stated:

> you should know that the President of Montesquieu, whom you so frequently cite without understanding, despite his distinguished origins, the elegance of his style, the profundity of his science, and all the qualities which have gained him such universal fame throughout Europe, even amongst ourselves . . ., loses all his fine gifts and appears to transform himself into another man when he speaks of us. He commits a thousand errors, not born of his own intention, but [derived] from the bad information supplied by people little-worthy of associating with such an outstanding man. . . .[15]

Therefore, while Spanish intellectuals tended to be attracted to foreign literature for its science, they were sometimes repelled by its prejudice; and although they remained receptive to its influence, they assumed a defensive posture in the face of its criticism. Their ambivalence reinforced their desire to identify with earlier Spanish reformers. It also directly influenced their interpretation of the decline of Spain. The onus was upon them not only to defend their culture, but to prove that, devoid of the character defects attributed to them by outsiders, Spaniards were as capable of attaining unlimited prosperity as was the rest of mankind.

Their strong sense of nationalism was provoked early in the 1780s by an article appearing in the new *Encyclopédie Méthodique* published in France. In a volume devoted to Geography, an obscure writer by the name of Masson de Morvilliers composed an essay entitled, "What is owing to Spain?" Responding to this rhetorical question, he argued that Spain had contributed nothing to European civilization for the past ten centuries.[16] His imperti-

---

15. Quoted from Julian Mariás, *La España Posible en Tiempo de Carlos III*, Madrid, 1963, p. 39.

16. R. Herr, *op. cit.*, pp. 220-230. There are numerous other accounts of this controversy, one of the most famous intellectual debates during the reign of Charles III.

nence was deeply resented and his article elicited a flood of replies. One of the most famous was the *Oración Apologética por la España* published in 1786 by Juan Pablo Forner. Unlike Cadalso, who earlier had muted his criticism of Montesquieu, Forner condemned wholesale the intellectual achievements of Northern Europe. "Spain is surrounded by adversaries," he wrote, "and the first is France. Her sophistry slanders Spain; and what are her arms? The first is ignorance."[17] Expressing his unqualified admiration for the accomplishments of Spaniards in the traditional fields of law and theology, he contended that Spain possessed no need for a Descartes or a Newton. The country had already produced "eminently just legislators and excellent practical philosophers who preferred the ineffable pleasure of serving the interests of humanity to the idle occupation of constructing imaginary worlds in the solitude and silence of a study."[18]

Spanish reformers were no more willing to condone Masson de Morvillier's bigotry than was Forner. Nevertheless, his *Oración* involved them in a controversy fought out mainly in the pages of *El Censor*, a leading reform periodical of the period.[19] An undiscriminating repudiation of the new sciences undermined those very instruments which they considered to be essential to perform an operation on Spain and restore the country to health. Also, they viewed as dangerous any attempt to bestow new dignity upon traditional Spanish studies because it would extend into the present the sterility of their past intellectual life. Neither desiring to side with the foreign critics of Spain, nor to reject the scientific knowledge available outside their national boundaries, they found need to establish another response to men like Masson de Morvilliers which preserved the momentum of their reform movement while it embodied their strong sense of nationalism. The response was fashioned in part by Juan Sempere y Guarinos, a leading bibliophile. In 1785, he commenced publication of a six volume work entitled, *An Essay . . . on the Best Writers of the*

17. Quoted from María Jiménez Salas, *Vida y Obras de D. Juan Pablo Forner y Segara*, Madrid, 1944, p. 252.

18. *Ibid.*, p. 254.

19. *Ibid.*, pp. 279-303 provides large extracts from this controversy. See also Patricio Redondo, *Extracto de un discurso sobre el del Censor Número CXX cuyo Lema infernal es su voz*, Madrid, 1786.

Reign of Charles III. In it he described the contents of the major books authored by Spaniards of his generation. He replied in effect to foreign critics by illustrating "the restoration, progress, and actual state of Spanish literature," showing how it was no longer "in the same miserable state as it has been for the past century and a half."[20] In addition, he tried to convince those who scorned foreign literature of the debt owed by progressive Spanish writers to outside influences. "One will not read in my work," he argued, "those excessive hyperboles and absolute improbabilities which the ignorance, vanity or false patriotism of their authors have perpetrated in others."[21]

Sempere y Guarinos also firmly placed the ideas of his contemporaries in the context of a national reform tradition. In 1801, he began publication of his *Spanish Library of Political-Economics* in which he analysed the important economic tracts written by Spaniards during the late sixteenth and seventeenth centuries. In this area of endeavour he was not an innovator. Eighteenth century reformers had always acknowledged the works of their predecessors, and sometimes published new editions.[22] The tempo of this activity quickened in the 1770s and 1780s, precisely when they were becoming increasingly sensitive to foreign criticism. The Count of Campomanes edited a number of "ancient" texts in the *Appendices* to his *Popular Education*, and in 1787, Antonio Valladares y Sotomayor founded the periodical, *Semanario Erudito*, designed to disseminate "the instruction that many wise Spaniards left us."[23]

Advertising the works of their predecessors proved to be one way in which reformers constructed their own brand of intellectual nationalism. Although both Jovellanos and Sempere y Guarinos, for example, conceded that political economics was the invention of their own century, the latter argued, nevertheless, that "the particular circumstances" existing in Spain, notably the

20. Juan Sempere y Guarinos, *Ensayo de una Biblioteca Española de los Mejores Escritores del Reynado de Carlos III*, Facs. ed., 6 vols., Madrid, 1969, I, p. 1.

21. *Ibid.* IV, p. iv.

22. A partial list of works re-published in the eighteenth century is given by José Muñoz Pérez, "La España de Carlos III y su conciencia de período histórico," *Estudios sobre Historia de España*, Manuel Fernández Alvarez, ed., Madrid, 1965, p. 373.

23. Quoted from R. Herr, *op. cit.*, p. 191.

experience of decline, made the discipline "of more ancient origins" there.[24] Similarly, the former urged his compatriots "to read above all the works of our Spanish economists" in addition to those of contemporary foreign writers.[25] Hence, they conferred upon a minor but relatively traditional area of Spanish intellectual activity the aura of prestige attached to a new and developing science.

Despite this praise, Spanish reformers generally considered the writings of their predecessors to be full of inaccuracies, inconsistencies, and contradictions. Campomanes confessed that "in those times the principles of economics were not well understood;" and Jovellanos, observing the "horror" accompanying the first manifestations of Spanish decadence, concluded that "our science of economics" then "hardly offered us a constant maxim for good government."[26] Such comments were obviously not intended to detract from the considerable achievements of the early Spanish "economists," whose occasional and scintillating insights gave them the stature of being men of genius in a pre-scientific age. Rather, they were intended to reveal the gulf separating a primitive from a modern form of economics, to heighten the reformers own sense of intellectual accomplishment, and to indicate that the usefulness of these earlier tracts lay more in the present than it had in the past. Jovellanos underlined this attitude when he wrote:

The ancient economists, although inconsistent in their

24. Juan Sempere y Guarinos, *Biblioteca Española Económico-Política* III, Madrid, 1804, pp. vi-vii. Jovellanos viewed this science as being "of this century, and perhaps of our own generation." See "Informe de la Sociedad Económica de Madrid al Real y Supremo Consejo de Castilla en el Expediente de Ley Agraria. . . ," *B.A.E.* 50, p. 83. In an article published shortly after the presentation of this paper, J. A. Maravall shows how eighteenth century Spanish Reformers in general appealed to the history of their country, often embracing in the process the discipline of history, in order to identify cultural precedents for those activities and modes of thought which they considered to be most essential to the development of Spain. See J. A. Maravall, "Mentalidad burguesa e idea de la Historia," *Revista de Occidente*, 107, February 1972, pp. 250-286.

25. Gaspar de Jovellanos, "Discurso dirigido a la Real Sociedad de Amigos de País de Asturias sobre los medios de promover la felicidad de aquel Provincia," *B.A.E.* 50, p. 440.

26. For Campomanes' view see José Muñoz Pérez, "La Idea de America en Campomanes," *Anuario de Estudios Americanos* X, 1953, p. 232. Jovellanos stated his opinion in "Elogio de Carlos III," *B.A.E.* 46, p. 313.

principles, deposited in their works an incredible number of facts, calculations, and arguments, as excellent as they are indispensable for a knowledge of the civil state of the nation and the influence of her political errors. There was lacking only an assiduous and wise hand to select through them and bring to light the true principles. The indefatigable magistrate, (an obvious reference to Campomanes) read and abridged these works, published the inedited, unearthed the unknown, made comments, rectified the opinions, and corrected the reasoning of their authors. Improved by new and admirable observations, he presented them to his compatriots . . . and the light of economics spread.[27]

Employed in this manner, the seventeenth century "economic" tracts discovered by eighteenth century Spanish reformers played a vital role in shaping their analysis of Spanish decadence. They could not be relied upon to suggest a comprehensive diagnosis of the disease afflicting Spain; however, they could disclose the earliest symptoms of that disease and place current economic problems in their proper historical perspective. Bernardo Ward, an Irish immigrant to Spain whose *Proyecto Económico*, published in 1762, exerted a profound influence on reformers, emphasized the need for such an approach in dealing with current economic problems. He wrote:

Various are the causes normally given [to explain] the decline of Spanish industry from the flourishing state in which it existed two centuries ago. So many efforts having been made unsuccessfully to restore it during the past two reigns . . . casts doubt on whether what are considered to be causes really are. As it is difficult to remedy the disease without discovering its true origin, this point ought to be examined with all the attention possible.[28]

It was Campomanes who endeavoured most to meet Ward's challenge. He edited and republished the works of his predecessors, counselling political economists of his own genera-

---

27. Gaspar de Jovellanos "Elogio de Carlos III," *B.A.E.* 46, p. 316.
28. Bernardo Ward, *Proyecto Económico. . .* , Madrid, 1762, p. 100.

tion to study "the history, customs, and laws of the country" because those "who ignore them will not be sure what economic matters require discussion."[29] He also encouraged the various Economic Societies established throughout Spain during the reign of Charles III to undertake provincial histories, and he proposed the publication of books examining in detail the decline of Spain from the reign of Philip II.[30]

Because Campomanes and his contemporaries failed to produce these comprehensive works of historical scholarship, they tended to rely upon the writings of Spain's "ancient" economists to provide the details required to construct their analysis of decline. In addition, they made full use of the works of contemporary political economists. One of the most influential sources employed was Cantillon's *Essay on the General Nature of Commerce*, translated into Spanish by Jovellanos.[31] Cantillon's interpretation of Spanish decadence was important not because it deviated substantially from earlier theories, but because it placed Spain's economic crisis in the context of a recurring economic phenomenon. Utilizing a form of quantity theory, he illustrated the effects produced by a massive influx of bullion into Spain from the Americas. This influx, he argued, provoked a price inflation making Spanish commodities uncompetitive in world markets and causing her industries to collapse, her population to decline, and her silver to escape into foreign hands. This experience, however, he did not see as unique to Spain. Even those countries whose flourishing industries and commerce had allowed them to reap advantages from the collapse of the Spanish economy would inevitably experience the same rise in wages, rents, and prices, the same uncompetitiveness, and lacking special precautionary measures, the same decline.[32]

Cantillon and other current political economists, therefore,

29. Quoted in Ricardo Krebs Wilckens, *op. cit.*, p. 167.

30. Juan Sempere y Guarinos, *Biblioteca Española Económico-Político* I, p. 12.

31. Gaspar de Jovellanos, "Discurso dirigido a la Real Sociedad de Amigos del País de Asturias," *B.A.E.* 50, p. 440. He wrote: "I translated this work from the French many years ago for my own use, and would have preferred it to all others if that of Condillac, published later, had not surpassed it in order and clarity."

32. Richard Cantillon, *Essai sur la Nature du Commerce en Général*, Henry Higgs, ed., London, 1931, p. 185.

provided Spaniards with the theory necessary to help them comprehend their experience of decline. More than this, they encouraged amongst Spanish reformers a tremendous sense of optimism. Cantillon, for example, maintained that wise and vigorous government could arrest the onset of an economic recession. Similarly, he implied that good government could overcome the problems resulting from the experience of a collapse. Such, he noted "is approximately the circle (of economic growth and decline) which may be run by a considerable State. . . . A capable minister is always able to make it commence this round."[33] On the basis of such welcome scientific observations, Campomanes began to argue that Spain's very impoverishment represented her greatest asset by enhancing her ability to compete with wealthier countries.[34] He and other reformers believed the conditions to be ripe for a restoration of Spain's former prosperity. Persuaded by this optimism, they tended to make the disease afflicting their nation as implicit in a preconceived cure as they assumed the cure would be implicit in a detailed diagnosis of the disease.

Their intellectual dexterity becomes evident in their analysis of Spanish decadence. They refused to admit to any basic defect in the climate or physical geography of Spain which might account for her poverty relative to the nations of Northern Europe. This was a general attitude, and earlier reformers had often echoed those panegyrics discoverable in classical sources by describing Spain as a virtual "paradise of God."[35] Eighteenth century writers tended to be more subdued in their praise. Ward considered Spain to possess "great advantages" and her soil to be superior to that available in either France or England![36]

33. *Ibid.*, p. 259.

34. R. Krebs Wilckens, *op. cit.*, p. 175. Wilckens argues that Campomanes inherited this idea from David Hume, and Hume's views were very similar to those of Cantillon. See David Hume, *Writings on Economics*, Eugene Rotwein, ed., Madison, Wisconsin, 1955, p. 63.

35. Pedro Sainz y Rodríguez, *op. cit.*, pp. 48-49. See also Manuel Colmeiro, *Historia de la Economía Política en España*, 2 vols., Madrid, 1863, II, pp. 80-82. He shows how the belief in a fertile Spain was part of the belief in a past "golden age." This was a very popular notion as shown by Miguel Herrero García, *Ideas de los Españoles del Siglo XVII*, Madrid, 1966, pp. 45-50, and María Teresa Perez Picavea, *op. cit.*, pp. 175-177.

36. Bernardo Ward, *op. cit.*, p. xiv.

Similarly, Francisco Cabarrús, another immigrant and the founder of the ill-fated Bank of San Carlos, noted his desire to determine "the means to raise (Spain) to her greatest splendour, by employing advantageously the gifts with which Providence and nature have distinguished these regions."[37] These observations contradicted those expressed by foreign travellers who almost invariably described Spain as being dry, arid, and naturally poor. Even some Spanish reformers were more bluntly realistic. Jovellanos wrote: "the climate of Spain is generally hot and dry, and consequently there is a great amount of land which, for lack of irrigation, either produces nothing or only some sparse pasture."[38] Yet their realism was also tempered by their refusal to admit to any relationship between Spain's "horrendous decadence" and her geography.[39] To make such an admission would have been tantamount to rejecting all hopes for regeneration.

Likewise, they refused to attribute Spanish decadence to any basic defect in their national character. The penchant of European intellectuals to personify nations became increasingly pronounced from the period of the Renaissance.[40] Eighteenth century writers indulged shamelessly in the pastime, and proved capable of producing brilliant character assassinations. Spaniards received a great deal of attention, and failed to be pacified when the attacks, as with Montesquieu, wore the veil of scientific reasoning. Montesquieu explained the Spanish character in terms of the country's climate. The intense heat made men passionate and violent. It also made them prone to subtle reasonings, similar to those found in scholastic theology. He considered Spaniards to be naturally phlegmatic and vain. The first characteristic made them unsympathetic to work; the second, manifested in a cult of

37. Quoted from Alberto G. I. Novales, *Las Pequeñas Atlántidas: Decadencia y Regeneración Intelectual de España en los Siglos XVIII y XIX*, Barcelona, 1959, p. 77.
38. Gaspar de Jovellanos, "Informe de . . . Ley Agraria," *B.A.E.* 50, p. 127. In the same text, however, Jovellanos also argued: "those great states, and especially those which, like Spain, enjoy an extended and fertile territory, ought to look upon [agriculture] as the first source of their wealth."
39. Gonzálo Anes Alvárez, *Las Crisis Agrarias en La España Moderna*, Madrid, 1970, p. 180. Jovellanos stated the accepted opinion unequivocally in "Informe de . . . Ley Agraria," *B.A.E.* 50, p. 101. "One cannot attribute the present state of agriculture to the climate. . . . Bética had a flourishing agriculture under the Romans . . . and also under the Arabs. . . ."
40. Julio Caro Baroja, *op. cit.*, pp. 78-79.

nobility, made them disdain manual labour. Hence, they were without doubt "the most invincible enemies of work."[41]

Such general criticisms were not unknown in Spain itself. Seventeenth century writers often lamented the idleness of their people. González de Cellorigo, writing in 1600, attributed Spain's decline to the sloth of Spaniards; and Andrés de Mendo, in 1656, observed that "we complain of the absence of people, but our only real complaint is the absence of people who apply themselves to work."[42] Eighteenth century economists, while no more tolerant of laziness, refused to see the indolence of Spaniards as a congenital defect. Hence they refuted the charge as expressed both by foreigners and their own predecessors. Early in the century, Géronimo de Uztáriz, the leading exponent of Colbertian mercantilism in Spain, produced quantitative evidence to prove that when their manufactures had flourished, Spaniards had been industrious; and using similar evidence, Ward argued that "it constitutes . . . proof that indolence is either not a national vice, or is a vice which can be remedied."[43] Most reformers agreed that idleness was a solvable problem, a consequence not a cause of economic decline.

Their reasoning indicates clearly the essence of the economic analysis of Spanish decadence produced during the reign of Charles III. Only those things susceptible to human remedy were allowed to qualify as causes of Spain's decline and to account for her poverty relative to other Western European nations. For this reason, they attributed the collapse of their economy to two factors above all others, bad government, and the general lack of practical, scientific knowledge available in the seventeenth century. "The state of cultivation," wrote Jovellanos, "has always conformed to the existing political situation of the nation," and no natural advantages "have been powerful enough to overcome the impediments which this situation [has created] to block its progress."[44] He and others drew heavily upon the outspoken criticism of government policies voiced by seventeenth century

41. Julian Marías, op. cit., p. 26.
42. Manuel Colmeiro, Historia de la Economía-Política, p. 24.
43. Gerónimo de Uztáriz, Theorie et Pratique du Commerce et de la Marine, 2nd. ed., Hamburg, 1753, pp. 30-35, and Bernardo Ward, op. cit., p. 105.
44. Gaspar de Jovellanos, "Informe de . . . Ley Agraria," B.A.E. 50, p. 82.

writers, and condemned the Habsburgs for their wars, the support which they gave to guilds, in particular the *Mesta*, and to entails, their commercial and colonial policies, and their disastrous fiscal system. These "mistakes" were not blamed entirely on the perfidy of the Spanish Habsburgs, but were also linked to the intellectual sterility of Spain. "Our bad intelligence and our bad leadership," wrote Ward, "have generally been the cause of our backwardness."[45] This view was confirmed by Campomanes when he wrote: "all nations have suffered their eclipses and decadence and this ought to be commonly attributed . . . to their lack of calculation and reflection on the original causes weakening industry and the useful occupation of the people."[46]

What was required to cure the economic ills debilitating Spain, therefore, was to replace bad government with good government, and faulty intelligence with a sound intelligence. For this reason, the analysis of Spanish decadence produced by eighteenth century reformers reflected what they considered to be their own strengths. If the lack of a practical knowledge had been at fault in the initial failure of Spaniards to arrest their economic collapse, that lack had been overcome. They prided themselves on their awareness of the true principles of politics and economics, and attempted to disperse this knowledge by means of the Economic Societies. "For our happiness," exclaimed Campomanes, "those calamitous and obscure times have passed. Good books are sought and respected without distinction to when or in what countries [they were written]."[47] If Spain had suffered from bad government, that situation had also changed. The leading reformers praised their Bourbon monarchs for promoting the new sciences and for legislating necessary reforms. Jovellanos considered the state of agriculture in 1794 never to have been so good. This "salutary fermentation," which included population growth and industrial expansion, he associated with "legislation not only more vigilant but also more enlightened." It was as clear to him as it was

---

45. Bernardo Ward, *op. cit.*, p. 102.

46. Quoted in Juan Sempere y Guarinos, *Biblioteca Española Económico-Político* I, p. 8. This opinion was widespread and was the basis for promoting major educational reforms. See John H. R. Polt, "Jovellanos y la educación," *Simposio sobre el Padre Feijoo y Su Tiempo* II, Oviedo, 1966, pp. 315-338.

47. Quoted in R. Krebs Wilckens, *op. cit.*, p. 37.

to others that "the heavens have reserved to the Bourbons the restoration of Spain's splendour and strength."[48]

The belief that Spain was ready to recommence or had already recommenced "the round" of economic growth described by such writers as Cantillon was widely held by reformers. Drawing their maxims for good government from the works of contemporary political economists and their specific facts and frame of reference from their Spanish predecessors, they worked to stimulate this development. In the process they achieved a number of important reforms, including the liberalization of the grain trade and the freeing of commerce between Spain and her colonies. Nevertheless, the glowing optimism of men like Jovellanos peaked too soon. Just as he was claiming a major victory in his *Ley Agraria*, an economic tract completed in 1794, Spain was beginning to experience a series of subsistence crises which continued sporadically until 1815.[49] These crises, characterized by high prices, low productive yields, famine, and population decline not only placed in jeopardy earlier reforms, especially the free circulation of grains, but also proved that the major structural weaknesses of the Spanish economy had not been removed. The optimism inherent in the economic analysis of Spanish decadence became progressively undermined by events.

The economic recession suffered by Spain during the last decade of the eighteenth century and the first two decades of the nineteenth century coupled with the political uncertainties created by the Napoleonic invasion produced the climate of disillusionment in which the ideas expressed by Léon de Arroyal and others began to spread. Arroyal differed from moderate reformers in a number of significant ways. Whereas they lauded the implementation of specific reforms, and claimed to be solving Spain's major

48. Gaspar de Jovellanos, "Informe de . . . Ley Agraria," *B.A.E.* 50, p. 81 and "Elogio de Carlos III," *B.A.E.* 46, p. 313.

49. The debate over agricultural reform in Spain began seriously in the 1760s and it was in 1787 when Jovellanos received a commission from the Madrid Economic Society to compose a report on the subject. Hence, the "Informe" represented his thinking between then and 1794 during a period when Spain experienced two famines, one in 1788 and the second in 1792. See Gonzálo Anes Alvárez "El Informe sobre la Ley Agraria y la Real Sociedad Económica Matritense de Amigos del País" *Economía e Illustración en la España del Siglo XVIII*, Barcelona, 1969, pp. 95-138. See also by the same author *Las Crisis Agrarias*.

problems and restoring vitality to the nation, he extended the period of Spain's decline into the present, lamented the failure of the government to transform the feudal structure of the economy, and blamed the failure on the administrative structure of the state. For this reason, he concluded that economic reform was an impossibility without preliminary political and constitutional reform. He accused other writers of confusing the causes of Spain's economic debility with the consequences, just as they had accused their predecessors of the same failing. Instead of condemning government policies contrary to the ideals of freedom of commerce and economic liberty, as did they, he condemned those contrary to freedom of speech and political liberty, lamenting in particular the emasculation of the Spanish *Cortes*. Armed with these new criteria for analyzing the decline of Spain, men like Arroyal helped to usher in the political turbulence of nineteenth century Spain.

C. Jago

Utility, Material Progress & Morality in 18th Century Spain

The economic history of eighteenth century Spain was marked by a modest degree of recovery in contrast to conditions in the preceding century.[1] The expansion of commerce, the emergence of more sophisticated forms of capitalistic enterprise and the gradual if incomplete liberalization of a once rigidly mercantilist economy which took place under the Bourbons, however, was not welcomed by all segments of opinion. Study of the extensive literature written by ecclesiastical moralists during the eighteenth century indicates that many churchmen were gravely troubled by the moral and social implications of economic change. The problem of the relationship between religious attitudes and material development is, of course, complex as the long debate over the Weber thesis has shown. The effect of Catholic thought upon economic life is no less complicated a question to resolve. The moral philosophy of the church, derived from Aristotle and St. Thomas Aquinas, developed principles on usury, avarice and the use and purpose of wealth which were not compatible with the values of an emerging capitalist society. In theory and in fact the church accomodated itself to the process of change, although the interminable disputes among theologians and canonists over the legitimacy of business practice reveal that the compromise was not a comfortable one.[2] Moreover, the elaborate legalistic arguments used to justify certain commercial and industrial operations did not filter easily into that vast and more unsophisticated literature,

1. For a general discussion of the economic situation in eighteenth-century Spain, see, Jaime Vicens Vives, Jorge Nadal, *An Economic History of Spain*, 3rd ed., Princeton, 1969, chapters XXXV-XXXVII.
2. J. T. Noonan has studied the struggle within the church on these questions. *The Scholastic Analysis of Usury*, Cambridge, Mass., 1957.

manuals of piety, sermons, pious biographies, etc. published by ecclesiastics for the spiritual direction of the faithful.[3]

Spain had seen its share of debate among theologians and canon lawyers over such questions as the taking of interest, the doctrine of the just price and the danger of avarice in commercial undertakings.[4] These issues continued to attract attention in the Spain of the Bourbons, but the forum of discussion shifted away from learned exchanges in Latin treatises and academic halls to open confrontations between clerics and merchants and to the publication of works designed to convince the faithful of the evils resulting from a general obsession with the acquistion of riches. The latter had long been a preoccupation of churchmen, but the increasingly violent tone of the spiritual guides, sermons, catechisms and similar works written during this period suggests that the chronic pessimism of many clerics had become more foreboding than ever before. Preachers dwelt increasingly on the vice of avarice in their sermons as they saw the pursuit of riches in their time as a sign of a deeper spiritual malaise that had led Spaniards to accept "doctrines which promote the corruption of customs and give free rein to the appetites."[5] Spain, indeed, seemed to have arrived "at those dangerous times of which the Apostle preached, when, men . . . abandon all respect and law as the dominant passion of each individual becomes the only arbiter of his actions."[6]

Catholic moralists directed their admonitions to all members of the church, but they made it clear that of all Christians, the merchant was especially vulnerable to the sin of avarice. The suspicion with which they viewed the individual engaged in business arose from the limited place assigned to commerce by the church in the transitory human society that lay before eternity.

3. For a study of literature of this kind written in France during this period, see, B. Groethuysen, *La formación de la conciencia burguesa en Francia durante el siglo XVIII*, Mexico, 1943.

4. Noonan, *The Scholastic Analysis of Usury*, pp. 283-86.

5. Francisco de Bocanegra y Xibaja, archbishop of Santiago, *Declamación oportuna contra el libertinae*, Madrid, 1779, p. 24.

6. Fray Bruna de Zaragoza, *Instrucción católica y convencimiento racional de los heterodoxos y libertinos*, 2nd ed., Zaragoza, 1804, p. 4. A good study of traditional thought in eighteenth century Spain is R. Labrousse, *La doble herencia política de España*, Barcelona, 1942.

Moralists admitted that trade constituted a legitimate field of endeavour imposed by the divine commandment that men should love their neighbours and by man's original lot in the world when he found himself "destitute of all assistance."[7] In these circumstances, reason dictated that men should come together to aid one another and that one of the ways that they might do so was through commerce which existed to serve "the common utility . . . for the benefit of all."[8]

The restricted sphere of action assigned to commerce by the clerical moralists reflected their belief in a corporate and hierarchical social order. In a society divided by nature and divine providence into well defined classes, some with a more exalted function than others, the place of commerce, agriculture and the artisan trades was necessarily inferior to that of the nobility and the clergy. Churchmen admitted that the former were required for the physical survival of the body politic, and they recognized their contribution to the common good, but they made it clear that this form of service on behalf of the general welfare did not merit the rewards and privileges given to those responsible for the salvation of men and the defense of the realm.[9] For the moralists, the position of the merchant was especially ambiguous; he was needed to supply the goods which men required to live but the very nature of his profession encouraged him to sacrifice the interests of society as a whole for his personal profit.

Defenders of the traditional morality, then, did not deny the contribution of the merchant to the well-being of society nor did they question his right to a profit and a reasonable standard of living as long as both respected the interests of the common good. Ecclesiastical moralists accepted the legitimacy of "the discrete and virtuous search for material things."[10] As a result of original sin, men were bound to labor on this earth and to acquire whatever worldly possessions were necessary to sustain "the

---

7. Alejandro Aguado, professor of theology at the University of Alcalá, *Política española para el más proporcionado remedio de nuestra monarquía*, 2 vols., Madrid, 1746, II, pp. 172-74.

8. *Ibid.*, p. 208.

9. *Ibid.*, pp. 56, 64, 118.

10. Antonio Arbiol, *Desengaños místicos a las almas detenidas o engañadas en el camino de perfección*, 7th ed., Zaragoza, 1729, p. 82.

decency of their households."[11] The moralists, indeed, suggested that a connection existed between prosperity in this world and the attainment of felicity in the next.[12] Concern with material things and the motivation of work itself, however, had to be directed towards the ultimate purpose of human existence for "without divine benediction, the individual who works does so in vain."[13] Moreover, the decent life which men might legitimately seek on earth was to be one of temperate prudence. Men were warned that worldly prosperity was transitory and that while they should work "moderately and avoid idleness" in order to fulfill their familial obligations, they must not let "all their hearts be occupied" with such concerns: "regular and virtuous work must be tempered . . . so that it does not occupy the soul but only the body."[14]

The hard work, long hours and preoccupations of the businessman naturally attracted the hostility of the moralists. The author of one of the most popular manuals of piety complained of merchants who defied divine providence by becoming slaves to their affairs, "working at all hours, . . . lamenting whatever brief period they take to see the good of their souls; . . . as they pass all of their miserable and laborious lives concerned with temporal possessions."[15] The line between decent and avaricious labour was seen as a fine one since greed could be introduced "nearly unperceived because little by little the individual becomes addicted to the profits which he is making."[16]

An excessive preoccupation with business interests was the fatal sign of avarice which moralists saw as the root of all evil. Nowhere did clerics become more wrathful than when they were denouncing the wickedness of the avaricious who had erected "idols of gold" as their gods.[17] Avarice, they maintained, prevented man from fulfilling his obligations towards God and his

---

11. Antonio Arbiol, *La familia regulada con doctrina de la sagrada escritura*, 5th ed., Madrid, 1725, p. 304.

12. *Ibid.*, p. 308.

13. *Ibid.*, p. 304.

14. Arbiol, *Desengaños místicos*, p. 82.

15. *Ibid.*, p. 81.

16. *Ibid.*, p. 82.

17. José Climent, bishop of Barcelona, *Pláticas dominicales*, 3 vols., Barcelona, 1799, II, p. 78.

neighbour. The greedy man refused to assist the poor whom he regarded as idlers; he refused to remain content with his state in life but developed instead "a great anxiety to acquire the goods that he did not possess.[18] Here again it was the merchant who was most likely to fall into this most terrible of vices. The very nature of his occupation revolved around the handling of money and "in commerce it is difficult to develop a desire for reasonable profit without the desire for riches."[19] The moral dangers implicit in commerce could be avoided only if merchants directed their consciences "faithfully and rightly ... in matters involving self-interest," and this could be done only with the advice of their spiritual directors.[20]

Ecclesiastical moralists were convinced that only a small minority of the merchant community was avoiding avarice in its business enterprises. The Jesuit missionary preacher, Fr. Pedro de Calatayud, observed that in his journeys across Spain he had noted "many injustices and illicit profits in the purchase and sale of wool and other products:" while the archbishop of Burgos complained that usurious commercial practices were common throughout the kingdom and another bishop declared that the problem would be difficult to control "so many were the injustices, so enormous the iniquities" being committed in the name of commerce.[21] All this was bad enough, but even more scandalous for the moralists was the way in which merchants boldly rejected their counsel.[22] Calatayud attacked merchants "who close their eyes ... in order

18. *Ibid.*, p. 79. On this theme see also, Bocanegra y Xibaja, *Sermones*, 2 vols., Madrid, 1773, I, pp. 260-62; Matías Sánchez, *El padre de familias brevemente instruido*, Madrid, 1792, p. 29.

19. Pedro de Calatayud, Respuesta a una consulta que me hace un comerciante de Bilbao sobre la compra de lanas, 1764. Biblioteca Nacional, ms. 5809, fol. 309.

20. *Ibid.* Several guides were published to provide merchants with the information which would enable them to distinguish licit from illicit business practices. See, for example, José Manuel Domínguez, *Discursos jurídicos sobre las acceptaciones, pagas, intereses y demás requisitos y qualidades de las letras de cambio*, Madrid, 1732; Miguel de Hualde, *El contador lego, especulativo y práctico sobre varios assumptos de aritmética civil*, Madrid, 1758.

21. Calatayud, *Tratados y doctrinas prácticas sobre ventas y compras de lanas merinas y otros géneros*, Toledo, 1761, p. 1. José Xavier Rodriguez de Arellano, *Pastorales, edictos, pláticas y declamaciones que hacia a su diocesi*, 7 vols., Madrid, 1775, V, p. 410; Miguel de Santander, auxiliary bishop of Zaragosa, *Doctrinas y sermones*, 5 vols., Madrid, 1800, I, p. 330.

22. Rodríguez de Arellano, *Pastorales, edictos* V, p. 410.

not to see what is illicit and ugly in their affairs . . . lest they be obliged to restore what they have improperly earned."[23] Still more aggravating was the ease with which those engaged in commerce reconciled their religious beliefs with questionable business practices. One moralist cited the example of merchants who frequented the sacraments but whose attention was concentrated "on their wretched little interests," while the archbishop of Burgos lashed out against businessmen whose homes were "little theatres . . . of devotion" as hypocrites seeking to hide the corrupt source of their wealth.[24]

The issue which most aroused the anger of the moralists was the perennial question of usury. "Who are the rats of the field," asked Calatayud in a popular catechism; the reply was quickly forthcoming, "those merchants and dealers who suck the blood from peasants and nobles with their illicit profits."[25] It is true that theoretical arguments were worked out which permitted the use of a wide range of capitalistic business practices and that some ecclesiastics interpreted these more liberally than others, but Spanish moralists of the eighteenth century generally adhered to a strictly conservative interpretation which saw the potential for usury in every commerical transaction.[26]

Moralists objected to usury because they believed that it perverted the nature of commerce and exalted the selfish concerns of the merchant over the welfare of society as a whole: "self-interest has been raised upon the throne; to this merchants look, to this they sacrifice tranquility, health and their souls."[27] The specific form of mercantile greed which most provoked ecclesiastics was the use of the anticipatory payment to purchase

---

23. Calatayud, *Tratados y doctrinas*, prologue.

24. Arbiol, *Desengaños místicos*, pp. 82-3; Rodríguez de Arellano, *Pastorales, edictos* V, pp. 419-20.

25. Calatayud, *Cathecismo práctico y mui útil para la instrucción y enseñanza de los fieles*, 8th ed., Seville, 1761, p. 255; Rodríguez de Arellano, *Pattorales, edictos* VI, p. 201.

26. An important exception was the Basque cleric, Jose María Uría Nafarrondo who published a work in 1785 which defended the moral probity of merchants in their operations, although even he admitted that he had undertaken his book to refute the widespread opinion that "merchants are public usurers and thieves." *Aumento del comercio con seguridad de la conciencia*, Madrid, 1785, p. xxi.

27. Santander, *Doctrinas y sermones* II, p. 338.

raw materials and artisanal products from peasants and craftsmen who sold their goods at lower prices in return for cash advances. Such a practice, the moralists held, flagrantly violated the purpose of commerce, the mutual rendering of assistance among men, and the principles of justice because it led to the merciless exploitation of the worker denied a just price for his labours by the avaricious merchant intent only upon maximizing his profit. The archbishop of Burgos summed up the feeling of the moralists when he lamented the fate "of that poor workman who, though working day and night to earn enough to eat, is paid badly or not at all because they have lowered the price of his goods without reducing the amount of labor necessary to produce them, and they have done so with arrogant pride, rejecting the dictates of their consciences by refusing to render honest work its just reward."[28]

The issue of the anticipatory payment produced one of the sharpest conflicts between moralists and businessmen in the 1750s and early 1760s when Fr. Pedro de Calatayud challenged the great merchant *consulado* of Bilbao for indulging in the practice.[29] The Basque mercantile corporation, one of the most successful and active in the kingdom, had extensive commercial interests both within Spain and abroad. A convenient geographical situation made the city a busy port of export for Spanish raw materials destined for northern Europe. Much of the *consulado*'s export trade was made up of wool and iron purchased from herdsmen and forge owners of modest economic circumstances. The Basque merchants paid for these materials in advance in return for a price lower than the going market price at the time of delivery. Calatayud, whose preaching missions had made him familiar with the areas where the *consulado* made its purchases, denounced the custom as usurious as he directly attacked the Basque merchants for brutally exploiting the economically defenseless.[30] The Jesuit's charges set off a bitter public debate which eventually was carried to the highest circles of government before it was resolved. The *consulado* engaged its own theological consultors to reply to the

28. Rodrïguez de Arellano, *Pastorales, edictos* V, p. 426.
29. An account of this conflict can be found in T. Guiard, *Historia del Consulado y Casa de Contratación de Bilbao*, 2 vols., Bilbao, 1913-1914, II, pp. 611-22.
30. Calatayud, *Tratados y doctrinas, passim.*

accusations and eventually appealed to the Council of Castile. The Council ordered a ban on the circulation of the Jesuit's published works in the Basque Provinces, although Calatayud remained unrepentant, convinced that he had spoken "with equity and reason according to God and the truth."[31]

In Madrid, early in the 1760s, another clash took place between a Dominican, Fray Antonio Garcés, and a no less formidable opponent than the Cinco Gremios Mayores, the great corporation of guilds that dominated the commerce of the city.[32] In several public sermons, Garcés, "with zeal and in the name of doctrine," reproached the guilds' practice of paying interest to those who had lent them money for fixed periods of time. The arguments presented by both sides rested on their respective interpretations of the large body of literature that had been written on the legitimacy of taking or giving interest. What is significant about the dispute is that it was carried on vociferously and openly, leading the guilds to complain that Garcés had provoked "a kind of public clamour" against them as they appealed to the king for redress.[33] They eventually had the satisfaction of hearing that their affairs had not been conducted illicitly and that their members were "men of integrity and holy doctrine."[34]

In both of these cases, the state came to the defense of the merchant community against clerical attack. It is significant, however, that Calatayud and Garcés did not scruple from launching their offensive against two of the most distinguished and influential merchant corporations of the kingdom. Spectacular public conflicts of this sort were not frequent in the eighteenth century, it is true, but the vast spiritual literature of the period shows that many ecclesiastics viewed the campaign against the immorality of business practice with great sympathy. Moreover, it is reasonable to assume a connection between the growing

31. Calatayud, Respuesta a una consulta, fol. 309.

32. Vicente Palacio Atard provides a summary of this dispute in *Los españoles de la Ilustración*, Madrid, 1964, pp. 98-102.

33. *Representación hecha al Rey N. Sr. por los Diputados Directores de los Cinco Gremios Mayores, sobre lo que predicó contra sus contratos el Rmo. P. Mtro. Antonio Garcés*, 1763, in *Semanario Erudito*, 34 vols., Madrid, 1787-1791, XXVII, p. 240.

34. Resolución de S. M. sobre la legitimidad de los préstamos a interés hechos a los Cinco Gremios Mayores de Madrid, 1764. Biblioteca Nacional, ms. 11265.

resentment of moralists at the exploitation of peasants and artisans and the social impact of economic change. There is some evidence to suggest that the fate of the rural agriculturalist rested increasingly in the hands of speculators whose resources allowed them to dominate economically weak suppliers to their own advantage. The same can be said for the use of the anticipatory payment by merchants dealing with artisans, for here too there were signs of the spread of a putting-out system among manual tradesmen.[35]

The intervention of the state in these two conflicts reflected the concern of the eighteenth century Bourbons with problems of material development and their determination to overide the traditional scholastic opposition of clerics to the economic changes deemed essential to the restoration of national strength. Educated opinion was also concerned with the question of the economy. This was especially true during the reign of Charles III (1759-1788). Books, periodicals and articles dealing with economic issues proliferated; in nearly a hundred towns, local notables formed economic societies to encourage agriculture, industry and commerce. This widespread preoccupation with economic questions did not emerge from any theoretical agreement among partisans of material progress, for there were often differences of opinion on specific policies. For conservative ecclesiastics, however, the seemingly universal emphasis upon material development appeared as a dangerous sign of moral degeneration.

The most spectacular conflict between clerical moralists and advocates of economic progress took place in the 1780s in Zaragoza. In the Aragonese capital, the local economic society, one of the most active in Spain, sought to promote "utilitarian" culture through the establishment of academic chairs of mathematics, botany, chemistry, agriculture, moral philosophy and civil

---

35. A royal decree of August 12, 1774 thus complained of "the insatiable greed" of speculative silk merchants. Ministerio de Hacienda, Ordenes Generales de Rentas, XXI, fols. 123-24. And in 1770, a master of the lace industry of Valladolid complained that although some forty masters worked at that trade in the city, the making of lace had declined "because of a lack of resources among its individuals, in such a way that most of the masters see themselves forced to work . . . for the merchants of the city." *Descripción natural, geográfica y económica de todos los pueblos de España*, Madrid, 1771, IV, no. 83, p. 123.

economy.[36] Of the several chairs created by the society, the most important was that of civil economy. The inaugural lecture was given on October 24, 1784 by Lorenzo Normante y Carcavilla, attorney of the Royal Councils and member of the College of Lawyers of Zaragoza, who exalted the study of the economic sciences as the foundation of material progress: "If the centuries of Augustus, of the Medici and of Louis XIV were centuries of letters and the fine arts, the century in which we live will be, perhaps, the century of true philosophy, of patriotic love, of the useful arts and sciences."[37] Normante singled out for special praise the pragmatic education being given by the economic society of Zaragoza because it served "to reveal the means which will lead to the public felicity." "After religion, can the Amigos del País of Aragón find any objective more worthy or employ themselves in anything greater," he asked rhetorically.[38]

Normante later published several works which, among several economic topics discussed, treated the question of luxury in a manner calculated to arouse defenders of the traditional morality. There was little new in Normante's work which drew heavily on the ideas of the French economist, Melon, but the rigor of the author's language and his ill-disguised contempt for the religious interpretation of luxury which, he observed, "represents nothing but vague, confused and even false ideas," prepared the ground for a violent clerical counter-attack.[39] Normante was interested in the question of luxury primarily for economic reasons. He believed that "industry is the source of wealth and national power," and thus attacked the use of sumptuary laws to restrain expenditures on luxury goods and maintained that the effect of such legislation upon the economy was disastrous because it encouraged consumers to purchase foreign manufactures.[40] Here Normante echoed what had become familiar doctrine to many eighteenth-

36. For a discussion of the society in Zaragoza, see, Jean Sarrailh, *La España ilustrada de la segunda mitad del siglo XVIII*, tr. J. Gaos, Mexico, 1957, part II, chapter V; Jose Alvárez Junco, "La labor educativa de la Sociedad Aragonesa de Amigos del País," in *La Real Sociedad Bascongada y la Ilustración*, San Sebastian, 1969, p. 14.
37. Quoted in *ibid.*, p. 24.
38. *Ibid.*
39. Lorenzo Normante y Carcavilla, *Espíritu del Señor Melon en su ensayo político sobre el comercio*, Zaragoza, 1786, p. 38.
40. *Ibid.*, pp. 38, 44.

century economic writers; as early as 1740, the mercantilist author, Bernardo Ulloa, had deprecated sumptuary laws in Spain because "they have not had any favorable effect."[41] The preoccupation of the state with industrial development had gradually reduced the importance of sumptuary legislation in Spain. No significant laws of this kind were issued during the rule of Ferdinand VI (1746-1759), and only four were promulgated during the twenty-nine year reign of Charles III.[42] The state's declining interest in controlling luxury was further encouraged by changes in fashions and fabrics which made effective regulation of consumer tastes difficult. Moreover, during the last third of the century, the crown had begun to dismantle, albeit incompletely, the elaborate guild and industrial regulations which had militated against the introduction of new and more attractive products by Spanish manufacturers. The orientation of the state's economic policy in a more liberal direction, however, early aroused the suspicions of conservative moralists like Francisco Bocanegra, the archbishop of Santiago, who in 1779 lashed out against "that intolerable luxury which they wish to sanctify in the name of the utility of the state."[43]

Had Normante left his discussion of luxury on the level of economic necessity, it is unlikely that his restatement of ideas already in general circulation would have provoked more than passing controversy. He did not rest his case, however, on economic considerations alone but chose to venture onto the field of morality where defenders of traditional moral values were ready to do battle. Normante admitted that indulgence of the passions could create difficulties for society, but he maintained that little could be done about this, and, more significantly, he declared that the exercise of the passions lay behind the accomplishments of successful men: "the soldier displays bravery because of ambition; the merchant acts out of greed; both engage in their work impelled by the desire to place themselves in a position to enjoy luxurious things, to live with special comfort and pleasure."[44] Normante

41. Bernardo Ulloa, *Restablecimiento de las fábricas y comercio español*, Madrid, 1740, p. 9.
42. Henri Bérindoague, *Le mercantilisme en Espagne*, Paris, 1929, p. 217, note 2.
43. Bocanegra y Xibaja, *Declamación oportuna*, p. 24.
44. Normante, *Pruebas del espíritu del Señor Melon*, p. 37.

then went further and asserted that indulgence of the passions for material comfort brought with it substantial economic benefits for the rich man "knowing that his wealth may soon be consumed unless he seeks the means to preserve it or to acquire new riches, works with eagerness."[45]

Normante argued that attempts to control luxury were unacceptable because they served "to enchain the liberty of the citizens," and because they pushed the state into an area — the regulation of personal morality — where it did not belong, at least insofar as the disposition of private property was concerned. It was not the affair of the state, he contended, to concern itself with the moral effect of luxury upon the individual. If a man chose to ruin himself, both spiritually and materially, by excessive indulgence on luxury goods, the responsibility was his alone. It is true that Normante foresaw a few situations in which luxury would have to be controlled, but he saw these as exceptional and in general held that "luxury not only should be permitted, it should be encouraged."[46]

It should be kept in mind that Normante's defense of luxury represented an extreme position among Spanish authors who treated this subject. Most authors dwelt upon the potential economic benefits to be derived from luxury, and those who felt compelled to consider the moral side of the question did so by seeking to prove the compatibility of luxury with traditional moral values. Juan Sempere y Guarinos, who wrote the most detailed work published in Spain on the question of luxury during this period, best represents this more widely held moderate view of the subject. Sempere maintained that it was incorrect to see evil in the mere possession of worldly goods for "vice cannot exist simply because of the things which man uses."[47] He contended that sin resulted only from the excessive and disordered use of material goods, and that it was only in this context that luxury could be regarded as evil. In other circumstances, it served a beneficial purpose by providing employment and bringing eco-

45. *Ibid.*, p. 39.
46. *Ibid.*, pp. 39, 42.
47. Juan Sempere y Guarinos, *Historia de luxo y de las leyes suntuarias de España*, 2 vols., Madrid, 1788, II, p. 195.

nomic advantages to the state.[48]

Defenders of the traditional morality were highly suspicious of even this restrained advocacy of luxury, but it was the more audacious work of Normante which called forth their wrath. The angel of divine retribution could not have been more aptly chosen; he was the celebrated Capuchin, Fray Diego de Cádiz, an ascetic and emotional monk whose fiery preaching had won him a considerable reputation across Spain. Cádiz was by no means the ignorant Spanish friar of legend. He had been well trained in theology, philosophy and the scriptures. His moral philosophy was rigid and uncompromising, and on more than one occasion, his frank denunciations of what he saw as immorality involved him in difficulties with influential figures stung by his sharp preaching. Cádiz had developed a terrible vision of Spanish society in his own time as one which was sinking deeper and deeper into a morass of corruption and libertinism.[49]

In November 1786, the friar arrived in Zaragoza to preach an Advent mission and to give a series of spiritual conferences for the clergy of the city in the Seminary of San Carlos. In the course of the latter, he attacked Normante, especially for his statements on luxury, the taking of interest and the necessity of limiting the number of religious in Spain. Subsequently, Cádiz made a formal accusation before the local officers of the Inquisition.[50]

The charges of Cádiz set off a public uproar in Zaragoza as a controversy developed between partisans of the economic society and conservative moralists. In the city, crowds rushed to hear the friar, now publicly attacking the economic society for seeking to secure the ruin of the church through the teaching of its chair of civil economy.[51] Prominent members of the local clergy supported the Capuchin who believed that he saw "in every ecclesiastic a St. Peter with sword in hand" ready to halt the progress of libertinism. Several clerics defended the position of Cádiz in

48. *Ibid.*
49. For a biography of Fray Diego de Cádiz, see, Jose Calasanz, *Vida del Beato Diego de Cádiz*, Rome, 1894, p. 165.
50. There is a brief summary of this controversy in Sarrailh, *La España ilustrada*, pp. 278-80.
51. Alvárez Junco, "La labor educativa," p. 26.

print.[52] Fray Jerónimo de Cabra, a Capuchin colleague of Cádiz, compared Normante to Calvin and Molinos, the Spanish Quietist, and numbered him among "the deceivers of the people."[53] Fray Jerónimo was especially outraged by Normante's emphasis upon material progress as necessary for securing the public felicity. He scornfully dismissed Normante's pledge of religious orthodoxy and denounced his concern with economic questions as "nothing less than an occupation full of pride and curiosity, . . . highly distracting for the attainment of the knowledge and love of God, the one necessary and indispensable thing for every man."[54] Another critic of Normante took up the theme in a different form and asserted: "what arrogance is to be observed in the prideful man who pretends, indeed who already thinks, that through reliance upon human wisdom and without any respect for the divine, he has risen to the heavens and placed his chair of learning above the stars."[55]

Normante's defense of luxury came under especially bitter attack. For ecclesiastical moralists, luxury was nothing less than "an abominable vice," a sign of that extraordinary relaxation of customs" which appeared in times when men "were subjugated by their passions." To assert, as Normante had done, that an individual might construct a palatial residence solely for his amusement and pleasure was to justify "the vanity, the pride, the grandeur . . . and the delights which are completely contrary to reason . . . and to the holy law of the Lord."[56]

The economic society of Zaragoza regarded the campaign against Normante as an attack upon itself. Normante appeared before a general assembly of the society and offered a defense of his position which received the enthusiastic support of the membership. The society then launched a counter-offensive of its own. It first appealed to other societies and received fourteen expressions of support and then elected to by-pass any attempt to

52. Calasanz, *Vida del Beato Diego de Cádiz,* pp. 139-40.
53. Fray Jerónimo de Cabra, *Pruebas del espíritu del Señor* Melon y de las proposiciones de economía civil del Señor Normante, Madrid, 1787, pp. 95, 74.
54. *Ibid.,* pp. 15-16.
55. *Carta confidencial a Dn. N. de N. de la cautela con que se han de leer las dos cartas del Correo de los Ciegos de Madrid,* Madrid, 1787, p. 75.
56. Cabra, *Pruebas del espíritu del Señor Melon,* pp. 75-85.

defend itself before the Inquisition in favor of a direct appeal to the king and the Council of Castile. The society, in its letter to Charles III, described the denunciations of Cádiz against the "perverse, accursed century" in which "error" was being preached to the ruin of the church."[57] It also complained of the public hostility being directed against it in Zaragoza as a result of the friar's sermons. The society acted wisely by taking its case to Madrid. The Council of Castile had been responsible for encouraging the formation of the economic societies, and the Council was irritated at yet another example of clerical hostility towards its projects for reform. It named a commission of three more liberally disposed ecclesiastics to examine the charges levied by the Capuchin friar. The commission acted quickly and concluded that there was "nothing unorthodox or reprehensible" in the writings of Normante and it recommended that his works be allowed to circulate freely. Once the state had rendered its decision, the immediate controversy came to an end. Normante continued to teach and, in fact, held his chair of civil economy until 1801.[58] There was nothing that conservative clerics could do about the state's decision, but it is clear that the triumph of Normante and the society of Zaragoza rankled for some time afterward.[59]

The debate over luxury reveals once again the extent of the unease and pessimism that gripped clerical moralists as they contemplated the world about them. To a degree, they were correct to see that economic conditions were undermining the providential and hierarchical social order which they cherished as an ideal. The transformation of society which they so deplored, of course, was very far from being complete in spite of their conviction that a final collapse into libertinism was imminent. The legal structure of the society of orders remained intact, and material progress was too sporadic and uneven to have profound social effects. The grim determination with which the clerical moralists combated the nascent forces of economic and social

---

57. Sarrailh, *La España ilustrada*, p. 280.
58. Alvárez Junco, "La labor educativa," p. 26.
59. Fray Diego de Cádiz remained convinced of the rectitude of his stand long after the events in Zaragoza. "Carta del P. Fr. Diego Josef de Cádiz . . . al editor," in Miguel de Santander, *Doctrinas y sermones*, I, p. xi.

change indicates, however, that any transformation of Spanish society, no matter how limited its character, was not to be accomplished without vigorous opposition.

W. J. Callahan

Political Patronage
in 18th Century England

To twentieth century critics convinced of the virtues of political democracy, eighteenth century English society can scarcely appear other than thoroughly corrupt. They would probably regard as typical the story told in 1831 – during the debates on the first Reform Bill – by the Lord Advocate. He spoke thus of the county of Bute, with a population of 14,000 and only 21 qualified voters:

> At an election in Bute, not beyond the memory of man, only one person attended the meeting, except the sheriff and the returning officer. He of course took the chair, constituted the meeting, called over the roll of freeholders, answered to his own name. ... He then moved and seconded his own nomination, put the question to the vote, and was unanimously returned.[1]

This is admittedly a Scottish story, and probably apocryphal at that. But one could equally well point to that most notorious of English pocket-boroughs, Old Sarum – for long the property of the Pitt family. At a bye-election there in 1728 the young Henry Fox, at the outset of a political career during which he was to take full advantage of the patronage system to acquire a fortune and a peerage, nearly caused one of those electoral upsets which at once delight and confound modern psephologists. Though a candidate, Fox did not appear in the borough, but he was informed of the result by Thomas Winnington, who wrote: "It was your fortune to lose the election by one vote only, for [Thomas] Pitt, not

*Paper presented at a joint symposium on "Patronage in Politics and The Arts" sponsored by the McMaster Association for Eighteenth Century Studies and the Department of Classics held on February 19, 1972.

1. Quoted in Thomas Erskine May, *Constitutional History of England*, F. Holland, ed., London, 1912, I, pp. 240-1.

suspecting any opposition, had but two voters there except the person who voted for you."[2]

An electoral system in which some 50% of the 489 English seats were under the control of private patrons or Government Departments lent itself naturally to tales such as these, and to the resultant myth of a legislature elected by corrupt methods in order to extend further the vested interests of its members. It was no secret that extensive literary activities of Horace Walpole (member of Parliament for Callington, 1741-54, Castle Rising 1754-57, and King's Lynn 1757-68) were partly subsidised by his enjoyment of the triple sinecures of Usher of the Exchequer, Clerk of the Estreats, and Comptroller of the Pipe for no less than 59 years; or that his vitriolic bias against Henry Pelham and the Duke of Newcastle in *Memoirs of the Reign of George II* owed much to their refusal to let young Horace get his hands yet further into the till. Equally assiduous in the search for preferment was General Charles Churchill (member of parliament for Castle Rising 1715-45), the illegitimate son of Marlborough's brother and the father of an illegitimate son, Charles Churchill (member of Parliament for Stockbridge 1741-47, Milborne Port 1747-54, and Great Marlow 1754-61), who married the illegitimate daughter of Sir Robert Walpole. Between them father, son, and daughter-in-law managed, except during the 1750s, to hold court offices of one kind or another from 1718 to 1782. It was not too difficult to achieve a modest competence through Parliament.

It is appropriate to quote the most prominent of living English historians to have addressed himself to the importance of patronage in eighteenth century England. In his Ford Lectures, J. H. Plumb remarked:

> What Sir Robert Walpole and the Whigs did was to make certain that political and social authority should devolve by inheritance. . . . And power by inheritance means a world run by patronage. . . . Patronage has been, and is, an essential feature of the British structure of power, no matter how various the costumes it may wear. In the eighteenth century

2. Quoted in Earl of Ilchester, *Henry Fox, First Lord Holland*, London, 1920, I, p. 30.

it scarcely bothered to wear a fig-leaf. It was naked and quite unashamed. . . . It was patronage that cemented the political system, and made it an almost impregnable citadel, impervious to defeat, indifferent to social change. And yet there are historians who dismiss eighteenth century patronage as little more than private charity. This is absurd, and arises from considering the pecuniary rewards of place only. Place was power; patronage was power; and power is what men in politics are after. After 1715 power could not be achieved through party and so the rage of party gave way to the pursuit of place.[3]

It would be both dishonest and immodest of me to conceal the fact that the only absurd historian identified in the accompanying foot-note is J. B. Owen, and I may perhaps be forgiven for quoting the offending passage from *The Rise of the Pelhams*:

The myth that Walpole and later Henry Pelham controlled the House of Commons by virtue of 'every man having his price' will not bear close examination. A solid core of placemen was a useful and reasonably dependable basis for an administration; under eighteenth century conditions its existence was inevitable, even indispensable. But a Government that had no coherent policy, no administrative talent, and no debating strength could never hope to build up and maintain a working majority in the Lower House. Patronage was necessary; it was not, and never could be, sufficient. Its primary purpose was to provide seats and salaries for the 'men of business,' on whose work and abilities the security of the Government depended; for the rest, it had the character of private charity rather than public corruption, and as a constitutional lubricant between executive and legislature it was always of subordinate significance. In a century that lacked the bitter controversial issues of its predecessor, the indifference of parliamentary majorities was too often mistaken for subservience. In normal times it was unneces-

3. J. H. Plumb, *The Growth of Political Stability in England, 1675-1725*, London, 1967, pp. 188-9.

sary to buy votes; a competent administration could count on the predisposition of the ordinary member to support the King's Government. When feeling ran high, the demands of conscience and prejudice frequently deprived ministers of this initial advantage. But on such occasions the efficacy of political corruption was unlikely to be great. An impassioned man seldom consults his purse. The appeals of eighteenth century politicians were made to the reason or to the passions, not to the pockets of their fellow-members.[4]

I do not wish to pretend that my views and those of Dr. Plumb are necessarily as irreconcilable as the juxtaposition of the above two passages might seem to suggest. Patronage was certainly essential to the relative political and social stability of eighteenth century England. In an era of mixed government, before well-disciplined and nationally organised parties had emerged, and when the royal Closet was still on a higher political level than any Cabinet, nominal or efficient, the most basic ingredient promoting harmony between the King and his ministers on the one hand and the Commons on the other was of necessity the complicated nexus of interests created by the web of patronage. Without the nucleus of a substantial body of placemen in Parliament, and without the electoral resources to keep them there, chronic political friction would have become characteristic of English government. David Hume was after all merely stating a commonplace when in 1741 he made the oft-quoted remarks:

> The Crown has so many offices at its disposal, that, when assisted by the honest and disinterested part of the house, it will always command the resolutions of the whole, so far, at least, as to preserve the ancient constitution from danger. We may, therefore, give to this influence what name we please, we may call it by the invidious appellations of *corruption* and *dependance*; but some degree and some kind of it are inseparable from the very nature of the constitution, and necessary to the preservation of our mixed government.[5]

4. John B. Owen, *The Rise of the Pelhams*, London, 1957, p. 62.
5. D. Hume, *Essays, Moral, Political and Literary*, London, 1862, p. 25.

If, therefore, I disagree with Dr. Plumb, it is because he seems to me inclined too much to disregard the "honest and disinterested" part of the House. I do not believe that *all* men in eighteenth century politics were merely after power and patronage; two generations of Tories under the early Hanoverians and a large body of country gentlemen during the second half of the century gave the lie to this notion. I do not believe that the contemporary political system was impervious to defeat. I do not believe that after 1715 the rage of party merely gave way to the pursuit of place. Patronage could not save Walpole from defeat in 1742 any more than it could save Lord North from defeat in 1782. Nor could it prevent the elder Pitt, who ostentatiously scorned to cultivate a connexion of his own, from achieving between 1757 and 1762 a position of dominance unequalled by any other politician during the century. It could not muzzle the denunciations of men so far apart politically as Edmund Burke and Thomas Paine. In 1770 Burke could claim that "the power of the Crown, almost dead and rotten as prerogative, has grown up anew, with much more strength, and far less odium under the name of Influence;"[6] and in 1776 Tom Paine echoed the words of his future arch-opponent:

> That the crown is the overbearing part in the constitution needs not be mentioned, and that it derives its whole consequence merely by being the giver of place and pensions is self-evident, wherefore, though we have been wise enough to shut and lock a door against absolute Monarchy, we have at the same time been foolish enough to put the Crown in possession of the key.[7]

Both men of course were merely voicing a detestation of placemen and pensioners that had been the common plaint of country members since the days of Charles II, if not earlier. But the particular animus against the Crown had to await the accession of George III and the fall from royal favour of the rump of the

---

6. *The Works of the Right Honourable Edmund Burke*, London, 1906, II, p. 11.
7. W. M. van der Weyde, ed., *Life and Works of Thomas Paine*, New York, 1925, II, p. 106.

Walpolian-Pelhamite Whigs. A system of patronage which had been welcomed when it operated to their advantage became obnoxious when they were on the outside looking in, instead of the inside looking out. The culmination of their protest came with Dunning's celebrated motion of 6 April 1780, "that the Influence of the Crown has increased, is increasing, and ought to be diminished"[8] — a motion that would scarcely have been passed by a House of Commons dedicated only to the pursuit of place. Nor for that matter would such a Commons have passed significant measures of economical reform under the second Rockingham ministry in 1782, or have provided as many as 174 members to vote for the younger Pitt's proposal for parliamentary reform in April 1785. The eighteenth century House of Commons was a surprisingly independent body, much more so in fact than its twentieth century successor.

Having said all this, it is fair to add that there were few members of Parliament in the eighteenth century who did not seek, and obtain, some small mark of favour for themselves, their relatives or their constituents. In an age when members were paid no salaries, some compensation was expected for the expense of getting oneself elected, maintaining a house in London during the parliamentary sessions, and aiding the King and his ministers in the government of the nation. Indeed, a man who was granted no favour was regarded as a fellow of little consequence. But whether these favours were sufficiently substantial to affect political behaviour is quite another matter. Nor should we forget that for every successful applicant there were many who were disappointed. The First Lord of the Treasury and its Secretary may have been the eighteenth century forerunners of the modern Government whips supplying emollients that formed the precursor of later party discipline, but theirs was at times a thankless task. The Treasury has been well described as a place "where numberless sturdy beggars apply, who cannot all be satisfied, nor all with safety refused," and when patronage reached its peak during the 1750s, Chesterfield could lament wryly that there was scarce enough pasture for the beasts to graze upon.

8. W. Cobett, *The Parliamentary History of England*, London, 1814, XXI, p. 347.

The true extent and nature of political patronage can be assessed only through an examination of its actual operation. This can be a tiresome and exacting task, but it is one which must be attempted. Let me first turn to the English electorate of the period, an electorate which returned 80 county and 409 borough members to the House of Commons. Of the forty two member counties none could be said to be under the influence of a single individual or family. The Earl of Sandwich, it is true, frequently wielded a decisive influence in the return of one or both members for Huntingdonshire, but this was due to his local standing rather than to any power of coercion. Otherwise, in perhaps some fifteen counties, a tacit agreement was frequently reached between a local magnate and the country gentlemen, whereby the latter nominated one member, and the magnate the other — usually one of his own sons. This was merely a convenient way of avoiding contests that could prove prohibitively expensive. In the famous contested election of 1754 in Oxfordshire the extant Tory election accounts show an expenditure of £20,068-1-2, and it is extremely unlikely that the Whig candidates spent less.[9] The even more celebrated Yorkshire election of 1807 was rumoured to have cost over £200,000. Even without a contest, money was lavishly spent. When Philip Yorke, eldest son of Lord Hardwicke, was elected for Cambridgeshire in 1747, there was never the slightest hint of opposition. Nonetheless it cost Hardwicke £2,188-14-6 to get his son returned and this was said to have been one of the cheapest elections in the county for many years.[10] For our purposes it is sufficient to note that Government influence in County elections was at best trivial, and of the top-ranking politicians of the century, Henry Pelham, who represented Sussex for no less than 32 years, was the only county representative. Equally, no private individual commanded such an interest in a county that ministers could call upon his services to ensure the return of a government nominee.

With the 203 English boroughs the position was of course very

9. See R. J. Robson, *The Oxfordshire Election of 1754*, Oxford, 1949.
10. P. C. Yorke, *The Life and Correspondence of Philip Yorke, Earl of Hardwicke*, Cambridge, 1913, II, pp. 161-2.

different. They boasted a bewildering array of franchises. In a dozen, virtually all adult males had the vote; in another 37 the "scot and lot" franchise was almost as wide; in 92 the privilege rested in the hands of the freemen, of whom a corrupt mayor and corporation were frequently wont to create many more immediately before a general election; in another 27 boroughs, voting was confined to members of the actual corporation; and in the remaining 35 burgage boroughs — the closest of all — the vote was actually attached to particular plots of land, the purchase of a majority of which ensured control of the constituency. Yet it would be wrong to assume that those boroughs with the smallest electorates were necessarily the most venal or the most easily manipulated. Few were more independent than Bath with its 32 voters, or Devizes with its 38; few were more open to bribery on a massive scale than Gloucester with its 1500 or Bedford with its 1000. Nor should one imagine that corruption came from above. Those enfranchised looked upon their votes — as indeed did the Courts of Law — as a species of property on which they were entitled to expect a return at least once in seven years, and more often if the Almighty or the King's ministers willed it so. As with placemen in the House of Commons, so with electors. The system was not unlike that of a welfare state in miniature, confined to the politically active part of the population. The difference between 25 guineas a head to the freemen of Grampound and free wigs and upper dentures for the entire community is perhaps less than one might at first sight imagine. Bribery is now on a massive scale, and the muck is more evenly spread; but it is doubtful whether the motives of electors or elected have essentially changed. What is endearing about the eighteenth century is that, except in a handful of open constituencies, borough electors showed little interest in the politics of the candidates. They were unashamedly interested in the depth of those candidates' pockets, in the benefits they might gain for the locality, or in the amount of support they enjoyed from local magnates; but only rarely did they show any concern for the way their representatives were likely to vote in the House of Commons.

In the course of the fifty years between 1734 and 1784 — the only period I have studied in any detail — the over-all position was remarkably stable. Between 220 and 245 seats were during this time under the control of private patrons or Government departments such as the Treasury, the Admiralty or the Post Office. Of these the Government had a reasonably firm grip on some 20 to 25 seats, and wielded a less decisive influence on a further 20 to 35, which for convenience we may call "quasi-Government" seats, and in which they had to depend on the management and co-operation of a local magnate. Here Cornwall, where at one time or another Lords Falmouth and Edgcumbe, and the Buller and Eliot families, each aided the Treasury in returning four to six members, was the most rewarding area for the Government. But if these often fragile alliances broke up, it was anybody's guess whether the seats would remain in the Government's possession or follow the dictates of the local patron; and in many cases the latter, if the omens seemed auspicious, would seize the initiative and try to convert to his own allodial property what had once been the fief of the Crown. It was the attempt of John Roberts (former private secretary to Henry Pelham) to do precisely this that caused an irate Postmaster-General, the Earl of Leicester, to denounce Roberts in a phrase that must remain the classic definition of a civil servant. Leicester called him "an ink-shitting prig."[11]

In essence, then, any Government might in a general election hope to return a minimum of perhaps 40 and a maximum of 65 members for seats that were wholly or partially under its control. A further 170 to 200 seats were in the hands of private patrons. Here for the most part there was relatively little concentration of power. The Duke of Newcastle, the greatest borough-monger of the century, could never in his private capacity return more than nine members (frequently only seven), and he was in a class of his own. The Cornish families mentioned above could each influence four to six seats, but usually only with Government or other support (e.g. from the Prince of Wales). Otherwise another eight patrons might return three or four members each, but the great majority had to be content with either one or two. I suspect, though until much more work has been done on the subject I

11. Devonshire MSS., Leicester to Devonshire, 16 October 1757.

cannot be certain, that towards the end of the eighteenth century and the beginning of the nineteenth, the picture began to change; and that private patrons began to gain ground at the expense of the government and build up borough empires equal to, or greater than, that of the Duke of Newcastle. But that is another story.

It is now time to ask two crucial and closely related questions. How far was borough patronage used for purely political purposes, i.e. how many members were returned by patrons solely for political reasons? And how far did the system of borough patronage contribute towards the production of a Government majority in the House of Commons? In attempting to answer these questions, I shall analyse the results of the general election of 1741, the one with which i am most familiar. In this particular election 241 members were returned for private, Government, or quasi-Government seats. Forty-one members came within the two latter categories and, as might be expected, were supporters of the Administration at the time of their return. But two points should be noted. Eight of them deserted the Government on major issues during the life of the subsequent Parliament, and 25 of them were already office-holders and therefore under a more material obligation towards the Government than that issuing from their free return to Parliament. If the prime purpose of patronage was to influence the votes of as many members as possible, offices would surely have gone to some and safe seats to others.

The remaining 200 members were returned by private individuals. Of these, 111 found their way into Parliament through the good offices of patrons who were themselves Government supporters; 89 via the medium of Opposition patrons. Immediately, of course, one is reminded of the obvious fact that borough patronage could benefit the Opposition as well as the Government, though one would naturally expect the latter to be more favourably placed. But the situation is more complicated than that. Of the 111 returned by Government patrons, no less than 42 were actually the patrons themselves, and it is scarcely necessary to point out that few members of the eighteenth century House of Commons were more independent than those who returned themselves for their own private boroughs. They could thumb their noses at both King and ministers, as is indicated by the fact

that ten of the 42 changed sides at least temporarily during the life
of the ensuing Parliament. A further 41 out of the 111 were
relatives of the patrons, and it is abundantly clear that the prime
determining factor in their return was kinship rather than politics.
Two of them were actually known Opposition supporters at the
time of their election, and a further 14 subsequently ratted on the
Government on major issues. This leaves us with a rump of only
28 members returned by Government supporters solely because
they were expected to vote on the ministerial side; and even here
one of these went over to the Opposition.

When one turns to the 89 members returned by Opposition
patrons, the picture is essentially the same. Thirty-one were the
patrons themselves, of whom 14 subsequently crossed the floor on
at least one vital occasion; 28 were related to the patrons, 6 of
whom were actually confirmed supporters of the Administration,
and a further eight of whom later deviated from the political line
of those patrons; and only 30 were returned for purely political
reasons, of whom no less than 8 later turned their coats.

Where do all these wildly confusing figures leave us? Of the
241 members who were returned for close borough seats, only 99
owed their return exclusively to political reasons, and seventeen of
these turned out to be unreliable on occasions when their support
was most needed either by Government or by Opposition. Of
these 99, 69 were originally Government supporters, and 30
known members of the Opposition. The Government's advantage
was therefore a mere 39. Even if one includes all the 241
members, regardless of their identity or of the reasons for their
return, the Government advantage rises to only 71, of whom no
less than 35 — almost half — ratted on the Government on at least
one major occasion. It seems clear that the effect of borough
patronage was not to supply the Government with a large,
subservient body of voters in the House of Commons.

We may indeed look at electoral patronage from two different
vantage points. Firstly, from the point of view of the individual
borough patron, its purpose was to provide a seat in Parliament for
himself (if he was a Commoner and sought membership) and for
any of his relatives with similar ambitions, regardless of their
political complexion. If he then happened to have a surplus of

seats, he would be open to approaches from either Government or Opposition leaders, according to his own political sympathies. Candidates returned for these seats normally bore the entire cost of their elections. Secondly, from the point of view of the Government, the purpose of patronage was above all to provide safe seats for the men of business and other office-holders whose presence in Parliament was regarded as essential, but who had no boroughs of their own and could not afford to compete in the open market. Government and quasi-government boroughs were sufficient to provide for most of these men. After that, the Government negotiated with politically sympathetic private patrons who happened to have surplus seats available at a price to known Government supporters. In round figures the market price for such a seat was probably about £1,000 in 1715, £1,500 by 1741, £2,000 by 1754, £2,500 by 1761, and £3,000 by 1780. We might here pose a number of hypothetical questions. What political obligation, if any, was incurred by John Smith, a wealthy merchant and Administration supporter, who sought a way into Parliament via the First Lord of the Treasury, Lord Brown, who, on receipt of £2,000 from Mr. Smith, paid that sum over to his friend and fellow minister, Lord James, who in turn promptly returned Mr. Smith to Parliament for one of his boroughs? Did Mr. Smith feel that he was morally obliged to continue supporting Lord Brown's government because its leader had arranged his return to Parliament? Or did he feel a greater obligation to Lord James, whose borough he represented, and who might well break politically with Lord Brown during the life of the ensuing Parliament? Or, having paid the market price for his seat, did Mr. Smith regard himself as wholly independent? No set answer can be given to any of these questions, since everything depended upon personal inclinations and upon unpredictable political circumstances. But the questions serve to illustrate the highly intricate net-work of conflicting obligations that could arise from the system of borough patronage.

Before leaving the field of elections, a few words should be said about that mythical engine of corruption, the Secret Service fund. The late Sir Lewis Namier of course exploded this particular legend some forty years ago, since when it has been widely accepted that a relatively small proportion of that fund went to members of Parliament or were spent on elections. To be more precise, some £25,000 from this source was provided for the general election of 1754, £50,000 in 1774, £62,000 in 1780, and £32,000 in 1784. In 1761 the young naive George III, reacting against the supposed corruption of his grandfather's reign, refused to contribute a single penny; and there is no reason to believe that his refusal in any way affected the outcome of the general election of that year, at which anyway a handsome Government majority was returned. We may gain a clearer idea of the relative importance of Secret Service expenditure by looking more closely, for example, at the general election of 1754. In all, £25,495 was spent — enough at current market prices to purchase some twelve seats out of the 558 in the House of Commons. Even the £62,000 spent in 1780 could have commanded no more than 21 seats — approximately 4% of the House. But of course Secret Service expenditure did not take this straightforward form. In 1754, £8,030 — almost a third of the total amount — was squandered on five unsuccessful candidates in Oxfordshire, Wallingford, Reading and Worcester. The remaining £17,465 was distributed among 21 candidates, all of whom were duly returned to Parliament. But in virtually every case the candidates contributed amounts from their own pockets equal to or greater (sometimes substantially greater) than that provided from the Secret Service fund. Here again, one may conjecture on the political obligation incurred by John Smith who, having spent £3,000 of his own money, received a further £500 from the fund — sufficient in the event to carry the election. He may well have felt that his duty towards the King, or towards whoever happened to be First Lord of the Treasury at that particular time, was severely limited. At all events, it is clear that the main purpose of the Secret Service Funds, as far as electoral expenditure was concerned, was to subsidize known Government supporters who ran into financial difficulties in the later stages of their campaigns, and to assist candidates in a few open constituencies (e.g. Oxfordshire in 1754 or Westminster in 1784) where the Government felt that its prestige was at stake. It cannot be emphasized too much that the overwhelming majority of members financed their own elections — which produced a much more independent House of Commons than we are likely to see in the twentieth century.

So much for electoral patronage; what of financial inducements offered to those who were already members of the House of Commons? The string of Place and Pension Bills promoted by Country members from the 1670s to the 1780s might suggest that the House was dominated by placemen and pensioners. Such in fact was not the case. Secret Service pensions were never popular with members of Parliament, and while Newcastle was at the Head of the Treasury between 1754 and 1762 only 35 members were in receipt of such pensions – the total amount paid to each varying from a mere £200 to £4,700.[12] In most cases these pensions were in the nature of temporary charity and their political influence was negligible. Placemen were of course vastly more numerous than pensioners. In 1741 there were approximately 160, in 1754 some 150, in 1760 around 220, and in 1780 about 160. If one were to add to these (and it is not clear that one should) those serving officers in the army and navy who held nothing but their commissions, the numbers would rise to 180, 180, 250, and 190 respectively. In other words, by stretching the definition of a placeman to its utmost limit, only one-third of the membership of the Commons normally held office, save during the Seven Years War in the late 1750s and early 1760s, when the all-embracing nature of the Pitt-Newcastle coalition, the large number of army and naval officers, and the rise in the number of Government contractors, temporarily swelled the proportion to almost one-half. Such offices of course varied widely in importance and in emoluments. At the highest level were the members of the Cabinet and other effective heads of departments. Almost equally vital to the Government's survival were the embryonic civil servants, e.g. the Secretaries to the Treasury, Admiralty, Board of Trade etc. Indeed, many of the actual members of the Boards of Treasury, admiralty, and Trade and Plantations were more like civil servants than acitve politicians. But most of the so-called Court and Treasury Party were men of meaner mould – sinecure-holders, Court officials, Governors of Military establishments, judicial

12. Sir Lewis Namier, *The Structure of Politics at the Accession of George III*, 2nd ed., London, 1957, p. 217.

officers etc. They aimed above all at security of tenure, and — however they might originally have achieved preferment — chose to avoid identification with any particular set of politicians. It was this mentality, rather than any incipient insanity, that led Thomas Hervey, Superintendent of the King's Gardens and Waterworks, to explain his desertion of Sir Robert Walpole in December 1741 by remarking: "Jesus knows my thoughts; one day I blaspheme, and pray the next."[13] Indeed, one of the great ironies of patronage was that the serried ranks of the Court and Treasury Party were most prone to division when their support was most needed. At times of political crisis some of them paid little heed to William Pulteney's witticism — made admittedly in quite a different context — "dividing is not the way to multiply." When a minister was in imminent danger of falling, the Court and Treasury Party was placed in a dilemma. If they were to stand by him and he were to fall, the incoming ministers might seek to wreak vengeance upon them; if they were to go over to opposition and he were to recover, he might seek similar vengeance. Politicians may come and politicians may go, but the Court and Treasury Party wanted to go on for ever. What then was a poor sinecure-holder or Court official to do? The great majority of course stood firm, and a few whose gambling instincts had not been eroded by the fruits of office took their courage in both hands and crossed the floor of the House. But a significant minority preferred to play safe, and invented excuses to keep away from the House and avoid committing themselves until the issue became clear. Thus Lord Hervey could lament at the time of the Excise Bill crisis of 1733:

> A great many in the King's service, Madam, are said openly to have declared themselves against this measure, and many more are thought to have taken the quiet part of lying by only till things are ripe for a revolution in the ministry, at which juncture it is expected they will break forth and show themselves not less inveterate enemies to Sir Robert Walpole than the others, though they have had a little more caution in appearing so.[14]

13. W. S. Lewis, ed., *The Yale Edition of Horace Walpole's Correspondence*, London, 1958, XVII, p. 244.
14. John, Lord Hervey, *Some Materials Towards Memoirs of the Reign of George*

And on the eve of Walpole's fall in December 1741, young Horace Walpole could disgustedly point out that there were 41 of his father's supporters who could not, or would not attend[15] — a sentiment that was echoed by Lord Hartington.[16] Indeed, whenever a ministry was overturned in the Commons in the eighteenth century, the actions of the placemen were almost invariably decisive. The Opposition found an issue on which it could stir independent opinion to the extent that the Government's majority dropped to a dangerously low level of about twenty. Then a few rats and more numerous abstainers among the Court and Treasury Party sufficed to swing the balance in favour of the Opposition. Again and again these symptoms manifest themselves — at the time of the Excise Bill (when Walpole avoided defeat by dropping the measure), at his fall, when Carteret was at the height of his unpopularity in 1744, and in the dying days of North's ministry in February and March 1782.

Fortunately for the members of the Court and Treasury Party, they did not often have to declare their primary allegiance — which, by definition, was to the King — during the reigns of George I and George II. Loyalty to the King and to the Old Corps politicians (the Walpoles, Pelhams, Yorkes etc.,) could conveniently go hand in hand. But when George III produced a series of ministries in bewilderingly swift succession during the 1760s, the allegiance of the Court and Treasury Party to the King stood out with unprecedented clarity, and — in the pages of Edmund Burke — they achieved an undeserved notoriety as the first and most important element of the "King's Friends" — a title which they had in fact merited since the days of Danby and Charles II. Rockingham would have done well to have heeded the King's advice in January 1766: "if you continue firm, I don't doubt of success, but if you in the least seem to hesitate, the inferiors will fly off."[17] Sir Robert Walpole had learnt this long before, but Rockingham was too inexperienced a politician to appreciate the

II, Romney Sedgwick, ed., London, 1931, I, p. 161.

15. W. S. Lewis, ed., *Yale Edition*, XVII, p. 251.

16. Devonshire MSS., Hartington to Devonshire, 30 January 1742.

17. Hon. John Fortescue, ed., *The Correspondence of King George III*, London, 1927, I, p. 218.

situation, and the resulting defection of King's Friends so undermined confidence in his ministry that it withered away a few months later.

Yet even in quiescent political times it would be misleading to assume that every office-holder in the House of Commons was a reliable Government supporter. Of the 157 placemen in the Commons in 1741, no less than 33 were actually members of the then Opposition — nineteen holding office under the Prince of Wales, six enjoying their sinecures for life (and therefore thoroughly independent) and eight being judicial officers. Nor were the remaining 124 wholly reliable, at least nineteen of them subsequently ratting on the Government over an issue that in modern times would occasion a three-line whip. Places were normally rewards for past services rather than bribes for future subservience, and no Government in the eighteenth century could ever hope to survive by virtue of patronage alone. A coherent policy, debating and administrative talent and a chief minister who sat in the House of Commons and could act as the essential liaison between the House and the King, were more necessary to the achievement of political stability than a handful of Government boroughs and an admittedly substantial body of placemen; though I must emphasize again that this does not mean that patronage was not a vital part of the political system.

It remains to conclude with a few comments about the decline of patronage, although the full story would go far beyond the chronological limits of this article. Trivial reductions in the number of placemen were effected by Place Acts of 1700, 1701 and 1742; but early Country agitation for significant reform bore relatively little fruit. The first significant decline took place — ironically enough — during the first two decades of George III's reign, though by accident rather than by design. As Ian Christie has shown,[18] Dunning was wholly wrong when in 1780 he claimed that the Influence of the Crown had increased. Nonetheless a majority of members voted for his motion in the firm conviction that he was correct, and we can scarcely blame them for not

18. I. R. Christie, "Economical Reform and the 'Influence of the Crown,' 1780," in *Cambridge Historical Journal* 12, p. 144.

having read Christie. It was the mounting cost and ill-success of the American War of Independence that first gave teeth to the rising movement for economical reform which, in one form or another, was to make the first major inroads into the patronage system. But we should remember that economical reform meant different things to different people. To Edmund Burke and his fellow-Rockinghams, it meant exclusively the reduction of the supposedly sinister Influence of the Crown; to Christopher Wyvill and the country petitioners of 1779-80 it also meant the reduction of Government expenditure; for Shelburne and the younger Pitt the Influence of the Crown held no terrors — their interest in economical reform stemmed from the desire to economize and the need for administrative reform. So the ball was set rolling by the much-vaunted but scarcely sweeping measures of the second Rockingham ministry in 1782 — Clerke's Act disqualifying Government contractors from sitting in the House (though the 37 contractors of 1761 had shrunk to 15 by 1782); Burke's Civil Establishment Act which, among many other things, abolished some 34 offices, 22 of which were held at that time by members of the House of Commons; and Crewe's Act, which disfranchised revenue officers but which, as Betty Kemp has shown,[19] had little practical effect. These were the measures that attracted attention, for they were political measures directed against a sovereign who was soon to get his revenge by defeating the Fox-North coalition which, born of an agreement (dictated by North) that there should be no further economical reform, survived long enough to produce a further barely disguised and abortive instalment in the shape of Fox's India Bill, thereby attempting to transfer East India Company patronage from the Crown to seven members of the coalition. It was left to the younger Pitt to accelerate the process by which placemen were excluded from the House — not by dramatic acts of the legislature, but by piece-meal administrative action. As a result, there were by the 1820s no more than 60-70 office-holders in the Commons. The fact that Lord Liverpool could maintain his ministry from 1812 to 1827 without substantial patronage to aid him merely underlines the moral that its

19. B. Kemp, "Crewe's Act, 1782," in *English Historical Review* 68, p. 258.

indispensability in eighteenth century politics has been exaggerated.

What else is there to say? Dr. Plumb has his point of view, and I have mine. Perhaps in the last analysis we merely reflect different emphases, interests and values. At all events I remain an unrepentant apologist of the essential independence of the House of Commons in a highly individualistic and idiosyncratic era.

J. B. Owen